Testing Second Language Speaking

GLENN FULCHER

D0171312

PEARSON
Longman

London • New York • Toronto • Sydney • Tokyo • Singapore
Hong Kong • Cape Town • Madrid • Paris • Amsterdam • Munich • Milan

Pearson Education Limited

Head Office:
Edinburgh Gate
Harlow CM20 2JE
Tel: +44 (0)1279 623623
Fax: +44 (0)1279 431059
www.pearsoned.co.uk

First published in Great Britain in 2003

© Pearson Education Limited 2003

The right of Glenn Fulcher to be identified as Author of this Work has been asserted
by him in accordance with the Copyright, Designs and Patents Act 1988.

ISBN 0 582 47270 9

British Library Cataloguing in Publication Data
A CIP catalogue record for this book can be obtained from the British Library

Library of Congress Cataloging in Publication Data
A CIP catalog record for this book can be obtained from the Library of Congress

10 9 8 7 6 5 4 3 2 1

Typeset in 10/12pt Baskerville by Graphicraft Limited, Hong Kong
Printed and bound in Malaysia

The Publishers' policy is to use paper manufactured from sustainable forests.

APPLIED LINGUISTICS AND LANGUAGE STUDY

GENERAL EDITOR

CHRISTOPHER N. CANDLIN

Chair Professor of Applied Linguistics
Department of English
Centre for English Language Education &
Communication Research
City University of Hong Kong, Hong Kong

Error Analysis:
Perspective on Second Language
Acquisition
JACK C RICHARDS (ED.)

Contrastive Analysis
CARL JAMES

Language and Communication
JACK C RICHARDS *and*
RICHARD W SCHMIDT (EDS)

Reading in a Foreign Language
J CHARLES ALDERSON *and*
A H URQUHART (EDS)

An Introduction to Discourse Analysis
Second Edition
MALCOLM COULTHARD

Bilingualism in Education:
Aspects of Theory, Research and Practice
JIM CUMMINS *and* MERRILL SWAIN

Second Language Grammar:
Learning and Teaching
WILLIAM E RUTHERFORD

Vocabulary and Language Teaching
RONALD CARTER *and*
MICHAEL McCARTHY

The Classroom and the
Language Learner:
Ethnography and Second-Language
Classroom Research
LEO VAN LIER

Listening in Language Learning
MICHAEL ROST

An Introduction to Second Language
Acquisition Research
DIANE LARSEN-FREEMAN
and MICHAEL H LONG

Process and Experience in the
Language Classroom
MICHAEL LEGUTKE *and*
HOWARD THOMAS

Translation and Translating:
Theory and Practice
ROGER T BELL

Language Awareness in the Classroom
CARL JAMES *and*
PETER GARRETT (EDS)

Rediscovering Interlanguage
LARRY SELINKER

Language and Discrimination:
A Study of Communication in
Multi-ethnic Workplaces
CELIA ROBERTS, EVELYN DAVIES *and*
TOM JUPP

Analysing Genre:
Language Use in Professional Settings
VIJAY K BHATIA

Language as Discourse:
Perspective for Language Teaching
MICHAEL McCARTHY *and*
RONALD CARTER

Second Language Learning:
Theoretical Foundations
MICHAEL SHARWOOD SMITH

Interaction in the Language
Curriculum:
Awareness, Autonomy and Authenticity
LEO VAN LIER

Phonology in English Language
Teaching:
An International Language
MARTHA C PENNINGTON

Measuring Second Language
Performance
TIM McNAMARA

Literacy in Society
RUQAIYA HASAN and
GEOFF WILLIAMS (EDS)

Theory and Practice of Writing:
An Applied Linguistic Perspective
WILLIAM GRABE and ROBERT B KAPLAN

Autonomy and Independence in
Language Learning
PHIL BENSON and PETER VOLLER
(EDS)

Language, Literature and the Learner:
Creative Classroom Practice
RONALD CARTER and JOHN McRAE
(EDS)

Language and Development:
Teachers in the Changing World
BRIAN KENNY and WILLIAM SAVAGE
(EDS)

Communication Strategies:
Psycholinguistic and Sociolinguistic
Perspectives
GABRIELE KASPER and ERIC KELLERMAN
(EDS)

Teaching and Language Corpora
ANNE WICHMANN, STEVEN FLIGEL-
STONE, TONY McENERY and GERRY
KNOWLES (EDS)

Testing Second Language Speaking
GLENN FULCHER

Errors in Language Learning and Use:
Exploring Error Analysis
CARL JAMES

Translation into the Second Language
STUART CAMPBELL

Strategies in Learning and Using a
Second Language
ANDREW D COHEN

Managing Evaluation and Innovation in
Language Teaching:
Building Bridges
PAULINE REA-DICKINS and
KEVIN P GERMAINE (EDS)

Reading in a Second Language:
Process, Product and Practice
A H URQUHARD and C J WEIR

Writing:
Texts, Processes and Practices
CHRISTOPHER N CANDLIN and
KEN HYLAND (EDS)

Disciplinary Discourses:
Social Interactions in Academic Writing
KEN HYLAND

Experiential Learning in Foreign
Language Education
VILJO KOHONEN, RITTA JAATINEN,
PAULI KAIKKONEN, JORMA LEHTOVAAR

English as a Second Language in the
Mainstream:
Teaching, Learning and Identity
BERNARD MOHAN, CONSTANT LEUNG
and CHRISTINE DAVISON

Researching Pedagogic Tasks:
Second Language Learning,
Teaching and Testing
MARTIN BYGATE, PETER SKEHAN
and MERRILL SWAIN (EDS)

Learner Contributions to Language
Learning:
New Directions in Research
MICHAEL BREEN

For my mother, Joan.
And to the memory of my father, Norman.
Without whom nothing would have been possible.

Testing Second Language Speaking

APPLIED LINGUISTICS AND LANGUAGE STUDY

GENERAL EDITOR

CHRISTOPHER N. CANDLIN

Chair Professor of Applied Linguistics
Department of English
Centre for English Language Education &
Communication Research
City University of Hong Kong, Hong Kong

For a complete list of books in this series see pages v–vi

Contents

List of tables and figures   x
Preface   xi
Acknowledgements   xvi
List of abbreviations   xx

1 The history of testing second language speaking   1

2 Defining the construct   18

3 Tasks for second language speaking tests   50

4 Rating scales   88

5 Test specifications   116

6 Raters, training and administration   138

7 Evaluating second language speaking tests   171

8 Researching second language speaking tests   199

Appendices   226

References   256

Index   277

List of tables and figures

Table 1.1 FSI rating factors   12
Table 1.2 FSI weighting table   12
Table 1.3 FSI conversion table   12
Table 1.4 A comparison of the ILR and ACTFL rating scales   15
Table 2.1 A pragmatic scale   41
Table 2.2 A framework for describing the speaking construct   48
Table 3.1 A framework for describing tasks   57
Table 4.1 A framework for describing rating scales   91
Table 4.2 The relationship between actual and predicted scores   103
Table 4.3 Questionnaire with speaking items   110
Table 4.4 Descriptors mapped to the common reference levels
           of the Common European Framework   111
Table 4.5 The fluency scale for the Common European
           Framework   112
Table 6.1 Inter-rater reliability on an FSI-type speaking test   141
Table 6.2 Features of accommodation   148
Table 7.1 FSI rating components reported to discriminate at
           each level in the FSI rating scale   183
Table 7.2 The relationship between ACTFL scores and years
           of study   184
Table 8.1 A factor matrix for ratings of TA performances   205
Table 8.2 Multitrait-multimethod matrix   208
Table 8.3 Results of the Bolus *et al.* Generalisability Study   212
Table 8.4 A Facets map   214

Figure 3.1 Communicative potential of task types   52
Figure 4.1 EBB for communicative effectiveness   106
Figure 4.2 EBB for grammatical accuracy   106
Figure 4.3 The Skehan model of speaking test performance   114
Figure 4.4 An expanded model of speaking test performance   115
Figure 5.1 Test specification format   130
Figure 7.1 The Functional Trisection   177

Preface

Testing second language speaking has become extremely important since the Second World War. When it was realised the American service personnel were often ill equipped to communicate, that their inability to speak in a second language might be 'a serious handicap to safety and comfort', the push for tests of second language speaking began in earnest. From the needs of the military, the practice soon spread to colleges and universities. Today, speaking tests are available from all major test producers, for a multitude of purposes.

This book offers a comprehensive treatment of testing speaking in a second language. It will be useful for anyone who has to develop speaking tests in their own institutions, which is becoming an increasingly common requirement placed upon teachers who may have no training in test development. For teachers this book contains a generic programmatic approach from design to implementation that can be adapted to local conditions. Teachers are also asked to evaluate tests for use by their institutions when there is a need to use speaking tests produced by agencies like Educational Testing Service or the University of Cambridge Local Examinations Syndicate. The book provides clear guidance about the kinds of questions teachers may ask, and how to evaluate the answers. But it is never prescriptive.

The book is also intended for students of Applied Linguistics, languages and Teaching English to Speakers of Other Languages (TESOL). It brings together in one volume a summary and critical analysis of research into testing second language speaking. There is a wealth of examples, not only of task types that are commonly used in speaking tests, but of approaches to researching speaking tests, and specific methodologies, that students may have to use in their own projects. The approaches and methodologies are presented with examples from the literature, and are carefully referenced for follow-up study.

It is a 'practical' text for teachers and students. But it is not *just* a practical text. There is a theoretical framework, drawing on our evolving understanding of validity in language testing, which underpins the discussions and examples. We argue that practical decisions in speaking test development only make sense when we understand *why* we make those decisions. There is no one 'correct' decision in any testing context. We are faced with many possible choices, and the process of making those choices is a crucial aspect of understanding what the scores from our speaking tests might mean. Establishing what scores from a speaking test might mean is part of constructing, or evaluating, a *validity argument* (see the discussion at the beginning of Chapter 5). Readers are introduced to how validity arguments are constructed, what they may contain, what evidence can be presented to support them, and how we can evaluate them. Validity arguments are never 'static'. They are dynamic, fallible, endlessly evolving, attempts to investigate test score meaning. Ultimately we judge them by their utility and plausibility.

For teachers and students of language testing alike, this book tries to provide a theoretical backdrop to the issues raised. And so it cannot avoid philosophical matters. There is no running away from questions of *meaning* and *interpretation.* Statistical analysis will always play a part in language testing, but the ultimate challenge, as Davidson (2000) so eloquently reminds us, is how we utilise the range of tools at our disposal to address questions that are essentially *human* and *social* in essence. The same applies to qualitative approaches to researching second language speaking tests. Investigating how test takers do tasks, their affective reactions, the language they use, are all legitimate areas of enquiry that enhance our understanding of what we are doing when we test second language speaking. The interpretation of qualitative evidence to support a validity argument is just as problematic as the interpretation of quantitative evidence, as we shall see in Chapter 8.

The quality of a validity argument is subject to the evaluation of the community of language testing specialists, those who take the tests, the consumers of test scores, and society at large. Placing a book in this context also makes it relevant, we hope, to language testing researchers, and all those stakeholders who have an interest in how test scores are used to make critical decisions about the lives of individuals.

Although perhaps better left to the judgement of the reader and reviewers, we would like to think that this book is therefore about language testing in general, as well as the testing of second language speaking in particular. It adopts a pragmatic stance. There is no suggestion that there is one 'right' way to do things. But we do argue that there is a responsibility to be systematic and deliberate in test development, employ a variety of analytical techniques, and present validity arguments that are open to scrutiny. So it is different from Underhill (1987), which is a polemic against statistical analysis, while still managing to provide a useful list of task types for speaking tests. And while we spend many pages evaluating the American Oral Proficiency Interview, this is not the primary focus of the book, as it is for Johnson (2001). Rather, we are concerned about what we can learn from the tradition of the Oral Proficiency Interview to improve the quality of validity arguments.

Just as our approach to language testing cannot exist in some kind of limbo separate from our conception of society and the rights of the individual test taker, nor can it remain isolated from history. Testing second language speaking has a history, albeit a relatively short one. The first large-scale test of speaking was developed and implemented to exclude immigrants from the United States, because there was a loophole in the 1924 Immigration Act. If readers of this book think that such practices are long gone, they need only read Shohamy (2001). And if we reflect on why we have the linear rating scales that we use today, we need only look back to the first rating scales constructed for the military in the 1950s.

All of the considerations outlined above have influenced the structure and content of this book. It is structured so that it can be read from Chapter 1 to Chapter 8. However, some readers may wish to turn directly to a chapter that addresses a particular issue in the testing of second language speaking. The following outline of the book, which is broken down into four sections, may be useful in deciding upon priorities. Chapter 1 is essentially historical. Chapters 2 to 5 are concerned with the process of design and development of second language speaking tests. Chapter 6 deals with raters and interlocutors, training, administration and finance. Chapters 7 and 8 look at evaluation and research. This is an artificial compartmentalisation, but may nevertheless be useful.

In **Chapter 1** we look in some detail at the history of testing second language speaking. It looks at the political and military impetus behind testing speaking. Not all of the story is particularly pleasant. But for the most part, testing speaking was conducted for the benefit of the test takers, whether it was to ensure their safety in military operations or place them in the right class at school.

In **Chapter 2** we turn to the *construct*. We attempt to define what is meant by the term 'construct', and then ask how we can define the construct of 'speaking', or its constituents. This is particularly important. If we can't define what we think we are testing, the scores from a speaking test are hardly likely to be meaningful. When we have defined what we are looking for, we can go on to consider how we wish to elicit speech from test takers that will provide the basis for giving a score. This is the subject of **Chapter 3**. The use of tasks in second language pedagogy, second language acquisition research, and second language speaking tests is reviewed. We tackle the thorny problem of 'what makes a task difficult', before presenting a range of task types used in second language speaking tests within a test task framework. Having elicited a performance, a speech sample, we have to score it. **Chapter 4** outlines the types of rating scales that can be employed, and describes in some detail four distinctive approaches to the development of rating scales for second language speaking tests. **Chapter 5** is designed to draw together everything from Chapter 2 to Chapter 4. We begin by discussing what is meant by a *validity argument*, and how this encompasses our construct definition, the tasks we use, and how we score the performances on the tasks. These are brought together in the test specifications for a test of second language speaking. But it is not just a matter of sitting down to write test specifications. The process of producing test specifications is characterised as non-linear, and decidedly 'messy'. We provide four examples of test specifications for speaking tests, and a generic template for specifications based on the work of Davidson and Lynch (2002).

Chapter 6 moves us into getting ready for 'live or 'operational' testing. What does it mean for a rater to be 'reliable'? And is it necessary for a rater to be reliable? Rater reliability studies are reviewed, and we consider approaches to rater training and certification. In recent years, just as much attention has also been paid to the interlocutor in the speaking test. We consider the sources of interlocutor variability in second language speaking tests, and how this can be controlled through training. Equally important, although not frequently discussed, are local performance conditions. These conditions are defined as the administration of the speaking test, and the environment in which it takes place. We look at these issues from the perspective of how variations in administration or environment can impact on the score that an individual test taker may get. But we recognise that the administration of the speaking test may be deliberately altered for some test takers with disabilities. We outline the types of 'accommodation' that may be offered test takers with disabilities, such as deafness. We discuss how this impacts upon our definition of the construct, and how we might report scores from the test. Last, but not least, we look at how much it costs to design a test of second language speaking. A working budget is presented that draws on all the processes described in Chapters 2 to 6. The cost of the process is significant, especially for institutionally developed speaking tests where resources may be limited. We look at what is lost in validity claims through cutting corners to reduce costs, and what may be lost through court action if costs are cut and high stakes decisions retained.

Chapter 7 offers a view of how we may evaluate tests of second language speaking. Drawing upon the discussion in Chapter 5 it presents three validity arguments, with a review of the literature associated with each argument. The first argument is the most traditional, and for which there is a wealth of literature. It is the argument for the validity of the Oral Proficiency Interview, which is termed the 'FSI tradition of testing speaking'. The second argument is more recent. We consider the claims made for testing second language learners in pairs or groups, and evaluate the evidence presented for the proponents and opponents of this format. Thirdly, we look at the validity argument for 'indirect' (semi-direct, simulated) tests of second language speaking. In each of the three examples we ask how plausible the arguments are, given the probability that further evidence or rationales may be presented to change the nature of the validity argument in the future. We conclude this chapter by outlining a validity model based upon the work of Messick, which summarises the types of questions we may ask about any validity argument, and the sort of evidence that could be provided to support a particular validity argument. **Chapter 8** considers the type of evidence that may be offered to support or undermine a validity argument, while acknowledging that there is no one-to-one mapping between the source of evidence and the argument. Various approaches to analysis are described and discussed, under the headings of 'quantitative' and 'qualitative' methods. It is argued that this is an artificial distinction. Quantitative methods always involve human interpretation. Qualitative methods usually have a quantitative component, but equally involve human interpretation. The methods that we select to study tests of second language speaking are chosen because of their utility for addressing the validity questions that are most pressing in assuring the quality of our argument, and fairness to those who would take the test.

It is sometimes claimed that testing second language speaking is a much more difficult undertaking than testing other second language 'abilities', 'capacities', 'competencies', 'skills', or whatever other labels we may wish to use. Perhaps because it is the 'ability' that makes us human. Perhaps because speaking is fleeting, temporal and ephemeral. But the paucity of books on testing second language speaking might suggest that testing speaking is difficult. It is hoped that this book will fill the gap for those who are concerned with testing or assessing this most intrinsically human of capacities.

Acknowledgements

I am extremely grateful to Chris Candlin of Macquarie University, and the Editor of the Longman Applied Linguistics series. His timely and insightful comments at every stage in the preparation of the manuscript, and his encouraging advice and guidance, have made the writing process a pleasure.

Others have kindly given up their valuable time to read chapters and give much-needed critical feedback. Their input has contributed greatly to this book, but any shortcomings or deficiencies remain solely my responsibility. My particular thanks go to Brian North (Eurocentres), Alastair Pollitt (University of Cambridge), Bernard Spolsky (Bar-Ilan University) and Lynda Taylor (University of Cambridge Local Examinations Syndicate). I am also deeply indebted to Elizabeth Harvey (University of Surrey) who worked with me on the budgets for developing a test of second language speaking. She spent many hours working on the spreadsheets from which I created the examples in Chapter 6.

A special thank you is needed for Fred Davidson (University of Illinois at Urbana Champaign). His contribution to the development of my ideas has been especially significant. Whether through debate, feedback on parts of this book, or reading texts that he has recommended, I have never ceased to learn. The arguments in this book that are judged to show particularly clarity of thought, I owe largely to Fred, whether he agrees with those arguments or not.

Writing a book is not something that one does in isolation. I have been extremely fortunate to have excellent friends and colleagues to discuss issues in language testing, and they have helped to shape my views. My membership of the TOEFL Committee of Examiners (CoE) at Educational Testing Service (ETS) has been particularly valuable in this respect. I owe a debt of gratitude to all the members of the CoE with whom I have served, and the many ETS staff members with whom I have worked, too many to name individually. Also of immense importance has been my membership of the CoE Research Subcommittee. The quality of the discussions, but especially the friendship of its members, has been a great support while writing this book. My thanks to Merrill Swain (University of Toronto), Micheline Chalhoub-Deville (University of Iowa), Mary Enright and Rob French (ETS).

Of course, without Charles Alderson (Lancaster University) this book would not have been written. Over the years he has been a constant source of support, professionally and personally. My interest in testing second language speaking began when I was an English teacher in the Eastern Mediterranean. I couldn't understand why my students didn't get the grades that I predicted, and I began to ask questions that I couldn't answer. One of those questions concerned the efficacy of rating scales in testing speaking, which eventually became the research project that Charles Alderson supervised. My association with Lancaster and the staff of the Department of Linguistics and Modern English Language remains a constant source of inspiration, for which I am grateful.

Since completing my PhD at Lancaster I have taught language testing to many postgraduate students in TESOL. And probably learnt more than I have taught. So my thanks also to those many students, but especially the distance learning students who contributed their valuable experiences to Chapter 6.

The publishers are grateful to the following for permission to reproduce copyright material:

American Council for the Teaching of Foreign Languages for *The ACTFL Proficiency Guidelines: Gateway to Testing and Curriculum* Foreign Language Annals 17, 5, 475–489 by J. E. Liskin-Gasparro 1983 Revised 1985; The British Council for an extract from 'Specifications for an English language testing service' by B. Carroll published in *Issues in Language Testing* ed. J. Alderson and A. Hughes; Fred Davidson for an extract from *Assessment of Speech Acts: Role Playing Difficult Requests* from Virtual Specbank published on www.deil.uiuc.edu; Disability News Service Inc for the article 'Test score flagging tested in court' by Mike Irvin © The Disability News Service Inc. 'This work was performed under a subcontract with the Board of Trustees of the University of Illinois for the Great Lakes ADA Center, and funded by the U.S. Department of Education, NIDRR #133D60011'; Hodder & Arnold for an extract from 'Task difficulty in speaking tests' by Glenn Fulcher and Márquez Reiter published in *Language Testing* Vol. 20, no. 3; Multilingual Matters Ltd for an extract from 'Choosing and using communication tasks for second language instruction and research' by T. Pica, R. Kanagy and J. Falodun published in *Tasks and Language Learning: Integrating Theory and Practice* ed. G. Crookes and S. M. Gass; Ordinate Corporation for SET-10 Demo Test as featured on www.ordinate.com; Oxford University Press for extracts from *Language Testing in Practice* by L. Bachman and A. Palmer © Lyle F. Bachman and Adrian S. Palmer 1996, and UCLES for an extract from CUEFL Basic Level 0203/1 1988 © UCLES 1988.

Table on page 15 from The ILR oral interview: origins, applications, pitfalls, and implications in *Die Unterrichtspraxis*, 16, copyright 1983 by American Association of Teachers of German, reproduced with permission of American Association of Teachers of German in the format textbook via Copyright Clearance Center (Lowe, P. 1983); Table on page 41 from *Principles of*

Pragmatics, published by Longman, reprinted by permission of Pearson Education Ltd (Leech, G. 1983); Image and tasks on pages 68–69 from *ELSA Handbook 2003*, LCCI Examinations Board, reprinted by permission of EDI plc; Images and Chapter 3 extracts on pages 70–73 from *Test of Spoken English, Sample Paper, ftp://ftp.ets.org/pub/toefl/004954.TSE.pdf*, reprinted by permission of Educational Testing Service (ETS 2000); Images on pages 74–75 from *Preliminary English Test, Part 3, Sample Materials*, reprinted by permission of Cambridge ESOL (UCLES 2001); Images on pages 76 and 77 from *Presentation, Certificate of Proficiency in English, Part 3, Revised CPE Specifications and Sample Papers*, reprinted by permision of Cambridge ESOL (UCLES 2002); Chapter 3 extract from *Information Gap. Business English Certificate 1, Task 1, Sample Papers*, reprinted by permission of Cambridge ESOL (UCLES 1997); Chapter 3 extract and Table 8.4 from *Measuring Second Language Performance*, published by Longman, reprinted by permission of Pearson Education Ltd (McNamara, T. F. 1996); Image on page 85 from *Certificate in English Language Skills, Handbook and Samples*, reprinted by permission of Cambridge ESOL (UCLES 2002); Figures 4.1 and 4.2 after figures in Constructing rating scales for second language tests in *English Language Teaching Journal*, 49, 1, reprinted by permission of Oxford University Press (Upshur, J. and Turner, C. 1995); Figure 4.3 from Tasks and language performance assessment in *Researching Pedagogic Tasks: Second Language Learning, Teaching and Testing* edited by M. Bygate, P. Skehan and M. Swain, published by Longman, reprinted by permission of Pearson Education Ltd (Skehan, P. 2001); Table 4.3 from Scaling descriptors for language proficiency scales in *Language Testing*, 15, 2, reprinted by permission of Arnold Publishers (North, B. and Schneider, G. 1998); Table 4.4 from *The development of a common framework scale of descriptors of language proficiency based on a theory of measurement*, PhD Thesis, published by Thames Valley University/Peter Lang Publishing, Inc., reprinted by permission of Peter Lang Publishing, Inc. (North, B. 1996/2000); Figure 5.1 adapted from *Testcraft: A Teacher's Guide to Writing and Using Language Test Specifications*, © 2002 by Yale University, published and reprinted by permission of Yale University Press (Davidson, F. and Lynch, B. K. 2002); Images on pages 132–133 from *VOTE: Oral Testing*, reprinted by permission of British Council English Language Services Department ELT Group (British Council 1983); Table 6.2 from Cross-cultural pragmatics in oral proficiency interview strategies in *Performance Testing, Cognition and Assessment. Selected papers from the 15th Language Testing Research Colloquium*, University of Cambridge Local Examinations Syndicate, *Studies in Language Testing 3*, edited by M. Milanovic and N. Saville, reprinted by permission of Cambridge University Press (Berwick, R. and Ross, S. 1996); Figure 7.1 from http://www.languagetesting.com/scale.htm, reprinted by permission of American Council on the Teaching of Foreign Languages; Table 7.1 from Five coocurring factors in speaking proficiency in *Measuring Spoken Language Proficiency* edited by J. R. Firth, published and reprinted by permission of Georgetown University Press (Adams, M. L. 1980); Table 8.1 from The structure of oral communication in an educational environment: a comparison of factor-analytic rotational procedures in *Issues in*

Language Testing Research, First Edition edited by J. W. Oller, © 1983, reprinted with permission of Heinle, a division of Thomson Learning (Hinofotis, F. B. 1983); Table 8.2 from The construct validity of the FSI oral interview in *Language Learning*, 31, 1, reprinted by permission of Blackwell Publishing (Bachman, L. F. and Palmer, A. S. 1981); Table 8.3 from An introduction to generalizability theory in second language research in *Language Learning*, 32, 1, reprinted by permission of Blackwell Publishing (Bolus, R. E., Hinofotis, F. and Bailey, K. M. 1981); Appendix 5 extract from The construct validation of some components of communicative proficiency in *TESOL Quarterly*, 16, 4, copyright 1982 by TESOL, Inc., reproduced with permission of TESOL, Inc. in the format textbook via Copyright Clearance Center (Bachman, L. F., Palmer, A. S. and Palmer, A. 1982).

In some instances we have been unable to trace the owners of copyright material, and we would appreciate any information that would enable us to do so.

List of abbreviations

ACTFL   American Council on the Teaching of Foreign Languages
AEI   ACTFL/ETS/ILR
ANOVA   Analysis of Variance
APA   American Psychological Association
ASLPR   Australian Second Language Proficiency Ratings
ASTP   Army Specialized Training Program
CASE   Cambridge Assessment of Spoken English
CELT   Comprehensive English Language Test
CIA   Central Intelligence Agency
CPE   Certificate of Proficiency in English
CS   Communication Strategies
CTT   Classical Test Theory
CUEFL   Communicative Use of English as a Foreign Language
DLI   Defense Language Institute
EAP   English for Academic Purposes
EBB   Empirically derived binary-choice boundary definition scale
ELTS   English Language Testing Service
ENS   Educated Native Speaker
ETS   Educational Testing Service
FCE   First Certificate in English, UCLES
FSI   Foreign Service Institute
HeST   Hebrew Speaking Test
ICT   Interactional Competence Theory
IELTS   International English Language Testing System
ILR   Interagency Language Roundtable
IRT   Item Response Theory
ISLPR   International Second Language Proficiency Ratings
L1   Primary language(s)
L2   Second or non-primary language(s)
LCCI   London Chamber of Commerce and Industry
LEP   Limited English Proficiency
MLA   Modern Language Association
MTMM   Multitrait-Multimethod

OET	Occupational English Test
OPI	Oral Proficiency Interview
PST	Portuguese Speaking Test
ROPE	Recorded Oral Proficiency Examination
SLA	Second Language Acquisition
SOPI	Simulated Oral Proficiency Interview
TAs	Teaching Assistants
TLU	Target Language Use
TOEFL	Teaching of English as a Foreign Language
TOPT	Taped Oral Proficiency Test of Spanish
TRP	Transition Relevance Place
TSE	Test of Spoken English
UCLES	University of Cambridge Local Examinations Syndicate
VPA	Verbal Protocol Analysis
WENS	Well Educated Native Speaker

Chapter 1

The history of testing second language speaking

It is often remarked that language testing is one of the youngest fields of research and practice in Applied Linguistics (Alderson, 1991a). And the theory and practice of testing second language speaking is the youngest sub-field of language testing. During the heyday of modern language testing research through the First World War and into the 1920s, little if any atten-tion was paid to testing speaking. Despite some notable exceptions, it was not until the Second World War that the testing of second language speaking became a focus of interest (Fulcher, 1997).

In this first chapter we will first consider the testing of speaking up to the Second World War, look at how the war changed the way in which speaking was taught and tested, and then trace the movement of innovation in a military context to universities and schools. This chapter shows that it is important for us to understand the intimate connection between the develop-ment of speaking tests and political/military language needs; political and military events have had a deep impact upon the form and scoring of many modern speaking tests. We will also see that the problems encountered with speaking tests from the very early days have not disappeared. By placing our consideration of testing speaking into a historical context we can more fully appreciate why speaking tests that we are familiar with today look the way they do.

TESTING SPEAKING BEFORE 1939

In the United States where most of the language testing research was being conducted, there was an overwhelming concern with achieving reliable scores from tests. 'Reliable' meant that the scores from tests were consistent over a number of administrations, assuming that the conditions are the same and there is no impact on the scores from learning, familiarity or fatigue. It was argued that the testing of speaking could not produce reliable scores because the process relies upon judges who will be swayed by many uncon-trollable factors (see Chapter 6). Learners would therefore get different, or inconsistent, scores depending on the person making the judgement and the range of factors that may impact upon the speaking test at the time (Heyden, 1920). It was also considered impractical when testing large numbers of learners.

Although the phrase 'oral test' appears in language testing prior to the war, it did not mean that learners were required to speak in the test. Rather, it referred to the testing of pronunciation, usually requiring the test taker to write down the pronunciation of a written word using phonetic script. For example, in 1913 the Association of Modern Language Teachers instituted a committee to consider university admissions tests in French, German and Spanish that had an aural and oral component (Spolsky, 1995: 35). A test of speaking was abandoned because of problems with reliability. It was admitted that 'no actual oral test is included in this examination'. But it was also claimed that 'no candidate could pass it who had not received abundant oral, as well as aural training' (Committee on Resolutions and Investigations, 1917: 252). The aural component of the test was a 10-minute dictation, and writing answers to questions spoken by the examiner. Similarly, in his pioneering work on language tests for New York Schools, Wood (1927: 96) acknowledges the importance of using 'conversational materials' that can be used to hold individual speaking tests with students as a valid method of assessing students, but remained with paper and pencil tests because speaking tests would be 'subjective' and logistically difficult to put into operation.

We will return to these two problems again throughout this book. The concerns of early language testers have not disappeared. Reliability and practicality issues are major drivers of research into semi-direct tests of speaking, and the automatic (machine) scoring of speech samples today.

Language testing practitioners avoided the complex problem of testing speaking until 1926. Instead they concentrated on the 'new-type' multiple choice tests as reliable, objective measures of language ability. The first true speaking test used in North America was The College Board's English Competence Examination, introduced in 1930 for overseas students applying to study at US colleges and universities (College Entrance Examination Board, 1929). The 1930 test was specifically designed by the College Board at the request of the Association of College Registrars in 1927 (Spolsky, 1995: 55), and the request was made because of the 1926 requirement of the United States government (Commissioner of Immigration) that schools and colleges indicate the 'exact knowledge of English language a student must have before he can be admitted'. The College Board realised that it was essential to test whether a student was capable of speaking intelligibly in an academic context, and their solution was the first academic speaking test in a foreign language.

This format of the whole test was:

1. *Reading I*
   Four short passages, the first a simple narrative, the second a historical passage or a text of some topical interest, the third a critical discussion of a social issue, and the fourth a scientific text. Questions were primarily true/false.

2. *Reading II*

One longer passage on a critical or theoretical topic that would present the opportunity to test understanding of key ideas.

3. *Dictation*

One regular dictation, and one to be produced from memory after listening.

4. *Speaking*

A conversation with ten topics prepared for the examiner. The criteria for assessment were:

- Fluency
- Responsiveness
- Rapidity
- Articulation
- Enunciation
- Command of construction
- Use of connectives
- Vocabulary and idiom

The examiner graded each criterion on a three-point scale of: proficient, satisfactory and unsatisfactory. Interestingly, the examiner was also asked to record whether the test taker was shy. This is an early sign of interest in individual differences that may be a threat to the valid interpretation of test scores.

5. *Writing*

A 250–300 word essay on a selected topic.

The purpose of section 4 of the 1930 test was to ensure that a potential student in a US university could express him or herself intelligibly in spoken English. The criteria for assessment were not articulated, and we do not know anything about the training provided to examiners. Nevertheless, we may observe the interest in attempting to define what is important about speaking – defining the construct through enumerating the key features for assessment – and considering at least one factor that may affect scores but which is not related to the construct (construct irrelevant variance).

This innovative test design was not only the result of a very practical requirement to know whether a student would be able to speak once enrolled on an academic programme in a North American university. It was also designed to play an important role in US immigration policy.

Inter-war immigration policy was itself influenced by intelligence testing. During the First World War over 1.75 million men had taken the Army Alpha or Beta tests (the world's first mass-produced intelligence tests), or individual assessments for those whose intelligence was too low to attempt the Beta tests. The results were published by race (Yerkes, 1921), and the conclusions drawn were that:

(a) The average mental age of white Americans was in danger of decline because of breeding with more feeble-minded peoples. Yerkes calculated the average mental age as approximately 13. This estimate is just slightly higher than the definition of a 'moron':

> Going down the scale of mental development it has become customary to call those mental defectives who have a mentality of from eight to twelve years, morons; those who range from three to seven, imbeciles; and those of two or under, idiots.   (Goddard, 1919: 60)

(b) Many European immigrants, particularly those from Southern or Eastern Europe, had extremely low innate intelligence compared with those from Northern Europe.

(c) Coloured people are the least intelligent, their level of intelligence being directly correlated with the deepness of the colour of their skin.

Despite serious problems with the tests themselves, data collection and interpretation (see Gould, 1981), the First World War experiment with testing had a major political impact in the United States. On 6 December 1923 Calvin Coolidge said that:

> American institutions rest solely on good citizenship. They were created by people who had a background of self-government. New arrivals should be limited to our capacity to absorb them into the ranks of good citizenship. America must be kept American. For this purpose, it is necessary to continue a policy of restricted immigration. It would lie well to make such immigration of a selective nature with some inspection at the source, and based either on a prior census or upon the record of naturalization. Either method would insure the admission of those with the largest capacity and best intention of becoming citizens. I am convinced that our present economic and social conditions warrant a limitation of those to be admitted. We should find additional safety in a law requiring the immediate registration of all aliens. Those who do not want to be partakers of the American spirit ought not to settle in America.

He reiterated the view that America should remain American when he signed the 1924 Immigration Act, designed to keep the unintelligent foreigner out of the United States. He was merely responding to the fear of the day, the popular conception that allowing additional immigration would reduce the intelligence of the American population. This view was most clearly expressed by Brigham (1923, quoted in Gould, 1981: 260):

> The decline of American intelligence will be more rapid than the decline of the intelligence of European national groups, owing to the presence here of the negro. These are the plain, if somewhat ugly, facts that our study shows. The deterioration of American intelligence is not inevitable, however, if public action can be aroused to prevent it. There is no reason why legal steps should not be taken which would insure a continuously progressive upward evolution.
>
>   The steps that should be taken to preserve or increase our present intellectual capacity must of course be dictated by science and not by political expediency. Immigration should not only be restrictive but highly selective. And the revision of the immigration and naturalization laws will only afford a slight relief from our present difficulty. The really important steps are those looking toward the prevention of the continued propagation of defective strains in the present population.

Brigham may not have won the battle to 'prevent the propagation of defective strains' of human being in the United States, but he did get a restrictive immigration law that was based on strict eugenic principles (Brigham later repudiated these views when he moved to Princeton University). The Act was the first to introduce an immigration quota law, establish a preference quota system, non-quota status and consular control system. Immigration to the United States from the target nationalities fell swiftly. But there was a loophole in the 1924 Immigration Act. It allowed visas to be issued to non-quota applicants who had been accepted to study at a school, college or university in the United States. As a result the number of applications for student visas immediately began to rise dramatically. Spolsky (1995: 55) reports that in 1926 the Commissioner General of Immigration wrote that:

> The experience of the bureau in the past two and one half years is to the effect that many non-quota immigrant students gain admission to the United States totally unfit, because of insufficient knowledge of the English language.... Therefore, it is requested that all schools indicate in the certificate of admission the exact knowledge of the English language a student must have before he can be accepted.

The College Entrance Examination Board was given the task of providing this test by the American Association of Collegiate Registrars. It was used effectively until 1935, when funds to operate the test ran out, and the item pool had been over-exposed.

The fact that immigration needs led to the development of the 1930 speaking test shows the link that often exists between developments in language testing and political initiatives. These pressures still exist today, in the development and use of tests to regulate immigration, or determining the residential status of asylum seekers (Hawthorne, 1997; Shohamy, 2001).

In the United Kingdom the story was somewhat different. While testing speaking in the United States was frequently seen as 'desirable but not feasible', the University of Cambridge Local Examinations Syndicate (UCLES) were not hampered by concerns over reliability or measurement theory. A sub-test of spoken English was included in the Certificate of Proficiency in English at its introduction in 1913 (Roach, 1945). The examination consisted of:

I. *Written*
  (a) Translation from English into French or German (2 hours)
  (b) Translation from French or German into English, and questions on English Grammar (2½ hours)
  (c) English Essay (2 hours)
  (d) English Literature (The paper on English Language and Literature [Group A, Subject 1] in the Higher Local Examination) (3 hours)
  (e) English Phonetics (1½ hours)

II. *Oral:*
  Dictation (½ hour)
  Reading and Conversation (½ hour) (marked only for pronunciation)

Unlike in the United States, the primary purpose of an examination in the United Kingdom was to support the syllabus and encourage good teaching and learning (Brereton, 1944). As speaking was valued, it was therefore included in the examination on these grounds alone. When the Lower Certificate (now referred to as the First Certificate in English, or FCE) was introduced in 1939 there was a speaking test in the first form of the paper. Despite the early use of speaking tests in the United Kingdom there is little documented evidence of how they were designed or administered.

TESTING SPEAKING IN THE WAR YEARS

The Second World War was a watershed in the history of testing speaking. It was realised very early that many of the soldiers did not have the language skills that were required to carry out their duties. It is significant that Kaulfer's important 1944 article in the *Modern Language Journal* concludes with the words 'Foreign Languages for Global War and Global Peace!'

The Army Specialized Training Program (ASTP) was created in 1942 in order to address the communication problems of American service personnel through the delivery of language programmes that focused on speaking in the fields of engineering, medical and area studies/language (Spolsky, personal communication). The first learners started following the new syllabuses in early 1943 and some 140,000 soldiers received intensive instruction in the year that the ASTP operated. It was suspended by the US government in April 1944.

The ASTP was the first language instruction programme with the specific aim 'to impart to the trainee a command of the colloquial spoken form of a language and to give the trainee a sound knowledge of the area in which the language is used' (Angiolillo, 1947: 32). It is therefore not surprising that the criterion for success should be different from everything that had gone before. An individual was rated as 'expert' or 'competent' in the language following an ASTP programme. An 'expert' is an individual who 'can both comprehend and speak the language as well as a person with the same amount of formal schooling should speak his mother tongue', and a 'competent' individual 'can readily comprehend the language as spoken by one adult native to another and can speak the language well enough to be intelligible to natives on non-technical subjects of military importance'. The shift in pedagogy towards teaching speaking had lead to the leap from assessing grammatical knowledge to ability to perform. The use of the verb 'can' is extremely significant. Kaulfers (1944: 137) reflects this change in thinking and practice when talking about what new tests might look like:

> The urgency of the world situation does not permit of erudite theorizing in English about the grammatical structure of the language for two years before attempting to converse or to understand telephone conversations. . . . The nature

of the individual test items should be such as to provide specific, recognizable evidence of the examinee's readiness to perform in a life-situation, where lack of ability to understand and speak extemporaneously might be a serious handicap to safety and comfort, or to the effective execution of military responsibilities.

Kaulfers argued that pencil and paper tests were incapable of measuring the ability to speak in real-life conditions. The claim that they can measure speaking ability relies on the 'correlational fallacy' (see the discussion of correlation in Chapter 8). The fallacy is the conclusion that if there is a correlation between results on a paper and pencil test and a speaking test, the two tests are measuring the same construct. 'It simply cannot be taken for granted that ability to express oneself in writing is correlated with a like ability to speak the language extemporaneously' (Kaulfers, 1944: 140). Kaulfers argued for five-minute performance tests with three difficulty levels, each containing three items. The difficulty level of items and levels would be established through the use of bilingual subjects.

Interlocutors would be educated in the language being tested to a high level, and the raters would be trained using samples presented on phonograph. The interlocutor and rater would be different individuals. Kaulfers suggests that the test be administered in pleasant surroundings, and that the interviewer should be friendly and informal, but businesslike. The test would begin with informal talk to relax the test taker before the start of the actual test. The structure of the proposed test was:

1. Securing Services
2. Asking for Information
3. Giving Information

An example of an item in section 1 is: 'How would you tell a native speaker of Spanish to get you a doctor?' These performance tests were never designed and put into practice, but the foundation for new types of speaking test had been built.

The only test development in relation to the new ASTP programmes was undertaken at Queen's College, New York. Agard and Dunkel (1948: 55) reported that in 1944 they were unable to find any examples of published tests of speaking in the literature, and so designed their own to assess ASTP students. The criterion for success was 'communicative ability'. Barnwell (1996: 86–7) records that this was a three-part test:

1. *Picture description*
   The test taker is required to look at a sequence of pictures and describe what is portrayed in each.

2. *Sustained speech*
   The test taker is given a topic and required to deliver a short talk without preparation. An example of this task for a lower level learner is:

   > You are talking with a Spanish-speaking person who has never been to the United States. Describe to him the town or city in which you live. [If further

stimulus is necessary before time is up]: This person is also interested in what a North American home looks like. Describe to him the home in which you live.

3. *Directed conversation*

A prompt was delivered on a phonograph in the target language, and a voice in English would then tell the test taker what to do.

Parts 1 and 3 were rated on a three-level rating scale. The higher the score, the more successful the test taker was in communicating the intended message. Part 2 was linguistically based, using grammar, fluency, vocabulary and pronunciation as criteria for success. This college-based work in the testing of speaking is a clear precursor of the first published test of speaking, the Foreign Service Institute (FSI) Oral Proficiency Interview (OPI).

In the United Kingdom the testing of speaking also had a military focus, but new thinking about speaking test design and laying foundations for in-novations were slower to emerge. Much of the language teaching that went on in the United Kingdom, and those parts of the world over which the Allies had control, was done by the Army Education Corps. Much of this was teaching English to Allied Forces in Europe. The UCLES' tests were used to assess the learners' progress and 'as an encouragement to regular study under conditions that were often difficult' (Roach, 1945: 37). However, the test structure did not change at all from that introduced in 1913. Rather, it was the test users who had changed. The existing test was seen as providing adequate 'encouragement' to study, and an appropriate syllabus for the mili-tary. The main concern in the United Kingdom was:

> (a) How far it is possible to coordinate the standards of oral examiners in modern languages by means of joint examining, and (b) whether standards could be defined, for examiners both near and far, by some more positive means than rather sketchy and abstract instructions.   (Roach, 1945: 4)

The Roach studies during the war related to the reading aloud section of the CPE and the lower certificate, not to the conversation. A pass was awarded for a score of 8/20, a good pass for 12/20, and a very good pass for 16/20. Roach was concerned with establishing and maintaining these 'standards' across all language groups taking the test, and all examiners including new ones. The meaning of the scores is determined by the exam-ination board, and this meaning is learned by the examiners through familiarisation with the system over a period of time through practice. The examiners learn to 'feel' the standard by which they must grade. Thus, Roach was investigating whether joint examining and discussion of test takers would result in the 'feel' for the standards being passed on. This was con-ceived of entirely in terms of inter-rater reliability, or the extent to which two or more examiners would agree with each other on the scores awarded to a single learner. Roach concluded that standards are acquired in a fairly short period of time.

TESTING SPEAKING IN THE COLD WAR

Prior to the Second World War the American Council of Learned Societies ran language programmes for military personnel and diplomats in 'languages of potential military and diplomatic importance' (Liskin-Gasparro, 1984b: 17). With the realisation that American personnel were ill-equipped to deal with the linguistic demands which were placed upon them during the war, the FSI was set up in order to teach foreign languages which would be needed in overseas posts (Kramsch, 1986b: 366).

The initial impetus to the development of speaking tests was undoubtedly military need, but it was not until 1952 that it became necessary to measure the speaking skills taught by the FSI Instructors when the Civil Service Commission decided to create a register of personnel documenting their familiarity with foreign languages and cultures (Liskin-Gasparro, op. cit., 18–19). A committee with the responsibility for developing a test of speaking produced the first public, widely used rating scale (or scoring rubric) which consisted of six bands. Band (or level) 1 represented no ability to use a language, while band 6 represented native-speaker ability. No information is available concerning the choice of 6 bands as opposed to any other number, and no evidence is available to explain why a minimum of band 4 was required for diplomatic personnel. Sollenberger (1978: 5) states that 'to avoid complicating the task, no effort was made to separate the components of language proficiency'. What was developed was thus an intuitive six-band holistic rating scale with 'weak' descriptors only for the lowest and highest bands.

Political and bureaucratic problems held up work on and implementation of the 1952 testing procedures until 1956, when a survey discovered that personnel still did not possess the required speaking skills for their roles. In 1956 the FSI was given the responsibility to provide evidence of foreign language proficiency for all Foreign Service personnel. Sollenberger (1978) reports that one of the initial problems which the FSI faced was that the rank and age of officers tended to influence the raters' judgements. The FSI developers had identified one aspect of what today would be called test bias.

In 1958 the FSI testing unit further developed the 1952 scales by adding a checklist of five factors for raters, each measured on the six-point scale. These five factors were accent, comprehension, fluency, grammar and vocabulary (Adams, 1980). This was the first step towards developing multiple trait rating, even though the components were to be used as a check on a single holistic score (see the extended discussion of rating scales in Chapter 4). Further, although it was claimed that the rating procedure was 'a highly accurate predictor', the limitation of the system was also acknowledged to be that it did not measure 'effective communication' (Sollenberger, 1978: 7–8). Thus, from the very earliest days in the development of modern rating scales for speaking tests the roles of linguistic competence and communicative ability were issues of which the testers were aware.

Confidence in the new testing procedures developed by the FSI was so high that during the 1960s the method was adopted (and adapted) by the

Defense Language Institute, the Central Intelligence Agency (CIA) and the Peace Corps. Quinones (no date) details the way in which the CIA adapted the FSI system for its own use, the most important feature of which was the use of multiple raters and an averaging system for their marks in an attempt to increase reliability.

In 1968, partly as a result of experiences of language needs during the Vietnam War, these diverse agencies came together to produce a standardised version of the levels, which today is known as the Interagency Language Roundtable (ILR) (Lowe, 1987). This scale is still in use by the American security services and the Defense Language Institute (DLI).

These early developments in testing speaking thus generated interest in holistic versus multiple trait rating, bands and their descriptors, test bias, the difference between linguistic and communicative criteria for rating, and reliability. All of these areas are very high on the agenda of language testers today.

TESTING SPEAKING IN EDUCATIONAL CONTEXTS

The substantial use of the FSI system by the Peace Corps outside the control of the government agencies introduced the new testing system to academics and teachers (Liskin-Gasparro, 1984b: 22), and in the 1970s it was adopted by many universities and states for the purpose of bilingual teacher certification. The process of introducing the FSI system into universities and schools began with the development of the Testing Kit Workshops (Adams and Frith, 1979), initially for teachers of French and Spanish. Inter-rater reliabilities for speaking test scores between teachers and FSI raters were reported to be consistently over 0.84. The teachers used in this rating process had not been subjected to a lengthy period of rater training, and the confidence shown in the FSI system most probably came, in part, through the assumption that the rating scales in themselves possessed a degree of 'psychological reality', rather than being a mere artefact of the training. However, as we shall see, this was never addressed in research.

Barnwell (1987: 36) provides three other reasons why the FSI approach to testing speaking became generally popular within a short space of time. Firstly, as a direct test of speaking ability, the FSI was seen to have high face validity. Unfortunately, claims of high face validity have often resulted in claims of validity for all speaking tests (see Chapter 7). Others have warned of the dangers of this approach, as no evidence is involved in the construction of a validity argument (Stevenson, 1981; Messick, 1989). Secondly, inter-rater reliability had been shown to be high. Thirdly, by the late 1970s there was a growing interest in the notional/functional approach to teaching English, and it was widely perceived that the direct speaking test was a natural testing adjunct of new teaching methods. Thus, the relationship between teaching methodology and testing was recognised, and the importance attached to face validity may be seen in that context.

In 1979 the work of J. B. Carroll (1967) became the focus of considerable attention. Carroll had administered the speaking test to college majors of French, German, Russian and Spanish in the United States, and concluded that very few college majors in these foreign languages were capable of achieving a level above 2/2+. Level 3 in the FSI rating system was set as the minimum for professional working proficiency. Carroll's study was replicated in 1979 by the Educational Testing Service (ETS) (Liskin-Gasparro, 1984b: 27), and it was argued that if the ILR approach to testing speaking was to be used by universities, colleges and schools, the rating scales would have to be developed to allow more discrimination below the ILR 2+ level. The rationale was simply that it would not be appropriate for students to spend many hours of study on the foreign language and register no progress at all on the rating scale. This led directly to the involvement of ETS and the American Council on the Teaching of Foreign Languages (ACTFL) to alter the ILR rating scales to suit the new purposes for which speaking tests were being used outside the government (Liskin-Gasparro, 1984a: 447, 1984b: 25; Lowe, 1983: 232, 1985a: 13, 1987; Clark, 1988: 4–10).

In 1979 the President's Commission on Foreign Language and International Studies presented its report 'Strength through Wisdom: A Critique of US Capability' to President Carter. Among its recommendations was the setting up of a National Criteria and Assessment Program to develop language tests and assess language learning in the US, citing the work of the FSI as a valuable step in this direction.

ACTFL was given the role of producing National criteria, and the ACTFL Provisional Proficiency Guidelines appeared in 1982 (ACTFL, 1982), the complete Guidelines in 1986 (ACTFL, 1986), and the revised Guidelines in 1999 (ACTFL, 1999). The Guidelines gave birth to the Proficiency Movement (see the discussion of testing and curriculum in Chapter 7).

FSI TO ACTFL: THE FOCUS ON RATING SCALES

The early history of testing speaking focused almost exclusively on the development of rating scales, or rubrics, for the test (Fulcher, 1987: 78). Task design and the role played by tasks in tests was a concern that was to arise at a later date.

The FSI rating scale

The first FSI interviews were conducted by a native-speaker interviewer who was selected on the criteria of 'friendliness' and 'interest' to elicit the speech sample, and a rater who need not be fluent in the language, but who was sensitive to errors which the student might make (Wilds, 1979). The interview would last between 10 and 40 minutes. The procedure used was for the interviewer to begin with simple social formulae, and from there to proceed to elicit grammatical structures from the candidate. After this, a role-play or a prepared dialogue would be used. Elicitation techniques were prepared in advance. The rater would take notes, and grade the candidate on a six-point scale across five factors, as presented in Table 1.1.

Table 1.1   FSI rating factors

Accent	foreign	_:_:_:_:_:_	native
Grammar	inaccurate	_:_:_:_:_:_	accurate
Vocabulary	inadequate	_:_:_:_:_:_	adequate
Fluency	uneven	_:_:_:_:_:_	even
Comprehension	incomplete	_:_:_:_:_:_	complete

A weighted scoring system was devised by Wilds which was derived from the multiple correlation between each of the factors and the overall rating assigned. The weighted score was then converted into one of the FSI levels. This process (ETS, 1970) is illustrated in Tables 1.2 and 1.3.

Table 1.2   FSI weighting table

Proficiency description	1	2	3	4	5	6	
Accent	0	1	2	2	3	4	____
Grammar	6	12	18	24	30	36	____
Vocabulary	2	8	12	16	20	24	____
Fluency	2	4	6	8	10	12	____
Comprehension	4	8	12	15	19	23	____
			Total ____				

Table 1.3   FSI conversion table

Total score from weighting table	FSI Level
25	0+
26–32	1
33–42	1+
43–52	2
53–62	2+
63–72	3
73–82	3+
83–92	4
93–99	4+

From Table 1.2 we can see that grammatical accuracy is given the highest weighting in deriving the final scores. It is often claimed that this is still the case with the most recent ACTFL scales, and is the point of some contention between ACTFL proponents and their critics (van Patten, 1986). The

components which are chosen for criteria in a rating scale, and the importance of each of those components, is an area of research in which little
progress had been made, apart from the work done by Adams (1980), until
very recently (see Chapter 4). However, in 1958 when descriptors were for
the first time written to give content to the levels of the FSI scale, a process
was begun which provided the opportunity to conduct research into the
relationship between the test and actual language production. The 1958 FSI
band descriptors are given in full in Appendix 1.

It should be noted that the FSI band descriptors were developed in
such a way that they could be applied to all languages. In other words
it was considered to be a 'common measure' (Clark, 1980), and this
explained the very real problems in ensuring that an S-3 in French was
not more difficult to obtain than in other languages, as reported by
Sollenberger (1978).

The scale ranged from no proficiency whatsoever, to native speaker ability.
The concept of the 'native speaker' as an assessment criterion has affected most
rating scales since the FSI, and is one to which we shall return in Chapter 4.

The assessment carried out was global, but despite Sollenberger's view
that there was no attempt to isolate components of speaking ability, we have
seen that component scales were developed and a weighting system constructed. The component scales, given in full in Appendix 2, were used only
in the training of FSI raters, and in live tests as a check on the accuracy of the
global score awarded. However, there is no published evidence to suggest
whether this practice was successful or not.

The FSI descriptors contain a mixture of linguistic and non-linguistic criteria. There are undefined degrees of accuracy to be achieved for each level
in each scale, mixed with references to the types of task or the situation in
which the student would be expected to operate outside the test situation.
This mixture of criteria is another aspect of the original FSI descriptors
which has been passed on to successive generations of rating scales, and is
frequently criticised (Matthews, 1990). If prediction from a test situation to a
wider number of non-test situations is the purpose of the speaking test, then
it is often claimed that the rating scale contain descriptions of those skills or
abilities which researchers can demonstrate underlie successful performance
across a range of situations, or to specify tasks or situations which could be
demonstrated to allow generalisation to other tasks or situations.

Each of the scales assumes linear development in language proficiency
from zero to perfect, native-speaker speech. Each band represents an increase
in the accuracy of the language used, with similar modifiers being used in
each rating scale. The grammar scale appears to hinge around the progression of modifiers from 'constant', to 'frequent', 'occasional' and 'few' errors.
At band 1 grammar is 'entirely' inaccurate and at band 6 we expect 'no more
than 2 errors' – a specific number, the choice of which does not seem to
have been justified. Nowhere is it suggested what kinds of errors typify each
band, and there is no indication that the scale is linked to any consideration
of a sequence in which students acquire certain grammatical forms. The

reference to 'major patterns' in band 2 may seem to suggest that the authors of the scale did have some notion of the grammatical forms that they would expect to occur in earlier and later bands, but these are not listed or described.

The situation is similar with the FSI fluency rating scale. In band 1 we are told that 'conversation is virtually impossible' while in the last band it is 'as effortless and smooth as a native speaker's'. The concepts that dominate the bands between the extremes are those of speed of delivery, hesitation and 'unevenness', modified by 'very', 'frequently' and 'occasionally' in bands 2 to 4. These concepts are not defined. Speed of delivery may vary considerably among non-native and native speakers of a language, and 'unevenness' appears to be linked to 'rephrasing and groping for words', something which appears to be frequent in native-speaker speech (Fulcher, 1987). The nature of hesitation and its causes do not seem to have been investigated, and without a theory underlying the possible reasons for hesitation it would seem unlikely that the concept could be applied in such a linear fashion to non-native learners.

As the FSI provides the model which many other rating scales have adopted, these concepts, despite being poorly defined, have found their way into many other rating scales produced since the FSI with little or no change. The problem has been that the descriptors produced by the scale writers come from intuitive judgements about how language competence develops, and how this competence is used in a performance test.

The ILR rating scale

The ILR rating scales were produced in 1968 in the attempt by various government agencies to standardise their procedures. The ILR rating scale contained 6 bands, with plus points at 0, 1, 2, 3 and 4, giving 11 possible levels of proficiency. The 'Capsule Characterisations' of these levels is provided by Lowe (1985a: 14) as follows:

Level 0: No functional ability.

Level 0+: Operates with memorized material, and short lists.

Level 1: Survival. Consistently creates with the language. Tends to operate in the present time. Uses short sentences.

Level 2: Concrete. Operates in past and future as well as present time. Can use paragraphs (combining sentences into limited connected discourse).

Level 3: Abstract. Thinks in the target language. Supports opinions and hypothesizes. Handles unfamiliar situations and topics. Can use organized discourse. General vocabulary is controlled with only sporadic errors in basic grammar, but with some errors in frequent complex structures and more errors in low-frequency complex structures. Can use colloquial and careful formal speech.

Level 4: Representation. Tailors language to suit the audience. Discourse is well organized and a controlled use of synonyms.

Level 5: Educated Native. Functions equivalent to a well-educated native speaker. Absolutely appropriate discourse in a wide range of contexts from colloquial to careful formal speech.

The scale begins with no ability and ends with native-speaker ability, although there are a number of additional assumptions made:

- present tenses are used before past and future
- control of discourse begins with the ability to use paragraphs (band 2)
  - although what a 'paragraph' is in speech is not explained
- the ability to use colloquial and formal speech is a feature of band 3
  - although we are not told which of these is used prior to band 3
- awareness of audience and the puzzling 'use of synonyms' is a feature of band 4

As in the FSI scale, precise definition of terms is avoided, although there is some indication as to why this is the case. Lowe (1985a: 15) claims that the ILR rating scale was developed on the basis of Gestalt psychology, arguing metaphorically that one does not have to 'test the soil to tell that you are on a mountain: one need only rely on the overall shape of the terrain'.

The ACTFL/ETS rating scale

The ACTFL rating scale, described by Lowe (1987), was specifically designed with a larger number of levels in order to discriminate more accurately between students in non-government settings at the level below 2/2+ following the studies by Carroll and the ETS. Table 1.4 is taken from Lowe (1983: 232) and demonstrates how the ACTFL levels relate to the ILR rating scale.

The categories at the lower end of the continuum have been expanded to increase the amount of discrimination possible, while at the higher end all the categories from S-3 upwards have been collapsed into the single category 'superior'.

Table 1.4 A comparison of the ILR and ACTFL rating scales

ILR	ACTFL
5	
4+	
4	Superior
3+	
3	
2+	Advanced Plus
2	Advanced
1+	Intermediate High
1 (strong)	Intermediate Mid
1 (weak)	Intermediate Low
0+	Novice High
0 (strong)	Novice Mid
0 (weak)	Novice Low

Republished with permission of American Association of Teachers of German, from 'The ILR oral interview: origins, applications, pitfalls, and implications' by P. Lowe in *Die Unterrichtspraxis*, 16, © 1983 by American Association of Teachers of German; permission conveyed through Copyright Clearance Center, Inc.

The descriptors used to define the ACTFL levels are given in full in Appendix 3 from the ACTFL Guidelines (1986).

The ACTFL scale is marked by an increase in the amount of information which is provided for the rater, but the lack of detailed explanation of the terms used or potential exponents in actual speech continues to be a mark of the prose descriptions. No empirical evidence is available to confirm that new criteria introduced into the rating scale such as 'discourse', 'interactive' or 'communicative' strategies do discriminate between the students at the proposed ability levels where these occur. Indeed, Lowe (1985a: 16) states that 'the use of the system remains implicit' which means that rater training is essential for any practical use of the scale (see Chapter 6). Finally, we make the observation that the mixture of linguistic and non-linguistic criteria is increased in the ACTFL scale, indicating task type and topic area which may be dealt with at a given level of ability. This is often seen as the confusion of criteria, which may make validation studies extremely difficult (Bachman and Savignon, 1986; Matthews, 1990).

The ACTFL Guidelines were revised in 1999. These are given in full in Appendix 4. The most obvious change is that the order of the bands or levels has been reversed, with Superior coming first. ACTFL (1999: 14) argues that this

> emphasizes that the high levels are more closely related to the level above than to the one below, and represents a considerable step towards accomplishing the functions at the level above, not just excellence in the functions of the level itself. Second, it allows for fewer negatives and less redundancy in the descriptions when they refer, as they must, to the inability of a speaker to function consistently at a higher level.

Secondly, the Advanced level is now divided into three sections: High, Mid and Low. This, it is argued, is to allow finer discrimination among more advanced learners. Nevertheless, it remains essentially an *a priori* construction with little published evidence to support the usefulness of these levels.

DIGEST

This chapter has not attempted to document every change to the CPE, or record each new development in speaking tests in the United States (like the pioneering work of Upshur, 1971). Nor has it attempted to provide an extended critique and discussion of the rating scales that have been discussed. That will be presented in Chapter 4.

The main purpose of this chapter has been to show that tests of speaking have always been thought of as important, but that they were too unreliable and impractical to use in the kind of large-scale language testing that emerged in the 1920s with a rapidly expanding educational system. Despite the use of a traditional unstructured speaking test on the 1913 CPE, of which we know very little, the main thrust in the development of tests of speaking stemmed initially from the requirements to stem immigration in the late 1920s, and more importantly by the need to ensure that military personal could carry out their duties safely and effectively. After the Second World War it was the continuing pressure from the US Administration to register the language capabilities of diplomatic and military personnel, and prepare the country for future conflict, that led to the first large-scale speaking test development programme at the Foreign Service Institute.

The military model was updated, and exported to schools and colleges. The ILR is still in use, and few speaking tests do not owe something in their design and scoring system to the ACTFL oral proficiency interview.

It is important to note that the 'construct' – what is being measured – is defined within the rating scale. The bands or levels of the rating scale are intended to describe levels of language proficiency that 'exist' in the real world, whether the descriptions are phrased in terms of language elements or functional ability. But the question of 'what it means to be able to speak' was infrequently raised until the 1970s. This is the topic of the next chapter.

Chapter 2

Defining the construct

Lado (1961: 239) wrote: 'The ability to speak a foreign language is without doubt the most highly prized language skill, and rightly so. . . . Yet testing the ability to speak a foreign language is perhaps the least developed and the leased practiced in the language testing field.' Lado argued that this was because of 'a clear lack of understanding of what constitutes speaking ability or oral production'.

Asking questions like 'What is speaking?' or 'What constitutes speaking ability?' is a matter of *construct definition*. The purpose of this chapter is to look at ways in which we might define the construct of speaking. In order to do that we must first understand what a 'construct' is. We frequently use the word 'concept' to talk about abstractions such as 'achievement'. We can't observe 'achievement' directly, but teachers talk about what their students have 'achieved' based on all the observations of performance that they make in the classroom. 'Achievement' is defined in terms of the observable behaviours that are of interest in a particular learning context. A construct is frequently said to be a concept that is deliberately defined for a 'special scientific purpose'. Kerlinger and Lee (2000: 40) argue that a construct differs from a concept in two important ways: it is defined in a way that can be observed and measured, and that the relationship between different constructs constitutes a theory. We add the proviso that theory is always contingent upon evidence, and evidence upon theory, in an endless refinement of our understanding of the utility of theory for the practice of assessment. If we are to define 'speaking' as a construct it is therefore necessary for this construct to be associated with 'things' that can be observed, and that these 'things' can be scored. Such definitions are said to be 'operational'. The relationship of 'speaking' to 'reading' or 'listening' for example (to use Lado's 1957 terminology – which is not necessarily useful today) may then constitute a theory of 'language use'. This is a gross oversimplification, but helps to clarify the meaning of the term 'construct', and it focuses on the key point that any construct definition needs to be operational if it is to be useful to the language tester.

Lado (1961) drew attention to the fact that that there was no operational definition of the construct 'speaking'. His solution to the problem of construct

under-definition was to test linguistic elements in order to eliminate variables that might be confounded with the construct, such as 'talkativeness' or
'introversion'. Lado wished a test of speaking to be a language test, and to
avoid anything that would 'muddy' the construct and the interpretation
of the scores. This approach is often called the 'trait theory' approach to
construct validity. More recently there has been a tendency to admit that
sometimes, when contextual factors clearly impact upon discourse and test
score, it may be more appropriate to include the contextual factors in the
construct definition (Chapelle, 1999a). This may be most appropriate in tests
of speaking for specific purposes (Douglas, 2000), where the definition of
the construct, the selection of tasks and the scoring procedure are designed
to collect evidence for ability to speak in a small sub-set of contexts, such as
service encounters or air traffic control. In these cases a full description of
the target language use domain (Bachman and Palmer, 1996) forms the
basis for test design, as the inferences made from scores are not to 'speaking
ability' but to 'speaking ability in x, y or z context'. In other words, test
purpose should drive the definition of the construct, its range and generalisability. But there are many other factors that could be included in the definition of the construct. If we accept the view that conversation is co-constructed
between participants talking in specific contexts, our construct definition
may have to take into account such aspects of talk as the degree of interlocutor support. We discuss these more complex aspects of construct definition
within the context of Interactional Competence Theory.

So this chapter aims to consider what types of 'things' (in the broadest
sense) might contribute to an operational definition of 'speaking' that will
inform the design and development of a test of speaking, including the
mode of delivery, tasks and method of scoring. However, it is not claimed
that the list is exhaustive in any way. No operational construct definition can
ever capture the richness of what happens in a process as complex as human
communication, even if the speaking test is mediated by tape or computer.
Nor is it being suggested that a test of speaking should test everything that we
will attempt to put into our list. Choices will depend upon test purpose and
the extent to which scores need to be generalisable to other contexts.

The qualifications of the last paragraph may seem defensive, but they are
not. We saw in the first chapter that one of the reasons for the spread of
testing speaking from the military to educational contexts was the assumption that there was some 'psychological reality' underlying the descriptors of
the rating scale. This is a mistake. The constructs we use in testing speaking
should be those which are *useful* for the testing purpose. We should not
assume that any description, any rating scale, captures some psychological
reality that exists in the language competence of all speakers for all time
in all contexts. Different constructs are useful for different test purposes. Or,
to put it another way, 'The relation of tools to what they manipulate is simply
a matter of utility for a particular purpose, not of "correspondence"' (Rorty,
1999: 65). We can therefore only consider what we have learnt about what it
means to 'speak', and use such descriptions to construct 'constructs' that are

useful for our testing purposes; the construct definition we decide upon should not be evaluated by its correspondence to psychological reality, but its utility in making inferences from test scores, and its value in helping us to construct a validity argument that supports the link between a test score and what we claim it means.

To approach this from a slightly different angle, the field of applied linguistics has been burdened for decades with the neo-platonic distinction between 'competence' and 'performance'. The former is intra-individual, the latter inter-individual. For some, the former is 'real' and the latter 'incidental'. For others the former is merely a 'heterogeneous capacity' and the latter 'observable reality'. When discussing communication strategies (CS), for example, Kasper and Kellerman (1997b: 3) write that:

> Identification of CS depends to a great extent on what one considers a CS to be, and in this respect, it matters very much whether one conceives of CS as intraindividual or interindividual events.

But it does not matter, except with regard to the research methods that might be employed, for example in a choice between analysing hesitation phenomena or retrospective verbal protocol analysis (see Chapter 8). The distinction between what is inside (knowledge, competence, capacity, etc.) and what is external (interaction, communication, co-construction, etc.) is fluid. The two interact. My 'competence' in Chinese is non-existent; I cannot co-construct discourse and meaning in Chinese. My competence in Greek is fair. I have a 'knowledge' of the vocabulary and structure of the language. Through interaction with other speakers of the language I have gained other competencies which are useful in new situations, but not all. The strategies that I use to interact are simultaneously internal and external to myself. I am recognisable as myself when I speak in a variety of contexts, and yet in context my speech is always contextually bound. The internal/external, competence/performance distinction is useful for some purposes, and not for others. The 'absolute' choice of analysing hesitation phenomenon or employing retrospective verbal protocol analysis is illusory: both contribute evidence about the study of speaking strategies *from a different perspective*. When talking about constructs in this book there is no explicit distinction between the internal and the external, although for some aspects of construct there may be a focus on one or the other. The focus depends upon the utility of the construct definition for test purpose: sometimes it is necessary to be a trait theorist, and at other times to try and increase score-task dependency, sometimes to score grammatical accuracy, and at other times the quality of a group interaction.

From what we know about speaking and testing second language speaking from research, we can therefore 'pick and mix' to make a construct. All we have to do is provide a rationale and empirical evidence to support the 'mix' we end up with in terms of test purpose. One attempt to define the speaking construct for an academic context states that 'the available research does not provide a firm foundation for constructing a specific test of speaking as part of second language academic communicative competence' (Butler *et al.*, 2000: 3). If by 'firm foundation' the authors mean that there is a 'real' or 'true' or 'best' construct definition for 'second language academic communicative competence' the search for it will be as futile as our failure to reach agreement on the meaning of 'communicative' in language teaching and testing. What Butler *et al.* end up doing is recounting the key aspects of the sociological and speech act theory approaches to describing speech, but do not suggest which 'features' of 'speaking' might be included in a construct definition for 'second language academic communicative competence'.

Firstly, we include a discussion of learning to speak in a primary, and then second language. Following this, the remainder of chapter is more like the sweet section of a highway service station where you can select from the choice on offer to make up your pic'n' mix bag. The selection is a brief presentation of approaches to describing speaking , with references only to key studies in the field, followed by a consideration of speech as co-construction. The selection is not exhaustive by any means, but presents the range of more common choices for inclusion in construct definition for tests of second language speaking.

LEARNING TO SPEAK

Learning to speak primary languages

Most speakers grow up learning more than one language; they are bilingual or trilingual because of the speech they hear in their environment. Monolingual societies are the exception, rather than the rule. But whether we use one or more than one language in our daily lives, the outer form of speech is sound. Sounds are meaningful because of the inner representation or meaning of the sounds in the language that the speaker and listener share. It is the ability to speak and understand the speech of others that makes us different from other species. It is also the factor that makes us more alike, whatever our primary language background, than anything else that might help to define the word 'human'.

There is considerable variation in language use among speakers of the same language too. Individuals often have their own 'way of speaking'. This 'idiolect' is part of what it means to be an individual. Each individual shares a 'dialect' with others from the same speech community, identifying the individual as a member of a group within society. And in society each individual participates in a range of speech situations. These situations require the use of different types of speech, which may take the form of stylistic variations ranging from friendly conversations to formal exchanges in business meetings. Or they may take the form of participation in highly specialised genres such as courtroom presentations or delivering lectures in physics. Nevertheless, the variability that is often so striking cannot hide the fact that speakers have more in common than what separates them: the ability to use language to communicate.

The ability to communicate and the steady development of speech are so natural that most people find it unremarkable. Speaking is an ability that is taken for granted, learned as it is through a process of socialisation through communicating (Hall, 1995). Linguists, applied linguists and language teachers are unusual in this respect. Speech is a focus for their study and attention.

A great deal of effort has gone into describing linguistic and communicative 'competence' – underlying mental abilities that make speech possible (Canale and Swain, 1980; Bachman, 1990). Applied linguists have also made much progress in describing variability in speech in different contexts. We know that discussing the weather with our next door neighbour is likely to be a very different speech event from negotiating a contract with a supplier of raw materials. We also know a great deal about how speakers cooperate to co-construct talk. But the definitions are not so robust that we can easily define a construct for a particular test of speaking, even in a first language. Rubin and Schramm (1997: 34) echo Lado when they state that 'The validity of speech assessments suffers from a lack of construct definition.'

Learning to speak a second language

Learning to speak a second or third (non-primary) language is different from acquiring a primary language or languages. There are many theories about why this is so. One suggests that after a certain age we no longer have access to the innate 'language acquisition device' that makes the primary languages seem so easy to acquire. After the age of nine, it may be that humans must make an effort to *learn* to speak in another language. Learning (or acquiring) a language as a child is *something that happens*; learning a language slightly later in life is something you *do*. Language teachers more than others are aware of the years of effort that many learners need to put into learning a language, specifically learning how to speak. Even so, there are many learners who do not achieve their goal of being able to communicate at the target level.

It is unremarkable to observe that learning to speak a language as an adolescent or adult is much more difficult than learning to speak a primary language. It is perhaps equally unremarkable to observe that while children acquire speech as a matter of course, older second language learners have motives and reasons for wishing to speak the new language. These reasons and motives have frequently been used as variables in studies of language learning. The most common division is between integrative and instrumental motivations. This dichotomy is a useful fiction through which we might try to understand the reasons why learners wish to learn a language. For example, learners may hold beliefs about a target population that speak a certain language. These beliefs or sentiments, when positive, lead to a desire to make friends with people who speak that language, or to work in the country where the language is spoken. When learners hold beliefs and sentiments like these, they wish to 'integrate' to some degree with the speakers of the language they are learning. Perhaps more common is the learner who needs to speak a language to achieve some goal that is related to study, work or leisure. A businessman may need to speak French to arrange shipments of wine to British supermarkets. A German student may need to speak English to study law at a British university. In these cases, the language is instrumental to another primary need.

Our understanding of why learners wish to speak another language, what is known about variation in speech over a range of contexts, and what is known about the process of speech, have contributed to how second language speaking is taught. Methods underpinned by 'consciousness-raising' or 'language awareness' theories include analysis of spoken genres, looking at patterns of turn-taking, focusing deliberately on fixed interactive lexical phrases, and so on. Studying authentic dialogues is a common technique, followed by the use of controlled exercises like dialogue scripts. Other methods stress the use of communication in pairs, small groups and whole class discussion. Role-play and simulations are also used to create the conditions under which learners may acquire the speaking skills they need outside the classroom. The theory underpinning this approach is that interaction leads to the acquisition of needed skills and knowledge (see Chapter 3).

However, there is little methodological research upon which we can draw to make any firm statements about the effectiveness of any particular approach or technique in teaching second language learners to speak in the target language, and even less in how best to test speaking. Although little appears to have changed since language teachers were told 'As ye teach, so shall ye test' on purely intuitive grounds (Underhill, 1982: 18), we hope to show that these shortcomings can be overcome by a close consideration of how we might best select tasks for second language speaking tests for their utility in generating performances that can be scored in a way that supports our understanding of test construct.

It is important to define the constructs for speaking tests in ways that are relevant and meaningful for learners, or more abstractly the 'test-taking population' for whom a test is designed. The constructs should be driven by test purpose, taking into account the desires and motivations of those who will take the test, and be sensitive to the requirements of score users.

WHAT IS SPEAKING?

Speaking is the verbal use of language to communicate with others. The purposes for which we wish to communicate with others are so large that they are innumerable, and as this is not a book about human needs and desires we will not even attempt to provide examples. The outward manifestation of speech is found in sound waves. Its meaning lies in the structure and meaning of all language, whether this is written or spoken. But speaking nevertheless differs from written language in a number of respects (Halliday,

1985; Biber, 1988). It is common to note that it is usually (although not by any means always) less formal in use of vocabulary, uses fewer full sentences as opposed to phrases, contains repetitions, repairs and has more conjunctions instead of subordination. But none of these observations changes the fact that speech *is* language, and is governed by the same syntactic and semantic rules. Some researchers have even suggested that the difference between speaking and writing is not as great as has often been suggested, because the differences relate only to casual conversations and not the many other more conventional exchanges that speakers engage in every day. In other words, there is a wide variety of 'speech events'.

Nevertheless, there are some features of speech that are 'endemic'. Speech is organised in particular ways. Openings and closings of topics or conversations, the way in which certain features occur next to each other (questions–answers), and turn taking, can all be described. Secondly, there are types of interaction that tend to occur mostly in speech. Greetings, invitations, offers, apologies and so on, are often fairly fixed in form. There are also more general 'rules' of speech that are related to the context of the talk. In any situation the speaker needs to make choices in the use of language depending on the formality of the situation, the social status of the various speakers, and a range of other contextual variables. These are critical social/contextual considerations for testing speaking when selecting the interlocutors or considering the use of paired or group formats for the test (see Chapter 7).

'Speech' in so far as it can be separated from 'language' will consist of a mix of these features, which we will consider below. However, there is a psychological aspect to speech that needs to be considered. When writing, the writer has time to plan, produce and correct. The speaker cannot tackle the task of speaking in the same leisurely manner.

Speech is a 'real-time' phenomenon (Bygate, 1987). It has to be planned, formulated and articulated with considerable speed. The speed with which learners can produce speech that is appropriate to the context will depend upon a number of factors, including their control over the structure of the language, their lexical range, the ability to chunk formulaic expressions, and ability to monitor the effect of speech on the listener. All of this can be summed up in terms of the degree to which the whole process has become 'automatic', and no longer requires conscious attention. This concept of 'automaticity' in speech may be associated with a number of factors, including the complexity of the message the learner wishes to communicate, how familiar they are with the topic area, the speed at which processing is expected to take place, the degree of accuracy required in the context, and perceived 'penalties' of getting something wrong.

Speech is about making choices. Learners must choose how to interact in expressing themselves and forming social relationships through speech. Making the right choices for the context is very important: what level of formality is required? Is interrupting permitted? How should you address the person you have just been introduced to? The choices are both internal (psycholinguistic) related to language and processing, and external (sociolinguistic) related to context and the interactive nature of the speech event with other speakers.

Any construct of 'speaking' or 'speech' is obviously going to be multi-faceted. And however much we may try to define and classify, the kinds of choices that a second language speaker makes are going to be influenced by the totality of their current understanding, abilities (personal and cognitive), language competence and speech situation. The choices are also going to be influenced by the person or persons they are talking to. What kind of feedback is being given? How does the other person contribute to the conversation?

We now turn to our pic'n' mix counter. We begin by looking very briefly at speech as sound, and then consider the use of the traditional terms 'accuracy' and 'fluency' in relation to the psychological aspect of speaking. Strategies in speaking are then considered, before turning to the structural aspects of speaking, including opening and closing conversations, and taking turns. We consider the pragmatic aspects of speaking, such as rules of speech, doing things with words, and the management of roles and relationships through the use of speech. Finally, we look at the co-construction of discourse, and what it may mean for testing second language speaking.

PRONUNCIATION AND INTONATION

The outer manifestation of speech is sound. The speaker must first decide what to say, be able to articulate the words, and create the physical sounds that carry meaning. Second language learners therefore need a knowledge of the language they wish to speak, an understanding of the phonetic structure of the language at the level of the individual word, and an understanding of intonation.

At the level of word pronunciation, second language learners regularly have problems distinguishing between sounds in the new language that do not exist in languages they already know. In English, examples may be between the vowel sounds in the words 'rule' and 'put', or between the initial consonants in the words 'June' and 'chin'. Problems with pronunciation at the level of the word may be distracting for the listener, but they rarely lead to miscommunication or misunderstanding. When we design speaking tests we must decide whether assessing pronunciation at this level is relevant at all to the situation. This depends upon the test purpose. Pronouncing words in the way they would be pronounced in the standard variety of a language may be important to a newsreader, but for most learners testing pronunciation may only be a matter of general intelligibility.

At levels above the word, the possibilities for miscommunication increase. At the level of utterances, stress carries a layer of meaning in addition to the words. Stress is recognised as the increased volume on a syllable, and sometimes this word or syllable can be longer than those surrounding it. Stress usually occurs on words that carry the most meaning in an utterance (see

Brazil, 1985). Imagine a situation in which a customer goes into a supermarket and asks for a large cheese.

Can I have a CHEESE, one of the LARGE ones please.

Here we can see that stress falls upon the words 'cheese' and 'large'. This is not surprising, as these are the words that carry the burden of the meaning in the request. Stressed or prominent syllables also carry information on tone (voice movement) and key (voice pitch) that we normally associate with intonation. This request was actually made with a rise–fall tone on both stressed words, showing that this is the important information, and that it is new information for the listener.

The assistant took one of the smaller cheeses and began to wrap it. The customer then said to the assistant:

Sorry, I said wanted the LARGE one.

In this example, the stress falls on the word 'large', making it prominent, and hence the most important part of the message. In this example, the word 'large' was said in a slightly higher key than the rest of the sentence (realised as higher pitch in the voice), which indicates *contrast*. It was also spoken with a falling tone, which indicates that this is still new information for the listener. If the speaker uses a mid key (no change in pitch from what has gone before) and a fall–rise tone (indicating information that you expect to share with the listener), the utterance may come across as indicating that the speaker is exasperated by the inability of the assistant to get the order right. In other words, the specific choices made by the speaker at the level of intonation send the message 'I want the large one, not the small one'.

It is at this level of communication that learners may often cause misunderstanding when speaking to others, rather than at the level of single word pronunciation.

ACCURACY AND FLUENCY

The distinction between 'accuracy' and 'fluency' is common in the literature on language teaching activities (see, for example, Brown and Yule, 1983: 104; Brumfit, 1984), and in second language acquisition studies. In the SLA literature the difference is variously referred to as that between 'norm-oriented' and 'communicative-oriented' learners (Clahsen, 1985), or 'rule-formers' and 'data-gatherers' (Hatch, 1974), or 'planners' and 'correctors' (Seliger, 1980). In each case, the former of the two categories refers to students who concentrate on building up grammatical rules and aim for accuracy in production (at the expense of fluency), and the latter category refers to students who concentrate on communicating fluently, paying little attention to accuracy. The two concepts are frequently seen as being at opposite ends of a continuum in which at extremes speech is seen as accurate and disfluent (hesitant, slow, etc.), or inaccurate and fluent.

In language testing, the attention of raters has been drawn to the accuracy of structure and vocabulary in speech as one component of assessment, and the quality and speed of delivery as a separate component. This is an attempt at construct definition: the operational definition of two related but distinct components that make up the construct of speaking. The distinction is still actively used by researchers such as Foster and Skehan (1996) and Skehan and Foster (1997) to predict task difficulty in speaking tests (see the discussion in Chapter 4).

Accuracy

Teachers are aware that learners make errors when speaking. As Brazil (1995: 11) notes:

> Our 'experience of speaking', to use Halliday's term, is of something that begins, continues, and ends in time: it happens. As speakers, we know that causing it to happen is not always without its problems: our ability to put together what we want to say may not always be equal to the pressure to keep up with ourselves, so to speak, in the delivery of our message.

Some of these errors interfere with communication, and others do not. The technical term used to talk about the seriousness of errors is 'error gravity' (James, 1998). Let us consider two simple examples:

- John buy a newspaper every day
- Every day a newspaper buy

In the first of these two sentences, the learner has not added the -s morpheme to the verb 'buy'. This is said to be an error of agreement between the subject and the verb. In speech this may be noticeable, but it is unlikely to cause misunderstanding because it is clear who buys the newspaper every day. The gravity of the error is therefore said to be very low. In the second sentence, however, there is a much more serious problem. Firstly, there is no subject in the sentence. In many languages this is quite acceptable, but not in English. Secondly, the verb 'buy' has been moved to the end of the sentence, after the object 'a newspaper'. In English, the verb must come before the object of the sentence, whereas in some languages this is not a requirement. Notice that the movement of 'every day' to the beginning of the sentence is not a problem, as phrases like this, called 'adjuncts', have more freedom of movement in English. The second sentence breaks the rules of word order in the language and removes information that is essential for communication. Errors of accuracy like this seriously interfere with the intended message. The gravity of the error is very high.

In teaching speaking it is common to correct high gravity errors immediately. Low gravity errors can wait. Teachers have to set priorities like this in the day-to-day planning and implementation of the syllabus. When testing speaking it is similarly important to decide what types of errors should be penalised in the scoring, and which errors should be ignored or treated with leniency. We will briefly look at some of the more common errors that learners make when speaking. The examples given are taken from real performances on a test of speaking English as a foreign language (Fulcher, 1993). For a fuller discussion of the grammar of speech, see Brazil (1995).

Word order and omission

We have already considered an example of a word order error above. In most cases, these errors do interfere with communication to a considerable degree. In English, the sentence 'every day a newspaper buy' is extremely difficult to understand, especially if delivered at speed in a stream of speech. We have already noted that in some languages it is possible to omit the subject of a sentence completely, whereas in other languages it is not possible to do this. In languages where the subject can be omitted it has to be supplied by the listener from the context, and by using grammatical clues such as verb endings that are marked for person and gender. But in languages like English omitting the subject causes a problem with cohesion, so that the listener does not necessarily know who the speaker is talking about. Word order and omission errors are almost always high gravity.

However, it is often the case that errors in word order or omission are corrected very early in the learning process. Evidence suggests that errors of this type decrease rapidly as the learner moves beyond the stage of being a 'beginner'.

Pronouns and relative clauses

The incorrect use of pronouns or relative pronouns can cause difficulty for the listener, but these are not usually as serious as word order errors. Consider the following example, in which a learner is explaining that many fathers will only allow girls to remain in the family home after the completion of full-time education if they pay rent:

> her father don't er [pause] if if he if he like to live in the house he must paid er the rent

The error here is one of reference, and likely to cause a problem with cohesion. The error may indicate that the learner has not yet fully acquired gender marking in the pronominal system.

Learners with little command of a language usually avoid complex sentence structure, particularly the use of relative clauses. As they progress in learning the language, more experimentation occurs. This means that sometimes learners make more errors as they learn more (see the discussion of an approach to rating non-linear speech in Chapter 4). In teaching and assessing, we should be aware of the fact that sometimes quite serious errors are made simply because the learner is making progress in learning the language. In the following example a learner is pointing to a graph and explaining that point 'r' on the graph marks the place at which material bends when it is being tested for how much stress it can tolerate.

> then we have we have r is the yield er [pause] of the material

Complex sentence structure is beginning to emerge, but the learner does not yet have the ability to successfully construct the relative clause. Here is another example, taken from the speech of the same learner. Here, the learner is explaining from the graph the point at which the material begins to bend.

> it bends where the load is fourteen kilonewtons [pause] where is the elastic point

We could correct this sentence so that the final clause reads 'which is where the elastic point is'. This learner is at a fairly advanced stage of acquiring complex sentence structure, and is using her knowledge of the language to communicate very efficiently.

These examples illustrate that errors are a sign of learning, and should not always be treated as 'negative' evidence that are 'penalised' in speaking tests.

Tense

In some languages, such as English, tense selection is probably the most common problem in speech production. Yet, the use of an inappropriate tense has hardly any impact at all on the listener's ability to understand what the speaker means. Take this example from a test situation, in which the learner responds to a question about what he does for a living:

> I am in the Political Affairs Division for the last five years.

As this is not intrusive in conversation, tense errors are generally of low gravity. Unless this kind of accuracy is seen to be very important within a particular context, it may be appropriate not to use it as a criterion in scoring.

Prepositions

Mis-selection of prepositions is extremely common in English, even with more advanced learners. Look at the following example taken from the speech of a learner who is explaining that when a new medicine is imported into the country where she works, the government medical laboratory is required to check the quality of the drug and then register it for legal distribution.

> they are first checked from their quality and then registered here.

The situation is similar to that with using an inappropriate tense. It is fairly easy for the listener to understand precisely what is meant. Once again, such errors are not considered to be very serious, because the impact upon the ability of the listener to understand is minimal.

Fluency

The terms 'accuracy' and 'fluency' are part of the vocabulary of language teaching, and most language teachers have an intuitive understanding of what these terms mean. Even classroom activities are often classified as 'fluency' or 'accuracy' based. Fluency – or rather the lack of it – is most often described in metaphorical language. Lack of fluency is therefore said to be 'slow and uneven speech', which is 'hesitant' or 'jerky'. It is 'uneven' as opposed to 'smooth', and learners are often said to 'grope for words' or 'stumble' when speaking. Speech is sometimes described as 'disconnected' or having incorrect 'rhythm'. This is a prime case of construct under-definition in second language teaching and testing, and it is rare for 'fluency' to be associated with particular speech behaviours that can be observed.

The concepts of 'accuracy' and 'fluency' are related through the notion of automaticity, which we have already discussed. If speech is going to be fluent, the process of planning what to say, retrieving the necessary grammar and vocabulary, and speaking, needs to be automatic. It is when speech becomes more noticeably automatic that we describe a speaker as being 'fluent'.

In second language testing, however, 'fluency' is a much more difficult concept than 'accuracy'. If a student speaks accurately, he or she is capable of constructing sentences and longer stretches of language that follow ac-ceptable rules of usage. It is relatively easy to point to examples of good and poor usage. The concept of fluency is much more fluid than this, and we must try to establish some speech phenomena that we could say are markers of fluency or disfluency (see Fulcher, 1996b). We could point to the follow-ing as phenomena that we may wish to consider as helping to define what we mean by 'fluency' (or lack of fluency):

- Hesitations consisting of pauses, which can be unfilled (silence) or filled (with noises like 'erm').
- Repeating syllables or words.
- Changing words.
- Correcting the use of cohesive devices, particularly pronouns.
- Beginning in such a way that the grammar predicts what comes next, but the speaker changes the structure of the utterance part way through.

As we have mentioned in the discussion of accuracy, it is quite possible that errors indicate that a learner is at a more advanced stage of learning the language. Something similar may be observed with regard to fluency. For example, a learner may pause for two or three seconds between propositions. The pause may be filled or unfilled. Does this indicate that the learner needs to pre-structure speech and is therefore at a stage where speech is not auto-matic? Or is this an example of content-planning hesitation – something which expert speakers do all the time when they are considering what to say next? All speakers pause as they speak to plan what they wish to say. The fact that observable speech phenomena are therefore not 'linear' (that is, more pauses does not necessarily equal less fluency) is problematic for testing speaking, which has traditionally relied on linear scales for scoring.

We will investigate this issue further when we consider rating scales and how we score student performances in Chapter 4. To conclude this section, we note that accuracy and fluency are associated with automaticity of performance and the impact that this has on the ability of the listener to understand. The quality of speech therefore needs to be judged in terms of the gravity of the errors made, or the distance from the target forms or sounds. But we also need to take into account that many errors are also only made once the learner has enough language to be able to experiment. What we know about non-linearity in language development should therefore also inform our approach to scoring.

STRATEGIES FOR SPEAKING

Canale and Swain (1980: 31) define strategic competence as 'coping' when a speaker has difficulty communicating because of a deficiency in grammatical or sociolinguistic competence. Bachman (1990: 106) changed the definition of strategic competence to 'a general ability, which enables an individual to make the most effective use of available abilities to carry out a given task'. It is the mechanism by which other components of a model of Communicative Language Ability are utilised in a specific speech event. In other words, it was no longer seen as a way of coping with problems, but as a more general cognitive capacity to manage communication. In Bachman and Palmer (1996) strategic competence is broadened to include metacognitive strategies, such as setting goals in communication, assessing what is said, and planning utterances.

However, if we intend to put 'strategic competence' in our construct definition we need to be able to define what it is that we would observe in speech that would provide evidence of strategy use. From this point of view, the more practical approach to strategy definition for testing speaking is the analysis of speech (Færch and Kasper, 1983; Yule and Tarone, 1997). The taxonomies of strategies have multiplied in recent years (Kasper and Kellerman, 1997a), but we have already indicated that the division between 'internal' and 'external' models and the various taxonomies associated with them are merely different ways of looking at the same phenomenon. We therefore outline a more traditional description of strategies that provides details of what we could look for in test-taker speech.

Achievement strategies

Learners use achievement strategies when they wish to express themselves but have problems because they lack the knowledge of the language (grammar or vocabulary) to communicate. The learner tries to overcome this lack of knowledge by finding ways around the problem. The following list represents the most common achievement strategies:

- Overgeneralisation/morphological creativity: When learners need to use lexical items or expressions over which they do not have full control, it is likely that they will transfer knowledge of the language system onto these items. For example, if a learner knows that the morpheme /-ed/ is a past tense marker and wishes to use the past tense of the verb 'buy' he or she would say 'buyed' instead of 'bought'.
- Approximation: Primarily a lexical strategy, learners may replace an unknown word with one that is more general (using 'went' for 'drove'), or use exemplification ('tables' and 'chairs' for 'furniture').
- Paraphrase: If a learner cannot remember vocabulary immediately, it is common to paraphrase by using a lexical item that is a near synonym for the word needed. Alternatively, a learner may sometimes use circumlocution by trying to explain what is meant, or describe the concept for which the words are not known.
- Word coinage: Sometimes, learners invent a new word for an unknown word, as in the common example of using 'air ball' for 'balloon' (Váradi, 1983).
- Restructuring: After a learner has said something and realises that it has not been understood, it is common to begin again and try to communicate the same message using different words. The new attempt usually follows a different grammatical pattern.
- Cooperative strategies: In face-to-face communication it is possible for a learner who is having difficulty communicating to get help from the listener. Getting help can take the form of asking someone if they have understood, appealing directly for help in saying something, or providing an unknown word.
- Code switching: If a learner is speaking to someone with whom he or she has a language in common, a word or phrase taken from the common language may be used to overcome a communication difficulty.
- Non-linguistic strategies: Speakers usually share a common physical environment, unless they are communicating over the telephone. The learner can use gestures or mime, or point to objects in the surroundings in order to elicit language or help with communication.

Avoidance (or reduction) strategies

Unlike achievement strategies, avoidance strategies are used by learners who try to avoid having to use language over which they do not have control. Far from being creative with the language in an attempt to communicate effectively, learners who use avoidance strategies will only communicate those messages that they already have the linguistic means to convey. Avoidance strategies are usually classified into Formal and Functional avoidance.

- Formal avoidance: If a learner avoids using part of the language system it is difficult to detect. For example, if a learner does not use passive voice, even where passive would be more appropriate, this can only be seen through the overuse of the active voice. Some learners may also avoid talking about subjects for which they do not have the appropriate vocabulary to communicate. This is also difficult to detect, because the absence of something does not always indicate that the learner is actually avoiding using it.
- Functional avoidance: In many ways, functional avoidance is much more serious than formal avoidance. Its extreme forms can be seen in clear cases of topic avoidance and abandoning conversations. In the latter case, a learner may simply give up trying to put a message across, without any attempt to use achievement strategies or appealing for help. When this happens, utterances are usually left propositionally incomplete. A less serious form is semantic avoidance, in which a learner continues with the topic, but tries to avoid unknown lexis. This typically results in the overuse of delexicalised words, such as 'thing', giving the message a sense of vagueness.

Whether we wish to test strategy use depends upon the purpose of the test, and whether we are interested in the process of producing speech, as well as the product. Strategies are concerned with the relationship of the internal processes and knowledge base of the test taker to the external real-time action of communicating. For example, learners who may appear fluent in their speech could be using a strategy such as circumlocution to communicate more efficiently. If the use of such strategies is related to greater communicative ability, it may be appropriate to try to test the use of strategies.

However, we are also faced with the question of whether we can test strategy use. It is difficult to tell for certain whether a learner is or is not employing a particular strategy when speaking, and even more difficult to attribute purpose to the use of the strategy in a test situation. It is for this reason that there are few tests in which raters are asked to score strategy use. Yoshida-Morise (1998) analysed the strategy use of 12 Japanese test takers on the OPI, and found significant differences in strategy use between students rated from 1+ to 3 on only 6 of her 11 category strategy taxonomy. Further, where significant differences in strategic use were found, frequency of strategy use was non-linear. In the category of 'paraphrase', for example, the frequency decreases from a high use by test takers at the 1+ level through to 2+, but increases again at level 3. Yoshida-Morise struggles to explain the data, having to draw on U-shaped language learning phenomena (see Chapter 4 for further discussion), the likelihood that interlocutor accommodation changes across levels and the individual test taker's motivation to communicate, and anxiety levels caused by the asymmetrical nature of the interaction in the OPI (see 'Interlocutor training' in Chapter 6).

It appears likely that testing strategy use is likely to be a high inference process, similar to that of testing the construct of 'fluency'. This does not mean that it should not be attempted, only that it would require careful construct definition and research into scoring procedures that could take account of the range of factors that could affect strategy use.

STRUCTURING SPEECH

To the extent that most people think about the structure of conversations (or other types of speaking), it is believed that speaking is fairly random with people free to say what they want, when they want, how they want. In the communicative language testing literature this has emerged as the principle of 'unpredictability' (see Morrow, 1979; Fulcher, 2000). In fact, most speaking is a highly structured activity. The most obvious fact is that participants usually take turns to speak. But there is much more to the structure and predictability of speech than this. Anderson and Lynch (1988) referred to how speech is structured as part of 'interactional competence', which includes sequential organisation of speech, turn taking and repair. In what follows we will discuss some of the classic treatments of structuring speech. However, recent work has also considered how talk is sequenced and how turn taking operates in situations where speakers are equal and unequal in social power (Markee, 2000). This work is potentially important for discourse studies that look at the type of language elicited by different task formats, such as the paired speaking test as compared to the OPI (see Chapters 3 and 7).

Turn taking

When we take part in spoken interaction, whether this is with one other person or a group of people, everyone usually gets the chance to speak. How is it that listeners know when to become speakers and, as speakers, indicate that it is someone else's turn to talk? This question has been addressed most fully by Sacks *et al.* (1974).

A speaking turn normally comes to an end at a *transition relevance place* (TRP). These places in conversation are usually clearly recognised, because most speaking is structured in pairs of contributions that occur together naturally. These have been called 'adjacency pairs' because they occur adjacent to each other, and the first part must come first and the second part must come second. These are discussed below, because they are such an important part of understanding how speech works. Other indicators of a change in speaking turn can be syntax or intonation (see Brazil, 1985; 1995).

The current speaker in a conversation actually possesses a great deal of power. We have all listened to politicians on television who try to keep the floor as long as possible by saying things like 'I just have three points to make' and going on to list them. If someone interrupts before point three is complete, it looks as if the opponent is being rude. This strategy is not usually acceptable in everyday conversation. A speaker can also deliberately pass on the turn by asking a question, and thus specifying who is to speak next. Again, this invests the speaker with power. If the speaker does not select the next speaker, then any other speaker may contribute to the conversation.

As listeners, we are very adept at noticing transition relevance places. This accounts for why a new speaker often begins speaking before the previous speaker has completed. The small overlap between speakers is a result of the listener's ability to predict the TRP. Similarly, if two speakers begin speaking after a turn, it is usually the person who starts first who gets to continue. This implies that there are rules that we observe when taking turns.

The rules for turn taking have been described in the following way, where C is the current speaker and N the next speaker:

Rule 1 (applies at the first TRP of any turn)
(a) If C selects N in the current turn, then C must stop speaking, and N must speak next, transition occurring at the first TRP after N-selection.
(b) If C does not select N, then another (other) party may self-select, first speaker gaining rights to the next turn.
(c) If C has not selected N, and no other party self-selects under option (b), then C may (but need not) continue.

Rule 2 (applies at all subsequent TRPs)
When Rule 1(c) has been applied by C, then at the next TRP Rules 1 (a)–(c) apply, and recursively at the next TRP, until speaker change is effected.

There is an obvious benefit to listeners in anticipating TRPs, so that they may contribute to a conversation. As Sacks *et al.* (1974: 727) say:

> An intrinsic motivation is identifiable for listening. In its turn-allocational techniques, the turn-taking system for conversation builds in an intrinsic motivation for listening to all utterances in a conversation, independent of other possible motivations, such as interest and politeness. In the variety of techniques for arriving at next speakers, and in their ordered character, it obliges any willing or potentially intending speaker to listen to and analyze each utterance across its delivery.

We must consider the implications of turn taking for second language learners, especially when they are taking face to face speaking tests. Firstly, a second language learner must be a good listener if he or she also wishes to be a good speaker (Buck, 2001). This is not just to understand what another speaker is saying, but to decide when it is time to speak. Secondly, we should not assume that the learner's ability to speak well in the first language can be transferred to the second language. The turn-taking routines and conventions that apply to Anglo-American societies do not apply to all societies. In some speech communities, like that of Burundi, turn taking is pre-allocated by social rank (Hudson, 1980: 122). If person A is of higher rank than B, and B than C, then the turn taking order is A – B – C. In societies like Japan and Korea where social rank is reflected in language use, it is likely that learners will transfer the dominant or submissive turn-taking strategies to the second language that they might use in the first language. Young and Halleck (1998) provide an extended discussion of turn taking and topic development in the OPI across test takers and interlocutors from different cultural backgrounds.

If turn taking is considered important, it should be included as part of the test construct. This will have implications for the types of tasks that might be included in the test. As we will see in Chapter 7, Saville and Hargreaves (1999) explicitly defend the use of tasks where test takers are paired and have to talk to each other. They argue that this is the 'best' way to elicit turn-taking behaviour from test takers that is not dependent upon the 'unnatural' turn taking that occurs between a single test taker and powerful interlocutor/rater who manages the conversation in a sequence of questions/answers.

Adjacency pairs

The adjacency pair is usually considered to be the most fundamental unit of conversational structure (Schegloff and Sacks, 1973; Goffman, 1976), and is one way in which we can understand how turn taking works. Although its use has been questioned, in favour of a three-part unit of analysis (Tsui, 1994), it nevertheless remains important for our purposes. An adjacency pair consists essentially of a first and second part produced by two speakers. They must also be ordered, in that the first part must come before the second. Examples of adjacency pairs are:

question – answer
greeting – greeting
invitation – acceptance (refusal)
compliment – acceptance
request – compliance
offer – acceptance
complaint – apology

Although the first part usually predicts (or expects) the second part, it is possible for a speaker to select different second parts. This is discussed below. It is also common for an adjacency pair to be separated by an inserted sequence.

For example, in a question – answer pair, we could imagine the following sequence:

A: Have you got the time?
B: It's five o'clock

Goffman (1976: 259) offers the following example of how this conversation is more likely to proceed, when A is talking to a railway official in the United States.

```
┌──── A1: Have you got the time?
│      ┌──── B2: Standard or Daylight Saving?
│      │      ┌──── A3: What are you running on?
│      │      └──── B3: Standard
│      └──── A2: Standard then
└──── B1: It's five o'clock
```

These are variably called embedded, insertion or side sequences, which together make up a chain. Let us take an extended example from Levinson (1983: 305), where R labels a first part request and Q and A question and answer.

B: I ordered some paint from uh a couple of weeks ago some vermilion
A: Yuh
B: And I wanted to order some more the name's Boyd (R1)
A: Yes how many tubes would you like sir (Q1)
B: An-
B: Uhm what's the price now eh with VAT eo you know eh (Q2)
A: Er I'll just work that out for you (HOLD)
B: Thanks (ACCEPT)
A: Three pounds nineteen a tube sir (A2)
B: Three nineteen is it (Q3)
A: Yeah (A3)
B: Eh yes Uhm eh jus-justa think, that's what three nineteen that's for the large tube isn't it (Q4)
A: Well yeah it's the thirty seven ccs
B: Er, hh I'll tell you what I'll just eh eh ring you back I have to work out how many I'll need. Sorry I did- wasn't sure of the price you see (ACCOUNT for no A1)
A: Okay

Levinson points out that neither the initial request nor the initial question receives its second part, even though they are expected. However, when expected second parts are not forthcoming, there needs to be an account for their omission, otherwise the conversation would certainly appear odd. It is clear that adjacency pairs, despite the term used, need not be adjacent. Secondly, when a second part to an adjacency pair does not follow immediately, the embedded adjacency pairs in the conversation are seen as a preliminary to the introduction of the second part. Thirdly, if a second part does not occur, there must be an explicitly stated reason for its non-appearance.

Listeners must be able to understand utterances as questions or requests in order to be able to see when TRPs occur, and must be able to respond appropriately, either with a second part of an adjacency pair, or introduce an embedded sequence. Minimally, in a speaking test like the OPI it is essential for the test taker to recognise the question–answer sequence (He, 1998). In task types that require role-play or simulation of some kind a larger ability to understand and manipulate many types of adjacency pairs, included embedded sequences, is required.

Openings and closings

Conversations clearly have beginnings and ends, and in between there are moves from one topic to another. Openings of conversations seem to be fairly straightforward in their nature. Take, for example, two friends meeting.

> Hi, how are you?
> Fine thanks, and you?
> Okay. I'm just going for lunch. Fancy joining me?

Such sequences are fully describable in terms of adjacency pairs discussed above. When it comes to closing a topic, or closing a conversation, the closing is usually preceded by expressions that indicate that a closing is coming next. These are often called 'pre-closings', and often take the form of 'well', 'so', or 'okay', with falling intonation. These markers allow the next speaker to change topic if they wish. Look at this fairly typical ending to a conversation, from Levinson (1983: 316–17):

> Why don't we all have lunch?
> Okay so that would be in St Jude's would it?
> Yes
> Okay so
> One o'clock in the bar
> Okay
> Okay?
> Okay then thanks very much indeed George   **Pre-closing I**
> All right
> See you there   **Checking**
> See you there
> Okay   **Pre-closing II**
> Okay
> Bye
> Bye   **Closing**

In this example a pre-closing is interrupted by a checking procedure, after which the pre-closing begins again, before the final closing in the use of 'bye'.

If it is very important for speakers to be aware of how they can bring topics and conversations to an end, we may wish to include this in our construct definition for a test. In situations of unequal social power one speaker has the right to bring a conversation to an end without going through the normal closing routines. Teachers frequently do this, as in this example:

> Right, okay, you've done well and we can continue tomorrow. Bye.

It has often been said that the OPI is much more like this last example than using task types where the speakers have to open and close topics, and the conversation. If we wish to see if test takers can structure conversations, the opportunity to do so must be presented.

SPEAKING IN CONTEXT

We have looked at accuracy and fluency, strategy use and some of the ways in which speech is structured. In this section, we consider the context of speaking and some of the rules that govern speech, how we do things with words, and how speaking helps us to define who we are.

The rules of speaking and pragmatic appropriacy

Learners of a language may be able to use the grammar of a language, pronounce the sounds and speak fluently, but this may not mean that they communicate well. It has become an axiom of applied linguistics that 'There are rules of use without which the rules of grammar would be useless' (Hymes, 1971). Hymes continues: 'Just as rules of syntax can control aspects of phonology, and just as semantic rules perhaps control aspects of syntax, so rules of speech acts enter as a controlling factor for linguistic form as a whole.' The ability to communicate through speech is much more than the knowledge of the grammatical or phonological system of a language. Unless learners understand the 'rules' of speaking they may at best appear 'rude' or, at worst, cause offence. Much research has been conducted into these rules of speaking (Grice, 1975), and they are often taken into account in tests of speaking under terms like 'appropriacy' (Wolfson, 1983).

'Appropriacy' is a construct that is concerned with the way in which speakers use language according to rules of which they are hardly aware. Even speakers who have spent all their lives speaking and listening to a language would not be able to explain to another person what those rules are. Nevertheless, they do not break the rules when they communicate with others, unless they deliberately wish to achieve a certain effect. When speakers do this, they are aware that they are doing something 'wrong', but could not say why it was inappropriate for the context. Second language learners, on the other hand, may not be aware that something is inappropriate.

Let us take a rather harmless example from the field of address terms. Ervin-Tripp (1968) was among the first to study the use of address terms. That is, how we address each other when meeting or departing. Ervin-Tripp collected many examples of speakers using address terms, and attempted to analyse them. Many students address university teachers with the title 'doctor', as in 'Good morning, Dr Smith'. However, some learners may simply say 'Good morning, doctor'. This is not likely to cause offence, but it does sound 'wrong'. It violates the rule that titles should only be used on their own when the title refers to a job. Similarly, it is not appropriate to address a lecturer or a medical practitioner by their last name alone. This would certainly cause offence.

These 'rules of speaking' are pragmatic in nature (Thomas, 2003). They are conventions that must usually be followed. This brings us to a very important point in understanding 'errors'. If a grammatical error is made in speaking, or a word is used incorrectly, the listener is likely to be very patient and make a great deal of effort to understand what is being communicated. But if the 'error' is pragmatic the consequences are potentially serious. Breaking the rules of speech can result in serious misunderstanding.

At a more general level, we are concerned with what speakers *imply* when they speak. The most famous formulation of rules of speech regarding implication is that of Grice (1975), in what he called 'conversational implicature'. That is, we can *imply* something without saying it. Take this example from Grice (1975: 43):

> Suppose that A and B are talking about a mutual friend, C, who is now working in a bank. A asks B how C is getting on in his job, and B replies, 'Oh quite well, I think; he likes his colleagues, and he hasn't been to prison yet'. At this point, A might well inquire what B was implying, what he was suggesting, or even what he meant by saying that C had not yet been to prison. The answer might be any one of such things as that C is the sort of person likely to yield to the temptation provided by his occupation, that C's colleagues are really very unpleasant and treacherous people, and so forth. It might, of course, be quite unnecessary for A to make such an inquiry of B, the answer to it being, in the context, clear in advance.

The problem for learners of a second language is that they may imply something that they did not wish to communicate. This is important when speaking 'in the real world', and for some tests we may wish to include pragmatic appropriacy in our construct definition. The example that we will provide to illustrate how this may be taken into account in testing second language speaking is based on the 'Politeness Principle' (Leech, 1983: 79–103), which states that speakers should 'minimize the expression of impolite beliefs'.

These developments help us and learners understand why it might be unwise (in many circumstances) to use utterances like:

- Shut up
- Just clean the dishes, will you
- Help me with my homework now
- Can't you answer the phone?
- Bring the bill waiter

Leech (1983: 107) suggests a cost-benefit scale, in which speakers attempt to produce an utterance which maintains a benefit to the hearer, rather than a cost. This is illustrated in Table 2.1.

Indirect expressions are more polite because they increasingly allow the hearer not to do what is requested. Indirect requests are tentative, and both the hearer and speaker may retreat from a situation in which one or the other may lose face. Indirectness is seen as resulting in less cost and more benefit to the hearer. This attempt to make the option of refusing a request more acceptable is often termed 'negative politeness'. It is a device to avoid conflict, which speakers enter into when the cost to the hearer of the speaker's words may become intolerable.

Leech (1983: 123) therefore proposes that there are pragmatic scales, the cost-benefit scale, the optionality scale, and finally the indirectness scale. The latter is the length of the path connecting the goal of the utterance to its act.

Table 2.1 A pragmatic scale (extract from Leech, 1983: 108)

1	Answer the phone	Less indirect	Less polite
2	I want you to answer the phone		
3	Will you answer the phone?		
4	Can you answer the phone?		
5	Would you mind answering the phone?		
6	Could you possibly answer the phone?		
7	Etc.	More indirect	More polite

For example, 'give me the pen' is more direct than 'may I borrow your pen for a second'. To these, he adds the further scales of 'authority' and 'social distance'. In the former, we are concerned with which of the speakers has the right to make decisions that effect the hearer, and in the second, the extent to which factors such as age, experience, length of acquaintance and social rank, are likely to affect speech. With language learners from a variety of cultural backgrounds, the problem may not be so much that they appear 'impolite' when speaking, as that they come across as being too diffident. There are many cultures in which the teacher, or anyone in authority, should be treated with great respect. The sign of this respect is to remain silent unless asked a question, and then to answer it as quickly and briefly as possible. When a speaking test is designed with 'communicative' principles, including tasks that encourage or require test takers to ask questions of the interlocutor/rater, such problems should be taken into account. Similarly, learners should be made aware of the communications norms of speakers with whom they are likely to interact.

Fulcher and Márquez Reiter (2003) have taken the notion of pragmatic scales, authority and distance, to investigate how a range of tasks can impact upon test takers from two L1 cultural backgrounds. They discovered that there is variation in how test takers from a particular cultural background may use language that is perceived as inappropriate in speaking tests. In one task, for example, test takers were asked to perform a role play in which they played the role of a university student asking a professor if they could borrow a book. Social distance is high, as is the authority of the professor. The requests made by English L1 speakers were much more indirect than those of Spanish L1 speakers, as this example shows:

English
I was just wondering if you have the book and if I could borrow it?

Spanish
¿Me puedes prestas el libro?
(Could I borrow the book?)

While the utterance of the Spanish test taker is appropriate in a Spanish university context, it is unlikely to be pragmatically appropriate in university settings where social distance and authority require a level of indirectness that allows the professor to refuse without losing face. If pragmatic appropriacy is to be included in the construct definition, careful consideration will have to be given to the nature of the tasks that will provide evidence for the ability of the test taker to manage the pragmatic force of utterances.

Doing things with words

Speakers of a language do things with words, and learners must know how to do things with words in the language they are learning. Different languages have different ways of doing the same or similar things with words, and so we cannot expect the impact that words will have on the listener to be the same in two different languages. The study of how we do things with words is called *speech act theory*, originally developed by J. L. Austin (Austin, 1962).

Austin was not a language teacher or tester, but a philosopher. His primary intention in his work was to disprove the view that a declarative sentence is always used to describe some fact, either truly, or falsely. Austin claims that such sentences are actually performing actions, only some of which are merely stating some truth. He calls such sentences 'performatives', and provides examples (Austin, 1962: 5), such as:

- I do (in a wedding ceremony)
- I name this ship the *Queen Elizabeth* (uttered while smashing a bottle against the stem)
- I give and bequeath my watch to my brother (as occurring in a will)
- I bet you sixpence it will rain tomorrow

In each of these cases, the declarative sentence does not describe what the person is doing, it *is doing it* – or at least the language-related part of it (see McCarthy, 1998: 19–20 for a discussion of the interpretation of speech acts in a social context). These performatives can be distinguished from 'constatives', which are statements that do not 'do' anything.

If we 'do' things with words, it is not unreasonable to expect that the impact words, or rather utterances, have upon a hearer in one language, will not translate directly or even indirectly, into the second or foreign language. Different languages perform the same or similar speech acts in different ways. This becomes crucial when we deal with issues such as politeness, as discussed above.

For example, speakers do not normally say things like 'the door is open' with the intention only of stating the fact that the door is open. Nor is it very common to use imperatives like 'close the door!' to get someone to close the door. Many speech acts are indirect. Consider the following examples:

> We need a little less draught.
> The room's cold.

I'm freezing.
Were you born in a barn?

None of these are imperatives, but all have the effect of telling someone to close the door. And there are many more ways in which we could 'do' this through language. These examples are indirect speech acts. In a literal utterance, meaning and the form of the words coincide exactly, but this is very rare in spoken language.

Searle (1969) draws a distinction between the meaning of what a speaker says, and the literal meaning of an utterance. In a literal utterance, speaker meaning and utterance meaning coincide exactly, but this is extremely rare in spoken language.

In situations where learners of a language are likely to be faced with performing speech acts like requests or refusals, where politeness is important, we may wish to consider including the use of performatives into our construct definition.

Being things with words

Although it is very important to understand the role of rules of speech and speech acts in communication, they cannot explain why speakers speak the way they do in particular situations. Social contexts must be taken into account to achieve this.

Labov and Fanshel (1977) were among the first to argue that the social context of speech is critical to understanding the aspect of appropriacy that we have termed 'being things with words'. A simple example that we have already considered is that of the social status of different speakers. The degree of politeness required to a superior is different to that required when one is giving instructions to a junior in the workplace. The directness or indirectness of speech acts will therefore change. In other words, we will do things with words in different ways, in different contexts. It has been noticed many times that in the OPI the power relations between the assessor and the assessed are fixed, and that the context restricts test takers in their use of language. The resultant discourse has frequently been classified as a 'test genre', as a result (van Lier, 1989; Perrett, 1990; Lazaraton, 1992; Johnson, 2001).

Speakers also adopt and play roles in the use of language. In any particular context the role the speaker is playing will have speaking rights attached to it. Speakers of higher social status, for example, may have the right to initiate and close topics, and direct the conversation (Young and Halleck, 1998). Some speakers, like teachers and judges, even have the right to say who is to speak next and what they are to speak about.

So we not only do things with words, we are things through words, in that we define our status and role through speech; and it is the context and our place in it that dictates to a large degree what kind of language we use. Our being is defined by language, and status is one aspect of being, which is related to our role in the speech situation.

Consider the following (real) example, overheard in an office:

Boss: If we're to get this contract we have to move fast; these letters need typing up and faxing out today. The number's on the top of the front page.
Secretary: I'm busy with the petty cash; in any case, that's why we have the temp.

The boss issues an indirect instruction for the secretary to type some letters. The secretary is not being a secretary through language. Although she correctly interprets the utterance of her boss as an instruction, she refuses to comply. The words are seen as a direct threat to the accepted roles of the two speakers. There are only two possible outcomes to this exchange. The boss may indeed find the temporary secretary and reissue the instruction, in which case he has lost face (and probably control of the office). On the other hand, the secretary may be called into the boss's office, warned and be given a direct instruction to type the letters immediately. In this latter case, the secretary has lost face, and is now given no way to refuse without causing the initiation of disciplinary procedures.

One problem is that learners may be able to transfer appropriate speaking templates from their primary language to the language they are learning. But teachers and language testers should not assume that this is the case.

In this context we should also be aware that when a learner is speaking in a second language, he or she is 'being' a different person simply through the act of communicating in the new language. We are aware that to some extent we change when we speak in a second language. Language testers need to be sensitive to this when devising language tests. It may be appropriate to consider, for example, the extent to which role-play or simulation should be exploited with students from some L1 cultural backgrounds. In a simulation the test taker is asked to take on the persona of an imaginary character. This may be more than can reasonably be expected. The test taker is already playing a new role in speaking the second language, and very much aware that he or she is a 'test taker'. The task then requires the test taker to be yet another, third person. The situation is less complicated when learners play roles which are related to their jobs, as is the case with the Occupational English Test (OET), for example (McNamara, 1996).

INTERACTIONAL COMPETENCE

Interactional competence is most often defined in terms of how speakers structure speech, its sequential organisation and turn-taking rules, sometimes including strategies. Markee (2000: 54) can therefore claim that the notion of interactional competence 'converges with sociolinguistic notions of communicative competence' found in Bachman (1990) and Canale and Swain (1980). Interactional competence is therefore constituted from some of the elements that we have already introduced briefly.

However, McNamara (1997: 447) writes:

it turns out that the term *interaction* has in fact featured strongly in work in language testing, but from what seems on reflection to be a rather one-sided perspective. Potentially, there are two main senses of the term: (1) a loosely psychological one, referring to various kinds of mental activity *within* a single individual, and (2) a social/behavioural one, where joint behaviour *between* individuals is the basis for the joint construction (and interpretation) of performance.

McNamara argues that the approach to defining interaction as a construct in models of Communicative Language Ability, such as Bachman (1990), focuses on the first of these two uses of the term. Interaction is seen as an 'ability' within an individual. He proposes a 'more dynamic' understanding of social interaction, where strategic competence is removed from the knowledge of the individual, and places it firmly in the realm of performance within context, where a whole range of factors can affect the quality of the performance and test score. These factors would include the talk of the interlocutor, personality of the test taker(s), and the nature of the task. The inclusion of these factors, including the affective and volitional, and potentially many others, has been called 'opening Pandora's box' (McNamara, 1995). Some of these factors are discussed in Chapter 7 when we consider testing speakers in pairs.

Using this second definition of interaction as part of construct definition expands the traditional understanding of the construct to encompass the view that individuals do not speak alone, but that performances are constructed with others, or co-constructed. Speakers collaborate and assist each other, so that there is 'distributed responsibility' for sequencing talk, turn taking and communicating (Jacoby and Ochs, 1995). In supporting this view of interaction, reference is frequently made to the theoretical basis in Vygotsky. Language 'ability' could only be defined in relation to particular setting, and 'interaction would have to be viewed as a social, not a cognitive, issue' (Johnson, 2001: 196).

The co-construction of talk is also at the centre of Interactional Competence Theory (ICT), which is an alternative approach to the models of Communicative Language Ability with which language testing has traditionally worked. This approach was originally put forward by Kramsch (1986b). Within ICT talk is seen as locally situated and co-constructed by the participants in the communication:

The focus of the Canale and Swain framework is on an individual learner in a social context; that is, the framework helps us understand what an individual needs to know and do in order to communicate. Such exclusive focus on a single individual's contribution to communication should, we believe, be problematized in view of current research that has advanced the position that abilities, actions, and activities do not belong to the individual but are *jointly* constructed by *all* participants.   (He and Young, 1998: 5)

For He and Young, what the participants bring to an interaction include:

- A knowledge of rhetorical scripts (typical sequences of speech acts for particular communication purposes).
- Specific lexis and syntactic structures.
- Strategies for managing turn taking.
- Strategies for managing topics.
- Signalling boundaries (opening and closing topics and interactions).

We have considered all of these features in this chapter. What makes the ICT approach different is the claim that:

> Interactional competence is not an attribute of an individual participant, and thus we cannot say that an individual is interactionally competent; rather we talk of interactional competence as something that is jointly constructed by all participants (including an analyst if the interaction is subject to analysis). Equally, interactional competence is not a trait that is independent of the interactive practice in which it is (or is not) constituted.   (He and Young, 1998: 7)

The understanding of speech as co-constructed in all its forms, whether labelled as ICT or 'indigenous assessment' (Jacoby and McNamara, 1999), raises many problems for construct definition in testing speaking in a second language. Most of these are highlighted by the discussion of Young (2002), particularly in his multi-layered analysis of a naturally occurring conversation. Young demonstrates how many factors contribute to the co-construction of the conversation, including non-verbal behaviours. If talk in second language speaking tests is co-constructed in such ways, we have to ask many questions, such as how scores can be given to an individual test taker rather than pairs of test takers in a paired test format. Or how the contributions of the inter-locutor/rater can be taken into account when he or she is co-responsible for the construction of the talk.

These and other issues that arise from a more complex understanding of interaction are discussed in detail in Chapter 7, and to some extent in Chapter 6. We saw at the beginning of this chapter that Lado avoided testing speaking because of his fear that factors like 'talkativeness' or 'introversion' might contaminate the construct of the 'ability to speak'. We are no longer able to avoid these issues so nicely.

DIGEST

Speaking is a complex matter. Anyone who wishes to speak a second language must learn the grammar and vocabulary of the language, and master its sounds. Planning what to say, formulating the utterances and producing them need to become automatic if what the learner says is to be considered 'fluent'. The learner needs to be able to open and close conversations in acceptable ways, and manage the switch between topics. She needs to know the conventions of turn taking, when to begin speaking and when to stop. Cultural knowledge and sensitivity to social context is also very important. And speakers must maintain appropriate roles and relationships with other speakers in a variety of speaking contexts that differ with regard to a wide range of variables including social distance, power and authority.

Bygate (1987: 3) compares speaking to driving a car. This is a useful, if simplistic, comparison. He writes:

> What knowledge does a car driver need? Clearly he or she needs to know the names of the controls; where they are; what they do and how they are operated. . . . However, the driver also needs the skill to be able to use the controls to guide the car along a road without hitting the various objects that tend to get in the way; you have to be able to do this at normal speed; you have to drive smoothly and without getting too close to any dangerous obstacles. And it is not enough to drive in a straight line: the driver also has to be able to manage the variations in road conditions safely. . . . In a way, the job we do when we speak is similar.

We may continue the analogy to say that the purpose of testing second language speaking is similar to that of a driving test. The purpose of a speaking test is to collect evidence in a systematic way (through elicitation techniques or tasks) that will support an inference about the construct as we define it from the summary of the evidence (the 'score'). We will also usually be interested in the learner's ability to perform in a range of situations much wider than those that could be sampled during the test. The learner driver cannot be tested on all roads, in all possible weather conditions, or in all the potentially dangerous situations that may be encountered in the future. Similarly, the language learner cannot be tested in all speech contexts or on every task that could simulate potential situations in which he or she may have to speak in the future. From a sample performance, we need to make inferences about the likely success or failure of the learner's future performance in non-test contexts.

This is one of the key challenges in testing speaking: designing tasks that elicit spoken language of the type and quantity that will allow meaningful inferences to be drawn from scores to the learner's ability on the construct the test is designed to measure. In order to do this, the test must avoid two threats to its construct validity (Messick, 1989):

- Construct underrepresentation

This is the extent to which a test fails to capture important aspects of the construct the test is intended to measure. The danger in this is that the inferences that can be drawn from test scores is narrower than implied in the test. For example, if a test is made up of a 'reading aloud' and 'sentence repetition' tasks, scored according to accuracy criteria, it would be illegitimate to imply that the test score provided information about the test taker's ability to interact with others in a seminar.

- Construct-irrelevant variance

This is the extent to which test scores are influenced by factors that are irrelevant to the construct that the test is intended to measure. In other words, it is score variance attributable to anything that is not part of how we

Table 2.2   A framework for describing the speaking construct

---

Language competence

Phonology
• Pronunciation
• Stress
• Intonation

Accuracy
• Syntax
• Vocabulary
• Cohesion

Fluency
• Hesitation
• Repetition
• Re-selecting inappropriate words
• Re-structuring sentences
• Cohesion

Strategic capacity

Achievement strategies
• Overgeneralization
• Paraphrase
• Word coinage
• Restructuring
• Cooperative strategies
• Code switching
• Non-linguistic strategies

Avoidance strategies
• Formal avoidance
• Functional Avoidance

Textual knowledge

The structure of talk
• Turn taking
• Adjacency pairs
• Openings and closings

Pragmatic knowledge

• Appropriacy
• Implicature
• Expressing being

Sociolinguistic knowledge

• Situational
• Topical
• Cultural

---

choose to define the construct. The danger here is that the meaning of the score is not (entirely) related to the construct, but to some other factor that has nothing to do with the construct at all. As we have seen, Lado wished to remove construct-irrelevant variance by testing language elements. Most of the factors that could affect scores on speaking tests were classified as construct irrelevant. If we chose to leave task definitions outside the construct (as is usually the case), any variance attributable to the task type would constitute construct irrelevant variance.

To conclude this chapter we provide a summary of what we might wish to include in a construct definition for a test of second language speaking in Table 2.2. The model of presentation is adapted from Bachman and Palmer (1996). Changes to the Bachman and Palmer model have been made to account specifically for testing speaking. No attempt has been made to isolate separate categories for interactional competence, for as we have seen it is an approach to understanding the co-construction of speech that focuses on turn taking, or openings and closings, rather than suggesting completely new categories that should be included. The exceptions lie in how personality factors contribute to co-construction, and studies of how interlocutor/raters accommodate their speech to that of the test taker. Whether such aspects can, or should, be part of a construct definition is both controversial and unclear. We return to the discussion of these questions in Chapters 6, 7 and 8.

We have not considered how test designers arrive at a construct definition, the process by which the construct is defined. This is considered in more detail in Chapter 5. In the next chapter we turn our attention to tasks in second language speaking tests, the means by which the test designer elicits speech from test takers that provides the evidence for inferences to be made from scores to the construct.

Chapter 3

Tasks for second language speaking tests

The purpose of this chapter is to discuss tasks as the means by which we can elicit a sample of language that can be scored. Tasks need to be designed or selected for use that will strengthen the inferences that we can make from scores to constructs. For example, it is unlikely that we would wish to make a claim about a learner's ability to take part in a discussion from a task that requires the learner to read aloud; reading aloud a passage would not provide any information about a test taker's ability to use turn-taking strategies, open or close topics, or many of the other key constructs that we associate with taking part in a discussion.

Firstly we look at how tasks have been described in second language acquisition research and pedagogy, and then look at test task characteristics from the language testing literature. Any of these characteristics may be selected for the description of tasks in specific testing contexts, and a set are taken and applied to two tasks to show how we might use task descriptions. We then consider task difficulty, and ask what makes one task more difficult than another. Finally, we consider a range of task types and ask what type of language they may elicit, and for what purposes we might use that task type.

There is no attempt to provide a complete and systematic account of task types, which has been undertaken in other places. The purpose of this chapter is rather to provide an approach to describing task types that is useful in designing tests and writing test specifications (see Chapter 5), and to show how consideration of task type is directly linked to the kinds of construct-related claims that test designers may wish to make.

TASKS IN SECOND LANGUAGE ACQUISITION AND PEDAGOGY

In the testing of speaking it has always been argued that the primary concern in designing a test task is to elicit enough speech to allow a rating to take place. Valette (1977: 152) writes:

> Although a free expression test allows the students to demonstrate their linguistic creativity, one cannot simply put the student before a tape recorder or

in front of the class and say 'speak'. A testing framework that will facilitate student talk must be established. The following types of items have proven effective.

Valette then proceeds to categorise task types and provide examples of these task types, with an indication of what could be tested through each. The tendency to provide extensive lists of task types with a discussion of their relative advantages and disadvantages has continued in the literature on testing speaking (Madsen, 1983; Underhill, 1987; Weir, 1988). More recent books on language testing tend to avoid the discussion of task types.

However, the development of models of communicative competence (Canale and Swain, 1980; Bachman, 1990; Bachman and Palmer, 1996) have made it possible to look at task types in terms other than their general advantages and disadvantages for eliciting a 'good' ratable sample, because the models recognise that speaking takes place in specific social settings, between people with particular communicative goals. This change recognises an interface between the interests of language testers and those whose primary focus is the use of tasks in second language acquisition research, or pedagogy.

Candlin (1987: 10), for example, defines a task as:

> One of a set of differentiated, sequencable, problem-posing activities involving learners and teachers in some joint selection from a range of varied cognitive and communicative procedures applied to existing and new knowledge in the collective exploration and pursuance of foreseen or emergent goals within a social milieu.

This is not at all dissimilar to the three aspects of test tasks in Bachman and Palmer (1996: 44), that tasks are closely associated with a specific social situation, that task takers are goal-oriented, and that they involve 'active participation' of the learners. They therefore define a test task as:

> an activity that involves individuals in using language for the purpose of achieving a particular goal or objective in a particular situation.

Candlin (1987) defines tasks in terms of seven characteristics that are salient to their use in the classroom:

- Input or material used in the task
- Roles of the participants
- Settings, or classroom arrangements for pair/groupwork
- Actions, or what is to happen in the task
- Monitoring, or who is to select input, choose role or setting, alter actions
- Outcomes as the goal of the task
- Feedback given as evaluation to participants

Nunan (1989) offers an almost identical list, albeit with slightly different titles:

- Goals
- Input
- Activity

- Teacher role
- Learner role
- Settings

Characteristics like this can be used to describe tasks, and thus to select tasks for speaking tests that allow score inferences to generalise to the target language use domain outside the test.

Wright (1987: 49) argues that tasks have differing 'communicative potential', and suggests that tasks can be placed on a grid with two axes: task type and orientation (Figure 3.1). This moves task description towards processes required to undertake the task, as well as its characteristics.

In this model tasks can be placed along a cline of 'open' to 'closed'. In a closed task the outcome is almost pre-determined, and so there is an emphasis on goal convergence. Open tasks, on the other hand, have many different possible outcomes. Content-oriented tasks are likely to be more controlled in the use of discourse, whereas skills-oriented tasks are likely to be less structured and 'exploratory'.

Pica *et al.* (1993), drawing on the work of Candlin and others, also stress the two principal features of tasks: they are goal-oriented, and they require the learner to undertake some activity or work in order to achieve the goal. However, they present a task typology that also incorporates issues of process, breaking down task activities and goals into the following categories:

Interactional activity
- Interactional relationship
  1. Each interactant holds different information, supplies and requests information to complete the task
  2. One interactant holds all information and supplies it
  3. Each interactant holds all information
- Interaction requirement for activity of request/suppliance
  1. Each interactant is required to request and supply information
  2. One interactant is required to request and the other to supply

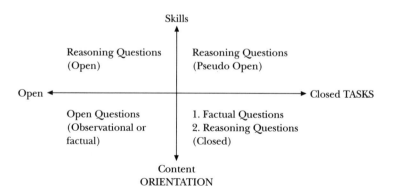

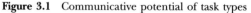

Figure 3.1 Communicative potential of task types
Source: After Wright, T. (1987) 'Instructional task and discoursal outcome in the LZ classroom' in C. N. Candlin and D. F. Murphy (eds) *Language Learning Tasks. Lancaster Practical Paper in English Language Education, Vol. 7,* published by Prentice Hall International, Inc., p. 49.

3. Each interactant is expected to request and supply but not required to do so

Communication goal
- Goal orientation
  1. Interactants have the same or convergent goals
  2. Interactants have related but divergent goals
- Outcome options
  1. Only one acceptable outcome is possible
  2. More than one outcome is possible

Pica *et al.* argue that comprehension of input, feedback on production and interlanguage modification are expected to take place when tasks fall under condition 1 in each of the categories. They conclude that the ideal task type for language acquisition is the jigsaw task (Geddes and Sturtridge, 1979), closely followed by information gap tasks.

In our discussion of task types for speaking tests later in this chapter, we will present a descriptive system that draws on the pedagogic work in task design as well as that in the language testing literature.

TEST TASK CHARACTERISTICS

Models of communicative language ability and use have never been subjected to validation (Fulcher, 1998: 282–3). Nevertheless they can provide a useful framework for interpreting the components of a construct, as we saw at the end of Chapter 2. In addition to the explicit consideration of construct, it is also possible to look at dimensions of the task type through a framework of task characteristics. Bachman and Palmer (1996) argue that it is critical to be able to identify the characteristics of language tasks so that it can be shown how performance on these tasks may be related to speaking in 'the real world'.

Bachman and Palmer (1996: 49) present their characteristics as a list:

Characteristics of the setting
- Physical characteristics
- Participants
- Time of task

Characteristics of the test rubrics
- Instructions
  - Language (native, target)
  - Channel (aural, visual)
  - Specification of procedures and tasks
- Structure
  - Number of parts/tasks
  - Salience of parts/tasks
  - Sequence of parts/tasks
  - Relative importance of parts/tasks
  - Number of tasks/items per part
- Time allotment

- Scoring method
  - Criteria for correctness
  - Procedures for scoring the response
  - Explicitness of criteria and procedures

Characteristics of the input
- Format
  - Channel (aural, visual)
  - Form (language, non-language, both)
  - Language (native, target, both)
  - Length
  - Type (item, prompt)
  - Degree of speededness
  - Vehicle (live, reproduced, both)
- Language of input
  - Language characteristics
    Organizational characteristics
       Grammatical (vocabulary, syntax, phonology, graphology)
       Textual (cohesion, rhetorical/conversational organization)
    Pragmatic characteristics
       Functional (ideational, manipulative, heuristic, imaginative)
       Sociolinguistic (dialect/variety, register, naturalness, cultural references
       and figurative language)
- Topical characteristics

The relevance of the list to task design in language testing is clear to see from the inclusion of the characteristics of the test rubric. From the remainder of the list, it is unclear as to which elements of the list are most important for task description in speaking tests. This may be because little research has been conducted into which task features need to be recorded in test specifications for speaking tests, so that task writers can produce sets of comparable tasks (see Chapter 5). However, the real reason for the development of TLU 'checklists' is related to the concept of 'authenticity' and its perceived relationship to validity claims. Bachman and Palmer refer to 'target language use (TLU) tasks' that exist in the 'real world', to which inferences from test scores need to generalise. The analysis of the TLU tasks provides the characteristics for the tasks to be used on the speaking test (Bachman and Palmer, 1996: 44–5). This is part of what they mean by 'authenticity' in the test task.

This is very similar to the approach to authenticity that was argued by Morrow (1979) in his definition of 'context' as the situation (physical environment, status of participants, degree of formality, speech acts performed). The 'authenticity' argument has been challenged many times (see Fulcher, 2000), and Lewkowicz (1997, 2000) echoes these challenges in relation to the Bachman and Palmer model. In particular, she questions whether it is possible to match test tasks to real-world tasks along all of the items in a checklist, and shows that 'authenticity' is really a concept rather than a construct, which is differentially interpreted by different test takers. It is a matter of perception rather than external reality. Or as Chapelle (2000: 161) put it, 'authenticity' is a folk concept, and models of TLU characteristics are attempts to simplify some 'reality' that we are unable to capture. (This most recent discussion of authenticity only rehearses what has already been said in the past (Widdowson, 1983: 30), that 'authenticity' is not simply a matter of copying situations, topics or discourses from the real world. It also echoes similar debates dating back to the 1950s, and impacting upon language testing in the 1980s (Spolsky, 1985).)

The level of detail required need not relate directly to proving the chimera of authenticity, but rather to describing tasks in ways that contribute to the development of test specifications.

Bachman and Palmer (1996: 50) also present the characteristics of the expected response:

Characteristics of the expected response
- Format
  - Channel (aural, visual)
  - Form (language, non-language, both)
  - Language (native, target, both)
  - Length
  - Type (selected, limited production, extended production)
  - Degree of speededness
- Language of expected response
  - Language characteristics
    Organizational characteristics
      Grammatical (vocabulary, syntax, phonology, graphology)
      Textual (cohesion, rhetorical/conversational organization)
    Pragmatic characteristics
      Functional (ideational, manipulative, heuristic, imaginative)
      Sociolinguistic (dialect/variety, register, naturalness, cultural references and figurative language)
- Topical characteristics

Relationship between input and response
- Reactivity (reciprocal, non-reciprocal, adaptive)
- Scope of relationship (broad, narrow)
- Directness of relationship (direct, indirect)

If speech is to be scored it is clear that we should be aware of what kind of language we expect from the tasks chosen for the test. While many of the characteristics of the expected response are similar to those in the pedagogic literature, the relationship between input and response is especially relevant to language testing because of the range of modes for the delivery of the prompt and the collection of the speech sample, from semi-direct (tape or computer mediated) tests, to pair simulations. Bachman and Palmer explain the features of the relationship between input and response in the following terms:

Reactivity
- Reciprocal: The test taker interacts with at least one other interlocutor, and gets instantaneous feedback on their performance.
- Non-reciprocal: There is no interaction of feedback.
- Adaptive: Each new task/item is selected depending upon the response to the previous item.

Scope of relationship
• Broad: Processing of significant amounts of input.
• Narrow: Processing small amounts of input.

Directness of relationship
• Direct: The response uses information supplied in the input.
• Indirect: The response includes information not supplied in the input.

A speaking task that required the test taker to describe a sequence of pictures would be (primarily) non-reciprocal, narrow in scope and direct; on the other hand, a pair of test takers discussing a topical issue would be reciprocal, broad and indirect.

The Bachman and Palmer model was designed to be generic, and applicable to language tests in general. More specifically related to the testing of speaking are Weir's (1993: 39) performance conditions:

• Processing under normal time constraints
  ❑ Tolerance of silence in short turns. Planning in long turns.
• Degree of reciprocity/participation in developing interaction.
  ❑ Equal speaking rights. Shared responsibility for continuance of the interaction.
• Purpose
  ❑ Reason for doing it (beyond demonstrating xyz features of spoken language).
• Interlocutors
  ❑ Number of participants in the interaction: dialogue, group discussion.
  ❑ Status: the social/professional status in real life of those involved: student, teacher, examiner, etc.
  ❑ Register: formal/informal
  ❑ Familiarity: participants known or unknown to each other.
  ❑ Gender: male or female examiners/interlocutors for male or female students.
• Setting
  ❑ Physical
• Role
  ❑ Appropriate to age and experience: friend/friend, undergraduate/supervisor, student/teacher.
• Topic
  ❑ Specificity, switching, familiarity, interest.
• Channel
  ❑ Telephone, face to face.
• Input dimensions
  ❑ Realistic task dimensions
• Size
  ❑ Processing appropriately sized input.
• Complexity
  ❑ Language used, subjects talked about
• Range
  ❑ Topics covered, lexical fields

Many of these categories are also under-defined. It is possible, for example that in many tasks it is not necessary to process language under normal time constraints, especially if a speaking task is designed with planning time in-cluded. It is also possible that even closed tasks like repeating sentences would penalise a student for a period of silence. Weir's conditions do, how-ever, contain the features of status and familiarity, which are oddly missing from Bachman's list. They are not discussed at length in the text, but as we shall see when considering task difficulty, they are more important predictors of difficulty than many other criteria that have been investigated to date (Plough and Gass, 1993; Fulcher and Márquez Reiter, 2003; Chapter 7). Also of importance in Weir's list is the inclusion of speaking rights and 'respons-ibility for continuance of the interaction', which opens the way to describing tasks in terms of the extent to which they might encourage the co-construction of discourse, as discussed in Chapter 2.

When we describe test tasks it is possible to use any of the categories presented above, as long as they are useful for the test design process and the subsequent analysis of how successful the tasks are in eliciting samples of language that can be rated. Test designers can select categories for task description that are salient to their own teaching and testing context. The utility of the descriptive framework can be evaluated with reference to the choices made when defining test construct (Chapter 2).

While each descriptive system has unique features, many overlap. This is the case with Bachman and Palmer's 'reactivity' and Pica *et al.*'s 'interactional activity'. In this analysis, we will use the characteristics presented in Table 3.1, which are generically useful in characterising tasks for speaking tests:

Table 3.1   A framework for describing tasks

---

1. Task orientation
   - Open: outcomes dependent upon speakers
   - Guided: outcomes are guided by the rubrics, but there is a degree of flexibility in how the test taker reacts to the input.
   - Closed: outcomes dictated by input or rubrics
2. Interactional relationship
   - Non-interactional
   - Interactional:
     - ❑ One-way
     - ❑ Two-way
     - ❑ Multi-way
3. Goal orientation
   - None
   - Convergent
   - Divergent
4. Interlocutor status and familiarity
   - No interlocutor
   - Higher status
   - Lower status
   - Same status
   - Degree of familiarity with interlocutor
5. Topic(s)
6. Situations

In order to show how this particular model can be applied, we present two examples of tasks that are very different in nature. The first is taken from PhonePass, which is the first computer administered and scored test of speaking. It is produced by Ordinate Inc. and can be found on their website (http://www.ordinate.com/ppass/ppuser/sampletest.jsp).

Task 1. PhonePass SET-10 Demo Test

Follow the instructions to read some sentences from among those printed in Part A. Read the sentences in the order requested. This order will be different from the printed order. Read aloud as smoothly and naturally as you can.

---

1. Traffic is a huge problem in Southern California.
2. The endless city has no coherent mass transit system.
3. Sharing rides was going to be the solution to rush-hour traffic.
4. Most people still want to drive their own cars, though.
5. Larry's next door neighbors are awful.
6. They play loud music all night when he's trying to sleep.
7. If he tells them to stop, they just turn it up louder.
8. He wants to move out of that neighborhood.
9. My aunt recently rescued a dog that was sick.
10. She brought her home and named her Margaret.
11. They weren't sure she was going to live, but now she's healthy.
12. I just wish she could get along better with their cat.

Task Orientation: closed. The test taker merely has to read the sentences aloud, in an order indicated by a computer-generated voice. The outcome of the task is entirely dictated by the rubric and the input, and no deviation is allowed.

Interactional Relationship: non-interactional. There is no communication between speakers.

Goal Orientation: none. In this task type there is no goal orientation at all, because there is no 'communication' taking place. It is feasible to have a computer-administered and scored task that did involve a convergent goal orientation, and an example will be given below. But for the most part computer-administered speaking tests cannot simulate divergent goal orientations.

Interlocutor Status and Familiarity: No interlocutor.

Topics: Home, travel, food.

Situations: variable.

This task type looks 'stilted' and 'unnatural'; it isn't what we normally understand by 'speaking'. Indeed, when we look back to the last chapter it is difficult to see what construct this task type could assess. However, reading aloud can be useful for some purposes. Ordinate claims that this task measures 'reading fluency', which is described as 'rhythm, phrasing, timing and pausing in reading aloud' (Ordinate, no date). The computer therefore calculates the rate of delivery, hesitations, omissions of words, repetitions, uneven or irregular phrasing. The task type is suited to eliciting evidence about whether the sound and speed is 'typical' of some notion of a 'standard' speaker of a specified variety of language, than any interactional or conversational ability.

Task 2. Communicative Use of English as a Foreign Language (CUEFL),
Test of Oral Interaction – Basic Level 0203/1, University of Cambridge Local
Examinations Syndicate, 1988.

You must talk with a teacher for about 5 minutes.

While you are talking, an assessor will be listening to what you and the teacher say.

As the end of the year approaches people all over the world will look back and think about it. What kind of year have you had? What were the best things about the last year for you?

You and your teacher are going to talk about this for about five minutes.

Topics you talk about could include the following:

- Study and/or work
- Health
- Travel
- People
- Special events
- Plus anything else you want to talk about

Task Orientation: open. While the input suggests topics it is made clear that the learner does not have to use any items in the list, and may talk about anything else that may have affected their life in the past year. The list is provided merely as support for those who may not be able to generate specific ideas.

Interactional Relationship: one-way. The learner is being asked to communicate opinions and views to the teacher; while the teacher may ask clarification questions, or encourage the learner through the use of appropriate back-channelling, it is clearly the case that the learner is intended to spend most of the time talking to the teacher. Communication is not co-constructed.

Goal Orientation: convergent.

Interlocutor Status and Familiarity: The interlocutor is a teacher, and therefore the status of the interlocutor is high. The teacher is one who has not taught the learner, and so familiarity is low.

Topics: Familiar topics about which the learner can *express* thanks, requirements, opinions, comment, attitude, confirmation, apology, wants or needs, information; *narrate* a sequence of events; *elicit* information, directions, or service.

This type of task requires the learner to speak on a topic provided and, while it is not capable of eliciting language upon which one could make judgements about conversational ability, it is possible to assess the accuracy of expression, the appropriate expression of opinion, or the ability to structure discourse. It could be used to assess language competence, and some aspects of strategic competence, such as restructuring utterances.

TASK DIFFICULTY IN PEDAGOGY AND SECOND LANGUAGE ACQUISITION

Brown and Yule (1983: 37–53) were among the first to discuss the difficulty of speaking tasks. Firstly they consider narrative tasks, in which learners are required to tell a story, often from a sequence of pictures like that described in Bachman (1981). They describe tasks that require learners to provide descriptions and instructions, and finally conversation or extended discourse tasks. They suggest a number of factors that will make tasks more or less difficult for each task type:

Narrative tasks
- Increasing cognitive load by requiring learners to undertake activities that are not directly related to telling the narrative, such as arranging pictures into a sequence before telling the story.
- The use of images that have different cultural implications for speakers of some languages. For example, some speakers may make assumptions about the place where the story is taking place that are incorrect because of their own cultural background.
- The proliferation of 'same-type' participants, usually characters of the same gender, where the learner can no longer use 'he' and 'she', or 'he' and 'it' to refer to the characters, but has to distinguish between two females, for example. Brown and Yule refer to this as 'communicative stress'.

Tasks requiring descriptions and instructions
- If learners have to describe a machine or object, and perhaps give instructions on how it is to be assembled, the more pieces there are, and the more complex the way in which they join together, the more complex the task will be. The same would be true in an information-gap task in which one

student was given a picture and asked to describe it for another student who would attempt to draw it.

- Cognitive load is increased by using culturally unfamiliar material, such as asking learners to describe pictures of objects that they have never encountered.

Extended discourse tasks

- Linguistic requirements for task completion, in terms of the difficulty of the language required to communicate.
- Cognitive requirements for task completion.
- Discoursal requirements for task completion, such as expected turn length.

Candlin (1987: 18–19) also considered how to sequence tasks for learners, also including the criteria of cognitive load and communicative stress, but adding:

- Particularity and generalisability. Tasks that follow a particular schema may be easier to do than tasks that are novel and need negotiation.
- Code complexity and interpretative density. Where the language of input is more complex, it is suggested that what the learner is asked to do with the input should be more 'straightforward' in order to avoid creating additional processing difficulties.

The exploration of task features that might make tasks more or less difficult within the second language acquisition literature has a somewhat different focus. The research of Tarone and Ellis emphasizes variability in performance task conditions such as physical setting, topic and participants. Tarone (1983, 1985, 1987, 1988) argues that variable performance by task and features of task shows that the construct of a 'stable competence' is untenable, and that performance data can only support the weaker construct of 'variable capability'. Similarly, Ellis (1985) argues for a heterogeneous capability that is manifested differentially depending upon task conditions in operation at the time of production. Fulcher (1995) first drew attention to the problem for language testing in adopting a variationist position. Fulcher argued that each test would be a test of performance in the specific situation defined in the task facets of the test situation, and that it would become impossible to generalise the meaning of test scores from any test task to any other task, or any non-test situation, unless there is a precise match between every facet of the test and the criterion. Tarone (1998) has since argued that the implication of a variationist position for language testing is that all speaking tasks must be carefully designed so that 'test elicitation conditions correspond with the authentic language use conditions that apply in the real-world situation or domain'. Using the notion of 'authenticity' in precisely the same way that is proposed by Bachman and Palmer (1996: 23–5), Tarone argues that scores from 'authentic' tests will inevitably lack reliability and generalisability.

The assumption underlying present SLA-influenced approaches to studying speaking tasks is that there is variation in test-taker performance by task characteristics or conditions, and that this variation leads to different scores (or estimates of speaking 'ability') under different test task conditions. This encourages the language test researcher to consider task features or conditions in relation to task difficulty, and how this may impact upon what inferences may be drawn from scores on speaking tests in relation to the tasks students are asked to perform.

There are a number of possible positions in relation to this argument (Chapelle, 1998, 1999a):

- The 'new behaviourism' position. Following the variationist argument, we may conclude that inferences drawn from scores may only be generalised to identical tasks in other tests or the real world.
- The trait theory position. Traditional trait theory assumes that the test scores are not task specific, or that tasks are for the most part interchangeable. The scores represent underlying constructs that enable speech, and from which we can generalise to other speaking tasks in other tests or the real world.
- The interactionist position. Some features of task may impact upon generalisability, and these need to be investigated. While the general degree of impact of some task features is usually small, it is these features that could be manipulated to make a test task specific to a particular situation in tests of speaking for specific purposes.

Part of the issue at stake is the extent to which the test task should be included in the construct definition. In Chapter 2, task type was omitted from the discussion of what might constitute a construct definition for a speaking test. However, it is only under the assumptions of trait theory that task types are irrelevant to the construct. In the new behaviourism, there is no construct other than the task description. The interactionist position is the middle ground, which admits that there may be contexts in which the task may be part of the construct definition.

TASK DIFFICULTY IN LANGUAGE TESTING

Research into task difficulty in speaking tests has not used the classifications outlined above, because they are related more to the classroom (to the kinds of interaction that promote learning) than the test, although Swain (2001) has recently revisited the one-, two- and multi-way classification to argue that multi-way tasks can be used to provide score meaning on more complex constructs (see Chapter 7). However, this does not mean that language testers should not frequently revisit the pedagogic literature for new ways of conceptualising task difficulty in speaking tests. For example, Pollitt (1991a) argued that in performance testing we make the assumption that all tasks are of equal difficulty, and suggested that performance tests might be constructed of a sequence of tasks with increasing difficulty, in analogy with the high jump in athletics. This early treatment of task difficulty in the language testing literature was merely applying the concept of sequencing from the pedagogic literature to language testing, although Pollitt did not suggest criteria that could be used to predict task difficulty in speaking tests.

While the structure of the interaction is important in test task design in order to ensure the elicitation of a range of discourse in speaking tests (Shohamy *et al.*, 1986), only psycholinguistic categories have been used in the empirical prediction of task difficulty. Similarly, the framework of test method facets as proposed by Bachman (1990) has not been used to investigate task difficulty, but for the comparison of content across tests (Bachman *et al.*, 1988; Bachman *et al.*, 1995). Douglas and Smith (1997), Skehan (1998a, 1998b), and Iwashita *et al.* (2001) have argued this is the case because (a) it is difficult to get agreement on precisely what each characteristic means, (b) there is no information on how or when method effects might influence scores, and (c) as an 'unordered check-list' the Bachman model would be difficult to use in research or task design. Rather, categories used from information-processing approaches have been used, particularly those put forward by Skehan (1998a, 1998b). Skehan has suggested that various (psycholinguistic) categories will affect task difficulty:

- Familiar information: the more familiar the information on which a task is based, the more fluent the performance will be.
- Structured tasks: where the task is based on a clear sequential structure there will be significantly greater fluency and accuracy.
- Complex and numerous operations: the greater the number of online operations and transformation of material that are needed, the more difficult the task. This may impact upon greater complexity, but at the expense of accuracy and fluency.
- Complexity of knowledge base: the more open the knowledge base on which a task draws, the more complex will be the language produced.
- Differentiated outcomes: as a task outcome requires more differentiated justification, the complexity of the language will increase.

For testing speaking, the claim is that the more difficult and complex the task, rated on these criteria, the more difficult the task will be. Foster and Skehan (1996) and Skehan and Foster (1997) report justification for the claims using three classroom activities: personally oriented tasks, narrative tasks and tasks where a choice and justification are required, scored for fluency, accuracy and complexity.

However, when this research has been replicated in a language testing setting it has so far proved impossible to predict task difficulty from these criteria (Brown *et al.*, 1999). Iwashita *et al.* (2001) and Elder *et al.* (2002) further investigated the possibility of establishing criteria for task difficulty in terms of task performance conditions. Modifying the Skehan model, they chose to investigate:

- Perspective: tell a story from one's own perspective, or from the perspective of a third person.
- Immediacy: tell a story with and without pictures.
- Adequacy: tell a story with a complete set of pictures, and with four or two pictures missing from the set.
- Planning time: with and without three minutes to prepare a task.

The McNamara *et al.* and Elder *et al.* study is unusual in that it combines both an analysis of the discourse produced from the tasks, and an empirical analysis of task difficulty, according to the criteria of fluency, accuracy and complexity. Learners were also asked to complete questionnaires regarding their perception of task difficulty. The study discovered that varying task conditions had no significant impact upon the discourse produced under test conditions, and no large significant relationship between task difficulty and task conditions. The feedback from test takers also provided no support for the model of impact of conditions on task difficulty.

The researchers say that their study 'failed to confirm the findings of existing research'. This is true in the case of research in classroom-based SLA investigation. However, in language-testing research, the lack of score sensitivity to variation in task has frequently been noted. The most striking example of this is the failure of researchers in English for Academic Purposes (EAP) tests to isolate 'specificity' of task. This story is summarised in Fulcher (1999), while Clapham (2000) acknowledges that specificity as a task condition has failed to generate enough score variance for it to be worth maintaining subject-specific modules in tests such as the International English Language Testing System (IELTS). Indeed, language for specific purposes testing (LSP) frequently struggles to discover what it is about an LSP test that makes it specific (Douglas, 1998, 2000), that is, easier for those with the specific (usually background) knowledge, and harder for those without it. Thus, while it has frequently been claimed that a lack of specialist knowledge in the topic of the test task makes the task more difficult for test takers without that knowledge, there is little evidence to suggest that this is the case in the language-testing literature.

This is not to question the view frequently supported by studies of test discourse that changes in task or task conditions result in changes of discourse (see Shohamy, 1983b, 1988, 1990; Shohamy *et al.*, 1986). It is evident that a change in task topic or number of participants will change the discourse produced by test takers (which is at the centre of Tarone's (1998) argument). What is in question is that *changes in discourse automatically translate into changes in test score,* and hence the estimate of task difficulty. Research has consistently shown that it requires gross changes in task type to generate significant differences in difficulty from one task to another, and even then the task accounts for little score variance. Using G-theory and multi-faceted

Rasch analysis, Fulcher (1993, 1996a) reports significant but extremely small differences in task difficulty that account for test score variance between a picture description task, an interview based on a text, and a group discussion. Similarly, Bachman, Lynch and Mason (1995) report significant but small differences between a task to summarise an academic lecture, and a task to relate a theme for the lecture to the test taker's own experience. Wigglesworth (2001) investigated the impact of task structure and familiarity, planning time and interlocutor, on task difficulty for a range of task types. She discovered that the significant effects were generally very small. If such gross differences have small impact upon scores, the results of the McNamara *et al.* study into conditions within the same narration task are unsurprising. Learner ability accounts for most score variance in these studies, and task difference, even if significant, accounts for only a small part of score variance. It is particularly important to note that in Skehan's (2001: 175) meta-analysis of task difficulty estimates within the framework summarised above, he concludes that the selection of task will affect test scores on the basis of p-values from the differences in accuracy and fluency scores by task. Fulcher and Márquez Reiter (2003) argue that the practical significance (as measured by Cohen's D, for example) is extremely important, and without such information it is always difficult to evaluate the claims of those who argue that task difficulties significantly vary and cause large changes in test scores. (For a discussion of the notion of 'practical significance' see Kirk, 1996.)

The only language testing studies to find large significant differences between how learners perform on tasks are those where the tasks are maximally different (as in Fulcher, 1996b and Bachman *et al.*, 1995) *and employ multiple rating scales.* Chalhoub-Deville (1995a) uses rating scales upon which all students are rated on all tasks and rating scales that are specific to some tasks. She reports using a modified ACTFL OPI, a picture narration task and a reading aloud task. Test takers were rated on 5 common scales, 8 specific scales for the interview, 7 specific scales for the narrative, and 1 specific scale for the reading aloud task. The first dimension discovered by Chalhoub-Deville relates to rating scales used in common across tasks (grammar and pronunciation), the second dimension relates to rating scales that were specific to a narrative task (creativity and adequacy of information), and the third to rating scales specific to an interview task (providing detail unassisted and length of subject's response). Upshur and Turner (1999) utilise only task-specific rating scales, for a story retelling task, and an 'audio-pal' task in which test takers sent a recorded message to an exchange student. Upshur and Turner found dimensions relating to each scale.

The rating scale specific approach to scoring speaking moves away from the traditional 'trait theory' approach to language testing, and towards what Chapelle (1999b) calls the 'new behaviourism', in which scores are not generalisable beyond the task types used. If speaking tasks and task conditions account for a significantly large portion of test score variance, the position of Tarone is upheld, and generalisability of score meaning is significantly reduced (see Chapter 8 for a discussion of Generalisabilty Theory). Linking rating scales to specific tasks is the inevitable end product.

However, in the two studies cited above, it is highly likely *that the use of specific rating scales has generated the large task-specific variance.* In other words, what is interpreted as task-specific variance is generated by the use of task-specific rating scales. Fulcher (1996b) has shown that rating scales that do not refer to specific task types, task conditions, or tasks, generate scores with most variance accounted for by test-taker ability. These findings support hypotheses regarding scale specificity and independence originally presented in Bachman and Savignon (1986), where it was argued that the inclusion of task-specific references in the ACTFL rating scales lead to difficulties in investigating construct validity, because test method facets (defined as error variance) were built into the scoring process.

This is not to suggest that designing rating scales that are specific to a certain task is something that language testers should not do. Chapelle (1998, 1999a) has argued that there may be situations when the nature of the task should be defined as part of the construct, if task conditions are relevant to the construct being tested. In such cases language testers need to abandon trait theory and move towards an 'interactionist approach' – where construct and task definition become intertwined. This may occur when designing a speaking test for a specific purpose (see Douglas and Selinker, 1992), or where tasks are designed on *a priori* grounds to elicit evidence for proficiency on a specific and carefully defined construct. However, this does not detract from present research findings that it is the rating scale that appears to invest the specificity in the task.

Fulcher and Márquez Reiter (2003) have argued that talking of task difficulty in speaking tests only makes sense *in relation to specific speakers.* They hypothesise that pragmatic task conditions are more likely to impact upon task performance, discourse and test score, and that pragmatic task conditions interact with the first language (L1) cultural background of the test takers. This approach to task difficulty draws more on the interests of pedagogy than has previously been the case in language testing, relating directly to the frequent claims that designing appropriate cultural contexts for language learning tasks is critical for learners to perform and acquire language (Kramsch, 1993). They investigated the degree to which various combinations of social power/distance and the degree of imposition of requests made in a variety of tasks affected task difficulty for two culturally different groups of speakers (English L1 speakers, and Spanish L1 speakers). It was discovered that there was a three-way interaction between social distance, degree of imposition and L1.

Task difficulty was moderately affected only in those tasks where the speaker was socially more powerful than the hearer but imposed high imposition on the hearer, and where the speaker is much less socially powerful than the hearer and makes a low imposition on the hearer. An example of the first situation is a task where the test taker is asked to play the role of a supervisor in an office, who approaches a junior and asks to borrow their personal laptop for the day. The second situation is represented by a task in which the test taker plays the role of a student, and is instructed to approach a professor and request to borrow a book that is not available in the library. In these tasks, the English L1 speakers found the tasks much more difficult than the Spanish L1 speakers, whereas in tasks that did not involve such extremes of social distance or imposition, there was no differential impact on task difficulty for either group. Nevertheless, social power and imposition did systematically predict task difficulty. In tasks where a socially less powerful person had to make a high imposition request, the task was seen as very difficult by both groups (such as asking your boss for a pay advance), while in tasks where a socially powerful person was making a low imposition request, the task was easier (such as asking an office junior to cover telephone calls for ten minutes).

These findings in language testing research are consistent with that in second language acquisition, that social distance affects communication (Varonis and Gass, 1985).

Despite the research undertaken to date, we know that it is not at all clear precisely what makes a task difficult or easy for a particular group of test takers. This is particularly the case because 'difficulty' does not reside in the task itself, but is an interaction of tasks, conditions and test takers, as argued by Bachman (2002). Teachers who have to devise their own tasks for speaking tests need to be aware of the problems with difficulty, and can choose frameworks for task development that may help isolate key features that affect the performance of their own students. For international testing, the problem is somewhat harder, as it is important to try to eliminate bias (here defined as differential construct unrelated difficulty for any sub-group of the test-taking population) from the tasks.

TASK TYPES IN SPEAKING TESTS

We have already considered two task types in order to demonstrate one framework for how speaking test tasks can be described. In this section we intend to follow the same format for a range of other tasks. This is not intended to be an exhaustive list of task types, but illustrative, drawing on descriptions provided in other sources (Bygate, 1987; Madsen, 1983; Underhill, 1987; Valette, 1997; Weir, 1988, 1993). The selection of tasks here is designed to highlight the approach to task description that has been discussed so far, to consider what type of speech each task may elicit, and suggest how this may be related to making meaningful inferences from scores to constructs.

The task types chosen are representative of the range of tasks that appear on many international and local/institutional tests of speaking, but they are not classified in traditional ways, for example as 'tasks suitable for tape-mediated speaking tests' or 'tasks suitable for extended speaking'. This is because many tasks can be used in both a semi-direct speaking test, or in a face-to-face interaction, and adapted to elicit different types of information. Even a closed repetition task can be included on a face-to-face interaction as part of a short pronunciation test for beginners. The way in which we classify tasks according to our scheme will, however, help us to see how we might select task types for specific tests. For example, a map-based speaking task that requires the learner to give directions to a destination may be identical in format in a computer-delivered test and a test with a human interlocutor; the only difference that may occur is in the coding of the interlocutor category. The interaction category may also change depending upon whether the interlocutor is intended to ask clarification questions or play a role.

Examples of task types

Repeat the sentence (PhonePass SET-10 Demo Test)

Please repeat each sentence that you hear.

Example: a voice says, 'Leave town on the next train.'
          and you say, 'Leave town on the next train.'

Task Orientation: Closed. The task outcome is completely directed by the input, to the extent that any deviation from accurate repetition of the input is considered to be an incorrect response.

Interactional Relationship: Non-interactional.

Goal Orientation: None.

Interlocutor Status and Familiarity: No interlocutor, or if an interlocutor is present, the interlocutor only acts in the role of providing the prompt.

Topics: Any short sentence with lexis that is not outside the ability range of the test taker.

Situations: These tasks usually lack context.

Repeat the sentence tasks are commonly used to test pronunciation, and the ability to reproduce stress and intonation. It is possible that repetition tasks are also sensitive to short-term memory processing, which may be overloaded in learners who have only just begun to learn a language. These types of tasks may not be of very much use beyond an elementary stage of language learning, as they seem to be incapable of discriminating at higher ability levels. Little research has been done to discover at precisely what point in the process of language learning repetition tasks provide less than useful information.

From ELSA Handbook 2003, *p. 56. Reprinted by permission of EDI plc. Contact LCCIEB Customer Service Team, +44(0)20 8309 3000, email: custerv@lccieb.org.uk.*

Part 6 Picture story

In this section you need to look at the 6 pictures printed below (1–6). The pictures show a story. First we are going to ask you some questions about the pictures. Then you are going to have a chance to tell the story. But first of all, you have 20 seconds to study the pictures and think what might be happening in each one, and how they connect together to tell a story. Study the pictures now, but do not start speaking yet.

(*20 seconds to study the pictures*)

OK, now we are going to ask you one question about each picture. You have 10 seconds to answer each question.

(*ANSWER THE QUESTIONS*)

Now it is your chance to tell the whole story. You will have 3 minutes to tell the story. Try to include as much detail as possible, and to make it as interesting as possible. Start the story like this: '**Mike really didn't feel like going to work that morning . . .**' Start telling the story after you hear the tone.

Task Orientation: Guided. While there may be some possibility for some individuals to alter the story creatively, most narrative tasks require the speakers to produce the expected story. Despite this, precisely how the test taker tells the story is not dictated.

Interactional Relationship: Non-interactional, or One-way, depending upon the mode of delivery. In this particular example the test is tape mediated, but it is a common task type in face-to-face interviews, where the interviewer may prompt, comment, or ask clarification questions.

Goal Orientation: Convergent. The primary aim of the test taker is to produce a monologue that will tell the story as efficiently as possible.

Interlocutor Status and Familiarity: No interlocutor, or a higher status interlocutor if used as a sub-task within a structured interview or other assessment procedure.

Topics: Short stories that can be visually depicted in 6–8 cartoons or pictures.

Situations: Variable.

Narrative tasks of this kind are frequently used to test the ability to recount events, and assess the test taker's ability to control time markers and past tense structures. It is difficult to claim that the task type can be used to infer to constructs beyond language competence, apart from an ability to report events in a specific purposes test. The task type remains especially popular for use in tests of speaking for younger learners, as telling simple stories is one of the first things that they are able to do in a second language. For the same reason they are more frequently used in tests for less proficient students.

Map, graph and text from ETS (2000) *Test of Spoken English, Sample Paper,* *ftp://ftp.ets.org/pub/toefl/004954.TSE.pdf. Reprinted by permission of Educational Testing Service, the copyright holder.*

Imagine that we are colleagues. The map below is of a neighbouring town that you have suggested I visit. You will have 30 seconds to study the map. Then I'll ask you questions about it.

1. Choose one place on the map that you think I should visit and give me some reasons why you recommend this place (30 seconds).

2. I'd like to see a movie. Please give me directions from the bus station to the movie theatre (30 seconds).

3. One of your favorite movies is playing at the theatre. Please tell me about the movie and why you like it (60 seconds).

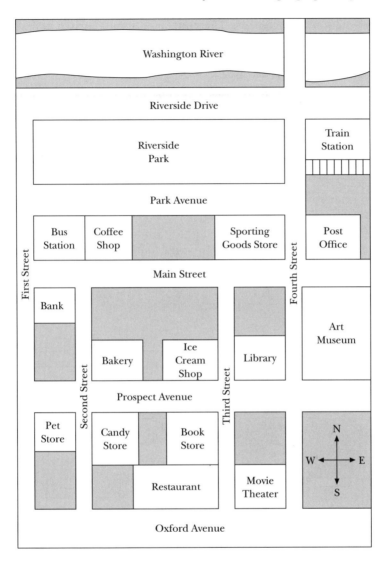

Task Orientation: Guided. Although question 2 requires the test taker to give an accurate set of instructions for someone to travel from the bus station to the movie theatre, the rest of the task is relatively open. In question 1 the test taker is allowed to select the destination and needs to come up with reasons that are neither provided, nor obvious. In question 3, the test taker is free to select any movie of his or her choice to talk about.

Interactional Relationship: Variable. In this particular example there is no interactional relationship, because it is tape mediated. However, such tasks can be one-way with an interviewer, or two-way if two candidates have partial maps and need to work together to complete tasks.

Goal Orientation: Convergent. The test taker is not invited to explore a subject independently and come to whatever conclusions they wish. Even in question 3 the movie must be one that the test taker likes, and only a justification for the choice is acceptable.

Interlocutor Status and Familiarity: Variable. Map-based tasks can be used with teacher interviewers, or as prompts for interaction with other learners.

Topics: Generally limited to places.

Situations: Providing directions and describing places for friends or colleagues.

---

4. The graph below presents the actual and projected percentage of the world population living in cities from 1950 to 2010. Tell me about the information given in the graph (60 seconds).

5. What might this information mean for the future? (45 seconds)

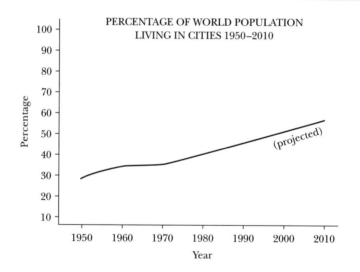

Task Orientation: Guided to Open. Graphs do not constrain the speaker in the same way that maps do, because the input is used to set the topic rather than the development of the discourse. The test taker is free to develop their own ideas in relation to the graph, apart from where a simple description is required.

Interactional Relationship: Variable. It is possible to use graphs in a variety of interactional situations, from no interaction where a monologic response is required, to multi-way interactions where a variety of related graphs are provided to different participants.

Goal Orientation: Variable. In the present example the first question is convergent, while the second question is divergent, requiring open-ended reasoning. The type of conclusion that the speaker comes to, and the views expressed, may differ from other participants in two- or multi-way interactions.

Interlocutor Status and Familiarity: Variable.

Topics: Variable. Graph type prompts can be used to elicit language in most topic domains.

Situations: Variable, but must be representable in graphic format.

The use of maps and graphics in speaking tests is favoured because, like pictures, they reduce the amount of linguistic input needed for the test taker to respond to the prompt. While maps are limited in the way they can be used, graphics have a much wider applicability, and are frequently used in tests of speaking for academic purposes. The norm is to require a description of the graph, followed by a long turn in which the test taker explains what the implications of the information might be for a particular audience. The interlocutor does not engage in open discussion unless the test taker cannot continue to speak. For this reason its use in semi-direct speaking tests is also favoured.

These task types are well suited to assessing sociolinguistic knowledge, and achievement strategies in extended explanation.

Picture Prompts (University of Cambridge Local Examinations Syndicate Preliminary English Test, Part 3, Sample Material 2001)

Task Orientation: Guided. Picture prompt items are very common in tests of speaking, providing the test taker with something specific to talk about, while allowing some flexibility in expression. It is possible to develop such tasks into open activities when the pictures are used as a springboard to wider discussions of topical issues.

Interactional Relationship: This task is intended to be two-way between the two test takers, while also offering the possibility for each to have a longer turn. While one test taker is the main speaker, the other may ask clarification questions or make comments. The interlocutor frame does not allow for the active participation of a third person, although it does allow for intervention if necessary, using prompts rather than direct questions. In many cases, however, these generate one-way interaction unless the test takers take the initiative to ask questions.

Goal Orientation: Convergent. The purpose of the task is to describe a picture and come to some agreement about its meaning.

Interlocutor Status and Familiarity: Same status, frequently familiar with each other. In paired tasks part of the aim is to reduce the social distance between the test taker and the teacher interlocutor by allowing two learners to inter-act. The rationale is to encourage different types of interaction that may generate a richer sample of language that may allow scoring on more complex constructs (see the extended discussion in Chapter 7).

Topics: Variable and extensive.

Situation(s): Variable.

SAMPLE TEST – SPEAKING

EXAMINER MATERIAL

PRELIMINARY ENGLISH TEST

| Part 3 (3 minutes) | Oral Test 4 (A Quiet Time) |

Tasks

Describing people and places; saying where people and things are and what different people are doing.

Interlocutor Frame

Say to both candidates:

> Now, I'm going to give each of you a photograph of people enjoying a quiet time.
>
> Candidate A, here is your photograph, (*Hand one of the photographs to Candidate A.*) Would you show it to Candidate B and talk about it, please? Candidate B. I'll give you a photograph in a moment.
>
> Candidate A would you start now please? _____ Thank you.

If there is a need to intervene, prompts rather than direct questions should be used.

> Now, Candidate B, here is your picture. (Hand the second photograph to Candidate B.) Would you show it to Candidate A and tell him/her about it, please? _____ Ready?
>
> Thank you.

Assessment

The candidates should talk about the photographs with little or no prompting. Specialised words such as 'hair-band' and 'crane' are not expected.

Retrieve the photographs before moving to Part 4.

| Part 4 (3 minutes) |

Tasks

Talking about one's likes and dislikes: expressing opinions.

Interlocutor Frame

Say to both candidates:

> Your photographs showed people enjoying a quiet moment in different ways. Now, I'd like you to talk together about the kind of things you like to do when you want to be **quiet** and the kind of things you **don't** like to do.

Assessment

The task is achieved if the candidates can talk, with little or no prompting, about the kind of things they like to do when they want to be quiet and the kind of things they don't like to do.

Time

Parts 3 & 4 should take about **6 minutes** together.

© UCLES 1997

Picture prompts provide considerable topical support for the test taker, but care must be taken to select pictures that do not include culturally alien images. Similarly, it is important to use pictures that do not require the use of descriptive vocabulary that is outside the expected range of the test takers for whom the test is being designed. The task type can be used to assess aspects of language competence, particularly vocabulary, extended turns, and sociolinguistic knowledge.

Presentation (University of Cambridge Local Examinations Syndicate, Certificate of Proficiency in English (CPE), Part 3, Revised CPE Specifications and Sample Papers, 2002)

For Oral Examiners' Use Only

| Certificate of Proficiency in English |
| Speaking Test |

| **Part 3   12 minutes** | **11 Changing Lifestyles** |

Interlocutor	Now, in this part of the test you're each going to talk on your own for about two minutes. You need to listen while your partner is speaking because you'll be asked to comment afterwards.
(A)	So *(Candidate A)*, I'm going to give you a card with a question written on it and I'd like you to tell us what you think. There are also some ideas on the card for you to use if you like.
	All right? Here is your card, and a copy for you *(Candidate B)*.
	Hand over a copy of prompt card 11(a) to each candidate.
	Remember *(Candidate A)*, **you have about two minutes to talk before we join in.**
	[*Allow up to 10 seconds before saying, if necessary:* **Would you like to begin now?**]
Candidate A	- -
_ *2 minutes*	
Interlocutor	**Thank you.**
	*Select **one** appropriate follow-up question for Candidate B:*
	• **What do you think?**
	• **Is there anything you would like to add?**
	• **Is there anything you don't agree with?**
	• **How does this differ from your experience?**
Candidate B	- -
_ *up to 1 minute*	
Interlocutor	*Address **one** of the following questions to both candidates:*
	• **Do you care about what you eat?**
	• **Do you think our diets have become healthier?**
	• **How confident can we be about food safety?**
Candidates	- -
_ *1 minute*	
Interlocutor	**Thank you.** *Retrieve cards.*

Prompt Card 11(a)

How are attitudes to food changing?

• **food production**
• **methods of preparation**
• **social importance**

For Oral Examiners' Use Only

11 Changing Lifestyles (cont.)

Interlocutor	Now *(Candidate B)*, **it's your turn to be given a question**.
	Hand over a copy of prompt card 11(b) to each candidate.
(B)	**Here is your card, and a copy for you** *(Candidate A)*. **Remember** *(Candidate B)*, **you have about two minutes to tell us what you think, and there are some ideas on the card for you to use if you like. All right?**
	[*Allow up to 10 seconds before saying, if necessary:* **Would you like to begin now?**]
Candidate B	
_ 2 minutes	
Interlocutor	**Thank you.**
	*Select **one** appropriate follow-up question for Candidate A:*
	• **What do you think?**
	• **Is there anything you would like to add?**
	• **Is there anything you don't agree with?**
	• **How does this differ from your experience?**
Candidate A	
_ up to 1 minute	
Interlocutor	*Address **one** of the following questions to both candidates:*
	• **To what extent is electrical equipment for the home good value for money?**
	• **Is technology in the home always beneficial?**
	• **How do you see technology for the home developing in the future?**
Candidate	
_ 1 minute	
Interlocutor	**Thank you.** *Retrieve cards.*

Prompt Card 11(b)

What changes have resulted from the introduction of technology into the home?

• **work**
• **free time**
• **communication**

Interlocutor	**Now, to finish the test, we're going to talk about 'changing lifestyles' in general.**
	Address a selection of the following questions to both candidates:
	• **To what extent can we change our lifestyle?**
	• **Which event of the last century do you think has had the most impact on**
_ 4 minutes	**people's lifestyles?**
	• **How influential is the media on the way we live?**
	• **What are the greatest threats to our quality of life?**
	• **Should we attempt to narrow the gap between the 'haves' and the 'have nots'?**
	• **Does more always mean better?**
Interlocutor	**Thank you. That is the end of the test.**

Task Orientation: Open. While the topic is provided, speakers may develop the theme in any way they wish.

Interactional Relationship: One-way, leading to two-way. The first part of this task requires the speaker to address the topic given for two minutes, making it an extended monologue. The task could have been ended at this point, but in the CPE it is extended to a discussion between the two test takers.

Goal Orientation: Divergent. Both test takers may present any views they wish, and are encouraged to do so through being asked what they do not agree with in the other test taker's presentation, and how their own experience differs.

Interlocutor Status and Familiarity: Same status, variable familiarity.

Topics: Variable.

Situations: Variable.

The innovative link between the presentation and discussion makes this a very flexible task, capable of eliciting language that can be scored in many ways. The presentation task can be directed towards specific topics, so it is useful in tests for specific purposes, and has been used in the Test of English for Educational Purposes (Weir, 1988: 83). The discussion and interaction also makes it an excellent task type for assessing strategic competence, textual and pragmatic knowledge, as well as sociolinguistic knowledge. The pairing of test-takers is now standard practice in most speaking tests produced by the University of Cambridge Local Examinations Syndicate (Saville and Hargreaves, 1999), and is discussed in more detail in Chapter 7.

Oral Proficiency Interview (OPI) From A. I. Weinstein, Steps in a Speaking Test, in Testing Kit: French and Spanish, *edited by James R. Frith, 1979*:

1. Warm up. Put the candidate at ease. Remember he or she is nervous. Engage in small talk; for example, ask about a former student of yours now at the post he or she just came from. Be natural, as you are in the classroom. Smile and be willing to laugh with (not at) the candidate.

2. Probe. Keep in mind the definitions of the levels. Now ask substantive questions at the lowest level you estimated during the warm-up. Let the candidate make his or her own test: this is best done by asking him what kind of work the candidate did at the last post, or what kind of work the candidate will do at the next one. Keep on asking more difficult questions until you think you're sure of the candidate's level.

3. Confirm. Ask one or two more questions at one level higher than your probes gave you. Make them long enough to insure a test of comprehension.

Task Orientation: Guided. In the traditional Oral Proficiency Interview, there is a face-to-face encounter with an examiner/interlocutor who asks questions from a suggested list in order to rate the performance. The questions selected by the interlocutor guide the test taker through the process.

Interactional Relationship: Two-way, between the test taker and the interlocutor.

Goal Orientation: Convergent. Although in principle the test taker could be allowed to develop their own ideas and begin to lead the conversation, this is actively discouraged in the interview. This is partly in 'fairness' to other test takers, but also because the interview is a structured encounter conducted for measurement purposes.

Interlocutor Status and Familiarity: The interlocutor is of higher status, and is always unfamiliar to the test taker.

Topics: Variable, but usually listed for each possible level in the rating system. Topics such as 'family and friends', 'food' and 'leisure' are assumed to be easier than topics like 'international diplomacy', which would be placed at a higher level. Topics and questions are selected by the interviewer according to the initial assessment of the level of the test taker in the warm-up phase, and then adapted as the prompt probe phase commences.

Situations: An interview, mainly constructed of questions by the interlocutor and answers provided by the test taker. Sometimes role-plays or other tasks are embedded within the interview.

The interview has been the most commonly used speaking test format, partly because the questions used can be standardised, making comparison between test takers easier than when other task types are used. Training interlocutors and raters is also considerably easier. Nevertheless, the test taker is primarily in a position of answering questions, and this limits the kind of inferences that can be made from scores. The interview has traditionally been used to test language competence. There is considerable scepticism about whether it is possible to test other competencies or knowledge because of the nature of the discourse that the interview produces, as first argued by van Lier (1989) and frequently repeated in the literature since (see, for example, Johnson, 2001).

Information Gap (University of Cambridge Business English Certificate 1, Task 1, Sample Papers 1997. Note: this task type was replaced in BECS in 2002, and is used here only as an example of an Information Gap task)

Candidate A

Your Questions.

You need to ask Candidate B for this information about a business centre.

Location	....
Name of Manager	....
Languages Spoken	....
Fax Service	....
Methods of Payment	....

Reverse side of Candidate A's card:

Information

This is the information about the other business centre. Try to answer Candidate B's questions.

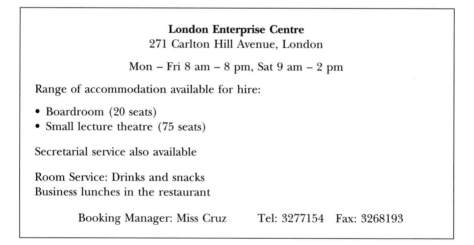

London Enterprise Centre
271 Carlton Hill Avenue, London

Mon – Fri 8 am – 8 pm, Sat 9 am – 2 pm

Range of accommodation available for hire:

• Boardroom (20 seats)
• Small lecture theatre (75 seats)

Secretarial service also available

Room Service: Drinks and snacks
Business lunches in the restaurant

Booking Manager: Miss Cruz   Tel: 3277154   Fax: 3268193

Candidate B

Your Questions.

You need to ask Candidate B for this information about a business centre.

Address of centre	....
Opening hours	....
Meeting rooms	....
Refreshments	....
Contact person	....

Reverse side of Candidate B's card:

Information

This is the information about the other business centre. Try to answer Candidate A's questions.

Bangkok Business Centre
53–57 Pacific High Road, City Centre

First-class professional service provided by Mr Jaffee (MBA) and staff
All reception staff speak Thai, English, Japanese

Range of accommodation available for hire:

- Photocopying and fax facilities: 1st floor, 7 days a week
- Translation service available: reasonable charges

All major credit cards accepted

Task Orientation: Guided. All relevant information is provided to the test takers. The task requirement is that they understand the question being asked by their partner, select the appropriate information from the card, and communicate this clearly and accurately.

Interactional Relationship: Two-way. This is a classic example of an information gap activity that Pica *et al.* (1993) argue is the most effective in task-based classroom learning. It is therefore not surprising that it is very widely used in face-to-face speaking tests in order to measure strategic, textual, pragmatic and sociolinguistic competences.

Goal Orientation: Convergent. The purpose of the task is to communicate and record information effectively.

Interlocutor Status and Familiarity: Same status, with variable familiarity.

Topics: Variable.

Situations: Variable.

It has been claimed that the primary advantage of information gap tasks is that the test takers 'genuinely' have to communicate. It is clear that they do have to ask questions, rather than simply provide answers as in an interview. As there is interaction it is possible to assess most aspects of strategic competence, although the question and answer structure limits the possibilities of assessing textual knowledge.

Role Play (from the Occupational English Test, Physiotherapists, in McNamara, 1996)

Candidate's card

Setting: Hospital clinic

Patient: An elderly person who is recovering from a stroke (CVA). The patient is making slow progress in learning to walk again.

Task: Talk to the patient about the following pieces of equipment:
  • A wheelchair
  • A walking frame
  • A walking stick

Explain the advantages and disadvantages of each one.

You would like the patient to be as independent in his or her movements as possible. You feel the frame is not appropriate. You want the patient to have a stick. You do not want the patient to have a wheelchair at this stage.

Role Player's card

Setting: Hospital Clinic

Patient: You are an elderly person who is recovering from a stroke. You feel you are making painfully slow progress, and don't really expect to be able to walk again.

You feel you should be allowed to have a wheelchair.

Task: Ask the physiotherapist when you will be given a wheelchair.

Insist on your need for this equipment. Explain that you feel that the painful exercises you are doing at the moment are pointless, and that you are pessimistic about your chances of making real progress.

Be difficult!

Task Orientation: Guided. Clear role cards are provided that specify the nature of the situation. In most role-plays test takers are not able to stray from the context, which makes them appropriate for testing English for use in specific purposes.

Interactional Relationship: Two-way, between a patient and a physiotherapist.

Goal Orientation: Divergent. The role cards set up the two test takers to disagree on the outcomes of the interaction.

Interlocutor Status and Familiarity: The physiotherapist is higher status within the hospital, and they are likely to be familiar with each other because of the course of treatment.

Topics: Mainly specific purposes.

Situations: Variable, mainly job-related.

As it is presented here, this task type is the closest to what Jones (1982) describes as 'simulations for assessment'. Role plays are frequently difficult for students who do not wish to assume the role that they are given, so it is important to ensure that the intended test takers are going to be prepared to accept the roles and suspend disbelief for the sake of the test (see *Being things with words* in Chapter 2). This is why role plays and simulations are more suited to specific purposes, and particularly job-related speaking tests, as is the case with the OET. It is one of the few formats that allows the test designer to collect evidence that would allow inferences to be made about 'expressing being', as well as most of the other constructs that make up a definition of speaking. Particularly important is the possibility of testing discourse co-construction.

Translating/Interpreting (from Stephen Zappala, Interpreter situations, in Testing Kit: French and Spanish, *edited by James R. Frith, 1979)*

> The examiner gives the candidate a detailed explanation in English of the role (s)he is to play with the interviewer in the target language. The candidate is then free to phrase his/her utterances in any manner that conveys the information required by the role. At the end of the role playing, the candidate, in the role of interpreter for the examiner, explains to the latter in English what took place and what the interviewer said.

It is the beginning of a workday at the office. Give your secretary instructions for the day. Among other things, ask her to cancel an appointment at 11:00 which you have with a professor from the National University because you must go to the airport to meet an official who is arriving from Washington. Instruct her about two letters which you wish to have written, and also ask her to remind you of an appointment you have at 3:00 with Dr Martin.

Translating/Interpreting (from anonymous, Requests Bridge, *Washington DC: Department of State, 1984)*

You have the opportunity to observe a slightly more experienced duty officer handling visitors to the Embassy. These encounters are on tape. You need not understand every word. Even the more experienced officer has difficulty understanding the visitor. You have two tasks: (1) identify the reason for the visit; (2) notice how the officer elicits the information, clarifies what s/he doesn't understand, and manages the encounter in spite of obvious language limitations.

Your teacher will provide you with the tape and leave the room. When your teacher returns report on the conversation in English.

Task Orientation: Guided. In the first example what is to be interpreted/ translated for the examiner is the outcome of a role-play, while in the second it is provided in a taped interaction between a member of the embassy staff and a visitor. The second of these is clearly more guided than the first. What is interesting to note in these examples from the FSI is the very early use of *integrative speaking tasks,* where the actual speech to be graded – in this case the interpretation/translation – depends on input that attempts to model the types of interaction the military test takers may be expected to undertake in their jobs.

Interactional Relationship: Two-way.

Goal Orientation: Convergent. The test taker should accurately interpret and translate an interaction between two people to the examiner.

Interlocutor Status and Familiarity: The interlocutor is higher status, and they are likely to be unfamiliar.

Topics: Mainly specific purposes, and particularly useful for job-related speaking tests.

Situations: Job-related tasks that require verbal reports of events.

Most examples in the literature relate to testing English for military/ diplomatic purposes (see Chapter 1). The very specific nature of this activity makes it very similar to a presentation without a discussion, but the integrative nature of the task deserves some comment. Unless the test taker can understand the aural input from the tape, or take part in the role-play, they will be unable to complete the actual test task. In many real-world situations this is often the case, although in language testing it is common to try to separate the assessment of 'different skills'. This type of task is worthy of further investigation in order to define more carefully the constructs that it may be testing, which are likely to be a mix of speaking-related constructs, listening-related constructs, and memory.

Discussion (from the University of Cambridge Certificate in English Language Skills, Handbook and Samples, 2002)

Candidate's Task Sheet

TASK 4   **VANTAGE, PART 2**

Most people wear different clothes on different occasions. To what extent are we influenced by fashion?

Choose 2 or 3 statements that best describe your own attitude towards fashion. Add other ideas of your own if you wish. Think about what you want to say and make some notes if you want.

- 'Being comfortable is the most important thing for me.'
- 'I love to follow fashion.'
- 'Fashion is fun, but I never wear things I don't like.'
- 'I can never find what I want in the shops.'
- 'I feel uncomfortable if I'm not wearing the latest fashion.'
- Other . . .

Compare your choice of statements with a partner and talk about the clothes you wear. Then the examiner will ask you about your discussion.

Is money an important factor in your choice of clothes?

Task Orientation: Guided. The test taker is asked to describe his or her attitude, which is then discussed with a partner. While choice of topic is open, the treatment of the topic and the expected outcome is firmly guided.

Interactional Relationship: Two-way, between two or three test takers. Discussion task types are sometimes used with an interlocutor/examiner.

Goal Orientation: Convergent or Divergent.

Interlocutor Status and Familiarity: Same status, variable familiarity.

Topics: Variable.

Situations: Conversation.

Frequently claimed to be the 'most natural' of task types (Underhill, 1987: 45), the discussion is designed to put test takers in a situation where the interaction may not resemble 'test-like' discourse. In principle it should be possible to assess most competences and knowledge using this format, but it remains problematic as a test task because of the assumed willingness of two test takers to 'chat' in front of an examiner (see the discussion in Chapter 7). For assessment purposes there is also the problem of how a score can be given to an individual when the interaction is co-constructed, even in a guided task. This should not deter language testers from using discussions, and trying to solve the problems that they generate, for there is evidence that in face-to-face interactions this type of task is greatly favoured by test takers in preference to some other task types (Fulcher, 1996a). The University of Cambridge Local Examinations Syndicate claim that this task type is capable of providing evidence from which we may draw inferences not only as to accuracy, but as to discourse management and interactional competence. If this is the case, the task type is capable of eliciting evidence for complex constructs.

DIGEST

We have argued that it is not useful to think about task types in terms of the mode of delivery. Each of the task types listed above could be used in a semi-direct test (which will be discussed more fully in Chapter 7), interviews with an examiner, or in the more complex paired or multi-way formats. The principle reasons for selecting task types for a test of speaking are:

• Will this task elicit a performance that can be scored (Chapter 4)?
• Will it be possible to make inferences from the score to the construct we intend to measure (Chapter 2)?

Task classifications can help the test designer to select the most appropriate set of tasks for a specific purpose, given that tests need to be short enough to be practical and economical, and long enough to be reliable and provide evidence to support valid inferences. The range and number of tasks in any speaking test are also important. Most speaking tests contain a range of task types that will allow inferences to be made from scores to constructs. Test designers should therefore ask themselves which mix of task types is most appropriate for the purpose of the test (see Chapter 5), and consider how it is possible to evaluate the selection made (see Chapter 7).

The task characteristics and task conditions that we use to describe the tasks should also reflect the type of variables that we might expect to affect task difficulty for the intended test takers. Even though evidence suggests that variations in these variables have limited practical effect on task difficulty, it is still important to ensure that some task characteristic or condition does not penalise some sub-group of the test-taking population.

We will look at the structure of tests, linking tasks to constructs, and tasks and constructs to rating scales, in Chapter 5.

In this chapter we have looked at a number of ways in which tasks have been described in the second language acquisition literature, the pedagogic literature, and the language testing literature. We have argued that it is possible to use or adapt categories from a range of sources that will provide a useful framework for characterising test tasks for our own purposes and contexts. One example of how this could be done was presented, and a range of speaking test task types were then presented using this framework.

In the next chapter we will consider the development of rating scales that can be used in the process of scoring.

Chapter 4

Rating scales

This chapter considers how we might score samples of spoken language and performances that are elicited by the tasks used in a second language speaking test. In this chapter we attempt to give an overview of this work together with an account of the four main approaches to scale development that are documented in the literature.

We begin by providing a definition of a rating scale and briefly outline the purposes for which they may be used. We then consider the main types of rating scales that have been used in the testing of second language speaking, and then consider at length four specific approaches to rating scale design. The first is the approach used in the FSI family of rating scales, probably the most influential in the history of testing second language speaking. While the methodology is not as explicit as the other three approaches to design that we discuss, the importance of the FSI tradition requires that we consider it in some detail. The other three are very explicit in their design methodology: data-based rating scale design (Fulcher, 1993, 1996b), empirically derived, binary-choice, boundary definition scales (Upshur and Turner, 1995), and scaling descriptors (North, 1996/2000).

Finally, we attempt to draw together the discussion of constructs, tasks and rating scales, in an expanded model of speaking performance in tests of second language speaking.

RATING SCALES IN SPEAKING TESTS

A rating scale, sometimes referred to as a 'scoring rubric' or 'proficiency scale', is defined as:

> A scale for the description of language proficiency consisting of a series of constructed levels against which a language learner's performance is judged. Like a test, a proficiency (rating) scale provides an operational definition of a linguistic construct such as proficiency. Typically such scales range from zero mastery through to an end-point representing the well-educated native speaker. The levels or bands are commonly characterised in terms of what subjects can do with the language (tasks and functions which can be performed) and their

mastery of linguistic features (such as vocabulary, syntax, fluency and cohesion). . . . Scales are descriptions of groups of typically occurring behaviours; they are not in themselves test instruments and need to be used in conjunction with tests appropriate to the population and test purpose. Raters or judges are normally trained in the use of proficiency scales so as to ensure the measure's reliability.   (Davies *et al.*, 1999: 153–4)

In this definition of a rating scale, it is claimed that the scale 'provides an operational definition of a linguistic construct', drawing on aspects of speaking presented in the framework of Chapter 2. This is the position taken by most of those who work with rating scales (Fulcher and Márquez Reiter, 2003), but it should not be taken for granted, as it rests upon an assumption that the rating scale will be used to (a) score speech samples, and (b) guide test developers in the selection of tasks for tests. Alderson (1991b) has suggested that there are other uses for scales:

- User-Oriented Scales: used to report information about typical or likely behaviours of a test taker at a given level.
- Assessor-Oriented Scales: designed to guide the rating process, focusing on the quality of the performance expected.
- Constructor-Oriented Scales: produced to help the test constructor select tasks for inclusion in the test.

The level of detail in each type of scale may be very different. In User-Oriented Scales it may be appropriate to phrase the band descriptors (we will use this term from now on to mean band or level descriptors) in terms of what the learner can do in the second language, or 'Can Do' statements. Assessor-Oriented Scales will need to contain construct definition, but it may need to be expressed in a way that can be processed in the limited time available to award a rating in a face-to-face speaking test. The Constructor-Oriented scale, on the other hand, may be much more detailed, and contain references to the types of task that are most likely to elicit the language sample required for the scores to be meaningful.

In this chapter we are assuming that the purpose of the rating scale is to guide the rating process. In other words, we are primarily considering the design of Assessor-Oriented Scales. The information needed by test constructors is considered in Chapter 5.

There are different types of rating scales used for scoring speech samples. One of the traditional distinctions is between *holistic* and *analytic* rating scales. The classic definition of holistic assessment is provided by Cooper (1977: 4) in the context of writing assessment. He says holistic assessment is:

any procedure which stops short of enumerating linguistic, rhetorical, or informational features of a piece of writing. Some holistic procedures may specify a number of particular features and even require that each feature be scored separately, but the reader is never required to stop and count or tally incidents of the feature.

Analytic assessment is the reverse, namely, counting or tallying incidents. For Hamp-Lyons (1991) holistic assessment can be broken down into 'holistic scoring', 'primary-trait scoring' and 'multiple-trait scoring'. These are defined as:

- Holistic scoring: A single score is given to each speech sample either impressionistically, or guided by a rating scale. This single score is designed to encapsulate all the features of the sample, representing 'overall quality'. This type of scoring is problematic because it does not take into account the constructs that make up speaking, but just 'speaking'. And if speaking is made up of constructs, 'speaking' is more like a theory than a construct. A single score may not do justice to the complexity of speaking.

- Primary-trait scoring: This approach assumes that one can only judge a speech sample in its context, and so rating criteria should be developed for each individual task. This would be the natural approach to scoring that would accompany the 'new behaviourism' associated with the variationist position in task research discussed in the last chapter.

- Multiple-trait scoring: Providing multiple scores for each speech sample, with each score representative of some feature of the performance, or construct underlying the performance. In the former case the multiple traits are task specific, as in primary-trait scoring. In the latter, by relating scores directly to constructs rather than tasks, the scores may be generalised across a range of task types. While it is clearly impossible to score each and every construct in even a simple definition of 'speaking', multiple-trait scoring does offer the possibility that the scores are sensitive to more constructs, with the added advantage that diagnostic information is also available for those score users who require it. The main disadvantage of multiple-trait scoring is that frequently raters cannot make the distinctions required to assign three or four separate grades for one speech sample. The tendency to give the same grade across categories, the 'halo effect' has come to be known as 'cross-contamination' (Alderson, 1981).

The two examples provided in Appendix 5 illustrate the key difference between analytic and holistic scales.

The first is an analytic scale devised by Bachman and Palmer (1982), consisting of three separate scales for each of the main traits of linguistic, pragmatic and sociolinguistic competence, each divided into sub-traits. Analytic scales of this type require the rater to pay attention to specific features of the trait and 'count' errors (accuracy), for example, or occurrences of non-native grammatical structure. However, what counts as 'extensive' vocabulary, or a 'large' vocabulary, or indeed what the difference between 'extensive' and 'large' is, is left undefined.

The second rating scale is the 1991 Interagency Language Roundtable (ILR) rating scale, the direct successor of the FSI rating scale for use in US government agencies. It requires the rater to score holistically, by attempting to match the speech sample with a particular descriptor, and each descriptor mentions a range of constructs.

Another difference between these two scales is that only the ILR scale contains references to the types of task that the test taker is able to undertake outside the test situation. This is what Bachman (1990: 344–8) refers to as the 'real-world' approach, whereas he refers to his own 1982 scale as an 'ability/interaction' approach that is more abstract, and relates more to constructs than tasks. As we have seen, the former 'real-world' approach limits the kinds of tasks that can be included in the test, whereas the latter are designed on the assumption that it is possible to generalise from test scores to real-world speaking situations that may not be modelled in the test tasks. We refer to this as the 'focus' of the descriptors.

The type of scale that is selected for a particular test of speaking will depend upon the purpose of the test. In a test of speaking for hotel receptionists, for example, the test developer may choose to use primary trait scoring with 'real-world' descriptions in the rating scale; this would directly link the assessment to the very specific functions of a hotel receptionist. Score meaning could only be generalised to those tasks on the test that mirror speaking tasks at the reception desk. For a test in English for Academic purposes a multiple-trait, ability type scale may be more useful, not only because it is necessary to generalise to 'ability to study in the second language', but because diagnostic feedback may be important to the test taker. A rating scale could fall into any of the categories in the framework of Table 4.1, but test developers should know why they choose a particular type for a particular testing purpose and make their decisions and reasoning explicit.

Table 4.1   A framework for describing rating scales

Orientation:
• User
• Assessor
• Constructor
Scoring
• Analytic Approach
• Holistic Approach
❑ Holistic scoring
❑ Primary-trait scoring
❑ Multiple-trait scoring
Focus
• Real World
• Construct

We now turn our attention to the different ways in which rating scales are developed.

APPROACHES TO RATING-SCALE DESIGN

The two basic approaches to rating-scale development are to use 'intuitive' methods, or to base the design upon some kind of empirical data. Each main approach can be further divided into three sub-categories. Each is briefly described below.

- Intuitive methods
  - ❏ Expert judgement. An experienced teacher or language tester writes a rating scale in relation to existing rating scales, a teaching syllabus, or a needs analysis. Informants may be used to obtain feedback on the usefulness of the scale.
  - ❏ Committee. As for expert judgements, but with a small group of experts who discuss and agree on the wording of the descriptors and the levels of the scale.
  - ❏ Experiential. Perhaps starting with expert judgement or committee design, the rating scale evolves and is refined by those who use it, so that over a period of time the users intuitively 'understand' the meaning of the levels in relation to sample performances. This is by far the most common intuitive method of scale development.

- Empirical methods
  - ❏ Data-based or data-driven scale development. This approach requires the analysis of performance on tasks, and the description of key features of performance that can be observed to make inferences to the construct.
  - ❏ Empirically derived, binary-choice, boundary definition scales. Expert judges are asked to take speech or writing samples and divide them into better or poorer performances. The reason for the categorisation is recorded, and used to write a sequence of yes/no questions that lead the rater to the score.
  - ❏ Scaling descriptors. In this approach many band descriptors are collected in isolation from a scale, and experts are asked to rank them in order of 'difficulty'. They are then sequenced to create the scale.

We will discuss an Intuitive experiential rating scale, and a rating scale relating to each of the empirical methods, in the next four sections. The selection of the rating scales for discussion has been made on the basis of the impact that the scales have had on the testing of speaking, their widespread use, and/or the explicitness of the design methodology. While there are other variants, the examples selected are typical of current theory and practice, and the related literature provides more information on the design process than that of other scales.

The FSI family tradition: Intuitive and experiential scale development

Wilds (1975: 35) writes that the FSI is

> very much an in-house system which depends heavily on having all interviewers under one roof. . . . It [the system] is most apt to break down when interviewers are isolated by spending long periods away from home base, by testing in a

language no one else knows, or by testing so infrequently or so independently that they evolve their own system.

The FSI scale, described in Chapter 1, became the model for the design of many other rating scales, including the ILR and ACTFL scales that are still in use today. It is both assessor- and user-oriented, and it has been widely used in the development of curriculum as well as in assessment contexts. The scales in the FSI family are scored holistically, and they have a real world focus. The original FSI was a semantic differential with the intermediate levels representing a relative amount of a quality between bipolar terms. Later these were supplemented by verbal descriptions of the intervening points, creating a Likert scale. These were expanded into the rating scales that have been copied widely (Lowe, 1985a: 19–25). Our discussion of the approach to rating-scale design within the FSI family is centred around a number of the principles upon which the designers adopted.

The educated native speaker

Adams and Frith (1979: vi) acknowledge that for the FSI scale descriptors there are no external criteria against which they can be assessed; rather each level within a scale is defined in relation to the other levels and the only key reference point, 'the ultimate standard, the ultimate criterion reference, is the proficiency of the educated native speaker'. The concept of the 'well-educated native speaker' was the starting point for the design of the scale.

In 1968 Perren noted that 'native' or 'native-like' language ability was a term which appeared in the top band of rating scales. 'What does this mean?' he asked. 'What kind of native, speaking about what, and to whom?' (Perren, 1968: 111). Perren recommended the development of scales based upon observations of the proficient second language speaker and not some notion of a 'native' speaker, but this has only been realised in data-based approaches to scale development. Intuitive scale development has depended upon the concept of the native speaker for the definition of the top band. Wilds (1975: 36) argued that the linguistic ability of a 'well-educated native speaker' was the 'absolute standard' upon which the FSI scales rested. The definitions of other levels were then hung upon this one peg through the principle of internal consistency.

Liskin-Gasparro (1984a) argues that the top of the ACTFL scale, representing educated native speaker abilities, is often achieved by students who have the opportunity to live in the country where the target language is spoken. Lowe (1983: 231) characterises the ILR oral assessment scale as ranging from 'no practical ability' to 'well-educated native-speaker ability'. One of the test's strengths for Lowe is that it judges the students' production in relation to 'language as it is spoken by well-educated native speakers'. It is not surprising to find that the Australian Second Language Proficiency Ratings (ASLPR) also depends upon the 'native-speaker yardstick' (Ingram, 1982: 8), and that the top band in the speaking scale represents 'native-like' proficiency (Ingram, 1985a: 4, 1985b: 222–5). In their latest form they have been renamed the International Second Language Proficiency Ratings (ISLPR) (Lee *et al.*, 1998), and still rely on the native-speaker concept for the structure of the scale (see Appendix 6).

The use of the concept of the educated native speaker for scale development has increasingly come under attack. The most significant problem with its use is that native speakers 'show considerable variation in ability' (Bachman and Savignon, 1986: 383). They argue that

> the ACTFL scale definitions are firmly rooted in the misconception that we can clearly identify native speakers and their standard of language performance.
>
> (Ibid., 385)

This can be seen in phrases from the band descriptors such as 'can be understood by native interlocutors', and 'using native-like discourse'. Bachman and Savignon conclude that the scale still contains 'the notion of a monolithic group of native speakers'.

Lantolf and Frawley (1985: 343) also argue that current scales contain 'an implicit notion of the mean linguistic behaviour of an ideal speaker'. The problem for them is similar to that of Bachman and Savignon: we do not know what an educated native speaker is. Lantolf and Frawley correctly state that when using the educated native speaker as a criterion, scale developers are concerned only with 'THE' native speaker, whereas in reality only types of native speaker exist. Lantolf and Frawley (ibid., 343) identify four 'types':

1. Idiolectal, or informants.
2. Statistical, or typical speakers.
3. Normative, or expert speakers.
4. Former, or speakers from historical records.

The ACTFL scale attempts to combine statistical and normative speakers on an intuitive basis. We may add that even 'expert speakers' may only be 'expert' within certain contexts, and not others. Jarvis (1986: 20) provides the example of a professor whose 'competence' (we might wish to say 'performance') varies depending on whether s/he is talking about an area of speciality, socialising at a cocktail party, or opening a bank account. Barnwell (1987: 39) can legitimately claim that what is being dealt with is an 'ideal' native speaker, not real native speakers, and Lantolf and Frawley are correct when they say that the concept of the educated native speaker 'is neither unitary nor reliable'.

Davies (1990: 52, 1991) has also demonstrated that the concept of the 'native speaker' is one which is not consistent, and no researchers have sufficiently defined the term to make it useful in a testing context. The results of studies generated by interest in 'World Englishes' also seriously cast doubt upon the notion of the 'educated native speaker' as construed by test developers (Kachru, 1992: 4–5).

In the face of these criticisms, Lowe (1985a: 47, 1987) has stated that native-speaker performance on AEI (an acronym for ACTFL/ETS/ILR) tasks would in fact probably fall in band 3, or 'Advanced'. 'Superior' performance is equivalent to educated native-speaker performance, which most native speakers cannot achieve. No empirical evidence is presented to support the claim, other than the appeal to the experience of testing 'adepts' who have used the scales over a long period of time. The appeal to experience is a key part of the claim to the usefulness of the scale in testing second-language speaking.

We return to the theoretical and (lack of) evidential basis for AEI tests in Chapter 7.

Scale descriptors and speech samples

Wilds (1979: 1) claims that 'the usefulness of the system is based on careful and detailed definition in both linguistic and functional terms of each point on the scale'. However, it is not clear that this is the case with the FSI family of tests. Jones (1975: 3) argued with reference to the FSI that

> One of the principal problems we are faced with is the construction of proficiency tests which measure language ability accurately enough to correspond to these definitions.

The problem faced by the scale designer is to develop a testing procedure that generates sufficient evidence to be scored, and a rating scale that describes the constructs to be measured. The correspondence between the speech samples generated and the descriptors in the rating scale has not been investigated, because reliable ratings depend upon 'experience'. Alderson (1991b), for example, reports that IELTS (International English Language Testing Service) band descriptors contained descriptions of performance which were not elicited by the actual tasks in the test. This echoes the work of Jones (1975: 4) who claimed that very little is known about tests such as the FSI, as 'no validation studies have been made with the definitions as the basis'. Jones (1981) adds that most oral testing procedures do not relate the elicitation technique to the scoring systems in any specific way.

A progression from zero to native speaker

Discussing the development of the ASLPR, Ingram (1982: 9) says that in the scales 'each definition exists in the context of the whole scale and in relation to adjacent definitions'. While he does not describe how the band descriptors were originally written, he claims construct validity for the rating scale by stating that the developers drew upon 'psycholinguistic research' (ibid., 19). However, he goes on to claim that the scale is not impressionistic, as it relies implicitly upon the concept of a 'universal pattern of language development'. Ingram (1985a: 4) makes a stronger version of this claim when he writes:

We have noted that rating scales such as the ASLPR are developmental in structure, i.e. the progression of behavioural descriptions attempts to reflect the way in which a second language develops from zero to native-like. Thus the scale is not arbitrary but related to the universal developmental schedule and a learner's rating indicates the stage of development he has reached in the developmental schedule.

This has come under criticism from Pienemann *et al.* (1988) because the notion of 'development' must be theoretically coherent and empirically verifiable. Further, the definitions of levels arrived at on the basis of the developmental process must be quantifiable, or validation studies cannot be carried out.

It would seem that these approaches to rating-scale development use unvalidated theories of second language acquisition, that correspond to the intuition and experience of the designers. Students must perform in such a way that they can satisfy a scale which 'intuitively' and inexplicitly reflects the subjective experience of the scale developer (see Chapter 7 for an extended discussion).

Terminology

The intuitive approach to scale development has led to a certain amount of vagueness and generality in the descriptors used to define bands. Such vagueness is sometimes seen as a strength (Wilds, 1979; Bachman, 1990: 341–6) on the grounds that it can be used in any testing situation. The disadvantages of general, vague terminology are lack of clarity and the possible 'meaninglessness' of the band for users, assessors or test constructors. Further, if the sequence of band descriptors is meant to reflect progression in second language acquisition it is important that the descriptors clearly reflect theory if validity studies are to address score meaning.

Schultz (1986: 373) claims that the ACTFL/ETS Guidelines provide testers and curriculum designers with a common terminology within which they can work for the first time. This optimistic view reflects the claims of Wilds (1979: 1) that key terms such as 'good' and 'fluent' used prior to the FSI descriptors were extremely vague and, being open to as many interpretations as there were raters, were in need of revision. Wilds' view is that the FSI descriptors are detailed enough to remove the uncertainty of interpretation which bald descriptions create. Wilds' view is echoed by Lowe (1983: 231) in relation to the ILR rating scale.

Typical band descriptors are, however, far from self-explanatory (Barnwell, 1989) and, as Matthews (1990: 119) notes, the bands

> are described in only vague and general terms and abound in qualifiers, so that only gross distinctions can be made with any confidence.

In an analysis of references to vocabulary knowledge in the ACTFL scale, Fulcher (1989) concluded that the descriptors were far too vague to be of any practical use within an operational oral testing procedure because they were not based on actual language production. Similar observations have been made with regard to fluency descriptors in intuitive scales (Fulcher, 1987; Matthews, 1990). Hieke (1985: 135) takes a particularly adamant stand on this issue:

> A glance at the literature on fluency reveals it to be replete with vacuous definitions, overlapping terminology, and impractical assessment strategies.

Mullen (1978a: 33) for example, considers fluency the 'easiest' aspect of oral assessment, as one need only consider pauses and fillers. Hieke (1985: 137) is probably correct when he argues that tests cannot be 'fair'

> as long as they (the descriptors) hinge upon prose statements to delineate levels while these are peppered with notions that cannot withstand close scrutiny.

Hieke's own suggestion is to develop a semi-direct test in which the candidate speaks into a tape recorder. The tape would then be used for grading fluency along the parameters: speech rate (syllables per second), length of runs (average number of syllables between pauses), and hesitation phenomena (stalls, repairs, parenthetical remarks, silent pauses, fillers, progressive repeats and false starts). This would be quantifiable, but the sheer increase in marking time per candidate over an oral interview would make the suggestion impractical unless scoring could be made automatic, as achieved in PhonePass, and discussed in a paper by Pendergast (1985).

While the terminology of the band descriptors is vague, it may be meaningful for experienced evaluators who have been trained and socialised in the use of the scale. However, it would be extremely difficult to say what this would mean for a given student at any specific band. Once again the issue of experience is provided as the most important reason for rating scales appearing to be meaningful and providing reliable results.

Alderson (1991b) points out that raters must rate to a common standard – which no one would wish to disagree with – but, in order to achieve this using intuitively developed scales, emphasis is placed on rater training and socialisation over time. The question that remains is to what extent the scales are meaningful once they are separated from the training which raters must receive in order to become certified raters. Training and socialisation may mask problems with the wording of bands in the scale by creating the illusion of psychological reality through high rater reliability.

The intuitive approach to the design of holistic rating scales is still the most common. The rating scales that belong to the FSI family are among the most important and widely used even today. We will therefore return to these rating scales in Chapter 7, where we provide an extended review and evaluation.

Data-based scale development

A different approach to rating scale development is one in which the band descriptors are developed through an empirically verifiable procedure, and

will have to be based on observed learner behaviour as opposed to postulated
or normative notions of how learners ought to behave.

(Pienemann et al., 1985: 2–3)

Observed learner behaviour must be quantifiable, and procedures developed for using the information in the construction of rating scales that
reflect the actual linguistic behaviour of students. In this way the close relationship between linguistic behaviour (which may or may not be specific to
the task or topic), the task and the scoring procedure is made transparent.
This is a 'data-based' or 'data-driven' approach to scale development with a
strong theoretical and empirical underpinning. Scales produced through this
approach are typically assessor-oriented, require holistic or multiple trait
scoring, and have a construct focus.

The example usually cited in this category of rating scales is that developed
by Fulcher (see North, 1993: 129). Fulcher (1987) initially questioned whether
the English Language Testing Service (ELTS) band descriptors characterised
the construct of 'fluency' in a meaningful way. An analysis of the rating-scale
descriptors seemed to show that the construct was directly related to repetition, hesitation, stumbling, propositional development and grammatical
accuracy. Fulcher then used discourse analysis to discover whether the assumptions underlying the scale (for example, that high repetition is a feature
of reduced fluency) were tenable. First language speakers were found to
use a great deal of repetition in conversation, mainly to reintroduce topics
that had been ignored by other speakers. Hesitation, also assumed to be
high in less fluent speakers, was found to fulfil two functions in L1 interaction. Firstly, at the end of an utterance in connection with certain fillers
that end in low key (see Brazil, 1985; McCarthy, 1991: 109–12), hesitation
acts as a turn-taking device. Secondly, it is related to propositional development. As speakers process meaning and translate this into speech they
frequently need to change the grammatical structure of the utterance to
complete the proposition. Hesitation can therefore indicate the online processing of propositional information. On the basis of discourse analysis,
Fulcher called for a 'data-based approach' that would build up a bank of data
that could be analysed to produce more meaningful band descriptors in
rating scales. Fulcher (1993, 1996b) designed a fluency rating scale based
on a larger database originally built for research into scale design for a
doctoral dissertation. This scale was intended to be one among many in a
multiple-trait scoring system; however, Fulcher could not provide divergent
evidence between scales (see Chapter 8 for a discussion of divergent validity
evidence).

The analysis of speech samples: coding speech

Initially speech samples were recorded from a range of speaking tests and
transcribed for analysis. The transcriptions were then coded for features of
fluency that had been described in the literature, and which suggested that

they were related to the perception of fluency. The six speech phenomena that were investigated were:

1. Fillers such as 'er(m)'.
2. The repetition of the first syllable of a word or a full word.
3. The negotiation of reference indicated by the re-selection of referring devices.
4. The re-selection of lexical items.
5. Anacolouthon.
6. Longer pauses, indicated in the transcripts and examples as two or three colons.

The initial problem that emerged from 'counting' pauses or repetitions stemmed from the fact that the number of pauses did not automatically translate into a perception of reduced fluency, as had been argued by Fulcher (1987). It was therefore necessary to introduce *explanatory categories* that would attempt to take account of why a pause occurred, or why there was word repetition. For example, some longer pauses may be interpreted by raters as indicating that communication has broken down. But it is also possible that the rater will consider certain pauses as being 'thinking time' in which the student is seriously considering the content of the next utterance. It has been observed that under these conditions raters are frequently prepared to award a higher band for 'natural language behaviour' (Meredith, 1978).

This leads to two further problems. Firstly, there is likely to be no one-to-one relationship between a speech phenomenon (like pausing) and the explanatory category (the suggested reason for the occurrence of the speech phenomenon). Secondly, the hermeneutics of classifying a speech phenomenon into an explanatory category is likely to require a high degree of inference.

This problem was identified by Long in 1983. Long (1983: 3) makes clear the difficulty faced by an approach to scale development which depends upon the analysis of actual learner speech when he comments on similar difficulties faced by any researcher who is working with spoken data. Although researchers recognise 'the bias in one person reporting events' they are prepared to do this in order to attempt a meaningful description of the phenomena which they observe rather than remain at the mundane level of simply reporting surface observations.

In data-based scale development it would be possible merely to observe the six speech phenomena which have been listed above, and to use the number of occurrences as a guide to scale construction. This would result in a 'low-inference' scale that could be used reliably, but the disadvantage would be that no inferences are actually being made about *why* the observed behaviour is occurring. When discussing the use of low-inference observational categories in connection to classroom observation, Long comments:

> The increase in reliability that these are designed to bring is largely mythical
> . . . and comes at a high price. A focus on overt behaviour may, for example,

'reliably' pre-empt the explanatory power of a study by precluding consideration of participants' intentions. (Long, 1983: 13)

If scores on speaking tests are to be meaningful higher inferences appear
to be inevitable in arriving at an explanation for speech phenomena, rather
than simply observing them.

As such, the second step in data-based scale development is to create
explanatory categories into which individual observations of speech phenomena can be coded. Consider the following categories, which are designed
to explain why a test taker pauses while speaking. For each category there is
a definition, followed by a short discussion. Speech fragments taken from
interview tests are used as examples.

1.   End-of-turn pauses: A pause may occur to indicate the end of a turn, especially
      when the utterance ends in low key, and is associated with fillers.

Discussion
The most frequent use of extended pauses in the data was at the end of a
student's turn (in the examples, a 'B' turn). This example is taken from the
speech of a lower-level test taker:

B>text says:: fifteen thousand womans went to er: prisons :: er :::: A> and since then B>
yeah A> has there been an increase or a decrease . . .

It appears that the students pause because they are not able (or willing) to
continue speaking. The interlocutor does not begin his turn immediately as
he is waiting for the student to continue. In speaking tests the interlocutor
frequently appears to be highly sensitive to the possibility that the student
needs time to plan what is going to be said next, and therefore the amount
of overlapping speech may be much less than in less formal interaction, and
the amount of silence between turns increases, something which would be
highly embarrassing in informal talk (Sacks *et al.*, 1974).

When turning to the higher-level test takers we discover that the amount
of this type of hesitation is somewhat different in format. For example:

A> . . . it sounds absolutely [fascinating B> it is]:: A> actually . . .

In this example the B turn overlaps with the previous A turn, and the
pause allows B to continue the conversation if B so desires. It is not taken up,
and so A continues not by asking another question to get the student to
complete the proposition (as it is already complete), but by continuing the
conversation. In speaking tests the experienced interlocutor does not really
wish to keep a turn for any length of time.

2.   Content-planning hesitation: pauses may occur to allow the student to plan the
      content of the next utterance.

Discussion
Hesitation seems to have a significant role in planning the content of the
utterance, as in these examples:

B> . . . some in the lungs:: from the lungs it goes er through the reticuloendothelial system . . .

A> why does it happen in this way B> what reason:: I I should say it must be the er: our er: con er: contribution to . . .

In the first example the test taker is considering the next step in a process which is being planned with the help of an input diagram. In the second example the test taker overtly indicates that content planning is going on, as the question which the interlocutor has asked is summarised before the pause occurs, and the beginning of the answer starts after the pause. This seems to be a case of the student 'thinking out loud'.

In the following example the test taker is thinking about her future plans. The pause after the filler is used to plan the content of the next part of the message.

B>my bother: I think that we'll we will be together A hm hm B> and er:: after that I want to: to be a judge . . .

3.   Grammatical-planning hesitation: pauses may occur when the test taker needs to plan the structure of the next utterance.

Discussion
Grammatical forward planning occurs when the speaker may know what to say, but is unsure how to say it. The planning stage needs time, and the execution may also contain other hesitations and structural reformulations.

A> . . . kind of a job do you want:: B> when I chose this subject: I:: I chose this sub I chose this subject because I think I can get any kind of job.

In this example it appears that the test taker wishes to say that the subject of study was chosen because of the ease with which she can get a job. The purpose clause, beginning with 'because . . .' contains the reason for the choice, but having begun with 'when' the test taker needs to produce a 'I did so because' to introduce the purpose clause. The use of 'when' activates colligational restrictions. The medium-length pause after 'I' and the two reformulations lead to the successful production of the purpose clause.

4.   Addition of examples, counter-examples, or reasons to support a point of view: pauses are sometimes used as an oral parenthesis before adding extra information to an argument or point of view, or break up a list of examples.

Discussion
A pause or a filled pause often precedes the addition of an example or reason when a test taker is presenting an argument, adding to or supporting what has already been said, as in this example:

B> . . . the television crimes and they are trying to mime them:: and er: the newspapers as well they don't erm: stick to the facts . . .

In the clause after the filled pause the phrase 'as well' overtly signals the additional nature of the information to support the argument. Higher-level test takers are more likely to use pauses or fillers to introduce an additional element to their argument. In this example the test taker argues that copying crimes on television is one cause of the increasing crime rate, but another cause may be the sensationalism of reporting in the written media. This was produced in response to a graph-explanation task.

Another example of the simple addition of examples is given in this extract.

B> . . . diarrhoea vomiting A> hm B> headaches and er: ataxia erm:: convulsions sweating A> it sounds pretty horrible B> yeah it is . . .

Very few examples of this category were found with lower-level test takers. When they did occur the most common use was that of adding to an utterance in order to give content to a general word which otherwise would have remained empty. Such general words are often referred to as 'delexical' in that they do not of themselves contain any specific meaning, and have to be filled out with reference to context or other parts of the discourse (Winter, 1978). This is the case in the following example where the delexical 'routine' is filled out with the specific information of going to the office and (after this) doing the work which is assigned by a superior.

Example 4.13

B> it's the same thing every day the same routine:: er I've got to go every morning to the office . . .

A sample transcript is contained in Appendix 7. This is from a higher-level test taker who would be thought capable of undertaking higher studies in an English-medium institution. A /1/, /2/, /3/ or /4/ in the transcript indicates that this is an example of pausing that falls into one of the four categories discussed above. Although the coders had access to the tapes of the speech, you may wish to see whether or not you agree with the classification from the transcript alone.

Quality control in coding data

When a methodology like this requires coding examples into high-inference categories a level of 'indeterminacy' is introduced. There is no one-to-one mapping between speech phenomena and the explanation for their occurrence, and it is always possible to challenging the coding. As a result, data-driven scale development needs to employ methods that control the quality of data coding and interpretation. These include double (or even triple) blind coding, and discriminant analysis.

The first of these two methods is a fairly obvious quality control system. Once the categories have been established two or more individuals use the transcripts and tapes of test-taker performance to code surface phenomena into the explanatory categories. The degree of agreement is a measure of the reliability of the coding. The second method requires all the speech samples to be drawn from speaking tests in which the test takers received scores.

Each of the test takers therefore 'belongs' in a category, such as 'band 4' or 'band 5'. Once the coding into categories has been completed, discriminant analysis can be used to ask the question: can we predict the score a test taker received *only* from the coding of speech phenomena into explanatory categories? This was attempted for 21 test takers in Fulcher (1993, 1996b), producing the following classification in Table 4.2.

Table 4.2   The relationship between actual and predicted scores

Score awarded in test	Predicted score in the discriminant analysis					Total
	1	**2**	**3**	**4**	**5**	
1	**3**	0	0	0	0	3
2	0	**4**	0	0	0	4
3	0	0	**7**	1	0	8
4	0	0	0	**4**	0	4
5	0	0	0	0	**2**	2
Total	3	4	7	5	2	21

The left-hand column is the score awarded on a speaking test, and the middle column the predicted score on the speaking test from the coding of the speech sample alone. The figures in bold show accurate prediction of scores, while positive numbers in cells off the diagonal represent misprediction. In this example only one test taker would have been predicted to have a score of 4 when they actually got a score of 3.

It should be pointed out that this method makes the assumption that the scores from the test of speaking that is being used at least rank orders the test takers on the construct in which the rating-scale designer is interested.

From categories to descriptors

A range of statistical evidence is used to understand which categories are the most important in discriminating between certain scores or bands on a speaking test. This evidence usually tells the scale developer that there is a non-linear relationship between the categories and the scores. That is, unlike the scales for holistic scoring that are premised on a gradual increase in fluency, or a decrease in error, there are actually sudden increases or decreases at particular levels, or even curvilinear patterns, in the evidence. Such patterns have frequently been found in second language acquisition research (see Lightbrown, 1985), but are not frequently taken into account in testing second language speaking. We will take the four categories relating to 'hesitation/pausing' that we have used as part of the definition of 'fluency' to explain what this might mean in practice.

On a test that divides test takers into 5 levels, with the top level indicating 'university readiness' and the bottom level a 'lower-intermediate' level of English, hesitation for grammatical planning falls rapidly between levels 2 and 3, and then tails off with very few examples at level 5. The reverse is the case with category 4, or the provision of examples, counter examples and reasons. These increase rapidly between levels 2 and three. However, with category 1 (end of turn pausing) there are few examples at levels 2, 3 and 4, a larger number at level 1 (breakdown in communication), and the largest number at level 5, where it has evolved into a turn-taking device. Content planning hesitation increases steadily from level 1 to level 4, but at level 5 the number of instances falls to below that of test takers placed at level 1.

Plotting the patterns onto levels enables the scale developer to use the descriptions of the categories to write the descriptions of the bands in the scale. Appendix 8 contains the full fluency rating scale. The numbers in square brackets indicate that the preceding part of the descriptor is derived from the description of a particular category. For a full list of categories, see Fulcher (1996b).

Scale stability

Once the rating scale had been constructed, a number of English as a Second Language Speakers were asked to take three separate tasks: a picture description task, an interview based on a text that was read immediately prior to the interview, and a group discussion. All test takers undertook each task, and their performances were rated on the fluency scale by 5 raters. Studies of the scores showed that within tolerable limits the results did not vary across tasks or raters.

The scale is very different in content from those in the FSI family of tests, as it rests on descriptions and explanations of discourse features from actual test performance. The level of descriptive detail is higher and, although still present to some extent, the use of expressions that indicate bands to be internally linked in a 'more than–less than' relationship is considerably reduced.

Another 'data-based' approach to scale is present in the next section. It differs from the approach of Fulcher, however, in that it does not employ the direct analysis of speech samples. It also differs in that binary-choice scoring is designed for use with a specific task. In other words, it is not assumed that scores can be generalised to other task types, and each task requires its own scale.

Empirically derived, binary-choice, boundary definition scales (EBBs)

Named and developed by Upshur and Turner (1995, 1999) and Turner and Upshur (1996), the EBB is assessor-oriented, uses primary-trait scoring, and has a real-world focus. In a method similar to Fulcher, the development procedure is to rank-order speech or writing samples, score them and then identify features that were decisive in allocating the samples to particular bands or score ranges. To this extent, EBB scales and the scales that use discourse analysis in their design methodology are modern uses of Thurstone's (1928) technique of sorting responses into piles, trying to discover what features distinguish between the responses in different piles, and then placing them on a scale (see Wright and Masters, 1982: 12–14). They differ, however, in that EBB scale development relies on expert judgement rather than the direct analysis of performance.

EBBs make no assumption at all about a theoretical, linear, process of second language acquisition. Rather, they rely entirely upon how sample performances are sequenced, and how these can be scored by asking raters to make a series of binary (yes/no) choices about

> features of performance that define the boundaries between score levels. They are, therefore, empirically derived, binary-choice, boundary-definition (EBB) scales. EBB scales are developed for particular tasks; a scale developed for the rating of one kind of writing task, for example, is not appropriate for a different writing task.

The steps in the design procedure for 6-level EBB areas follows (Upshur and Turner, 1995):

Step 1. Select performances to be rated, so that the range of performances covers the ability range that is to be tested.

Step 2. The individuals from a team of experts divide the performances into equal numbers of 'better' and 'poorer' performances impressionistically.

Step 3. The team of experts discuss why they placed the samples into the two piles, reconciling any differences they may have. As a team they are asked to write a single question, the answer to which would result in a sample being placed in the 'better' or 'poorer' group.

Step 4. The individual members of the team rank order the 'better' samples and score them as '4', '5' and '6' impressionistically.

Step 5. The team of experts discuss their rankings and reconcile any differences. The team then write criterial questions to distinguish level 6 performances from level 4 and 5 performances, and then level 5 performances from level 4 performances.

Step 6. Steps 4 and 5 are repeated for the 'poorer' performances.

This procedure was used to generate a rating scale for communicative effectiveness and a rating scale for grammatical accuracy to rate a task that required a test taker to re-tell a story seen on video in one minute. The recitation was recorded onto tape for scoring at a later time. The scales that were used to grade the recitations are produced in Figures 4.1 and 4.2.

Upshur and Turner (1995: 10) argue that the main difference between traditional scales and the EBBs is that instead of having a descriptor that attempts to define the 'midpoint' of a band, the questions on an EBB:

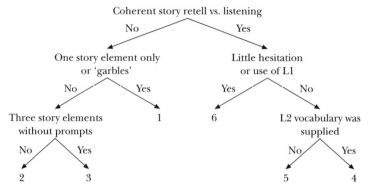

Figure 4.1 EBB for communicative effectiveness

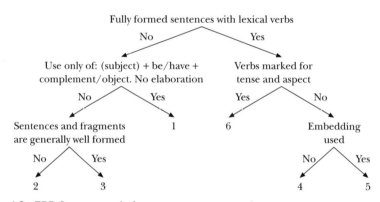

Figure 4.2 EBB for grammatical accuracy

After Upshur J. and Turner, C. 'Constructing rating scales for second language tests' in *English Language Teaching Journal*, 1995, 49, 1, p. 6, by permission of Oxford University Press.

describe the 'boundaries' between categories. Ratings are based upon the perception of differences rather than similarities. In this way the EBB scales are more like familiar measuring instruments.

The second claimed advantage is their simplicity. As they rely on a single judgement in answer to a criterial question, it is claimed that it reduces the problem in other scales of having co-occurring features in the band descriptor. With co-occurring features the problem has always been what score to award if a test taker does not 'fit' each part of one band descriptor, or if the performance relates to parts of different band descriptors, sometimes a considerable distance apart. This is because they do not assume that some features will be present or absent on the basis of any theoretical model, but only on simple criterion features described in the scale development process.

The EBB process clearly has a number of advantages. The first is that it is simple, and can be used to generate rating scales by teachers for locally produced speaking and writing tests. The second is that it is easy to use, and probably results in an increase in reliable scoring when used by teachers who have been on the team that developed the rating scale. Thirdly, as a primary trait scale, each scale is linked to a specific task. In a pedagogic context, especially if teachers are using a task-based methodology, these rating scales can provide a rich source of information on student progress. But this specificity is also the main weakness of the EBB approach. The meaning of the score relates only to the specific task that was used in the test, and its meaning cannot be generalised to any other test task, or any task in the real world, unless the criterion task is identical in every way to the test task. This is also compounded by a reliance on the use of expert impressionistic judgements to rank order the speech samples in the first place, making this 'data-based' approach one that still relies on the perception of a small group of individuals working within a particular context.

The lack of generalisability would certainly be troublesome for large scale tests, and it is unlikely that we will see EBBs used in tests provided by the large testing agencies. Despite this problem, the explicitness of the design methodology for EBBs is impressive, and their usefulness in pedagogic settings is attractive. They remain an excellent example of primary trait scoring.

Scaling descriptors

Developing rating scales through the scaling of descriptors is associated primarily with the work of North (1995, 1996, 1996/2000; North and Schneider, 1998) in the context of developing a common European framework for reporting language competency (Schärer and North, 1992; Schärer, 1996). The design method is empirical, it is user- and assessor-oriented, involves holistic scoring, and the focus is real-world in that the final descriptors are framed as 'can do' statements. In this approach scale developers collect large numbers of 'stand-alone descriptors' from as many different scales as possible, and re-sequence descriptors that can be calibrated onto new scales. The measurement model underlying this process is multi-faceted Rasch analysis.

The traditional approach to the use of Rasch analysis in the testing of speaking has been for the *post hoc* analysis of existing rating scales to address validity questions (Stansfield and Kenyon, 1992). Its use in the design of rating scales, therefore building validity questions into the design process, is a recent phenomenon. Fulcher used multi-faceted Rasch analysis (1993, 1996b) to investigate the scalability of the descriptors developed through the analysis of test-taker discourse, by modelling the effects of task, rater and rating scale on test scores. Similarly, Milanovic *et al.* (1992) used Rasch analysis to investigate the scalability of the Cambridge Assessment of Spoken English (CASE) rating scales prior to their operational use, and McNamara (1996) used Rasch to study the interactions of task, rater and ability on the OET. But these examples all take rating scales that have been developed according to some other methodology, and use Rasch analysis to investigate whether the scale is operating as intended. The scaling of descriptors using Rasch is therefore a distinctive approach: there is no focus for the rating scale created because the descriptors are not written by the designers, they are chosen only on the grounds of their fit to the measurement model. Before looking more closely at the scale design methodology we therefore consider briefly what the Rasch model is, and how it relates to the process of scaling.

The Rasch model

The Rasch model is a one-parameter model in Item Response Theory (IRT), which allows researchers to calibrate items and persons on a linear scale. A two-parameter model takes into account item discrimination as well as difficulty, while a three-parameter model can also account to some degree for guessing (when applied to objectively scored items). It uses a true interval scale that gives an estimate of the probability that a person or item will fall at a particular point on a scale (for a very accessible introduction to IRT see Baker, 1997). It is possible to fit persons and items to a scale using the Rasch model on three assumptions:

- The scale is unidimensional: all the items on the scale operate in the same way in measurement terms, even if they represent psychologically complex constructs (Henning, 1988; 1992a).
- The items are locally independent: the response to any single item is not influenced or determined by the response to any other item (Henning, 1989).
- There is no extensive guessing at work.

An extension of the simple model, multi-faceted Rasch analysis (Linacre, 1989), treats items, persons and raters/judges as 'facets' of the testing situation. Each 'facet' can be given a value on the same linear scale, representing item difficulty, person ability, and rater/judge harshness or leniency. This method is used to scale band descriptors because it provides information on the teachers who rate the 'difficulty' of the band descriptor, allowing for corrections to be made before the band descriptors are placed onto a scale.

Design process

North (1996/2000) followed a systematic process of four consecutive phases of analysis: (a) intuitive; (b) qualitative; (c) quantitative, and (d) replication.

PHASE A: Intuitive analysis
Step 1: North (1993) collected some 30 rating scales, the content of which was pulled apart into sentence-length descriptors, and placed into six proficiency levels.

This provided a 'pool' of 2000 band descriptors drawn from the language testing literature, and historical and operational tests.

Step 2: The 'pool' was classified into different types of communicative activities, and different aspects of strategic and communicative language competence. New descriptors were written to fill perceived gaps in the descriptive scheme.

PHASE B: Qualitative analysis with informants
Step 3: In a rolling series of workshops, pairs of teachers are given an envelope of band descriptors on confetti-like strips of paper and asked to sort them into 4 or 5 given, related categories. For each descriptor teachers mark those that they find particularly clear and useful. Several pairs will sort the same descriptors. Descriptors may be re-edited according to teacher comments (e.g. removing double negatives, or ambiguities.).

Step 4: The teachers read through the same band descriptors again, putting a circle around the ticks of those band descriptors that are relevant to their own teaching context.

Step 5: In other workshops, pairs of teachers are given the band descriptors for particular related categories, and asked to put them into three piles: 'low', 'middle' and 'high'; and then to divide each of these piles into two subdivisions, leaving six piles of descriptors. The performance of each descriptor in Steps 3–5 is recorded with codes in a detailed 'item history'.

Step 6: The descriptors interpreted most consistently are then used to construct overlapping questionnaires of approximately 50 descriptors each, each questionnaire being linked to the one immediately above and below by anchor items (items that they have in common). The result is a 'chain' of questionnaires, with balanced content, targeted at each of the levels, linked by the anchor items. These are then used for the main data collection.

PHASE C: Quantitative analysis with questionnaire data
Step 7: A rating scale is attached to each descriptor on each questionnaire. The rating scale is reproduced from North (1995: 451).

0   This describes a level which is definitely beyond his/her capabilities. Could not be expected to perform like this.

1   Could be expected to perform like this provided that circumstances are favourable, for example if he/she has some time to think about what to say, or the interlocutor is tolerant and prepared to help out.

2   Could be expected to perform like this without support in normal circumstances.

3   Could be expected to perform like this even in difficult circumstances, for example, when in a surprising situation or when talking to less cooperative interlocutor.

4   This describes a performance which is clearly below his/her level. Could perform better than this.

An example of a questionnaire is taken from North and Schneider (1998: 251), in Table 4.3.

Table 4.3   Questionnaire with speaking items

1	Can deal with common aspects of everyday living such as travel, lodgings, eating and shopping.	0	1	2	3	4
2	Can use public transport: buses, trains and taxis, ask for basic information, ask and give directions, and buy tickets.	0	1	2	3	4
3	Can cope with less routine situations in shops, post office, bank, e.g. asking for a larger size, returning an unsatisfactory purchase.	0	1	2	3	4
4	Can negotiate a price, e.g. for a second-hand car, bike.	0	1	2	3	4
5	Can get all the information needed from a tourist office, as long as it is of a straightforward, nonspecialised nature.	0	1	2	3	4
6	Can give simple directions and instructions, e.g. explain how to get somewhere; how to play a game.	0	1	2	3	4
7	Can provide concrete information required in an interview/ consultation (e.g. describe symptoms to a doctor) but does so with limited precision.	0	1	2	3	4
8	Can take some initiatives in an interview/consultation (e.g. to bring up a new subject) but is very dependent on interviewer in the interaction.	0	1	2	3	4

Step 8: A (preferably large) group of teachers are asked to rate a small sample of learners from their classes on the rating scale for each of the descriptors on the questionnaire.

Step 9: Multi-faceted Rasch analysis is conducted to construct a single scale from the descriptors on the chain of questionnaires covering levels from beginner to very advanced. The analysis discovers which items 'misfit' the model; this amounts to discovering which descriptors cannot be placed onto a unidimensional scale. These descriptors are removed from the scale. In linking the questionnaires together, various corrections need to be made for distortions arising from the statistical model and exaggeration by the teachers (North, 1996/2000: 208–22).

Step 10: Descriptors are identified that have a statistically significant differ-ence of difficulty across different language groups, or educational sectors. Such differences in difficulty could be caused by variation among teachers in the way they interpret the descriptors, or differences in curriculum. Some difference of interpretation in different contexts may be appropriate for profiling grids and checklists, but not for holistic scales.

Step 11: Determine the cut-offs between levels of attainment on the arith-metical scale according to
• Difficulty estimates, in order to have equidistant bands
• Natural gaps and groupings on the vertical scale of descriptors
• Comparing the pattern of gaps and groupings to levels on the source scales

This results in a map, like the one presented in Table 4.4 (North, 1996/ 2000: 274).

Table 4.4 Descriptors mapped to the common reference levels of the Common European Framework

Common reference levels	Finer level (Swiss)	Abbrev.	Cut-off	Range on scale (in logits)	Number of descriptors
C2	Mastery	M	3.9		3
C1	Effective operational proficiency	EOP	2.8	1.10	6
(B2+)	Vantage plus	V+	1.74	1.06	14
B2	Full independence (Vantage)	V	0.72	1.02	26
(B1+)	Threshold plus	T+	−0.26	0.98	18
B1	Threshold	T	−1.23	0.97	41
(A2+)	Waystage plus	W+	−2.21	0.98	37
A2	Waystage	W	−3.23	1.02	44
A1	Breakthrough	B	−4.29	1.06	15
–	Tourist	Tour	−5.39	1.10	5
	'smattering'				1

PHASE D: Replication
Step 12: Repeat the entire process with different teachers – and in this case also adding other languages (French and German as well as English) and other skills (Listening and Reading as well as Speaking). North (1996/2000: 339) reports a correlation of 0.99 in the scale values produced in the original study and those resulting from the replication study.

The result of this process is claimed to be a linear, equal interval, proficiency scale, based on a theory of measurement. Table 4.5 is the new Common European Framework scale for fluency once scaled descriptors are recombined. Elements of other scales can be detected in the wording, and it is worth comparing the descriptor for C2 and B1 with descriptors in the rating scale in Appendix 4, which was used in this study.

A measurement approach

The scale design methodology described above was produced within a specific context: the requirement for scaled definitions of the Council of Europe's Common European Framework for language teaching and learning (Council of Europe, 1996, 2001; Trim, 1997). The scale was meant to be used to assess learners of various first languages, learning a variety of second languages,

Table 4.5 The fluency scale for the Common European Framework

Proficient user	C2	Can express him/herself at length with a natural, effortless flow. Pauses only to reflect on precisely the right words to express his/her thoughts or to find an appropriate example or explanation.
	C1	Can express him/herself fluently and spontaneously, almost effortlessly. Only a conceptually difficult subject can hinder a natural, smooth flow of language.
Independent user	B2+	Can communicate spontaneously, often showing remarkable fluency and ease of expression in even longer complex stretches of speech.
	B2	Can produce stretches of language with a fairly even tempo; although he/she can be hesitant as he/she searches for patterns and expressions, there are few noticeably long pauses.
	B2	Can interact with a degree of fluency and spontaneity that makes regular interaction with native speakers quite possible without imposing strain on either party.
	B1+	Can express him/herself with relative ease. Despite some problems with formulation resulting in pauses and 'culs-de-sac', he/she is able to keep going effectively without help.
	B1	Can keep going comprehensibly, even though pausing for grammatical and lexical planning and repair is very evident, especially in longer stretches of free production.
Basic user	A2+	Can make him/herself understood in short contributions, even though pauses, false starts and reformulation are very evident.
	A2	Can construct phrases on familiar topics with sufficient ease to handle short exchanges, despite very noticeable hesitation and false starts.
	A1	Can manage short, isolated, mainly pre-packaged utterances, with much pausing to search for expressions, to articulate less familiar words, and to repair communication.

spread across a wide geographical area, with different educational systems and curricula. The results produced with the scale therefore had to be *consistent* and *comparable* across all of these variables. The approach adopted provides an adequate solution to this particular problem.

It does, however, bring one disadvantage, which is acknowledged by North and Schneider (1998: 242–3). Namely that the method is essentially a-theoretical in nature. It is not based upon 'empirically validated descriptions of language proficiency' or a model of the language learning process. It is, rather, an attempt to provide a working framework that is needed within a particular context, in the absence of a theoretical model upon which to base the framework. As North and Schneider (1998: 242) state:

The purpose of descriptors of common reference levels is to provide a meta-language of criterion statements which people can use to roughly situation themselves and/or their learners, in response to a demand for this. It is widely recognised that the development of such a taxonomy entails a tension between theoretical models developed by applied linguists (which are incomplete) on the one hand and operational models developed by practitioners (which may be impoverished) on the other hand.

DIGEST

This chapter has explained a framework for describing rating scales, and discussed four approaches to the design of rating scales where there is an associated literature that makes it possible for us to understand how they were developed.

Rating scales are important in tests of speaking because they are operationalisations of the construct that the test is supposed to measure, whether the description of the construct is 'thick' (Fulcher, 1996b), or 'thin' as in the scaling of descriptors. The band descriptor is a major part of the 'meaning' of the score, and delimits the type of inferences that can be made from the test score by the score user. This is true even if there is a difference between the rating scale for assessors, and the scale for users. The latter is reworded in terms that are more meaningful for non-language experts, such as university admissions officers.

Explicit and appropriate design processes for a particular testing context may not mean that rating scales can then be used in the way expected by the developers. Variation in the interpretation of descriptors and scales by individuals without training, or 'socialisation' into the use of the scale, has long been recognised (Wilkinson, 1968: 126). Rater training and characteristics are an important factor in the scoring process, but that is an issue that we shall return to in Chapter 6. Nevertheless, it is important to raise this matter here before presenting an expanded model of the test taking/rating process, to show the type of variables that may impact upon scores in speaking tests.

What we have considered in this chapter is the link between constructs, band descriptors and design processes to the types of inferences that we may make from scores on speaking tests. We conclude by considering the model of speaking test performance put forward by Skehan (1998a, 2001), which is based on previous models by Kenyon (1992) and McNamara (1995). This is reproduced in Figure 4.3.

The model presents three main affects on scores, namely:

- The interactive conditions of the performance
- The abilities of the test taker
- The task (as described by conditions or characteristics) used to elicit the performance

In the light of our discussion of constructs (Chapter 2), tasks (Chapter 3) and rating scales in this chapter, we may revise this model to expand our

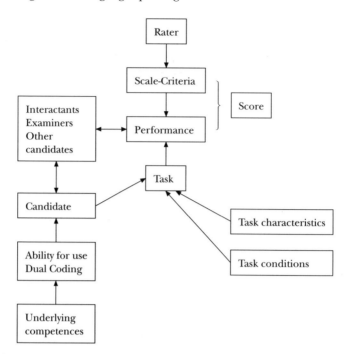

Figure 4.3   The Skehan model of speaking test performance

understanding of the role of the construct, task and scale in the meaning of the score; the revised model is presented in Figure 4.4. Skehan (2001: 169) describes Figure 4.3 as a 'programmatic model' that has evolved as a way to inform research into the testing of speaking. The expanded model in Figure 4.4 is also programmatic, and equally provisional upon future research that may lead to refinements and expansions. However, Figure 4.4 represents a significant expansion of the model of testing speaking, most noticeably (but not limited to) the following aspects:

- The model places construct definition at the heart of rating-scale and band-descriptor design, the understanding of what constructs are being looked for through the performance of a test taker, and the inferences that are drawn from scores. This is also related to the types of decisions that are made about test takers on the basis of test scores.
- The nature of the rating scale, its orientation, scoring philosophy and focus, affects the score and its meaning, which in turn relates to the type of construct claims that may be made.
- Task characteristics and conditions still play a role in understanding the meaning of the score, but these are now only a part of a larger system and interplay of variables at work in the model.
- Rater training, and rater characteristics, are acknowledged to play a role in the scoring process, as are local performance conditions at the time of the test (see Chapter 6 for a discussion of these issues).

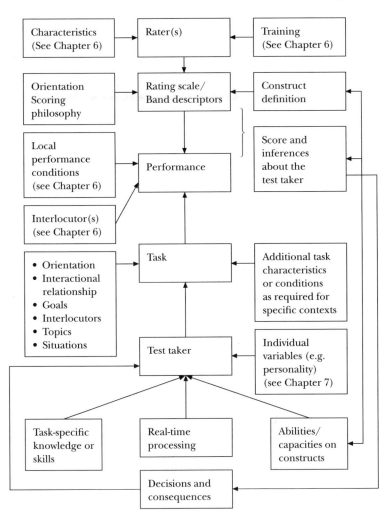

Figure 4.4 An expanded model of speaking test performance

The centrality of construct definition and its operationalisation in the rating scale in this model is not accidental. Research into construct definition and the relationship between score meaning and construct definition is at the heart of evaluating the utility of a speaking test for its specified purpose.

Now that we have considered the speaking construct, tasks to elicit performances that can be scored and how we can score performances, we turn to the process of creating test specifications for speaking tests. These are the 'blueprints' or 'plans' that test designers use to create a test and any subsequent forms (other 'versions') of the test that may be needed.

Chapter 5

Test specifications

In this chapter we try to show how it is possible to pull together many of the elements that we have discussed in previous chapters. Specifications for language tests are the 'blueprints' for speaking tests that contain a statement of the test construct, a description of the tasks that will make up the test, a statement about what kind of responses we expect test takers to make, and an explanation of how the performances are going to be scored. Of course, the specifications may also contain many other elements that need to be included for specific purposes or contexts. We consider some of those as well.

The chapter begins by placing test specifications firmly within the need to create a validity argument. We show that detailing why test design decisions are made, and creating the test specifications themselves, contribute to a validity argument that relates test score to constructs through inferences. Test specifications are dynamic, evolving, documents that should be related to the process of test design, piloting and revision.

In the second part of the chapter we define test specifications, and provide three examples of speaking test specifications from the literature. We provide a short commentary on each specification to draw out its key features. While it is not essential to have all features in every specification, many features will be required across a wide range of contexts in which we test speaking as a second language. We then look at writing test specifications, the components we may use, and some of the special considerations that are required in tests of speaking.

Finally we touch upon the issue of control and freedom in writing speaking tests, which parts of the test become 'fixed', which remain 'variable', and how we can ensure that test formats evolve, and don't become 'fixed in stone'.

THE VALIDITY ARGUMENT

Throughout the first four chapters of this book we have used the term 'validity' in the sense used by Messick (1989: 13), as 'an integrated evaluative judgment of the degree to which empirical evidence and theoretical rationales support the adequacy and appropriateness of inferences and actions based on test scores or other modes of assessment'. In Figure 4.4 we have shown that this concern with validity means that we need to focus on construct definition at many levels of the testing process, and we have argued that validity issues need to be considered at the very beginning of the test development process. This is because language testers now see providing empirical evidence and theoretical rationales as an *argument.*

This is a very different position to that which sees validity in terms of whether the test 'measures what it is intended to measure' (Hughes, 1989: 22). Rather than a quality that is present or absent, validity is seen as an argument that

> should present and integrate evidence and rationales from which a validity conclusion can be drawn pertaining to particular score-based inferences and uses of a test. (Chapelle, 1999b: 263)

The *argument* is not a once-and-forever phenomenon, but an ongoing enterprise. The argument encompasses all types of evidence that impact on our understanding of what the score might mean (Kane, 1992). This evidence includes the documentation of how a test is developed, the decisions made during the design process, and the reasons for those decisions, no matter how unimportant they appear at the time. The Standards for Educational and Psychological Testing (1999: 17) is very clear on this:

> A sound validity argument integrates various strands of evidence into a coherent account of the degree to which existing evidence and theory support the intended interpretation of test scores for specific uses. It encompasses evidence gathered from new studies and evidence available from earlier reported research. The validity argument may indicate the need for refining the definition of the construct, may suggest revisions in the test or other aspects of the testing process, and may indicate areas needing further study.
>
> Ultimately, the validity of an intended interpretation of test scores relies on all the available evidence relevant to the technical quality of a testing system. This includes evidence of careful test construction; adequate score reliability; appropriate test administration and scoring; accurate score scaling, equating, and standard setting; and careful attention to fairness for all examinees, as described in subsequent chapters of the Standards.

The 'evidence of careful test construction' implies that test developers should document the process of arriving at test specifications, as well as the specifications themselves. The types of activities that need to be documented are outlined for computer-based tests in Fulcher (2003), and can be adapted for tests of speaking to include the following:

• Identifying members of the design team in order to bring together the range of skills and knowledge required to undertake the design. What is the range of skills and knowledge required? Who are the members? What are their qualifications? The same documentation is required for members of the test review team, as experts are extensively used in any design effort (Standards for Educational and Psychological Testing, 43–4).

- Identifying the test takers. It is important to be as specific as possible about who the test is for, using characteristics such as: age range, gender, geographical location, first language(s), cultural factors that may impact on task/topic choice, and educational system.
- Defining test purpose. Why do these test takers need to take this test? Who will use the test scores, and what decisions will they take on the basis of the test scores?
- Defining the construct (see Chapter 2). Which constructs need to be included in the test in order for the scores to provide information that will directly address test purpose?
- Designing prototype tasks that elicit speech relevant to the constructs. This process is seen as the operationalisation of the constructs, and so the decisions made with regard to task types should be documented in order to show the theoretical rationale for this particular operationalisation rather than some alternative. If the test is for a specific speaking population and purpose, such as a test for airline staff, hotel receptionists or teachers, the process of designing prototype tasks will also involve conducting job analyses. These might include creating inventories of tasks undertaken by the target population, prioritising the inventory, and investigating the type of language used in those tasks.
- Piloting prototype tasks with small groups of learners in order to discover which tasks do not work as planned, and which can be included in the test after revision and further piloting. This critical phase of the work usually requires the use of protocol analysis (see Green, 1998), interviews (see Chapter 8) and observational studies of test-taking behaviours (O'Loughlin, 2001). The analysis of the feedback from test takers drawn from the entire range of ability of the test-taking population for whom the test is intended is used to revise the tasks and their rubrics, and to inform the development of scoring systems. This approach is also widely used in the development of work-based performance tests (see Mislevy *et al.*, 1998).
- Working on initial ideas for rating scales and band descriptors as prototyping continues through iterations of pilots with small groups of students.
- Writing and revising the task administration instructions, which tell the interlocutor in a face-to-face test how to conduct the task, or how the room is to be laid out in a simulated test of speaking (see Chapter 6).
- Commissioning appropriate research to support design decisions. Although the use of experts to both design and review construct definitions and tasks is essential, expert review cannot always provide the key to design decisions. For example, a speaking test is being designed to test the ability of speakers to communicate in an English L1 context. Five or six tasks have been selected to elicit spoken language that can be scored, but one appears to be much more difficult to score than the others, and produces consistently lower scores than other tasks. This task requires the test taker to look at a graph, prepare a response for one minute, and then describe and discuss the graph (see the Maps and Graphs examples in Chapter 3). Does the graph item provide unique and useful information on the construct,

or is the item biased in favour of test takers with good 'graph-reading skills' (construct irrelevant variance)? Or is it the case that some types of graph generate ratable speech, whereas others do not? (See Katz *et al.*, in press).

- Making explicit any constraints in test design. Unfortunately, it is not always possible to produce the test that a design team thinks may best operationalise the construct. For example, the team may wish to design a speaking test for tour guides that uses simulation tasks to emulate a range of speaking activities related to a job analysis, but is working within the constraint that the test takers cannot spend more than thirty minutes taking the test. In an international test of English for entrance to university level education it may be impossible to have multiple subject-specific speaking tests due to the financial cost in developing and maintaining multiple parallel modules.

Unlike older approaches to producing test specifications (Carroll and Hall, 1985: 11–23) these activities are not seen as discrete. Rather, they interact with each other as the initial look and feel of the speaking test begins to evolve. The structure of the development team may need changing, perhaps by bringing in additional expertise in particular areas of Applied Linguistics as the tasks begin to take shape. Test purpose and construct become more carefully defined as the team understands more about how real students react to prototype tasks, and evidence is collected about the kind of discourse that is produced in response to the tasks. Findings from specific pieces of research are fed into the design dialogue. As tasks are revised and piloted again the design team works towards ever more fixed ideas of what the test should look like.

The process is not linear, but dynamic. Documenting how and why decisions are taken is frequently not easy, because the process is much 'messier' than is frequently portrayed in step-by-step guides. But it is nevertheless important to try to document decisions, their rationales and any evidence presented to support a decision. The documentation is part of the validity argument linking the constructs to the tasks and the rating scale, through a record of design decisions. It shows in particular how the development team tries to avoid construct under-representation and construct-irrelevant variance as described at the end of Chapter 2, while trying to produce a practical test within budgetary constraints (see Chapter 6). Some refer to this as 'evidence-centred design' (Gitomer and Bennett, 2001; Kirsch, 2001; Mislevy *et al.*, 1999a, 1999b), a process in which the test specifications evolve through the process of collecting evidence during the design phase that supports the kinds of claims that the test designers wish to make about the meaning of scores. The design process, and the documentation of the design process, therefore becomes a critical part of the validity argument.

This position is implicit in the Educational Testing Service Standards for Quality and Fairness (2000b: 10) in Standard 1.3:

Standard 1.3
Document the development process used for existing products or services. Provide a plan for developing new products or services or revising existing ones.
The documentation or plan for a product or service, including research projects, should address development procedures, schedules, staff with major responsibility for the project, internal and external reviews, and fairness and accessibility issues. For products and services developed for a particular client, work collaboratively with the client, as appropriate, to establish the development plan.

The creativity of the dynamic design phase may last for a relatively short period of time if the test is a classroom progress test, or run to years for a large-scale international test upon which high stakes decisions are to be made. But an operational test cannot be released until there is considerable stability in how it will look and feel with regard to task types and content. Establishing this stability in the test requires the developers to make design decisions that become fixed features, and these are recorded in the test specifications.

DEFINING TEST SPECIFICATIONS

Alderson *et al.* (1995: 9) and Bachman and Palmer (1996: 176) define test specifications as the 'blueprint' for a test, used by test and item writers to produce forms of the same test. Alderson *et al.* point out, quite rightly, that these are different from what testing agencies or examination boards usually refer to as the test 'syllabus'. The syllabus is normally oriented towards the needs of test takers and teachers, whereas specifications are used by the test writers. Many examples of syllabuses are available from testing agencies, such as Educational Testing Service (www.ets.org) and the University of Cambridge Local Examinations Syndicate (http://www.ucles.org.uk/). These can be downloaded from their websites. Typical content covers the level of the test, who should take the test, its format, what is being tested, what task types are used, who the interlocutors are in a face-to-face test, and what the criteria for successful performances are. The criteria are extracted from rating scales, but presented in a format that is user-friendly.

The more detailed specifications for test and task writing relate to the overall format of a test, and to each of the individual tasks that are included within the framework. The specifications, as they evolve and become more fixed in response to all the information flowing in from piloting and other studies, become the basis for test/task writing, and for ongoing investigation of validity issues. These include:

• Writing many tasks that 'appear' the same, that can be placed into a task bank for creating parallel forms of a speaking test.
• Investigating whether speaking tasks elicit the processes or language that was predicted by the task writers.

- Varying the form of items in future versions so that the test evolves in line with future validity studies and new discoveries in language acquisition and applied linguistics.

For performance tests in English as a Foreign Language some of the earliest test specifications to be published were those for the English Language Testing Service (ELTS, the forerunner of IELTS), by Carroll (1980, 1981), which grew out of the practice of needs analysis (Munby, 1978). These required the use of taxonomies of functions to specify the types of tasks to be used in tests, and was very cumbersome to operate. More usable approaches have grown out of the work of Popham (1978), and are used more widely in educational measurement generally (Davidson and Lynch, 2002).

We will look at three speaking test specifications and comment on the features of each, before looking at the construction of test specifications.

Example 1. ELTS specifications (adapted from Carroll, 1981)

Category 1: Spec. 0   Student's background
Category 2: Spec. 1, 2, 3, 4, 5, 7   Setting
Category 3: Spec. 8, 9, 10   Manipulation of language
Category 4: Spec. 6   Target levels

Spec. 0: Identity and language of the test taker.
Spec. 1: Purpose of study and the type of English needed
Spec. 2: Settings for use of English (physical, temporal and/or psychological)
Spec. 3: Interactions involved (interlocutor, position, roles and social relationship)
Spec. 4: Instrumentality (mode of communication)
Spec. 5: Dialects of English (British, American, regional)
Spec. 6: Target levels on the features of text size, complexity, range and delicacy, speed and flexibility, tolerance conditions for error, style, reference, repetition and hesitation.
Spec. 7: Communication events and activities
Spec. 8: Attitudinal tone (e.g. pleasant–unpleasant; certain–uncertain)
Spec. 9: Language skills (from a taxonomy of 54)
Spec. 10: Micro-functions, such as persuasion, advising, invitation

Format: structured interview

Sample specification for the field of medicine

Spec. 0: Students coming from Saudi Arabia with an upper intermediate level of English.
Spec. 1: Postgraduate medical training. Medical studies in anatomy, surgery, general medicine, consultancy and casualty work.
Spec. 2: Hospital surgery wards, operating theatre, lecture rooms, seminar rooms, library, common room. Use of English 9 hours per day, 5 days per week while in the UK.

Spec. 3:   Learner–instructor, therapist–patient, adviser–advisee, consultant–client, leader–follower, adult–adult, professional–professional, professional–non-professional, senior–junior, equal–equal.

Spec. 4:   Face-to-face, monologue, dialogue.

Spec. 5:   British standard

Spec. 6:   Dimensions (max = 7): Size: 5, Complexity: 4, Range: 4, Delicacy: 5, Speed: 4, Flexibility: 5.

Tolerance Conditions (max = 5): Error: 4, Style: 3, Reference: 3, Repetition: 3, Hesitation: 3.

Spec. 7:   Diagnosis: questioning, rephrasing, comprehend garbled information, asking for clarification.

Instructing staff: groups or individuals, question to check, requests and instructions, write notes.

Conducting seminars: explain themes, question, correct, present seminars.

Spec. 8:   happy–unhappy, pleasant–unpleasant, cheerful–dejected, frivolous–serious, humorous–humourless, sensitive–insensitive, hoping–hopeless, courageous–fearing, cautious–incautious, caring–indifferent, wondering–unastonished, **formal–informal**, friendly–unfriendly, sociable–unsociable, unresentful–resentful, pleased–displeased, patient–impatient, grateful–ungrateful, honest–dishonest, disinterested–biased, respectful–disrespectful, praising–distracting, approving–disapproving, regretting–unregretting, temperate–intemperate, excitable–unexcitable, **willing–unwilling**, resolute–irresolute, inducive–dissuasive, **active–inactive**, concordant–discordant, authoritative–unauthoritative, **certain–uncertain**, intelligent–unintelligent, assenting–dissenting. Emphasis to be placed on those printed in bold.

Spec. 9:   Articulating sound in connected speech: strong/weak forms, word boundaries, allophonic variation. Articulating stress within words: accentual patterns, meaningful patterns, compounds. Recognising stress variations in connected speech: meaningful prominence. Manifesting stress in variations in connnected speech: rhythmic considerations. Recognising stress in connected speech: information units, for emphasis, for contrast. Manipulating stress in connected speech: emphasis, contrast. Producing intonation patterns: falling interrogative, falling imperative, rising interrogative, question tags. Intonation, expressing attitudinal meaning: rising interrogative, front shift, rising imperative, falling interrogative. Expressing information explicitly. Expressing information implicitly. Expressing conceptual meaning: quantity, definiteness, comparison, time, location, means, cause. Understanding and expressing communicative value in context with and without indicators. Expressing relations within sentence: structure elements, premodifications, postmodifications, disjuncts, negation, connectors, complex embedding, focus + theme. Using lexical cohesion: repetition, synonymy, hyponymy, antithesis, apposition, set/collocation, general words. Using grammatical cohesion devices: reference, comparison, substitution, ellipsis, time/place relaters. Using indicators for clarification. Initiating new discourse, and introducing new topics. Maintaining discourse through responding. Planning and organising discourse: classification, properties, process, change of state.

Spec. 10: Certainty, affirmation, probability, possibility, certainty, negation, conviction, intention, obligation, approval and disapproval, inducement, compulsion, prediction, give information, agreement and disagreement, concession. Proposition, substantiation, supposition, implication, interpretation and classification. Greeting, farewell, thanks, apology, good wishes, condolence.
(Many of these would need to be filled out with more detailed micro-functions.)

The first thing to notice about this specification is that it is related to what it is assumed a specific person (being representative of a group of people) will need to use English for during medical training. This approach to specification design implies that the first step is to conduct a needs analysis, which was not in fact done before these specifications were drawn up (Clapham, 1981: 113). But the real problem with this specification is that it is difficult to see how it would be used to generate test tasks and procedures. In other words, faced with a specification like this, would 5 teachers working independently produce tasks that look similar, are pitched at roughly the right level of difficulty (however that is defined), and elicit similar samples of language that can be scored according to the rating criteria used? While a test was constructed and operated for many years, and different forms of the test produced, it is difficult to see how these relate to the specifications in any clear way. Moving from a needs analysis to a test specification is not a simple task. This is why such functional approaches common in the early communicative approach to language testing are no longer in favour.

Example 2. An Exit Test for Adult Immigrants on a Conversation Course (adapted and shortened from Bachman and Palmer, 1996: 298–307)

Test Purpose
A low-stakes test providing evidence of ability to participate in small talk.

TLU domain and task types
Tasks to meet occupation, day-to-day pragmatic and social needs. Tasks to meet social needs include participating in small talk on a variety of topics such as the weather, family, living in the city, shopping, sharing experiences of applying for a job.

Characteristics of test takers
Refugees and newly arrived adult immigrants, of both genders. A wide variety of language and educational backgrounds, and social class.

Topical knowledge
Relatively diverse.

General profile of language ability
This will vary widely from beginning to advanced.

Definition of construct to be measured
Knowledge of vocabulary, syntax, textual knowledge, and topical knowledge.

Considerations of qualities of usefulness
Reliability: Testing procedures should be very similar across candidates, as the test is scripted. Rater training will be required, and agreement set high.
Construct validity: It will be necessary to investigate whether the scripted interview elicits a speech sample that can be rated.
Authenticity: Fairly low, as the set prompts do not follow 'ordinary conversational organization'.

Interactiveness
Language knowledge: a wide range is involved because of the complexity of the tasks.
Topical knowledge: Test takers talk about their own area of expertise.
Strategies: High, as they choose the area of expertise and many prompts allow open responses.
Affect: Positive.

Impact
This should be high as the test is closely related to the course objectives.

Test Structure
1. Warm-up. After greeting and explanation of test purpose, the examiner allows the test taker to select a topic for conversation from a list.
2. Initial questions: Yes/no and wh-questions to make the topic more specific.
3. Extended response questions: Test takers are required to provide.
4. Specialized vocabulary questions:
   - Elaboration questions: exactly what is (a/an) X? Tell me more about X? Can you describe X? What does it mean to do X?
   - Questions for particular items: What's the word for something that/ someone who _____? What do you call it when you _____?
   - Comparison and analysis: What's the difference between _____ and _____? Is it/Are they much like _____?

Textual organisation ability test
Elicit an extended response to rate textual organisation.

Hypothetical situations and supported opinion
The test taker is invited to talk about an area of expertise with regard to a previously unconsidered problem.

Example of an examiner test script for the topic 'children and schools'

1. Warm-up
   Good morning/afternoon/evening Mr/Miss/Mrs X. Please sit down. How are you today/this evening?
   [Test taker responses.] [Respond to test taker as appropriate]

   Do you know what the purpose of this test is?
   [Test taker responds. If test taker does not know the purpose of the test, explain as follows.]
   The purpose of this test is to give you the chance to talk about something that interests you so you can show us what you have learned in your conversation course.

   Mr/Miss/Mrs X, where do you usually speak the most English now?
   [Prompts: At home? Away from home (when you travel)? At work? In church? At school?]

   Who do you usually speak English with?
   What can you talk about best in English?
   [Prompts: Show or read list of 'Topics to talk about in English to test taker'.]

Children	Church
Field of study	Food
Friends and enemies	Hobby
Job	Movies
Parents	Politics
Reading	Shopping
Sports	Spouse
Teachers and school	Television
Travel	Vehicles
Weather	

2. Initial questions
   What different schools have you attended?
   Were most of your teachers men or women?
   Do you like school?

3. Extended response questions
   Was there any teacher you particularly disliked? Tell me about him/her. What did he/she do that you disliked the most? Did you learn a lot in his/her class anyway? Why?
   Was there any particular teacher that you really liked? What was he/she like?
   How were you selected for admission into school here? In your country? Why did you choose this particular school to attend?

4. Specialised vocabulary questions
   Can you describe a classroom in your school? What else was in the room? Exactly how were grades assigned in one of your classes? [Vocabulary questions: biased, incoherent, irrelevant, procedures, techniques, qualified, unqualified.]

5. Textual organisation ability test

What are the similarities and differences between the way students are admitted into colleges in your country and in the US?

What are the similarities and differences between the way and the time students select a major in your country and in the US?

What are the similarities and differences between the quality of education you receive in a school in your country and the US?

What are the similarities and differences between two classes you have taken here?

What are the reasons for and against studying in the US?

6. Hypothetical questions and supported opinion

If you were a foreign student advisor in your school here, how would you prepare students from your country for their experiences here? Why? If you were in charge of the university system in your own country, what changes would you make in the way students are chosen for admission? Why?

If you were a teacher, how would you treat your students? [Vocabulary questions: discipline, assignments, grading.] Why? Do you think your attitude has changed because of your educational experience here? How? Why?

A rating scale is provided as an appendix to the specification, and a description of how the performance is to be scored by two raters, giving independent grades both during and immediately after the test.

This example is much clearer than the ELTS specification. The first part is a generic description of the test, including its purpose, the construct(s) it is intended to test, the test structure with examples of the type of questions that may be asked, and a sample test that expands upon that structure on a particular topic. From this specification, if a group of teachers were asked to go away and produce new test forms for the topic areas of 'health and leisure' or 'travel and tourism' it is highly likely that they would be very similar in structure and form across topic areas. We could term these 'generative' test specifications, because they specifically aid in the construction of new forms. Where new forms look and feel similar, there is more chance that they will produce comparable results, which is important if scores are to be comparable (generalisable) from form to form.

Also important in this test specification is the explicit mention of the link between the scorability of the sample elicited, and the question of validity. Test specifications of this kind can be used to generate validity questions that become the subject for research. Of course, we have argued that the development of test specifications is a dynamic rather than a linear process. The question of whether or not the tasks in this test would generate a scorable speech sample should have been addressed during the phase of piloting prototype tasks, which leads to the specifications becoming more and more fixed. Nevertheless, the text specifications that are used to generate the operational test should provide useful guidelines regarding the types of validity evidence that need to be collected to create a validity argument.

Example 3. *Assessment of Speech Acts: Role-playing difficult requests.*
From Fred Davidson's *Virtual Specbank*,
http://www.deil.uiuc.edu/fgd/site/ltvshome.htm

General Description
This is a role-play assessment of the speech acts involved in making a difficult request. The situation in this role play is one of high imposition (on the part of the examinee), high distance, and high status differential. The roles, rights and obligations are unclear. The long-term relationship of the participants is not clear and possibly negotiable.

Prompt Attributes
The prompt material is written, possibly delivered by e-mail on a computer. It specifies the setting and task which the examinee will perform. It states that the examinee and person(s) to whom s/he is to speak are of the same gender. The prompt gives sufficient detail to establish the differential roles between the examinee and the person(s) to whom s/he is to communicate. The examinee is told to write his/her response.

Response Attributes
(1) To fulfil the task, the examinee is generally expected to:
　(a) show need/justification
　(b) display cultural knowledge and awareness of sociocultural and sociopragmatic values
　(c) display pragmatic ability
　(d) portray a tenor that shows deference and formality
(2) The examinee will also be rated along the following assessment criteria:
　(a) Does the examinee display justification for his/her request(s)?
　(b) Does the examinee use positive language in the request, with mitigators (no over-the-top language)?
　(c) Is the examinee clear in the request – does s/he do more than simply hint at what she/he wants?
　(d) Does the examinee's language fall within an American native speaker norm?
(3) The rating scale(s) sketched in (2) above would need to consider the following topics:
　(a) contextualised linguistic acceptability: word order, spelling, etc.
　(b) presence of strategies
　(c) pragmalinguistic ability (e.g. use of 'can' vs. 'could')
　(d) sociopragmatic ability
　(e) content, justification and relevance of the message
　(f) rights and obligations
　(g) clarity of the message

Sample Item
[Written prompt to the student]
You are in a survey course on world history. It is the middle of the academic term. Write a note to your professor in which you ask for a one-page study

guide sheet for a forthcoming midterm examination. You may assume that you represent a group of your peer students, if you wish. Your professor is a very strict and inflexible person. The professor maintains a distant relationship with students and is older than the students in your class. Assume that the professor is the same gender as yourself.

Specification Supplement
Issues for discussion and evolution of this specification:
(1) Should the written student prompt include guidance on how the examinee will be evaluated?
(2) In the sample item given, the examinee has the option to consider him/herself as a representative of a larger group. Should this be a required component of the specification?
(3) Following are some alternate assessment methods or facilitative tools that could be employed. These may necessitate new specs; alternatively, it may be possible to alter this spec so that it could encompass additional testing methods. Each alternative below is stated with particular reference to the actual SI above but should generalise to other SIs produced by this spec:
   (a) Leaving a note, vs.
   (b) Written speech used at the office hours; that is, in (a) the examinee would write a note or letter, whereas in (b) s/he would write whatever s/he would say in an office meeting. The level of formality would change in (a) vs. (b), as would length, possibly the strategies employed. The sociopragmatics of (a) and (b) may be very similar.
   (c) There could be two videos, one male and one female, of an opener by the professor.
   (d) The task could be oral but with interaction; i.e. it could be a full role-play between an examinee and an examiner, where the examiner plays the role of the professor.
(4) What is being tested – conversational ability or pragmatic knowledge?
(5) What is the ultimate use of this test's results?
(6) Should the test allow for opting out?
(7) What is the implication of the particular modality selected – spoken or written – with regard to rejoinders and interactiveness?
(8) Is this a holistic or analytic assessment of speech act performance?
(9) What language norms are expected in the examinee's responses? Of what group is the examinee a native? What is the *lingua franca* of the test setting?

The basic elements of this specification are not dissimilar to that of the example from Bachman and Palmer (1996), but the elements are more clearly specified using the headings derived from Popham (1978). While this specification is for a written response to the prompt, it is clear from the supplement that it could be done in face-to-face mode, or as a semi-direct speaking test The supplement is an important feature of this specification, which indicates how the task may be changed, or even evolve over time, indicating what issues the test designers would have to take into account if the alternative task types were to be piloted.

The precise form of a test or task specification for a speaking test is not fixed in stone. Precisely how the specification is laid out, and the type of information it contains, is dependent upon the test purpose, and the needs of the testing context.

WRITING TEST SPECIFICATIONS

We have stressed that test specifications grow out of a dynamic process of discussion, piloting and information collection through research. This process is not easy to describe, because it is frequently messy, and the types of activities in the early phases of test design are dependent upon the testing context. An example of the beginning of a principled test design process is the definition of constructs for the new TOEFL speaking test (Butler *et al.*, 2000; Douglas, 1997), after which task design is informed by a study of the domain to which inferences need to be drawn (Rosenfeld *et al.*, 2001; Waters, 1996). This is then extended to studies of prototype tasks, the language samples they elicit, and whether they can be reasonably scored using prototype rating scales (Cumming *et al.*, 2001). However, one of the few publications to show how the design of initial prototype performance tasks are piloted and analysed, revised and re-piloted, is provided by Mislevy *et al.* (1998) in the context of assessing dental hygienists.

This type of work is undertaken in what has come to be called an evidence-centred design process, where the record of test design and development decisions forms part of a validity argument. Following the principles of Messick (1992), Mislevy *et al.* (1999: 23) argue that:

> A fundamental tenet of the evidence-centred approach to assessment design (and of Messick's construct-centred approach as well) is that the characteristics of tasks are determined by the nature of the behaviors they must produce, to constitute evidence for the targeted aspects of proficiency. This perspective stands contrary to a task-centred approach, under which the primary emphasis is on creating tasks, with the target of inference defined only implicitly as the tendency to do well on those tasks. Valuable insights inform task design under this latter approach, to be sure. But the flow of the design rationale from construct to evidence to tasks makes our rationale explicit from the start – easier to communicate, easier to modify, and better suited to principled generation of tasks.

While we will not concentrate on the formal model developed by Mislevy for use within Educational Testing Service, we draw attention to the focus on precisely those elements that we have outlined as being critical in the development of tests of speaking, namely:

- Identifying the constructs about which we wish to make inferences.
- Identifying the relationships between constructs and behaviours in situations that call for their use.

Specification number: Provide a short index number.

Title of Specification: A short title should be given that generally characterises each spec. The title is a good way to outline skills across several specifications.

Related Specification(s), if any: List the numbers and/or titles of specs related to this one, if any. For example, separate detailed specifications may be given for each task type.

(1) General Description (GD): A brief general statement of the behaviour to be tested. The GD is very similar to the core of a learning objective. The purpose of testing this skill may also be stated in the GD.

(2) Prompt Attributes (PA): A complete and detailed description of what the student will encounter.

(3) Response Attributes (RA): A complete and detailed description of the way in which the student will provide the answer; that is, a complete and detailed description of what the student will do in response to the prompt and what will constitute a failure or success. There are two basic types of RAs:

    (a) Selected Response: Clear and detailed descriptions of each choice in a multiple-choice format.

    (b) Constructed Response: A clear and detailed description of the type of response the student will perform, including the criteria for evaluating or rating the response.

(4) Sample Item (SI): An illustrative item or task that reflects this specification, that is, the sort of item or task this specification should generate.

(5) Specification Supplement (SS): A detailed explanation of any additional information needed to construct items for a given spec.

Figure 5.1   Test specification format (after Davidson and Lynch, 2002: 14)

- Identifying features of situations that can elicit behaviour that provides evidence about the constructs.

We can see how this information is compiled into the specifications provided in examples 2 and 3 in the last section. The key elements in any test specification (reproduced from Davidson and Lynch, 2002: 14, which is adapted from Popham, 1978) are presented in Figure 5.1. The general description provides the summary of the construct (see Chapter 2) that underlies the test. It serves as a reminder of why this particular item or test is the way it is. The prompt attributes and responses provide the evidence trail for why a particular task or set of tasks was selected (see Chapter 3). Not only should the prompt attribute allow the generation of multiple forms of the same task, it should provide the basis by which researchers can generate research questions that will help to strengthen a validity argument. The response attribute section of the specification forces the test developer to state how a task is going to be scored before it is ever administered in an operational test (see Chapter 4). This may seem like a fairly obvious thing to consider at the design stage. But in many teaching and testing situations around the world it is still common for tasks to be designed and delivered operationally, and then for groups of teachers to hold meetings to look at sample responses in order to agree on how to score them *post hoc.* In my experience such meetings are the cause of extreme levels of frustration, and rarely result in agreed rating criteria.

The sample item or task is supposed to be a 'typical' example of the type of task that would be generated by the specification. As Davidson and Lynch (2002: 26) put it, the SI should 'bring to life' the language of the GD, PA and RA. Finally comes the specification supplement, which is optional, and may include any other information that is required to understand the specification. It may contain optional elements for item/task types, additional specifications of the physical situations/contexts for tasks, or more detailed lists of topics, or role-relationships, for example, should these be required.

When writing specifications for speaking tests there are a number of special considerations that the developers should take into account. Each situation and testing context may generate a different solution to each of these considerations, but they should be explicitly considered.

Specifications at the level of test and/or task

For many speaking tests a single specification may be appropriate. Davidson and Lynch (2002: 48–50) call this a 'procedure' specification. The example from Bachman and Palmer (1986) provided earlier also shows a single specification that encapsulates a number of separate tasks within a longer 'procedure' of testing speaking (the whole test). However, it might be appropriate to have specifications at two levels: the general specification of the procedure of testing speaking, including the various components and their timing, and more detailed specifications for individual tasks. For example, it is frequently the case that there are a variety of different task types embedded within a speaking test, perhaps including a descriptive activity and a short role play, in order to elicit a range of different language (Shohamy *et al.*, 1986). A picture description section within a longer procedure may be a sub-specification that could look like the following example, which was designed for learners at an 'intermediate' level of language learning.

Spec. no. 025
Title. Picture description component for OPI 21
GD: The picture description component is designed to elicit an extended sample of speech from the test taker in order to test monologic fluency, the ability to describe, compare and contrast, two pictures which should be familiar. The focus of the assessment is on achievement strategies to compare and contrast, using appropriate vocabulary to communicate with the interlocutor.
PA: The student is given two pictures of familiar scenes. The interlocutor says: 'I am giving you two pictures. Please take a minute to look at these. I will then ask you to describe each picture, and ask you one other question about them. You will then have three minutes to talk about the pictures. Do you understand what you have to do?' [Answer any questions the test taker may have.] After one minute, say: 'Would you describe the pictures for me, and then tell

me X.' In place of X insert: 'Would you prefer to go to A or B for your holiday?' 'Would you prefer to do activity A or B as a sport?' 'Would you prefer to do A or B as a hobby?' [If the test taker needs an additional prompt to continue speaking, ask: 'Why do you say that?']

When the test taker concludes, say: 'Thank you. I will take the pictures. We will now move on to the next part of the test.'

Each task must use two pictures that offer a contrast. These may be pictures of places (town/countryside, seaside/mountains, etc.), activities (surfing/ skiing, sailing/hiking), or hobbies (stamp collecting/gardening, reading/ listening to music). No specialised vocabulary should be needed to describe the pictures, or compare and contrast the themes or activities.

RA: The test taker will describe each picture. It is expected that they will identify the theme, activity or hobby, even if they need to use circumlocution if they cannot name the theme, activity or hobby. The description should allow a person who has not seen the picture to imagine what it contains. The test taker should then compare and contrast the two pictures with a reasonable degree of fluency. The performance is to be rated on the fluency rating scale in Appendix 4.4.

SI: 'I am giving you two pictures. Please take a minute to look at these. I will then ask you to describe each picture, and ask you one other question about them. You will then have three minutes to talk about the pictures. Do you understand what you have to do?'

Picture 1

Picture 2

[Wait for 1 minute]

'Would you describe the pictures for me, and then tell me where you would prefer to go for a holiday?'

[If the test taker needs an additional prompt to continue speaking, ask: 'Why do you say that?' Encourage the test taker to justify their choice.]

'Thank you. I will take the pictures. We will now move on to the next part of the test.'

There is no simple answer as to whether multiple specifications for individual tasks within a larger test should be drawn up, or whether simply to include them in one large specification. It depends upon the complexity of the speaking test procedure, and how best the test designers decide it is possible to generate all the multiple tasks that will be needed to compile operational forms of the test.

Teaching and the level of specificity

How specific should the description of the construct be in any given test specification? As Mislevy *et al.* (1999) argue, it can be at the level of the most general construct; in our case that would be 'speaking', or it could be a very long description of the discourse and strategic skills about which we wish to make inferences (Chapter 2). This relates to test purpose, and whether it is necessary for test scores, or even learner profiling, to feed back into the teaching and learning process (Davidson and Lynch, 2002: 10–12). For a proficiency test the description may be at a fairly generic level, but for a diagnostic profile it is likely that the construct description will run to pages, rather than a single summary paragraph. In these cases, much of the description can be placed in the specification supplement, along with the multiple-trait scales that would be needed to generate learner profiles. This is another reason why the design team often needs to spend considerable time discussing and documenting the purpose of the test, and the use to which the scores will be put.

Response attributes and speech samples

It is one thing to describe the expected response attributes, and another to show precisely what aspects of a response can be scored on the rating scale, and are relevant to the construct definition. During the process of piloting prototype tasks a lot of learner speech is generated. Sample responses can be included as part of the response attribute description in the test specifications. The transcript contained in Appendix 7 is a sample response attribute for a task that required a learner to interpret a graph, and the annotation explicitly relates test-taker speech to the rating scale in Appendix 8. Of course, this does not have to be done so explicitly for all speaking tests. It may be adequate to have two or three examples of graded responses to indicate what a response at key levels on a scale may look like. The addition of transcripts (and perhaps associated recordings) serves additional purposes. Firstly, task writers who are using the specification in their work can ask whether or not new forms are likely to generate similar discourse features. Secondly, key samples that are embedded in the specifications can be used as 'anchors' for selecting other key samples for inclusion in rater training materials (see Chapter 6 for a discussion of rater training).

TEST SPECIFICATIONS: CONTROL AND FREEDOM

In this final section, we look at the levels of control and freedom that are built into test specifications. Both are essential for the effective use of test specifications in speaking tests. Finally, we consider what Davidson and Lynch (2002: 64) call the 'set in stone phenomenon'.

The element of control should be clear from our previous discussion. The test specification tells the task writer what type of task should occur in each 'slot' in the test procedure. For example, what type of pictures should be used, and what type of language they should elicit. This control speeds up the process of producing new forms. It turns the production of similar item types into an efficient production line. The measurement advantage of this is that it is more likely that different forms of the test will elicit similar language samples, that the task difficulty (however defined) is more likely to be similar, and that scores are more likely to be reliable (Davidson and Lynch, 2002: 61–2). With this stability, we could also argue that the test is fairer to test takers. Test content is not likely to fluctuate wildly from form to form, making scores different depending on the form used for a particular administration. Nor are test takers likely to panic when they see some new unanticipated task. In terms of task writing, it is easier to produce many tasks for the 'task bank' much more quickly and easily when writing to a specification. Once large banks of equivalent tasks are created, it becomes much easier to select tasks from a sequence of banks to assemble a specific test form. This is a much more efficient use of resources than writing many different stand-alone test forms.

The specification also introduces freedoms. To illustrate this, we will use the example of the picture description task produced above. There are a number of elements that the task writer is not free to vary. These are:

- Only two pictures must be used.
- The two pictures must be thematically related, but contrastive.
- The picture content must not be culturally alien for the test takers.
- The interlocutor frame may not be varied.

Then there are elements that the task writer is free to vary. These are:

Theme of the pictures	Places
	Activities
	Hobbies
The pictures themselves	Town/countryside, seaside/mountains, etc.
	Surfing/skiing, sailing/hiking, etc.
	Stamp collecting/gardening, reading/listening to music, etc.

The themes are restricted to three, which have been found to generate the best language samples during piloting the prototypes of this task type. However, within the theme the task writer may select pictures from a potentially endless list of contrasts. The specification places no limit on the variability of topic at this level, other than that the test takers must be able to relate to the pictures culturally, and that the pictures should not require any specialised vocabulary.

The degree of freedom that is built into a specification should be explicitly discussed. Firstly, if the freedom allows the generation of task types that were not envisaged at the time of piloting, unwanted variability that may not be construct-related could be introduced into test scores. Secondly, the freedom should be deliberately built in at a level that allows the generation of different, but similar tasks. Part of the validity evidence to support the use of this task may be score invariance across tasks that differ at the level of the topic of the picture.

We have stressed that creating banks of tasks from specifications, from which forms can be generated, is much more efficient and effective than simply writing many forms. Over time, the tendency is for the specification to become set in stone. As Davidson and Lynch (2002: 65) warn:

> The power of a well-established test specification to guide practice is an important and dangerous power. A well-established spec – by its very reification – helps with test validity, because it clarifies the definition of the trait(s) [constructs] being assessed . . . It adds a nice air of stability and trust to any assessment system. But at the same time, the very trust we place in well-established specifications can mislead us to a false sense of security. We can become reluctant to change specifications because we don't want to relive the agonizing, costly, time-consuming process of spec creation.

There may be many reasons why it is essential to revisit test specifications periodically. Perhaps the most important is because our understanding of the construct has changed. If the discipline of discourse analysis adds something to our understanding of the construct of fluency, it may be time to update the general description, and perhaps the supplement, to a specification. The question then arises whether the rating scale needs to change, and perhaps the task itself. The test-taking population may change, in which case test purpose may also change. Are the constructs and the tasks relevant to the needs of the new test takers, and can appropriate inferences be drawn from the speaking test scores? Or perhaps the syllabus has changed, and the speaking test that was used to assess end of course achievement now doesn't match the aims and objectives of the teaching.

Specifications for speaking tests/tasks are not monolithic documents, but working plans and definitions, that should be frequently revisited. This is even more important in teaching contexts, where they can act as the explicit statement of the focus of learning. They can have a significant impact upon how teachers conceive of their role in the classroom, and act as a pivotal centre for discussion about the syllabus and curriculum. For testing agencies too, they act as a statement of what is being valued in learning and teaching, and what test-score users value when they make decisions about test takers. The fine balance between the need for stability in tests and the inevitable change in language education is one that needs to be constantly discussed and monitored.

DIGEST

In this chapter we have described a validity argument, and claimed that clear documentation of the test design process contributes to the validity argument. This includes documentation of decisions taken, rationales for the decisions, available empirical evidence and the test specifications themselves. We have shown that the process of writing specifications is not linear, but dynamic, requiring a number of simultaneous activities.

We have provided practical examples of how practitioners can work to develop their own speaking tests, drawing together insights from previous chapters. There is no 'one way' to get this right, but the guidelines in this chapter should make the process of test development and implementation easier, more transparent and more open to validity investigation.

In Chapter 6 we start with the assumption that we have designed our speaking test, and we turn our attention to the raters who will score it, the interlocutors who will administer it, how we train them, and the administration of tests of second-language speaking.

Raters, training and administration

In this chapter we turn our attention to what seem like more down to earth, *practical* matters. Issues like how we train raters and interlocutors, or how a room is laid out for a speaking test. But the practical matters are also extremely important for theoretical reasons. For example, the interlocutor may be exhorted to be 'friendly' (Underhill, 1987: 42–3) in a face-to-face speaking test, but this alone is really to miss the point. As we saw in Figure 4.4 the interlocutor (who may also be the rater) plays an important role in the testing process. The interlocutor interacts with the test taker. It is quite possible that the score is in some way *affected* by the interlocutor and the nature of the interaction. The question that we have to ask is whether this is inevitable in any act of communication in a speaking test. Or should the score be treated as 'independent' of the interlocutor and interaction?

The traditional view has been to treat this problem as a simple example of what we have referred to before as 'construct-irrelevant variance'(Messick, 1989). The test score is 'contaminated' by some aspect of the testing context that is not relevant to test construct. For example, if the same individual were to get different scores with different interlocutors, we may wonder whether the test score had any meaning at all *for that individual.* Depending upon test purpose we may, however, wish to accept this as inevitable (from a co-constructionist point of view) and merely attempt to control for some aspects of interlocutor behaviour.

We might also be concerned about the test-taking environment. If test takers in Centre A tend to get higher scores than test takers in Centre B, and Centre A has comfortable armchairs in wallpapered rooms while Centre B has wooden stools and grey concrete walls, should we suspect that the scores are contaminated by the environment? Perhaps the surroundings in Centre A serve to put students at their ease, leading to better performances.

As we have seen in Chapters 2 and 4, we could hold the position that in fact our ability to speak does 'change' depending not only upon whom we are speaking to, where, and about what, but under what conditions. With every change in each variable of the context in its broadest sense, the scores may also change.

Nevertheless, we would probably still agree that it is likely to be unfair on test takers in Centre B if their lower grades are lower *because* they attended Centre B and not Centre A. This is just not part of a notion of what is 'fair' in language testing. The conditions under which speaking tests are conducted are therefore standardised to a large extent.

Historically, most of the research effort has been into rater reliability. Rater reliability is concerned with the extent to which two or more raters are capable of agreeing with each other on the score they award to the same individual(s). The principle underlying the notion of inter-rater reliability is that it shouldn't matter to the test taker which rater they have in a test; test takers should get the same score irrespective of who is rating their performance. Rater reliability is also concerned with intra-rater reliability, or the extent to which the same rater awards the same score to the same individual over a period of time. If a rater cannot agree with him or herself over time, it is unlikely that an assessment of their agreement with other raters at a particular point in time will be meaningful.

We begin by looking at rater reliability and rater training. We then consider the important area of interlocutor training, and then turn to a brief consideration of the testing environment. We will look at issues surrounding accommodations for test takers with disabilities, and consider how their test scores are reported. Finally, we look at budgeting for speaking test design. This lengthy section on money is unusual in a book about testing. But it is very often not realised just how expensive it is to design a test that embodies many of the principles we have considered in previous chapters. And of course, the cost of testing is an extremely important consideration in the practicality of testing for many institutions.

RATERS AND RATER TRAINING

Rater reliability

Lowe (1987: 46) acknowledged that there had been few studies into the reliability (and validity) of the OPI even by the late 1980s. He refers to the experience of assessors with the use of the OPI and the successful placement of government personnel over a long period of time as justification for procedures used. Lowe (1986: 394) states that

> The ILR approach has permitted successful use of the WENS (well educated native speaker) concept as the ultimate criterion in government for over thirty years.

Wilds (1975) had already put forward the same argument. Above all, the tradition of AEI evaluation must continue unbroken (Lowe, 1986: 396). The point being made is that the top band in the scale is a fixed point capable of description, to which lower bands may be sequentially linked, and raters are capable of reliably using such a rating scale because of their understanding of this fixed criterion. (See Chapter 4 for a discussion of the native-speaker criterion.)

This is the experiential claim for reliability that is common to much work on testing speaking both within the AEI approach and elsewhere until the 1990s (Davidson and Bachman, 1990; Bachman *et al.*, 1995). Since then there has been a larger concern with rater agreement and severity by producers or large-scale speaking tests.

One study which is constantly referred to within the literature on the OPI is that of Adams (1978) on inter-rater reliability. Adams investigated the relationship between the five factors of the FSI rating scale (fluency, comprehension, grammar, vocabulary and accent) and the final rating of the students. The ratings of 834 tests conducted during the summer of 1978 in 33 languages were used in the study, and it was found that agreement between two raters was consistently in the order of 0.87 or higher. This single study is cited as justification more often than not for the reliability of scoring all forms of the OPI. Liskin-Gasparro (1984a: 483), for example, appeals directly to the Adams study in defence of the reliability of the ACTFL.

It has generally been claimed in the literature that high inter-rater reliability is not difficult to achieve in speaking tests. Harrison (1982: 2) is an exception to this rule, but he provides no evidence or rationale to support his view. Even Barnwell (1987: 36) who is a critic of the AEI approach to rating agrees that high rater reliability has been demonstrated. Barnwell (1986), for example, reports a study in which 7 teachers of Spanish were provided with 'brief' training in the use of the ACTFL rating scale and then asked to rate students from video recordings of OPIs. 41 per cent of grades were exactly the same as actual ACTFL scores, 45 per cent were within 1 band and 14 per cent 2 or more bands away. Barnwell concluded that this evidence shows that even untrained raters can reach acceptable levels of agreement.

Mullen (1978b) conducted a study in which two judges used four rating scales to rate the speaking performances of two groups of students. Each judge rated both groups of students on each of the scales, and it was found that there was no significant difference in the mean scores of the two groups, the judges, or the operation of the scales. Variance was primarily attributable to the difference between test takers, although a small interaction effect was found between judge and scale, and judge and test taker. Mullen concluded that inter-rater reliability was high when two judges were used. These findings are supported by other early studies by Clark (1975: 16–17) and Clark and Swinton (1980a). Hendricks *et al.* (1980) report an inter-rater reliability study in which an FSI-type procedure was used. 182 students from the University of Southern Illinois were tested, and taped interviews rated by two teams of raters made up from a pool of one instructor and three graduate assistants. The correlations are presented in Table 6.1.

Here, inter-rater reliability is acceptable in all but the assessment of pronunciation. The global score appears to be highly reliable. It must also be noted, however, that in this study the assessment was carried out by teams of

Table 6.1 Inter-rater reliability on an FSI-type speaking test (Hendricks *et al.*, 1980)

Group 1	Group 2					
	Global	**Pron.**	**Grammar**	**Vocab.**	**Fluency**	**Comp.**
Global	0.91					
Pronunciation		0.43				
Grammar			0.83			
Vocabulary				0.85		
Fluency					0.80	
Comprehension						0.89

raters working together rather than by individuals. This would probably have had the effect of inflating the correlations. So the results need to be treated with more caution than in other studies.

From studies of inter-rater reliability Mullen (1980) argued that two raters are required in any speaking test, as individual raters tend to have different patterns of rating. Indeed, most investigations of reliability in oral testing recommend the use of at least 2 raters (de Charruf, 1984) in order to avoid the possible impact that a single rater may have on the test score.

Lowe and Liskin-Gasparro (1986: 4) claim inter-rater reliability for the OPI to be within one plus point on the rating scale when using trained raters. In the light of the other studies reviewed here, this does not seem to be an unreasonable claim, and is borne out by research conducted using speaking tests outside of the US context.

An important series of studies conducted by Shohamy are most important in this context. Shohamy (1983a) reports a study in which a team of judges were asked to rate recorded tapes of interviews with 106 students of Hebrew at the University of Minnesota. Four weeks later 32 tapes were randomly selected for re-rating. Intra-rater reliability was found to be 0.99. A similar study (Shohamy, 1983b: 535) found inter-rater reliability to be 0.93. Reporting on the development of a new oral test for use in schools in Israel, Shohamy *et al.* (1986) describe four experimental tests (an oral interview, a role-play exercise, a reporting task and a group discussion), providing inter-rater reliabilities as 0.91, 0.76, 0.81 and 0.73 respectively. The very high correlation coefficient for the oral interview is not uncommon, although the reliability coefficients for the role-play exercise and the group discussion are somewhat lower. In Australia, a similarly high inter-rater reliability coefficient is reported for the ASLPR interview procedure (Ingram, 1982: 26, 1985: 249).

Morrison and Lee (1985) report on an oral test which was a simulation of an academic tutorial developed at Hong Kong University. The tests were videotaped and each student rated by a mixture of native and non-native speakers on a 5-band scale for the factors of general proficiency, use of grammar, pronunciation, fluency, communicative ability and academic potential. Inter-rater reliability was reported as 0.85 with no significant difference between the rating behaviour of native and non-native raters.

One study that reports much lower correlation coefficients is that of Jafarpur (1988). He used an FSI-type oral interview at Shiraz University, Iran, in which 3 raters scored the performance of 58 students on the five FSI factors. Inter-rater reliability was reported as lying between 0.58 and 0.65. Jafarpur concluded that there was a significant difference between the rating patterns of the 3 judges. However, the raters in this case were subject teachers, not language teachers, and had received no training (so-called 'naive' raters). This may very well account for such low correlations in this particular study.

The published evidence on inter-rater reliability suggests that high correlation coefficients are achieved when multiple trained raters are used to score performances. The correlation coefficients decrease in magnitude when untrained raters are used.

In all of these studies a correlation coefficient is reported as an inter-rater reliability statistic. However, the correlation coefficient does not take into account rater severity; that is, how severe or lenient a rater is (see Chapter 8). Bejar (1985) argued that, although there is often substantial agreement in the sequencing of test takers by raters, and hence high correlation coefficients, the severity of raters differs widely. Awarding the mean score of multiple raters is therefore suggested as a correction device for varying rater severity. The use of multifaceted Rasch techniques (see Chapter 8) has better allowed us to understand this aspect of rater behaviour. Programs like Facets (Linacre and Wright, 1990; Linacre, 1991) have made it possible to model the severity of raters more accurately than was previously possible. Using this technique McNamara and Adams (1991) have shown that the more double rating of writing samples takes place, the more reliable the scores, as it 'washes out' the differences between raters. McNamara (1996) also used this technique to investigate rater severity for the Australian *access:* test, and the Occupational English Test. He discovered a high degree of variability in rater severity. Fulcher (1993) also used multifaceted Rasch analysis to investigate the rating patterns of 5 raters. He discovered that consistency in severity was higher when the raters were using data-based rating scales than *a priori* rating scales, but that there were nevertheless significant levels of variability.

Rater training

This brings us to the issue of rater training. Wilkinson (1968: 121–2) argued that the training of raters is essential if they are to grade in the same way. Studies of rater training (Weigle, 1994) have shown that training reduces random error in rating, but that it is not possible to remove completely the differences in severity between raters.

In addition to the traditional solution of averaging multiple ratings, McNamara (1996: 127) raises the possibility of using estimates of rater severity to correct their ratings prior to releasing the results. He also suggests that the difference between raters may provide useful and insightful information. This suggestion reflects the theoretical position of Moss (1992, 1994), although McNamara does not discuss Moss's work. Moss questions the traditional requirement for reliability in tests. Rather, she wishes to stress the importance of 'contextualised judgements' where difference and diversity are valued. Talking of the usual requirement of score generalisability across raters (inter-rater reliability), Moss (1994: 9) writes:

> Initial disagreement among readers [raters] would not invalidate the assessment; rather, it would provide an impetus for dialogue, debate, and enriched understanding informed by multiple perspectives as interpretations are refined and as decisions or actions are justified. And again, if well documented, it would allow users of the assessment information, including students, parents, and others affected by the results, to become part of the dialogue by evaluating (and challenging) the conclusions for themselves.

While this is certainly the rationale for the way in which experts judge PhD dissertations, through discussion and dialogue, reflection on written work and interview, the time, cost and resources needed to implement the approach in the testing of large-scale second-language speaking is likely to be prohibitive.

A second reason for rater training is to try to affect the raters' interpretation of the rating scale. There is little point in building construct models to support the empirical development of rating scales if raters then pay no attention to it. As we have argued in Chapter 4, a large part of the meaning of a score on a speaking test is the descriptor that defines the level or band.

Barnwell (1989) conducted an inter-rater reliability study using the ACTFL rating scale to see if native speakers of Spanish reacted to foreign language proficiency in their language in the way predicted by the rating scale. Although this procedure had been suggested by Byrnes (1987) as a potential method of validating the ACTFL rating scale, Barnwell points out that the scale was developed intuitively. Barnwell hypothesised that inter-rater reliability between native speakers and ACTFL raters would be low. Barnwell taped four students doing an OPI and asked 14 native speakers of Spanish with a minimum of training in the use of the ACTFL rating scale to rate them. Barnwell found that the four students were placed in the same order of ability by all raters, but that three out of the four students were given vastly different band ratings by the native speakers and the trained ACTFL raters. The training of the ACTFL raters influenced the way in which they rate.

Barnwell (1989) suggests that the phenomenon of higher inter-rater reliability coefficients when using trained raters and lower coefficients when using untrained raters can be accounted for by the fact that trained raters undergo a period of 'socialisation'. During this period they begin to see 'speaking' in terms of the scale which they are using. By constant operation of the scale a high degree of reliability is achieved. Wilkinson (1968: 126) had previously argued in a similar vein that high inter-rater reliability could only be achieved when the assessors hold similar views about the nature of speaking. The process of rater training, the socialisation into a common view of spoken language, is described by Alderson (1991b: 64) as 'cloning', and in the AEI tradition as becoming an 'adept' (Lowe, 1986).

Although training reduces rater-related score variance, the fact that raters differ in their perception of what it is they are rating, and how, has therefore long been recognised. For example, McNamara (1996: 218–22) shows that in the Occupational English Test the raters are paying attention to grammatical accuracy rather than the communicative criteria embodied in the scale descriptors. Orr (2002) uses rater 'think aloud' protocols to identify the percentage of times FCE raters make judgements on the basis of criteria that are not contained in the rating scale. He concludes that raters frequently make judgements on the basis of their own personal constructs rather than the criteria in the rating scale.

Recently, the question has arisen as to whether these perceptions should be built into rating scales, so that the scale descriptors reflect rater perceptions. The assumption underlying such an approach is that rater training becomes less important for making consistent judgements than the parallelism between rater perceptions and descriptor content. Pollitt and Murray (1993) used Kelly's (1955) repertory grid procedure and Thurstone's (1959) method of paired comparisons to rank order speech samples. Once placed upon a scale the rater perceptions of why one sample was 'better' than another can be used to construct the verbal descriptors for the scale. In practice, this is precisely how Upshur and Turner (1995) approach the development of rating scales as well. Brown *et al.* (2001) also work on the assumption that rating scales can be constructed from the rater perceptions of speech samples. The real question here is whether information on the variety of perceptions should be built into the rating scales, or used as information to support rater training programmes (Brown, 2000). The former solution may just compound the problem of variable perception and its inevitable subjectivity by trying to pack as much of it as possible into a rating scale. In an attempt to mirror variable perception the method may simply produce a scale without meaning to anyone. If, on the other hand, the variable perception identified in these studies is taken to represent the types of variation that are likely to occur in a group of trainee raters, it may be possible to reduce more effectively the impact of the perceptions in the interpretation of a rating scale.

The practice of rater training

We have indicated that whether raters should be trained at all, and what the purpose of the training is, has been questioned. The radical solutions are to welcome the diversity of perception to a dialectic of assessment (Moss, 1992, 1994), or to build the diversity into the rating scale. But for all practical purposes, the objective remains to reduce the amount of variance in test scores due to the individual differences and perceptions of raters. The process of rater training is designed to 'socialise' raters into a common understanding of the scale descriptors, and train them to apply these consistently in operational speaking tests (Alderson *et al.* 1995: 108).

The pattern of training is common across institutions and testing agencies. During the piloting of a new speaking test, many sample performances are collected either on audio tape or video. These sample performances are scored as part of the process of creating the rating scale, or piloting the prototype tasks (see Chapter 5). A range of samples that typify each of the bands or levels on the rating scale are collected, and edited onto a single videotape. The video performances are used in two ways. One selection is provided to trainee raters as typical of a particular level. The trainees are usually required to attend a training session in which they watch the video, the trainer draws their attention to key features of the performance, and relates these to the rating scale. The trainees are invited to discuss each performance. A second selection of performances is then used in a certification procedure. The trainee raters are required to score a set of performances, of which as many as 80 per cent should be given the precise score that was awarded by the test developers, 15 per cent within one band, and no more than 5 per cent 2 bands away. Should the trainee rater not achieve these levels of accuracy they are not certified to rate operational speaking tests.

Re-certification for high-stakes speaking tests usually occurs at one- or two-year intervals. What little evidence there is for changes in rater consistency over time suggests random changes occur over a period of 18 months (McNamara, 1996: 237–8), but this is an area that requires further research before it is possible to recommend fixed times for re-training and re-certification on a sound empirical basis.

Rater training using samples typical of levels ('benchmark samples'), using at least 2 raters, and investigating drift from a standard, have resulted in the high levels of rater reliability across a wide range of performance assessments, including language tests (Brennan, 1996). To some extent these findings have justified the view that reliability in speaking tests is 'not a problem' (Bachman, 1988: 150).

Rater training and the validity argument

While this position is defensible, it is also misleading. Variation in severity between raters has now been identified as a cause for concern, as has the change in the severity of individual raters over time. There is also a more philosophical debate over whether reliability is necessary, or even desirable, as we have seen. However, for all practical purposes, it is necessary to maintain as much consistency in rater performance as possible. This is true in large-scale international speaking tests, and speaking tests used in specific institutions. But there is one more problem that needs to be addressed, and that is the relationship between rater training and the development of a validity argument for a speaking test.

Rater training *presumes* that the rating scale designed for the test is 'valid' and that training raters to use it in operational testing situations is legitimate. By 'valid' here, we mean that the rating scale has been constructed in some principled way, and that the level descriptors are meaningful for the purpose of the test, so that the inferences that score users make from the scores can be justified theoretically and empirically. Part of the validity argument will require using individuals to make judgements about sets of performances on sample tasks, and the consistency with which they are able to make those judgements contributes to validity evidence. If raters are trained, 'socialised' or 'cloned' before the validity argument is constructed, the training itself becomes a facet of the test that cannot be separated from the construct. This fusion contaminates any validity evidence that uses scores from these raters.

We could train a chimp to hit the keys of a piano in a sequence that we would recognise as a familiar tune. We cannot use the evidence of the tune-playing chimp in a validity argument for a theory of the development of musical ability in primates. In an ACTFL validity study (discussed in more detail in Chapter 7), Dandonoli and Henning (1990) took speech samples judged by trained ACFL raters to be typical of ACTFL levels, and jumbled the sequence. Two different trained ACTFL raters were then asked to match the speech samples to ACTFL levels. It is not surprising that they were able to do this accurately, but the evidence cannot be used as part of a validity argument for scale meaning (Fulcher, 1996b).

Raters should not be trained until after a validity argument has been constructed. This was the practice in the construction of the European Framework (North, 1996/2000), the data-based approach to scale development (Fulcher, 1993) and construct validity investigations that rely on scores from different groups of raters (Chalhoub-Deville, 1995b: 263). Two examples will help to make this argument clearer. In Fulcher (1993) part of the validity argument for a data-based rating scale was that the difficulty of achieving a particular band on a rating scale would be more consistent across tasks and untrained raters for a data-based rating scale than a scale constructed by other methods. The principle was that the rating-scale descriptors would be more consistently applied to new speech samples by raters, irrespective of the task being used, because the band descriptors described actual language use. If the raters had been trained before the data had been collected it would have been obvious that the raters would agree more highly because of the training, and not because of the quality of the descriptors. A second example comes from the growing interest in the process of rating, and what raters bring to the rating process. This research requires raters to reflect upon the rating process and verbalise what it is that they are paying attention to when making rating decisions (Milanovic and Saville, 1994). If raters have been successfully trained in a particular rating system, or socialised in the AEI tradition, for example, it is much more likely that they will 'think' in terms of the system that they are using. When using verbal reporting techniques (see Chapter 8) with trained raters the primary purpose of the research is to discover if the raters are applying the criteria in which they have been trained, or whether they are bringing personal construct-irrelevant criteria to the rating process. If the techniques are used with non-trained raters it may be possible to discover whether the raters can apply the descriptors of a new rating scale to samples with little training, or even use features that raters pay attention to in the construction of rating scales if there is significant agreement across raters. In summary, if rater scores are to be used as part of a validity argument, it is questionable whether the evidence is acceptable if the scores come from trained raters.

INTERLOCUTOR TRAINING

The role of the interlocutor in speaking tests has received growing interest because of our understanding of the interactive nature of discourse, and the observation that some types of speaking tests, particularly the OPI, are not 'natural' conversation (van Lier, 1989; Lazaraton, 1992; Perrett, 1990; Johnson, 2001). Interlocutors may differ along a range of parameters that introduce variation into the speaking test, which may affect scores (Brown, 2003). This variability in test discourse is not surprising, as it has been found in non-test discourse (see Varonis and Gass, 1988) and in studies of co-construction of discourse (see Chapter 2). However, the assumption is that such variation in a speaking test is a confounding variable that reduces our confidence in the inferences we draw from scores. The University of Cambridge Local Examinations Syndicate has tackled this problem through the introduction of interlocutor scripts for most of its speaking tests, in order to reduce the difference between the talk of different interlocutors (see the examples from Cambridge Tests in Chapter 3).

Most of the work on the impact of the interlocutor has involved discourse analysis of interview type tests, primarily looking at how the interlocutor accommodates to the level of the test taker (Ross, 1992, 1998; Ross and Berwick, 1992), while Berwick and Ross (1996) also present evidence to suggest that the extent to which interlocutors accommodate is also dependent upon their own cultural background and first language. This research on accommodation has shown that interlocutors vary their speech on a range of strategies that support the test taker. The features of accommodation are provided in Table 6.2.

Ross (1992) suggests that the degree of accommodation provided in a speaking test should be taken into account when giving the score, so that the role of the interlocutor in creating the discourse is explicitly taken into account. He also recommends that interlocutor training should include the study of various forms of accommodation and support, so that unnecessary support that may affect scores is not provided for the test taker.

Table 6.2 Features of accommodation (Berwick and Ross, 1996: 50–1)

Feature	Definition
Display question	The interviewer asks for information which is already known to the interviewer or which the interview believes the interviewee ought to know.
Comprehension check	The interviewer checks on the interviewee's current understanding of the topic or of the interviewer's immediately preceding utterance.
Clarification request	The interviewer asks for a restatement of an immediately preceding utterance produced by the interviewee.
Or-question	The interviewer asks a question and immediately provides one or more options from which the interviewee may choose an answer.
Fronting	The interviewer provides one or more utterances to foreground a topic and set the stage for the interviewee's response.
Grammatical	The interviewer modifies the syntactic or simplification semantic structure of an utterance so as to facilitate comprehension.
Slowdown	The interviewer reduces the speed of an utterance.
Over-articulation	The interviewer exaggerates the pronunciation of words and phrases.
Other explanation	The interviewer draws on the perceived meaning of the interviewee's utterance and elaborates on words or phrases within the utterance.
Lexical simplification	The interviewer chooses what is assumed to be a simpler form of a word or phrase which the interviewer believes the interviewee is unable to comprehend.

Similarly, Lazaraton (1996a) identified six types of interlocutor support in the CASE: priming new topics before they are raised, supplying vocabulary or helping to complete a test taker's turn, giving evaluative responses (the 'good' which is typical of teacher talk), echoing or correcting test-taker talk (modelling language for the test taker), repeating questions slower with over-articulation to improve test-taker understanding, reformulating questions as statements that only require the test taker to confirm or disconfirm the statement, drawing conclusions for the test taker based on an answer they have provided to a question, and rephrasing questions to help test-taker understanding. The variability in support provided by an interlocutor means that the test-taking experience is frequently very different for each test taker. Lazaraton suggests that rater training should focus on the variable aspects of interlocutor support to make the interactions more similar. Failure to take this type of variability into account is a direct threat to score interpretation and fairness to all test takers (Lazaraton, 1996a: 19).

Variation has also been established in the selection of topics by different interviewers in the OPI (Brown and Lumley, 1997; Reed and Halleck, 1997), and how they ask questions (Ross, 1998; Lazaraton 1996b; He, 1998). This has given support to the claim of Stansfield and Kenyon (1992c: 349) that the semi-direct oral proficiency interview, in which there is no interlocutor, is 'fairer' than face-to-face speaking tests.

Two significant studies in the literature have found no significant variation in interlocutor behaviours. Young (1995) found no variation in interlocutor discourse by test taker proficiency. He used the model of topical organization in dyadic discourse, originally presented in Young and Milanovic (1992) to investigate conversational styles in interview tests. O'Loughlin (2001) found no impact of the gender of the interlocutor on ratings, and more significantly found no evidence of differences that may be expected in the discourse of male and female raters.

What emerges from the research to date is that, while there appears to be substantial variation in interlocutor discourse at some levels, this may not translate into a significant difference in rating. However, Brown (2003) studied two IELTS interviews reported in an earlier study by Brown and Hill (1998), in which the interlocutors are significantly different in their 'difficulty'. She shows that they elicit qualitatively different performances from the test takers, and attempts to relate the performance to the rating through retrospective verbal protocols. The 'easy' interlocutor uses the full range of accommodations discussed above, while the 'more difficult' interlocutor uses more closed questions, accepts more minimal responses, and allows longer pauses between turns in the interaction (waiting for the test taker to speak). Questions were found to be more inexplicit, and topic shifts more unnatural. Many of the questions are statements intended to act as questions, or 'or' questions that do not elicit extended responses. Brown characterises the interactive style of the harsher rater as leading to a 'state of attrition' (Jefferson, 1993), where interaction dries up completely. The rater protocols show that the raters scored the interview with the more difficult rater less highly because of the overall impression that there was less test-taker talk in that interview.

The real question, as Brown is clearly aware, is whether it is preferable for the test taker to get a higher score because the interlocutor accommodates enough to provide scaffolding for the interaction (she refers to the less difficult interlocutor as 'teacherly' in style), or whether the non-accommodative style of the more difficult rater represents a 'better' test because it more closely approximates the norms of (English) L1 conversational strategies.

Brown also draws attention to the need for interlocutor (interviewer) training, but does not suggest what form this might take. This may be because interlocutor training has not been undertaken as seriously, or for as long, as rater training. The score variation associated with raters has simply been known about for much longer than that associated with interlocutors. However, there has been plenty of advice given about how interlocutors should and should not behave. Kaulfers (1944: 142) writes:

The deportment of the examiner should suggest cordial, but businesslike informality. The complete absence of stereotyped mannerisms suggestive of 'executive frigidity' or 'pompous austerity' will help set the examinee at ease, and thus enable him to do his best.

A particularly good example of interlocutor training is the British Council's *VOTE: Oral Testing* video (1983). The advice to interlocutors (demonstrated in the video) includes:

- Don't correct the test taker when they make mistakes
- Don't speak so quickly that the test taker has difficulty understanding you
- Don't whisper, cover your mouth, or mumble
- Don't speak too much
- Don't be condescending (e.g. following an error in speaking, don't say 'It's a bit difficult isn't it, speaking English'.
- Don't be offensive (e.g. make negative comments about the test taker's culture, etc.)
- Maintain eye contact with the test taker
- Don't engage in other activities (e.g. reading the assessment criteria, or candidate forms) during the test

A still from the British Council (1983) Oral Testing video. Don't whisper, cover your mouth, or mumble, when talking to a test taker. If they cannot understand what you are saying you will not be able to elicit a ratable speech sample.

A still from the British Council (1983) Oral Testing video. Maintain eye contact, and avoid engaging in other activities during the speaking test. This results in increased gaps between turns because the test taker is not engaging in meaningful exchanges.

The first of these pieces of advice is Lazaraton's (1966a) modelling language for the test taker. The next three are related to naturalness of delivery, perhaps echoing the more recent concern with over-articulation, along with providing balance in the exchanges between interlocutor and test taker. The other points are much more closely related with the concern to establish a neutral but friendly 'rapport' with the test taker that enables the elicitation of a ratable speech sample without providing undue scaffolding (McNamara and Lumley, 1997; Lazaraton, 1996a).

This type of approach is ideal for training interlocutors, as it is possible to demonstrate on video good as well as poor practice for which there is clear research evidence. It would also be possible, where resources exist, to undertake practice sessions with students, supervised by more experienced interlocutors. This may even be appropriate where the amount of uncontrolled interaction between interlocutors and test takers is seriously reduced through the use of interlocutor frames, as in the University of Cambridge Local Examinations Syndicate speaking tests (see Chapter 3).

What is important to take away from the discussion of interlocutor training is that there is evidence for variability within performance that may have a variable impact upon test-taker performance and scores. If this is defined as part of the construct, the variability needs to be understood so that it does not become a built-in feature of unfairness to test takers (Lazaraton, 1996a). If it is not defined as part of the speaking construct, it needs to be controlled through interlocutor training and interlocutor frames that limit the possibilities for construct-irrelevant variability to affect test scores.

LOCAL PERFORMANCE CONDITIONS

In this discussion of local performance conditions we consider the possible impact of administration and environment on test-taker performance.

Administration

The quality and practice of test administration in language testing is frequently not discussed, and there is very little research in this area. Advice is usually based upon experience and anecdotal evidence. For example, I once arrived at a centre selected for a large-scale speaking test administration in which my role was an interlocutor/rater. The test centre was locked, and the caretaker did not arrive until 5 minutes before the test was due to begin. When the examiners and test takers entered the building there were no ushers to indicate which rooms were to be used. The caretaker then opened a number of classrooms and indicated that we could use whichever rooms we wanted. The floors had been mopped the previous evening (at the end of the school week), so all the tables and chairs were stacked against one wall. It is not difficult to see that this led to a situation that was frustrating for all concerned, and it is highly likely that performances and scores on this test would have been affected by the poor administrative arrangements. Bachman and Palmer (1996: 233) similarly report anecdotal evidence:

> For example, we once witnessed a large-scale administration of a standardised test in which the test administrator obviously felt hostile to the test takers. We could actually hear a rumble of discontent among the test takers prior to the start of the test, which was probably not conducive to their performing at their best.

Here are a few more, kindly provided by some of my students who are involved in speaking tests in different parts of the world:

> I examine for [ ]. Last Sunday, I went to a kindergarten. I was shown into the interview room fitted out with Liliputian furniture. The chair was 18 inches high, and the table 27 inches. When I pointed out to a member of staff that this might not be the perfect set-up given my somewhat er.. generous proportions, she smiled inanely, flapped her hands and disappeared from the scene. I conducted a few interviews sort of 'a la sumo', then junked the chair and sat on the floor.   ['Furniture' by John Coomber, Taiwan]

At [ ] one time I had to give the end of year oral exam in a staff room which was supposed to be empty. Halfway through, a Portuguese history teacher came in and proceeded to sit down and read his newspaper. When I protested, he insisted he wouldn't make any noise or get in the way. My colleague and the student also voiced exception to the situation, and he eventually left in a huff.

['Unwanted visitor' by Kathleen Beesley, Portugal]

Once my students were scheduled to take the oral [ ] exam. I wanted the exam to start at 8:00, so I told the examiners to arrive around 7:45 and I told the maintenance staff to make sure the building and classrooms were open by 7:30. I arrived at the school at 7:30 and found everything locked. Punctuality is not people's strong point here, so I thought I'd wait about 5–10 minutes. The raters as well as the first few students who were scheduled to be examined began to arrive and everything was still locked. So first I had to apologise to the raters and then the students and I tried to amuse the external examiners with all kinds of stories and jokes until the maintenance staff arrived at 8:20!!!! I then decided to say a few words in a sarcastic tone of voice to the maintenance staff (in front of the students and examiners) to show our anger. The staff concocted some story about how the car wouldn't start. I said, 'Yeah, right, I believe that!' The test began at 8:30.

['Closed doors' by Moshe Roth, Israel]

This is why administrators are required to make all necessary arrangements in advance of the test date, to arrive well in advance of the examiners and test takers, and ensure that everything that they will need is in place. If recording equipment is required, or if the test is computer-mediated, technicians must have switched on and checked all equipment in advance. Technicians must also remain on hand throughout the testing period in case any equipment ceases to work and replacements are needed.

In speaking tests it is also essential that there is an usher who will ensure that as test takers finish the test they leave the site without coming into contact with test takers who are yet to take the speaking test. It is frequently the case that only three or four forms of a test are used in any single administration. If there is contact between students it is easy to pass on information about specific prompts or topics. The usher needs to be trained to behave in a friendly but professional manner, using enough authority to maintain a secure system, but doing nothing that would have a negative psychological impact upon a test taker prior to taking the test.

However, there is virtually no empirical evidence to support this advice. It is intuitive and anecdotal, and would therefore benefit from more careful study in the future.

Environment

The same applies to the test-taking environment. Little actual research has been conducted, but plenty of intuitively good advice is to hand. Alderson *et al.* (1995: 117) advise that the waiting room be large and comfortable, 'but not so large that it overwhelms the candidate'. The British Council (1983) also suggested that there were some environments that would encourage spoken communication more than others.

Stills from the British Council (1983) Oral Testing video. It is suggested that interlocutor and test taker are situated in a position where there is no table between them, the décor and lighting is cheerful, and the furniture comfortable and reasonably casual. There should be no items in the room that may distract the test taker from the test. Such an environment is likely to produce a less threatening context in which the test taker will perform to the best of his or her ability.

Bachman and Palmer (1996: 231–2) relate the testing environment to the test specifications, which for them include a description of the physical conditions in which the test takes place. If the test includes a formal work-related role-play, the testing situation may require a formal desk, a telephone and so on. This reminds us that the type of advice that has been typical in language-testing books over the years has generally related only to the OPI, and not other task types. Nevertheless, for all types of speaking test, it is usually recommended that the physical conditions should include good (preferably natural) lighting, an absence of intended or unintended strong smells (e.g. from the perfume of the interlocutor or the toilets next door), and appropriate heating or cooling. The last is particularly important in hot climates. The room should also be protected from distracting noise.

Noise is the subject of one of the few pieces of research to address the test-taking environment. Powers *et al.* (2002) conducted a study to discover if test takers who were undertaking a computer-based test of speaking, and hence speaking into a microphone, distracted other test takers who were taking computer-based tests of reading in the same environment. They discovered, perhaps not surprisingly, that the 'irrelevant' speech lead to an increase in the amount of effort that other test takers had to make to concentrate, increased their test anxiety and generally reduced their scores. It is not unreasonable to speculate that having multiple speaking tests in a large hall would be equally disruptive. Similarly, in semi-direct speaking tests that are held in language laboratories or computer suites, care needs to be taken to shield test takers from the sound of others speaking.

To the extent that our environment impacts upon what we do, and the quality of what we do, the local conditions in which speaking tests are held are worthy of serious consideration. More research is needed in this area, and test administration should be considered seriously by test designers, whether or not they decide to include this in the test specifications. For it seems at least intuitively likely that poor local test conditions will impact negatively on test scores, and variability in local test conditions in large-scale tests will introduce unfairness into the testing process.

We conclude this section with Standard 5.4 of the Standards for Educational and Psychological Testing (1999):

> The testing environment should furnish reasonable comfort with minimal distractions.

> Comment: Noise, disruption in the testing area, extremes of temperature, poor lighting, inadequate work space, illegible materials, and so forth are among the conditions that should be avoided in testing situations. The testing site should be readily accessible. Testing sessions should be monitored where appropriate to assist the test taker when a need arises and to maintain proper administrative procedures.

TEST ACCOMMODATIONS

Test accommodations are defined as modifications or adaptations of the testing situation or the materials 'to minimize the impact of test-taker attributes that are not relevant to the construct that is the primary focus of the assessment' (AERA, 1999: 101). In other words, accommodations should be provided to test takers with disabilities in order to avoid the disability contributing towards the test score. The provision of accommodations is therefore driven by validity concerns. In the United States much of the discussion regarding language and test accommodations concerns students with limited English proficiency (LEP) taking content tests in English (Stansfield and Rivera, 2001). This is clearly a 'disability' for LEP test takers, but we are more concerned in this context with any personal, individual, factor that may lead to an invalid score being awarded on a speaking test.

When teachers or language testers are designing a speaking test, they should ask themselves whether any individuals in the intended test-taking population may suffer from certain disabilities, and if necessary conduct research into the types of accommodations that will make the test fairer for that sub-group of the population. This is a matter for research, to establish that the provision of the accommodation does actually reduce the impact of the disability upon the test score. It should not be assumed, for example, that if a test taker is dyslexic, providing additional time for the test will automatically compensate for dyslexia. There needs to be an explicit logical and empirical link between a disability and an accommodation. On the other hand, failure to provide an appropriate accommodation for test takers with disabilities is likely to result in unfairness and, in many areas of the world, is also illegal. In the United States, for example, failure to provide accommodations for groups listed in the Americans with Disabilities Act could lead to litigation.

Individuals who may need test accommodations are those who suffer from:

- psychiatric disorders (not including test anxiety) (ETS, 2001)
- learning disabilities (ETS, 1999a)
- Attention-Deficit/Hyperactivity Disorder (ETS, 1999b)
- physical disabilities, such as blindness or deafness (APA, 1999: 102)

The types of accommodations that are normally provided include:

- Additional time for the speaking test.
- Provision of additional breaks during testing time.
- Reader (for the blind or an individual with reading specific learning disabilities), to read any textual prompts, or explain any graphical input).
- Braille copies of any textual prompts for the blind.
- Sign language interpreter for the deaf (translation of interlocutor speech and/or test-taker responses).
- Large print copies of textual prompt material for the visually impaired.
- Modified response formats for individuals with severe speech impediments.
- Provision of special furniture or other physical equipment (e.g. special chairs)

The problem with providing accommodations in tests is that they are highly likely to change the construct being tested. For example, if a speaking test is taken through the medium of a sign language interpreter, is the second language speaking test really a test of second language speaking? (See additional information from the National Task Force on Equity in Testing Deaf and Hard of Hearing Individuals at Gallaudet University, available online at: http://gri.gallaudet.edu/TestEquity/accommodations.html)

This brings us very conveniently to the vexed issue of score reporting.

REPORTING SPEAKING TEST SCORES: FLAGGING

We have already noted that it is important to report scores to users in ways that they can understand. Alderson (1991a) has suggested that this can be done through user-oriented scales, which may be simplified versions of the rater-oriented scales. However, a very real problem arises when there has been an accommodation in the test. This problem relates to the practice of 'flagging' scores. A *flag* indicates to the score user that the test taker has had the test modified in some way. In the 1985 edition of the Standards for Educational and Psychological Testing, the relevant standard reads:

> Until tests have been validated for people who have specific handicapping conditions, test publishers should issue cautionary statements in manuals and elsewhere regarding confidence in interpretations based on such test scores.
>
> (AERA, 1985: 79)

By 1999 this had been changed to:

When there is credible evidence of score comparability across regular and modified administrations, no flag should be attached to a score. When such evidence is lacking, specific information about the nature of the modification should be provided, if permitted by law, to assist test users properly to interpret and act on test scores.   (APA, 1999: 108)

This is also reflected in the ETS Standards for Quality and Fairness:

Provide appropriate and reasonable accommodations for people with disabilities, in accordance with applicable laws and client's policies.   (ETS, 2000b: 20)

In the 1985 and the 1999 Standards documents, and the 2000 ETS Standards document, the primary advice is that additional studies should be conducted to establish the equivalent meaning of scores on the standard test form taken by the majority of test takers, and forms with accommodations for specific disabled sub-groups. If this has been done the test is sensitive to the same construct across these sub-groups of the test-taking population and test format. However, if the accommodation changes the test construct the meaning of the score has changed, and so the testing agency is obliged to indicate that the score may not mean the same *in this context.*

After a speaking test we must ask whether it is appropriate to issue a certificate or report that indicates the test taker communicated through a sign language interpreter. Or should we report that because of a severe speech impediment a test taker was allowed to write answers to spoken questions? The problem with flagging accommodations is the possibility that the test taker is stigmatized in such a way that it impairs their educational or employment opportunities as a result of the flag. Consider the report of a court case relating to test score flagging in the following text box. The claim at the heart of the court case is that issuing a flag with a test score prejudices an individual's chance of college admission, and that an admissions officer may in some way be biased when dealing with an applicant who is forced to disclose a disability at the stage of applying to study at college. In research using survey and interview methods Mandinach *et al.* (2002: 2) report that Admissions Officers notice the flags when used, and:

Flagged scores are given the same weight as unflagged scores, and the flag has no impact on the chances of admission (surveys). Flagging helps to make admission decisions that are beneficial to the applicants with disabilities. Thus, respondents reported that the removal of the flag definitely will harm these students (interviews).

Guidance Counsellors also thought that the flag should remain, while disability service providers argue strongly that flags should never be used as it forces self-disclosure of disability, and may be harmful to the educational opportunities of the individual.

Test score flagging tested in court

This article is provided as a courtesy service of the Great Lakes ADA News Service under a subcontract with the Disability News Services and funded by the US Department of Education, NIDRR #133D60011.

By Mike Ervin
Copyright ©2000 The Disability News Service, Inc.

The Americans with Disabilities Act (ADA) case of Breimhorst v. Educational Testing Service (ETS), C-99-3387, challenges ETS's practice of using the words 'scores obtained under special conditions' to flag scores of test takers with disabilities who use accommodation.

Among the tests ETS administers are the Scholastic Aptitude Test (SAT), the Graduate Record Exam (GRE) and the Graduate Management Admissions Test (GMAT). In 1998, Mark Breimhorst of California sat for the GMAT because he wanted to attend business school. Breimhorst, who has no hands, received accommodations to take the test on a computer equipped with a track-ball, and to have the time limit extended by 25 per cent. When Breimhorst obtained his GMAT report, the disclaimer was attached to his score. He asked ETS to remove it, but the testing service refused. In August 1999, Breimhorst filed suit in US District Court for the Northern District of California, alleging test-score flagging violates the ADA and Section 504 of the Rehabilitation Act because ETS receives federal funding, as well as California civil codes.

Organizational plaintiffs include the International Dyslexia Association and Californians for Disability Rights with legal representation provided by Disability Rights Advocates of Oakland, California. The suit alleges the ETS disclaimer sends a 'stigmatizing message that people with disabilities obtain an unfair advantage when they receive accommodations, and that their scores should therefore be viewed with skepticism'. The suit contends ETS's practice also forces those with flagged test scores 'to disclose and explain away their disabilities to admissions offices, potential employers and other entities which receive the score reports'. The suit seeks injunctive relief to end the flagging practice, compensatory, treble and punitive damages.

On March 27, District Court Judge William Orrick denied a motion by ETS attorneys to dismiss all charges. Orrick wrote, 'If the testing provider complies fully with the requirement that its tests measure equally the abilities of disabled and nondisabled test takers, there would be no need for flagging.'

Tom Ewing, manager of media relations for ETS, said he could not comment on the case as long as litigation is in process.

This work was performed under a subcontract with the Board of Trustees of the University of Illinois, and funded by the US Department of Education, NIDRR #133D60011.

Of course, this is in the context of large-scale, high-stakes testing, in the United States. However, the ethical (and possibly legal) issues apply to all testing where the scores are going to be shared with others who may make decisions on the basis of the scores.

Phillips (1994) asks five questions about whether an accommodation is appropriate. He suggests that if we answer 'yes' to any question the accommodation may threaten any validity claim or argument that has been made by the test developer:

- Will format changes or alterations in testing conditions change the skill being measured?
- Will the scores of examinees tested under standard conditions have a different meaning than scores for examinees tested with the requested accommodation?
- Would non-disabled examinees benefit if allowed the same accommodation?
- Does the disabled examinee have any capability for adapting to standard test administration conditions?
- Is the disability evidence or testing accommodation policy based on procedures with doubtful validity and reliabilty?

We have already commented on the first two of these questions. With regard to the third, if non-disabled test takers could benefit from the accommodation, there is incentive to abuse the system by claiming a disability in order to get an accommodation, such as additional time. This leads to the final question, which requires that significant evidence should be collected to ensure that there is a disability before an appropriate accommodation is granted.

The issue of flagging in score reporting is primarily a concern for testing agencies that run large-scale, high-stakes tests. But readers of this section who use speaking tests in any way beyond that of a classroom progress quiz should also consider whether there is someone who might take your test who could be negatively affected because of a disability. Perhaps progress to the next level is dependent upon a 'good' score on the speaking test? Or perhaps the result will be recorded on a transcript of achievement?

No one who gives tests, produces scores and uses those scores for making decisions can completely avoid the ethical and fairness issues that surround some of the most practical aspects of how we administer tests and report scores.

BUDGETING FOR SPEAKING TEST DESIGN

Very little has been written about how much it costs to design and deliver a speaking test. And yet cost is a key part of whether or not it is practical to use a speaking test at all, whether a cheaper semi-direct test is to be used instead of a face-to-face interaction, and the number and length of task types that can be included. These considerations impact on the complexity of the test construct, and the potential generalisabilty of the score meaning. Referring to assignments submitted for a Language Testing module on an MSc in

English Language Teaching Management, Fulcher (2002) notes that most managers assume the resourcing of a language test development process to involve:

(a) cover for teaching hours of staff to write the test (typically one day)
(b) attendance at a training session for raters (perhaps an afternoon)
(c) some clerical support for typing and photocopying
(d) photocopying any test materials

Bachman and Palmer (1996: 161–2) are among the very few authors to address resource allocation and costs. They present a single table that covers physical resources, human resources, and honoraria paid to test takers for test piloting. They suggest that this can be undertaken in two phases. In the first phase resources and activities are identified, and in the second phase the cost is estimated in a budget. However, this model continues to suggest that test development is a relatively inexpensive process. For example, the 'test writers' are costed at $15 per hour, and will be required for 25 hours, giving a total cost of $375. These are the key personnel who do tasks such as collect material, write tasks, edit material, and undertake any recording that is necessary (ibid., 158). If a test is properly developed from prototype tasks through scoring systems, to test specifications, with appropriate studies to inform validity being conducted as necessary, the estimate of 25 hours is clearly inadequate as the maximum time allocated for test writing. Secondly, the Bachman and Palmer example does not set out the presuppositions that are necessary to cost a test development project and decide upon its practicality for the situation. All we are told is that it is a 'teacher-directed' project. But even in institutional programmes there may be infrastructure charge allocations for all activities, oncosts (such as National Insurance or contributions to pension schemes) that need to be allocated pro rata to staff activities, fixed costs depending upon timelines, and variable costs that change depending upon the number of iterations necessary in piloting prototype items. So, even if we assume that a very low-stakes teacher-devised test takes 25 hours to write, it is highly unlikely that the cost would be as low as $375 in real terms.

In what follows we are going to present a worked budget for the development of a speaking test. All budgets will look slightly different, because they depend upon local conditions, and the range of assumptions underlying the testing activity. However, the model that is presented here shows quite clearly the kind of costing implications that are attached to assumptions, and may be used by others as a way of evaluating the cost-effectiveness and practicality of implementing a speaking test.

Assumptions

1. The speaking test is being designed for a large language school in which the programmes have a significant speaking component in the syllabus. Numbers taking the test are expected to vary each year, but test volumes are expected to be approximately 240, in two administrations of 120. The

students are preparing for a prestigious national examination with a speaking component.

2. The test results are used to decide whether an individual is (a) ready to take the national test, and (b) should be promoted to the next level within the school. A poor performance in the test would result in the student being held in the same class until they were ready to take the test. The school cannot accept a large number of failures in the national test as this would have a negative impact upon its recruitment when comparative statistics are produced. The test is therefore high-stakes for the students and the institution.

3. Testing is not considered a 'core activity' of the institution. That is, the test is not going to be developed on a commercial basis for sale to other institutions. It is an internal activity.

4. It will not be necessary to design and research test accommodations.

Pre-activity costs

All institutions must allocate expenditure to income. That is, everything they spend on their activities should be accounted for by a source of revenue, whether this is public or private. In the case of this speaking test it is not being 'sold' as a core activity, in the same way that the language classes are being sold to students. It therefore doesn't attract any pre-activity costs. But what would such costs be, should the school decide to start selling the test to other institutions? These might include: dedicated/permanent staff salaries (for example, a share of the salaries of secretaries), a proportion of the rent or other building maintenance costs, rates or taxes, heating, lighting, or general office equipment. The principle is that any core activity must bear a proportion of the basic running costs (often referred to as the 'overhead' or 'infrastructure charge') of the institution.

Activity costs

Activity costs are those related to the tasks that need to be carried out and the related costs of those tasks. In what follows you will see that most of the activities listed are related directly to those we have discussed in Chapters 5 and 6, which describe the test development process.

1. Identifying the design team

For the development of this speaking test a project manager (testing specialist) is required. Three permanent teachers will be needed, secretarial time for clerical assistance (including taking minutes), an external teacher to support some activities and provide an independent point of view and a junior secretary to undertake some of the more routine typing. We will also need students to take our prototype tasks and be involved in the larger pilots of the new test, and we will have to pay them for their time. Example 6.1 identifies how much these people earn (based on rates in the United Kingdom).

Example 6.1 The cost of the design team

Salary costs: permanent staff
To discover the daily cost of permanent staff, add the gross annual salary to the additional annual costs to the employer (e.g. pension, holiday pay, bonuses, contributions, any hidden extra cost, etc.) and divide by the number of working days per year = daily cost.

N.B. the number of working days per year = number of days someone could work per year (e.g. excludes Sundays, public holidays, etc.) + number of days paid holiday entitlement per year

Staff member	Annual salary	Additional costs	Total cost	Working days	Daily cost
Specialist A	£38,603	£8486	£47,089	210	£224.23
Teacher A	£26,491	£5499	£31,990	215	£148.79
Teacher B	£24,435	£5040	£29,475	215	£137.09
Teacher C	£18,655	£3751	£22,406	215	£104.21
Secretary A	£13,310	£2740	£16,050	220	£72.95

Salary costs: external staff bought in for the project
For external staff will probably be bought in on an hourly rate of pay. The sum of the hourly rate of pay and any additional costs (see above) multiplied by the number of working hours in the day = daily cost.

Staff member	Hourly pay	Additional costs	Working hours per day	Daily cost
Teacher D	£24.00	£1.99	7	£181.93
Secretary B	£7.00	£2.83	7	£65.66

Type of work	Hourly pay	Additional costs	Paid by hour	Hourly cost
Test taker	£5.00	£0.00		£5.00

2. Identifying additional resources needed

Apart from the staff required to undertake test development it is highly likely that additional equipment or resources may be needed. This might include software for data analysis, stationery, toner for printers, paper, photocopying, telephone calls, the hire of rooms if suitable facilities are not available in the school, audio or video tapes, and so on. We will assume that this project requires some additional test analysis software at £1,000, stationery (communication with test takers, memos, etc.) at £50, 2 printer toners at £65 each (£130), 1,000 photocopies at 0.07p per copy (£70), and some telephone calls (£10). Videotapes will also be needed to record students during the piloting phase (£100) This is a total cost of £1,360 for resources, which may be an underestimate.

3. Defining test purpose

As we have seen, defining test purpose is one of the key critical activities at the start of the test design process. In the case of this school the purpose of the test is fairly clear, but it needs to be discussed and written out as part of the test specification very clearly as it will also form part of a document explaining to students and stakeholders (sponsors, parents) why the test is needed and what types of decisions will be made on the basis of the test. This is the public rationale for the test.

Example 6.2 Defining test purpose

Salary costs: permanent staff

Staff member	Daily cost	Days on activity	Staff costs
Specialist A	£224.23	1	£224.23
Teacher A	£148.79	1	£148.79
Teacher B	£137.09	1	£137.09
Teacher C	£104.21	1	£104.21
Secretary A	£72.95	1	£72.95
Subtotal permanent staff costs for activity =			£687.27

Salary costs: external staff bought in for the project

Staff member	Daily cost	Days on activity	Staff costs
Teacher D	£181.93	1	£181.93
Secretary B	£65.66	0	£0
Subtotal external staff costs for activity =			£181.93
Total staff costs for activity =			£869.20

---

4. Defining the construct

Defining the test construct is the most important of the activities the team will undertake. We have seen that this is essentially a group activity that leads into the process of writing test specifications and task types and, being iterative (see Chapter 5), requires a significant amount of time. Team members will also undertake relevant literature reviews and write these up as reports for the group. For this project we have estimated the need for 5 working days to decide what the test is supposed to measure and to write down the agreed construct definition.

Example 6.3 Defining the construct

Salary costs: permanent staff

Staff member	Daily cost	Days on activity	Staff costs
Specialist A	£224.23	5	£1121.15
Teacher A	£148.79	5	£743.95
Teacher B	£137.09	5	£685.45
Teacher C	£104.21	5	£521.05
Secretary A	£72.95	1.5	£109.43
Subtotal permanent staff costs for activity =			£3181.03

Salary costs: external staff bought in for the project

Staff member	Daily cost	Days on activity	Staff costs
Teacher D	£181.93	5	£909.65
Secretary B	£65.66	1	£65.66
Subtotal external staff costs for activity =			£975.31
Total staff costs for this stage =			£4156.34

5. Designing prototype tasks

In this activity the team write a wide variety of prototype tasks that are designed to measure the construct, which can be piloted on samples of students drawn from the test-taking population. This process will also include time to collect and evaluate appropriate prompt material. For our test we assume that one month will be enough to undertake this work.

Example 6.4 Designing prototype tasks

Salary costs: permanent staff

Staff member	Daily cost	Days on activity	Staff costs
Specialist A	£224.23	20	£4484.65
Teacher A	£148.79	20	£2975.80
Teacher B	£137.09	20	£2741.80
Teacher C	£104.21	20	£2084.20
Secretary A	£72.95	5	£364.75
Subtotal permanent staff costs for activity =			£12,651.20

Salary costs: external staff bought in for the project

Staff member	Daily cost	Days on activity	Staff costs
Teacher D	£181.93	20	£3638.60
Secretary B	£65.66	5	£328.30
Subtotal external staff costs for activity =			£3966.90
Total staff costs for this stage =			£16,618.10

---

6. Piloting and evaluating prototype tasks

Before tasks can be evaluating and refined, and selections made for inclusion in the final test design, students drawn from the target test-taking population need to attempt the tasks. The feedback from students and teachers will provide critical information on the appropriateness of the tasks for making inferences to the test construct. It is assumed that many tasks will be revised iteratively and re-trialled on another small group of students. For this reason we include the cost of using 80 students, each for a 1-hour period.

Example 6.5 Piloting prototype tasks

Salary costs: permanent staff

Staff member	Daily cost	Days on activity	Staff costs
Specialist A	£224.23	10	£2242.3
Teacher A	£148.79	10	£1487.90
Teacher B	£137.09	10	£1370.90
Teacher C	£104.21	10	£1042.10
Secretary A	£72.95	2	£145.90
Subtotal permanent staff costs for this stage =			£6289.10

Salary costs: external staff bought in for the project

Staff member	Daily cost	Days on activity	Staff costs
Teacher D	£181.93	10	£1819.30
Secretary B	£65.66	3	£196.98
Subtotal external staff costs for activity =			£2016.28

Type of work	Hourly cost	Hours activity	Costs
Students × 80	£5.00	1	£400.00
Subtotal student costs for activity =			£400.00
Total external staff and student costs for activity =			£2416.28
Total staff costs for activity =			£8705.38

7. Designing rating scales and band descriptors

Although this activity is simultaneous with the design and piloting of prototype items it can be budgeted separately in order to indicate that it is one of the key design activities within the process. After all, there is no point in designing wonderful new task types if the performances cannot be scored.

Example 6.6 Designing rating scales and band descriptors

Salary costs: permanent staff

Staff member	Daily cost	Days on activity	Staff costs
Specialist A	£224.23	10	£2242.30
Teacher A	£148.79	10	£1487.90
Teacher B	£137.09	10	£1370.90
Teacher C	£104.21	10	£1042.10
Secretary A	£72.95	2	£145.90
Subtotal permanent staff costs for activity =			£6289.10

Salary costs: external staff bought in for the project

Staff member	Daily cost	Days on activity	Staff costs
Teacher D	£181.93	10	£1819.30
Secretary B	£65.66	3	£196.98
Subtotal external staff costs for activity =			£2016.28
Total staff costs for activity =			£8305.38

8. Writing task administration and other administrative documents for inter-locutors/administrations/ushers

In order to ensure that the tasks included in the operational test are delivered in a standardised manner this documentation should be written up as carefully as possible by the team.

Example 6.7 Writing administration documents

Salary costs: permanent staff

Staff member	Daily cost	Days on activity	Staff costs
Specialist A	£224.23	2	£448.46
Teacher A	£148.79	2	£297.58
Teacher B	£137.09	2	£274.18
Teacher C	£104.21	2	£208.42
Secretary A	£72.95	0	£0.00
Subtotal permanent staff costs for activity =			£1228.64

Salary costs: external staff bought in for the project

Staff member	Daily cost	Days on activity	Staff costs
Teacher D	£181.93	0	£0.00
Secretary B	£65.66	1	£65.66
Subtotal external staff costs for activity =			£65.66
Total external staff costs for activity =			£65.66
Total staff costs for this stage =			£1294.43

---

9. Writing test specifications

Once again, the process of writing test specifications is not a discrete activity, as we have shown in Chapter 5. It goes on simultaneously with all the other test development activities. Nevertheless, the process of putting the pieces together into a document should be budgeted separately. The test specifications will be used to develop new forms of the test, and also acts as a key element in a validity argument.

Example 6.8 Writing test specifications

Salary costs: permanent staff

Staff member	Daily cost	Days on activity	Staff costs
Specialist A	£224.23	10	£2242.30
Teacher A	£148.79	10	£1487.90
Teacher B	£137.09	10	£1370.90
Teacher C	£104.21	10	£1042.10
Secretary A	£72.95	2	£145.90
Subtotal permanent staff costs for activity =			£6289.10

Salary costs: external staff bought in for the project

Staff member	Daily cost	Days on activity	Staff costs
Teacher D	£181.93	10	£1819.30
Secretary B	£65.66	3	£196.98
Subtotal external staff costs for activity =			£2016.28
Total staff costs for activity =			£8305.38

10. Designing training materials for interlocutors and raters, and under-
    taking training
When the test is ready to go into operational use the interlocutors and
raters will be drawn from the teacher population in the school, not just the
project team. We must therefore cost in time for the production of training
materials, and for actual training.

Example 6.9 Designing training materials for raters and interlocutors

Salary costs: permanent staff

Staff member	Daily cost	Days on activity	Staff costs
Specialist A	£224.23	0	£0.00
Teacher A	£148.79	15	£2231.85
Teacher B	£137.09	15	£2056.35
Teacher C	£104.21	0	£0.00
Secretary A	£72.95	0	£0.00
Subtotal permanent staff costs for this stage = £4288.20			

Salary costs: external staff bought in for the project

Staff member	Daily cost	Days on activity	Staff costs
Teacher D	£181.93	0	£0.00
Secretary B	£65.66	7	£459.62
Subtotal external staff costs for activity =			£459.62
Total staff costs for activity =			£4747.82

Example 6.10 Training raters and interlocutors

Salary costs: permanent staff

Staff member	Daily cost	Days on activity	Staff costs
Specialist A	£224.23	0	£0.00
Teacher A	£148.79	0	£0.00
Teacher B	£137.09	2	£274.18
Teacher C	£104.21	0	£0.00
Secretary A	£72.95	0	£0.00
Subtotal permanent staff costs for activity =			£274.18

Salary costs: external staff bought in for the project

Staff member	Daily cost	Days on activity	Staff costs
Teacher D	£0.00	0	£0.00
Secretary B	£65.66	0	£0.00
Subtotal external staff costs for activity =			£0.00
Total staff costs for activity =			£274.18

11. Basic research

In Chapter 5 we talked about some of the types of research that may be necessary to support test design decisions. It may also be necessary to conduct research that supports the inferences that the school wishes to draw from the scores. For example, we may wish to investigate the question of whether the test is capable of discriminating between students who have passed the national test and those who have failed. A budgetary allocation for investigating such questions should be established to support the validation argument.

Example 6.11 Research allocations

Salary costs: permanent staff

Staff member	Daily cost	Days on activity	Staff costs
Specialist A	£224.23	20	£4484.60
Teacher A	£148.79	20	£2975.80
Teacher B	£137.09	0	£0.00
Teacher C	£104.21	0	£0.00
Secretary A	£72.95	2	£145.90
Subtotal permanent staff costs for activity =			£7606.30

Salary costs: external staff bought in for the project

Staff member	Daily cost	Days on activity	Staff costs
Teacher D	£181.93	0	£0.00
Secretary B	£65.66	8	£525.28
Subtotal external staff costs for activity =			£525.28

Type of work	Hourly cost	Hours activity	Costs
Students × 20	£5.00	1	£100.00
Subtotal student costs for activity =			£100.00
Total external staff costs for activity =			£625.28
Total staff costs for activity =			£8231.58

The total cost of our test development project is £62,867.79 on a real-cost basis. But this is really what it costs to develop one form of a speaking test if all the appropriate steps for a fairly high-stakes test are to be followed. The figure would be higher if the test was for large-scale international testing. Of course, for low-stakes tests it is possible to decide which of the activities can be shortened, done by fewer people, or even left out. However, all such decisions to cut costs should be made explicitly, and the resulting inferences and decisions that are made on test scores adjusted accordingly. Institutions should be careful to get the balance of cost and claims/decisions right. While there is a significant cost (both direct and in 'lost opportunities') in careful test development, there is a significantly higher cost if a test taker subsequently takes the institution to court on the grounds that an unfair and unjustified decision, made on the basis of a test score, has negatively impacted on his or her educational or employment opportunities (Fulcher and Bamford, 1996).

There are other things that may have to be budgeted at the outset of a test. The examples provided will give a good idea of how this may be done, and so I won't continue to do this here. Probably one form of a test will not be enough for security reasons. And the test may be used for many years. So it is advisable to budget for the production of additional forms of the test. Training may have to be a yearly or six-monthly activity, depending upon how frequently current raters need to be re-certified, and the rate of staff turnover. Each year it will be necessary to review the test and the specifications to ensure that it is still appropriate for the inferences you wish to make and the decisions that are being taken. This may involve all the staff who use the test, perhaps for a half day, and a meeting of the test development team for another half day. This implies that the test specifications may evolve to reflect changes in curriculum or the national test, and once again these activities should be placed in the budget for future years. Last, but certainly not least, are the test running costs. Once the test becomes operational how many interlocutors and raters will be needed to process the expected number of test takers? How much will this cost? If each performance is rated twice, will this be done 'live' or will the second rating be done at a later time from audio or video tape? What are the resource implications? How many rooms will be required for testing? Will this impact on the normal teaching operations of the school, and is there a cost implication (perhaps from loss of revenue from core activities)?

In Chapter 1 we saw that one of the reasons for the widespread use of new-style (multiple choice) tests, even though the value of performance tests was acknowledged, was their practicality. This section has tried to show some of the financial and practical implications of using speaking tests. Testing speaking is certainly not a cheap option, and good budgeting as part of a test development project is an essential component in the assessment of practicality.

DIGEST

In this chapter we have tried to look at a wide range of practical issues, including rater training, interlocutor training, test administration, local test conditions, providing accommodations, score reporting and budgeting.

Throughout the discussion we have seen that it is really impossible to separate these practical issues from the central concept of validity. Even when it comes to looking at how much it might cost to design a speaking test from which we might make valid inferences we see that for many institutions there may need to be a trade-off between what they can afford and the degree of validity needed for the intended purpose of the test.

What is most important is that as teachers and test developers make decisions, often for practical reasons, they understand and document why decisions are taken, record the constraints under which the work is being undertaken, and state clearly what impact the decisions have upon what validity claims can be made.

In the next chapter we consider the evaluation of speaking tests and investigate the types of evidence that we may wish to consider when deciding whether the tests we develop or use are worthy of the validity claims made for them.

Chapter 7

Evaluating second language speaking tests

A test score interpretation always involves an *interpretive argument*, with the test score as a premise and the statements and decisions involved in the interpretation as conclusions. The inferences in the interpretative argument depend on various assumptions, which may be more-or-less credible. For example, inferences from test scores to nontest behavior involve assumptions about the relationship between test behavior and nontest behavior; inferences from test scores to theoretical constructs depend on assumptions included in the theory defining the construct. Because it is not possible to prove all of the assumptions in the interpretative argument, it is not possible to verify this interpretive argument in any absolute sense. The best that can be done is to show that the interpretive argument is highly plausible, given all available evidence.

(Kane, 1992: 527)

This chapter focuses on the types of evidence that may be presented to support validity arguments, which (hopefully) strengthen the bond between the test score and the inferences which we draw from the score. As Kane makes clear in the quotation above, there is never going to be an absolute guarantee that a test score means what we think it does. Validity is not an 'all or nothing' affair, it is an ongoing activity to improve an argument and gather evidence to support the argument. Deciding 'if a test is appropriate for a particular purpose' involves critically evaluating the plausibility of the argument and the evidence used to support the argument.

The first section of this chapter focuses on the AEI tradition of testing speaking, from the original FSI to the ACTFL. This is primarily because there has been more critical evaluation of the OPI than any other approach to testing speaking, partly because it has had a longer history than other speaking tests (see Chapter 1). The validity argument has been questioned on the grounds the approach lacks theory and what validity argument does exist lacks empirical support. Despite this, the ACTFL has been widely used in the design of foreign language curricula and teaching programmes. A number of empirical studies will be discussed, but the conclusion of this section is that the validity argument relies almost entirely on claims of face validity, and that the language testers' 'experience' of successfully working with the testing system for many years should reassure the critics and score users.

We then turn to a consideration of testing students in pairs, or groups. The University of Cambridge Local Examinations Syndicate introduced the paired format into all of its main suite examinations in the 1990s, and it has caused considerable controversy. Foot (1999a) in particular has raised a series of issues that questions whether scores from tests utilising the paired format can be used to make inferences to the speaking construct. For example, the score for one individual may be more sensitive to who he or she is paired with, rather than their own 'speaking ability'. UCLES are therefore obliged to construct a validity argument that supports the introduction of this practice. We consider the reasons for the use of the paired or group format in speaking tests, evaluate some of the currently available evidence, and argue that 'on balance' the most plausible argument is that the format provides an opportunity to test a much richer and more complex construct than is possible in the traditional interview. However, it is always possible that at some point in the future the plausibility of the argument may increase or decrease, as the argument evolves and further evidence is amassed.

From 'direct' testing (only implying that 'direct' involves interaction with a human interlocutor, and nothing more), we consider validity arguments surrounding what in this chapter we refer to as 'indirect' speaking tests (tests in which there is no human interlocutor), one form of which is the simulated oral proficiency interview, or SOPI. The traditional validity argument for indirect speaking tests has been that they measure the same construct as direct speaking tests. The evidence used to support this argument has been mainly correlational, and many studies have been conducted to show that scores on an indirect test can *predict* the scores on a direct test. The argument is that if scores on two tests are so highly associated that one can predict from one to the other, the tests must be 'construct-equivalent'. The strong form of the argument is found in Stansfield (1991: 206):

> An examination of the SOPI research, which has been carried out on different examinees, on tests of different languages produced by different test development teams, shows that the SOPI correlates so highly with the OPI that it seems safe to say that both measures test the same abilities. The SOPI has also shown itself to be at least as reliable as the OPI, and in some cases more so. Thus, it seems safe to conclude that it is as good as an OPI in many situations.

We look at the assumptions underlying this use of correlation, and consider the evidence presented to support the argument. With the publication of the work of Shohamy *et al.* (1991) and Shohamy (1994) the argument began to fail, as the assumptions and evidence were questioned. New evidence was produced using a broader range of methodologies, and we now find that it is no longer possible to support the construct-equivalent validity argument.

The three examples selected here are not meant to be typical of validity arguments in the testing of speaking. We encounter different validity arguments depending on test purpose, the type of test used, who the test takers are, how the scores are used and by whom, and on the political and social context that provides the 'test mandate' (Davidson and Lynch, 2002; see also Shohamy, 2001). The examples are very different, and are illustrative of the philosophical, methodological and sociopolitical issues that we may come across when evaluating the use of speaking tests in a range of contexts.

Finally in this chapter we consider the work of Messick (1989, 1992, 1995, 1996) as a model that can be used to help us focus on critical aspects of evaluating validity arguments.

THE FSI TRADITION OF TESTING SPEAKING

The FSI tradition of testing speaking has been extensively critiqued. We outlined the approach to rating-scale design in Chapter 4 and to reliability in Chapter 6. In this discussion we will talk about all the variations within this family. It will inevitably focus once more on the place of the rating scale within the testing system and the 'theory' of 'language proficiency' that it expresses. The further extended treatment of the FSI tradition in this chapter is quite natural, as it represents the earliest and most influential of all approaches to the testing of second language speaking, spreading from the military to schools and colleges, and becoming the basis for curriculum design in modern foreign language teaching in the United States (see Chapter 1).

We have seen that one of the most important issues with regard to the rating scales in the FSI family of tests is that none of them have any 'empirical underpinning' (Lantolf and Frawley, 1985; Pienemann *et al.*, 1988: 218), and that Lowe (1987: 46) admitted that there have been few studies into the reliability and validity of the FSI/ILR OPI. The assumption underlying the use of a rating scale is that each of the levels represents a higher level of language ability than the one before, and that the descriptors within a scale describe the construct being measured. But if research into how students acquire or use language has not been taken into account, the testing procedure can easily become the focus of criticism. The criticism usually arises in relation to particular words or concepts that appear in the scale descriptors. Pienemann *et al.* (1988: 219) criticise in particular the concept of 'weakness' in a scale, such as that in band 2+ of the ILR scale (see Chapter 4, Appendix 1). They argue that:

> Such descriptions are so vague and general as to be utterly unhelpful in distinguishing any second language learner from another. If 'areas of weakness' can be construed to mean areas in which learners' usage does not conform to the standard, then every language learner conforms to this description. Numerous research studies have shown that learners do not suddenly 'learn' a structure and begin to use it correctly 100 per cent of the time.... Even the most advanced of second language learners will therefore display 'weaknesses' in the areas cited.

Similarly, Valdman (1988: 121) has argued that:

> it is fair to say that although the OPI (Oral Proficiency Interview) may be experientially based, its theoretical underpinnings are shaky and its empirical support scanty.

We are frequently reminded that without a sound empirical basis for test design and development it makes little sense to investigate validity *post hoc* when results cannot be related to initial hypotheses and constructs. For example, Jarvis (1986: 21) argues that:

> After-the-fact inquiry is unacceptable and has historically degenerated into little more than validation of flawed systems.

The link between descriptors and language elicited by tasks

Another problem relates to the language of the band descriptors, where there is little or no evidence to show the link between the descriptor and language produced on an OPI task. The following example is not a transcript of an actual interview, but a constructed dialogue to exemplify the difference between a Novice-level conversation and an Intermediate-level conversation on the ACTFL taken from Liskin-Gasparro (1984a: 480).

Novice-level conversation

Teacher: Tell me about your family.
Student: (Silence)
Teacher: How many people are in your family?
Student: Four.
Teacher: Who are they?
Student: Mother. Father. Brother. Me.
Teacher: Tell me something about your brother.
Student: (Silence)
Teacher: How old is your brother?
Student: 14.
Teacher: What is his name?
Student: John.

Intermediate-level conversation

Teacher: Tell me about your family.
Student: I have four people in my family. I have a mother. I have a father. I have a brother.
Teacher: Tell me about your brother.
Student: My brother's name is John. He is 14. He plays football. He plays the violin.

It is claimed that this second example shows that the student has 'crossed the all-important threshold from operating with memorised material and isolated words and phrases at the Novice level to creating with language at the Intermediate level' (Liskin-Gasparro, 1984a: 481).

Constructed conversations produced *post hoc* to justify the band descriptors can hardly be used to support validity arguments. Much more sophisticated approaches to discourse analysis need to be applied to actual performances on test takes before it is possible to make claims of this sort.

The Functional Trisection

A further justification of the ACTFL rating scale descriptors is found in the Functional Trisection, which was designed to provide the scale with a functional/notional emphasis (Liskin-Gasparro, 1984b: 35). The Functional Trisection has also been used by other researchers in the testing of speaking, notably Adams *et al.* (1987) and Griffin *et al.* (1988). It is claimed that each level in the ACTFL rating scale contains statements about what the students can do in three areas: (1) the linguistic functions or tasks that a candidate can perform, (2) the context, or topics that can be handled, and (3) the degree of accuracy with which the message will be communicated or understood. In order to give content to these three 'functions', five linguistic factors are taken into account: grammar, vocabulary, fluency, pronunciation and sociocultural ability. The Functional Trisection for levels within the ACTFL rating scale is given here in full:

Level 0 (Novice categories are not separated)

Function: No functional ability.
Context: None.
Accuracy: Unintelligible.

Level 1 (Intermediate)

Function: Can create with the language, ask and answer questions, participate in short conversations.
Context: Everyday survival topics and courtesy requirements.
Accuracy: Intelligible to native speaker used to dealing with foreigners.

Level 2 (Advanced)

Function: Able to fully participate in casual conversations, can express facts, give instructions, describe, report and provide narration about current, past and future activities.
Context: Concrete topics such as own background, family interests, work, travel and current events.
Accuracy: Understandable to native speaker not used to dealing with foreigners, sometimes miscommunicates.

Level 3 (Superior)

Function: Can converse in formal and informal situations, resolve problem situations, deal with unfamiliar topics, provide explanations, describe in detail, offer supported opinions and hypothesise.

Context: Practical, social, professional and abstract topics, particular interests and special fields of competence.
Accuracy: Errors never interfere with understanding and rarely disturb the native speaker. Only sporadic errors in basic structures.

Level 4 (Superior)

Function: Able to tailor language to fit audience, counsel, persuade, negotiate, represent a point of view and interpret for dignitaries.
Context: All topics normally pertinent to professional needs.
Accuracy: Nearly equivalent to an educated native speaker (ENS). Speech is extensive, precise, appropriate to every occasion with only occasional errors.

Level 5 (Superior)

Function: Functions equivalent to an educated native speaker.
Context: All subjects.
Accuracy: Performance equivalent to an educated native speaker.

Functions are defined as the tasks accomplished, attitudes expressed and the tone conveyed. Context refers to topics, subject areas, activities and jobs addressed. Accuracy is the acceptability, quality and accuracy of the message conveyed. There appears to be a mismatch between the Functional Trisection and the rating scale it was designed to defend. The Novice descriptions (especially Novice High) do not correspond with either the description in the rating scale or the example of constructed speech provided by Liskin-Gasparro to exemplify the kind of language which might be expected from a test taker at this level. Further, the Superior level is broken down into three sections within the Functional Trisection implying that these represent a linear development in language proficiency, while in the rating scale the Superior category is not broken down into subcategories (see Chapter 1, Appendices 3 and 4). As we can see from Figure 7.1, the assumption is that each level is qualitatively and quantitatively more difficult to achieve than the previous level. Very little progress in learning a language is needed to gain a higher band in the early stages of language learning and much more progress needed to register improvement in the later stages (Lowe, 1985a: 21). Finally, there is a 'non-compensatory' approach to rating. This means that everything in a band descriptor must have been achieved before a test taker can be placed in a higher band. There is little justification for this strictly linear 'building block' view of language acquisition in the literature.

From testing to curriculum

Despite the problems, the model of language learning assumed by the successors to the FSI, the ACTFL/ETS/ILR (AEI) speaking tests, has become the basis for a whole approach to language teaching as well as language testing, the Proficiency Movement. The wide acceptance of the principles of the movement constitutes a strong claim for the validity of the AEI approach to testing speaking. For example, Lowe (1987: 47) claims that

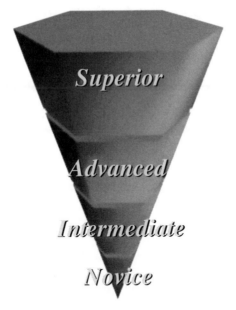

Figure 7.1   The Functional Trisection (http://www.languagetesting.com/scale.htm)

Its [the AEI model of language acquisition as represented in the band descriptors of the rating scale] ultimate utility may lie beyond testing per se in its effect on curriculum. In this case, teaching for the test – teaching for general functional foreign language ability – is not to be discouraged.

The strong form of this argument is that 'testing drives curriculum' (Lowe, 1983: 238–9). Similarly, Liskin-Gasparro (1984b: 35) claims that the ACTFL Guidelines are the first step in

creating proficiency-based curricula that respond to the need of the profession to define what students should be able to do with the language at various stages in the learning process.

However, limits to the usefulness of teaching to the test and positive washback effect on curriculum have been set. While accepting the importance of the ACTFL Guidelines for testing speaking, Brown (1985) has argued that the ACTFL global rating scale cannot be used for evaluation in the classroom as it does not provide adequate informative feedback to the learner. Similarly, Liskin-Gasparro (1984a: 486) writes that:

it is important to remember that the ACTFL Guidelines are not curriculum outlines, nor are they prescriptions for what grammatical structures to teach and when. They are a graduated sequence of proficiency states around which a foreign language program may be structured. The day-to-day activities that constitute the sequence of small steps in the context of the larger phases identified by the Guidelines, as well as the methods to be used, are still and always will be the province of the foreign language teacher.

Although limits are placed on the usefulness of the Guidelines in the classroom, this latter quotation amounts to a claim that the AEI band descriptors in the rating scales represent the way in which learners actually acquire language (Barnwell, 1987; Pienemann *et al.*, 1988). Language programmes are therefore often based around the ACTFL level descriptors (Magnan, 1986a: 429) and the oral proficiency interview elicitation techniques and tasks for each ability level used as teaching techniques (Magnan, 1986b). Clark (1988a) argues that washback from the AEI approach to testing has changed the way in which language is taught, introducing realistic communicative activities into the classroom.

Research has shown that the links between testing and teaching are not as clear as this (Alderson and Hamp-Lyons, 1996; Alderson and Wall, 1993; Bailey, 1996; Messick, 1996; Wall, 1997, 2000). There is no guarantee that the use of a particular type of test or testing system will automatically lead to better teaching. And there is always the basic concern whether the use of a descriptive system that has little theoretical or empirical support is capable of providing either a framework for teaching and learning, or a sound basis for the provision of feedback to language learners.

Rating scales

Among the most vehement critics of the Proficiency Movement and the rating scales upon which it is based are Lantolf and Frawley (1985, 1988), who believe that the whole approach to testing speaking is flawed.

With reference to the Proficiency Movement and the curriculum implications which have been implemented throughout the United States, Lantolf and Frawley point to a number of inconsistencies which cast doubt upon the whole process. They review two studies concerning the number of hours required to achieve the 2/2+ level. In Western Europe Brod (1982) claims that approximately 480 hours of study are needed to reach this level, while Lambert *et al.* (1984) claim that some 840 hours of intensive study are required. Given such different claims without any published evidence to suggest that either claim is accurate, Lantolf and Frawley ask how it is possible to proceed with curriculum reorganisation based upon descriptors from AEI tests.

Lantolf and Frawley (1985: 2–3) and Barnwell (1987: 40) also question the assumption that it is possible for students to achieve greater accuracy on familiar rather than unfamiliar task topics (ibid., 2–3). This is an explicit assumption of the rating scale band descriptors. Little evidence exists to suggest that there is a relationship between accuracy of language production and the degree of 'abstractness' or familiarity with the topic. The research into subject specificity in Language for Specific Purposes tests is relevant here, and we recall that it has been extremely difficult to isolate any subject or topic factors that contribute significantly to task difficulty, unless extremely obscure topics are chosen for test tasks (Fulcher, 1999).

Another assumption questioned by Lantolf and Frawley is that there is a difference in speech comprehension between speakers who are used to dealing with foreigners and those who are not. This difference is built into the band descriptors in a number of places, but it is an assumption which has not been verified. One of the few studies which has been used to support this distinction within the scales is that of Chastain (1980), which reported on reactions by native speakers to errors made in Spanish by intermediate students. The main problem with Chastain's study is that the 'errors' which were presented to the naive native speakers were constructed one-sentence examples written on paper. Chastain acknowledges the limitations of the study and states that the results would need to be subject to replication (ibid., 214). Van Patten (1986: 62) is particularly critical of this kind of generalisation, arguing that the lack of a speech database which could be used to support generalisations does not help the cause of the Proficiency Movement. We would also note that other researchers have come to the opposite conclusion, namely that native speakers unfamiliar with the L1 of the second language speaker are generally extremely tolerant of a learner's attempts to communicate, compared to the harshness of non-native teachers familiar with the student's L1 (Sheorey, 1986). Barnwell (1989) has studied naive target language speaker reaction to actual interview data, and found low agreement between them when judging the quality of second language speaker talk. He also discovered that they were unable to relate their perceptions of the second language speaker talk to the ACTFL/ETS rating scale without training.

Language acquisition

The main problem which Lantolf and Frawley (1985, 1988) see in the AEI rating scales is the underlying philosophical assumptions in the position taken with regard to how they represent levels of language acquisition.

They claim that the approach to testing developed is 'analytical' rather than empirical, but the analytical approach is presented as if it were empirical truth. The concept of the Functional Trisection is singled out for particularly harsh criticism. Lantolf and Frawley argue that the statements made by Liskin-Gasparro (1984b) and Lowe (1985a) 'may have nothing to do with real-world performance' and that 'such criterion-referenced tests *impose* competencies on examinees and measure the extent to which the person deals with the imposition' (Lantolf and Frawley, 1985: 339–40). They make a distinction between test language as reflected in the rating scales and real-world language.

Lantolf and Frawley (1985: 340) put their case in this way:

> An informal look at the logic of speaker-levels and linguistic guidelines for determining performance underscores our argument: (1) assume, from informal observation, that some speakers of L2 are better than others, and rank these speakers in groups labelled from one to five (or one to three, in the case of the ACTFL/ETS Guidelines); (2) with speakers grouped, abstractly, from one to five, decide how to put people into these groups; (3) define each

of these *a priori* groups in terms of linguistic criteria also organised from simple to complex (i.e. 1 to 5). It is not difficult to see the analytic logic here. The levels (1 to 5) do not exist except in terms of linguistic criteria which define them. That is, the logic of the levels and of their criteria is symmetric implication: X (levels) $\longleftrightarrow$ Y (criteria). What is a 'low-novice?' Someone 'unable to function in the spoken language'. What is someone 'unable to function in the spoken language?' A 'low-novice'. This logic does not yield criterion-referenced tests, but criterion-reductive tests: the criteria are the levels and vice versa.

Because the levels are criterion-reductive, many of the statements made by researchers concerning the levels and the criteria are understandable, if erroneous. Liskin-Gasparro states that the Guidelines are 'absolute definitions'. They must be 'absolute definitions' since they are analytic and reductive. The criteria, as absolutes, are then converted into requirements, because the criteria are required absolutely to define the levels. When the criteria are converted into requirements, one can argue, as Liskin-Gasparro and Omaggio do, that speakers must be judged in relation to their acquisition of the requirements: i.e. the acquisition of the analytically derived and absolute requirements which define each level – the acquisition of the so-called 'competencies which lie at each level'. With the criteria as analytic and reductive, it is impossible to evaluate L2 speakers with regard to the Guidelines. It is only possible to evaluate L2 speakers as they are in the Guidelines, because the Guidelines are absolute and reductive.

Lantolf and Frawley therefore claim that learners are being evaluated by a series of discrete stages through the law of non-contradiction: one cannot be in one level and in another. Level descriptors logically exclude all other levels. When it comes to applying these to the curriculum, this amounts to saying that the 'reductive definitions' are also teachable.

Further, because the definitions of the levels are measured against an 'educated native speaker' they claim that far from being a criterion-referenced test, the level descriptors are in fact norm-referenced. And, as we have seen in Chapter 4, defining a native speaker for the purposes of testing is extremely difficult.

Lantolf and Frawley (1988) refer to the 'psychometric posture' of the Proficiency Guidelines. They claim that the rating scale provides the 'illusion' that something is being measured, whereas in reality no metric exists. They provide as evidence the fact that the FSI has five levels within its scale, the ASLPR has nine, and Bachman and Savignon (1986) suggest that there are really only three. Lantolf and Frawley agree with Vollmer (1983) that 'proficiency' is what proficiency tests measure, and this will continue to be the case until a more empirical approach to rating-scale development and number of levels described is attempted, which is precisely what was undertaken in the work of Fulcher (1993, 1996b) and North (1996/2000) described in Chapter 4, and the work of Pollitt (1991b: 90). Unless it is possible to show that what is described in the bands of the rating scale relates to the way in which students acquire language and how they really speak, the rating scale and the model of acquisition of language it claims to describe will be open to this type of criticism (Pienemann *et al.*, 1988).

Validity concerns

As we have seen in Chapters 4 and 6, one of the main defences of the AEI approach to testing speaking is the 'face validity' of the tasks and elicitation techniques, and 'experience' in the use of the scale. Bachman and Savignon (1986: 381–2) argued that the fallacy of face validity lies in the notion that 'direct' tests (defined as 'valid') as opposed to 'indirect' tests (defined as not 'valid') lead to the production of 'normal' or 'real' language. 'Direct' tests have been considered automatically 'valid' by definition. The argument is tautologous. We have seen that this is the position of FSI and AEI proponents (Wilds, 1979; Lowe, 1983, 1986, 1987; Liskin-Gasparro, 1984a). Bachman and Savignon raise two objections to this position. Firstly, we have no definition of what 'normal' or 'real' speech is (or even if there is such a thing). The band descriptors do not provide any operational definitions. Secondly, the argument presented for validity using the claim of 'directness' confuses 'behavioural manifestations' with the construct. Bachman and Savignon (1986: 382) say:

> As with all mental measures, language tests are indirect indicators of the under-lying traits in which we are interested.

In this respect, all oral tests are indirect measures of the construct, and therefore it is illegitimate to rely on face validity. It is necessary to present a validity argument for every speaking test. Although the second of Bachman and Savignon's arguments is presented from a trait-theory position, which we may sometimes wish to dilute, it is difficult to disagree with their analysis.

Bachman (1988) argues that in order to investigate the construct of validity speaking tests it is necessary to separate the constructs to be measured from the tasks and elicitation techniques used. Although we have seen that there are some situations in which we may wish to include features of tasks in the definition of the construct (Chapelle, 1999b), this is more likely to be the case where there is a very good reason to do so on the grounds of the specificity of the test for a particular purpose, and where there is no need to generalise the ability to speak beyond the specific tasks contained in the test. The problem highlighted by Bachman is compounded where a single rating scale represents a global assessment of speaking ability, which has 'no basis in either current linguistic theory or empirical work in language testing' (Bachman, 1988: 63).

A response to Bachman came in a study by Dandonoli and Henning (1990) and Henning (1992b) which used a multitrait-multimethod (MTMM) design (see Chapter 8) to investigate claims that test method and trait (construct) were confused. In the MTMM the only test-method facet to be specified in the design was that of raters, and only two raters were used. Further, these two raters were trained and accredited ACTFL/ETS raters. It is thus quite possible that the results obtained by Dandonoli and Henning are an artefact of the rigorous training of the raters used (see Chapter 6). Secondly, in the Rasch analysis of speaking ability no test method facets were specified at all. Thirdly, two ratings of the same performance cannot be said to count as separate methods. Although the results do appear to be impressive, we are not only faced with the possibility that they too are an artefact of rater training, but they could have been caused by test-method facets such as the task or elicitation procedure. Fulcher (1996c) also points out that the speech samples used in the study were made 'such that one tape . . . was reliably judged to be at each proficiency level' (Dandonoli and Henning, 1990: 20). In other words, typical speech samples rated as such by trained raters were selected for the study, and then two more trained raters had to identify the levels of which the speech samples were typical. Impressive results were therefore to be expected if the training procedures were at all effective. Finally, Fulcher (1996c) reanalysed the correlation matrix presented in the study, and found that the correlations were so exceptionally high that the matrix was singular; in other words, despite small observed differences these were not significant, and there was no evidence for divergent validity.

Other empirical studies are also of note. Adams (1980) investigated the relationship between the five sub-scales on the FSI (fluency, comprehension, grammar, vocabulary and accent) and global ratings to discover which of the sub-scales successfully discriminate between learners at different ability levels. Bachman and Palmer (1981, 1983) conducted a multitrait-multimethod study to investigate the effect of method traits on the assessment of speaking and reading, in which one of the methods was the FSI testing procedure. Magnan (1986a) and Meredith (1990) conducted studies to discover whether the AEI testing procedure was capable of discriminating between groups of students who had been placed into teaching groups by other methods.

Adams (1980) used ratings of 834 tests conducted during the summer of 1978 in 33 languages. She used discriminant analysis in order to investigate the extent to which any factor was significantly contributing to the final score at any given proficiency level. Adams's results are presented in Table 7.1.

This table shows which of the five factors discriminate effectively at each level of the FSI rating scale. Although it would seem that different factors appear to be more salient at each level of the scale, it is almost impossible to relate the results theoretically to the FSI level descriptors, as there is no pattern to the discrimination. Nevertheless, Adams concluded that as the FSI raters first record a global score and then record the factor scores to explain it, the study showed that at certain levels raters are more sensitive to different aspects of performance. Adams uses this as an argument against the use of untrained raters as they cannot be aware of the complexity of the rating process in determining the proficiency of a student.

Bachman and Palmer (1981, 1983) observed that much speaking-test validation research was concerned with correlating scores on rating scales with external criterion tests. The criterion was often the FSI as it was assumed to be valid. Bachman and Palmer pointed out that an assumption is not a demonstration of validity, and called for construct validation research into

Table 7.1 FSI rating components reported to discriminate at each level in the FSI rating scale (Adams, 1980)

FSI level	Discriminating factors in descending order of significance
0+–1	Vocabulary
1–1+	Fluency Comprehension Grammar Vocabulary
1+–2	Comprehension Grammar Accent Fluency
2–2+	Fluency Comprehension Accent Vocabulary
2+–3	Grammar Accent Vocabulary Comprehension
3–3+	Comprehension Fluency Grammar
3+–4	Vocabulary Accent Grammar
4–4+	Grammar Vocabulary

the FSI. Using a multitrait-multimethod approach following Campbell and Fiske (1959) and confirmatory factor analysis after Joreskog (1969), Bachman and Palmer analysed the test scores on two traits (speaking and reading comprehension) measured by three methods (the FSI oral interview, translation and self-rating).

Reliabilities for the tests ranged from 0.85 to 0.99, and convergent validity from 0.46 to 0.97. For discriminant validity, 65 per cent of the results satisfied the criterion for speaking and 63 per cent for reading. Method effect was found to be prominent in the translation and self-rating methods, but not in the oral interview. The most important result for the FSI was the finding in the factor analysis that it loaded most heavily on the speaking trait (0.82) and had the lowest loading on the method factor (0.46). Bachman and Palmer (1983: 168) concluded that the oral interview maximises the effect of trait while minimising the effect of test method.

They felt confident that they had provided important evidence for the convergent and discriminant validity of the FSI. It is not without significance that this study is frequently quoted as one of the few which clearly provides evidence for the validity of the FSI oral interview, but is also taken, by implication, as providing evidence for the validity of the AEI rating scales and testing procedures also (Lowe, 1987: 46).

Magnan (1986a) and Meredith (1990) go some way toward providing evidence for validity by group discrimination for the AEI oral testing procedure which, while important (Clark, 1988a: 17–18), is a weak form of validity evidence.

Magnan (1986a) describes a study carried out at the University of Wisconsin to investigate the relationship between the level of study and the level of proficiency of French students as measured by the ACTFL rating scale. This investigation of validity by group differences used 40 students, 10 from each level of the French program. The learners were tested by a certified ACTFL interviewer and the interviews taped and rated by two independent raters from Educational Testing Service. Inter-rater reliability was reported as 0.72, which was not as high as Magnan had hypothesised it would be.

Magnan discovered some overlap between ACTFL band scores and level of study, which is presented in Table 7.2. However, this overlap could be accounted for by the rating error. Magnan (1986a: 431–2) justifiably concluded that there is, on the whole, a general relationship between years of study and proficiency ratings, except for the third and fourth year, where she argues that the ACTFL scale is not sensitive enough at the higher levels.

Meredith (1990) repeated Magnan's study using students of Spanish at Brigham Young University, and concluded that the ACTFL rating scale, as it stands, is 'a very blunt instrument'. After trying to make the rating scale more sensitive to years of language study, Meredith could only report a highest correlation of 0.57 between ACTFL ratings and length of study (ibid., 294).

The studies reported here are not part of a validation research agenda for a major approach to testing speaking. While some limited validity evidence has emerged from these studies, they do not constitute a validity argument. This is perhaps because of the over-reliance on the appeal to face validity.

Table 7.2 The relationship between ACTFL scores and years of study (Magnan, 1986a)

Year	Range	Median
1st Year	N-mid–I-mid/high	I-low/mid
2nd Year	I-low–Advanced	I-mid
3rd Year	I-mid/high–Adv/Adv+	I-high/Adv
4th Year	I-mid–Adv+	Advanced

Face validity in speaking tests revisited

Wilds (1979) maintained that the validity of the FSI was 'unquestionable' because the oral interview was based upon a demonstration of speaking ability in a 'natural context' related to living and working abroad, and that the rating scale used in the scoring procedure described that speaking ability. Face validity, defined as 'the degree to which students feel they are performing a real communicative act' (Bartz, 1979), was thereby pushed to the fore in discussions of validity.

Such claims need to be treated with extreme caution. In the evaluation of speaking tests we need to ask whether a reasonable, if partial, validity argument has been presented to support the use of the test for its purpose. However, because so many writers working with speaking tests have appealed to face validity we will consider the issues in a little more detail.

The notion of face validity in the literature on testing speaking has four related aspects:

(a) the speaking test is 'direct' (Clark, 1975: 14)
(b) it involves a natural context and real-life tasks which produce natural conversation (Wilds, 1979; Lowe, 1987: 46)
(c) the rating scale describes distinguishable levels of speaking ability demonstrated in the test (Liskin-Gasparro, 1984b; Lowe, 1985a) and
(d) experience leads to the consistent application of criteria (Liskin-Gasparro, 1984a)

The first has been severely criticised on the grounds that no test can be direct in this sense: speaking tests usually aim to elicit a speech sample, or performance provides evidence of competence to speak, so that score meaning can be generalised to other test tasks, and 'real-life' speaking contexts (Bachman and Savignon, 1986: 382–3).

The second has been questioned on the basis of studies of 'interview talk' which suggest that the interview generates a special 'genre' of language different from normal conversational speech (Silverman, 1976; MacPhail, 1985; van Lier, 1989; Perrett, 1990; Lazaraton, 1992; Young and He, 1998; Johnson, 2001).

The third has been questioned on the basis of analysis of actual speech in comparison to band descriptors (Fulcher, 1987, 1989; Perrett, 1990; Matthews, 1990), the scalability of the bands of the rating scale (Pienemann *et al.*, 1988), and the epistemology of the endeavour (Lantolf and Frawley, 1985, 1988).

The fourth has been questioned on the grounds that experiential claims to validity do not constitute either theoretical rationale or empirical evidence (Bachman and Savignon, 1986; Kramsch, 1986a, 1986b).

The reliance on face validity was also common in the early period of communicative language testing in Britain (Fulcher, 2000). Using 'real-life tasks' that elicited 'natural language' was for many years the touchstone of validity (Morrow, 1982: 56–7). A claim to face validity has often been all that is used to defend an entire testing system including its rating scale (Barnwell, 1987: 36). During the 1980s it was not surprising to find that writers such as Stevenson (1981, 1985a, 1985b) who rejected the use of face validity as the sole criterion for evaluating speaking tests were criticised by the communicative 'common-sense' school of testing speaking (Underhill, 1987).

The use of 'experience' as a validity claim is particularly troublesome. This is mainly because it is difficult to question the claim. Its strongest expression is found in Lowe (1986), written in response to criticisms by Kramsch (1986b) and Bachman and Savignon (1986). Lowe (1986: 392) writes:

> The essence of the AEI proficiency lies not in verbal descriptions of it, but in its thirty-year-long tradition of practice – making training in AEI proficiency testing a desideratum.

He argues that those who question the validity of the AEI rating scales do so because they are not among the AEI 'adepts': those who have been trained in the system and understand the words on the paper. Those who have not been trained are incapable of understanding the rating scale. The argument is bordering on the metaphysical. An external researcher cannot question validity because he or she is not an 'adept', an 'insider'. One has to join the cult to truly understand.

Experiential claims to validity without supporting rationales and empirical evidence should be treated with extreme caution. We must conclude that the AEI validity argument is implausible given the lack of support for its assumptions.

TESTING SPEAKING IN PAIRS

We have seen that the earliest example of testing speaking with pairs of learners occurs in the Foreign Service Institute Tests (see Chapter 3), and these are now common throughout the University of Cambridge Local Examinations Syndicate suite of tests. Taylor (2000) lists the reasons why UCLES introduced the paired format into the Cambridge examination suite in the 1990s (although it was optional on the First Certificate in English and Certificate of Proficiency in English in the 1980s):

1. Testing in the United Kingdom has always been closely linked to language pedagogy, and communicative language teaching has widely used pairwork in the classroom. The introduction of the paired speaking test therefore brings the test into line with classroom practice.
2. Work on the one-to-one interview format (Ross and Berwick, 1992; Young and Milanovic, 1992) had shown that the interaction in the test was asymmetrical because of the unequal power of the two participants. The paired format therefore allowed a range of different interactions between the test takers, and between the test takers and the interlocutor.
3. In (unpublished) studies UCLES discovered that in the paired format candidate turns were increased, and the length of each turn varied greatly

across the test. The amount of talking time attributable to the assessor was substantially reduced. It is therefore claimed that the language sample is 'richer' than in a traditional interview.

4. The number of functions observed in paired-format tests is said to be much higher than in the interview.

Saville and Hargreaves (1999) argue that the use of the paired format should be seen in the context of test design, in which a variety of tasks are used to elicit a wider range of language. The FCE contains an interview (3 minutes), an individual long turn for each of the test takers (4 minutes), a two-way collaborative task (3 minutes), and a three-way discussion between the two test takers and the interlocutor (4 minutes). They claim that this allows the assessment of construct features ranging from responding to questions to managing discourse, coherence, organisation, accuracy and appropriacy, turn-taking, topic initiation, negotiating and developing topics. Although Saville and Hargreaves do not use this language, what they are claiming is that the format and range of task types selected allow a broad range of construct features to be represented in the test.

This may be true, but one of the continuing problems is that the evidence upon which the claims about the paired-interview format is made has not been published (Foot, 1999a, 1999b), an ongoing problem with examination boards (Hamp-Lyons, 1987) whose internal research is frequently considered proprietary information. As long as evidence that could support a validity argument for the practice is not in the public domain it is easier for critics to question the practice. Foot (1999a) raises many of the appropriate questions that should be asked about the paired format, although I supplement these in the discussion.

Firstly is the issue of who is paired with who. Should the two test takers be familiar with each other, or does it matter if they are strangers?

- Does it matter if their first language is not the same?
- Should they be at roughly the same stage of learning the second language, or can they be at different stages?
- If the age, race, social class or profession of the two test takers is different, would it make a difference to how they would interact?
- What is the affect of personality differences between test takers?
- Should test takers be paired if one is extrovert and the other introvert, for example?

Secondly, in the paired format there is an interlocutor and an 'observer' whose only task is to rate the two test takers.

- What is the impact of this role on the test takers?
- The interlocutor also rates the two candidates, although he or she also participates in the interaction. Does this enhance the validity of the rating process?
- How do the raters assign grades to each of the test takers separately when, given whatever differences there may be in all the candidate variables

listed above, one may be supporting another, one may not be providing the other with an opportunity to show how well he can 'negotiate' or take turns?

Thirdly, what is the role of the interlocutor in cases where the two test takers are incapable (as a pair) of undertaking a task?

- How much should the interlocutor intervene?
- What is the effect on discourse and scores if 'significant' intervention is required, or if one (probably the stronger) test taker gets more talking time than the other? Foot (1999b) correctly observes that inability to manage paired tasks is likely to be higher in younger and less proficient test takers.

Fourthly, in a 15-minute interview with four tasks that have to be explained by the interlocutor, is the speaking time for each of the test takers enough to elicit a ratable sample of speech?

Fifthly, does the test format result in a reduction or increase in test-taking anxiety, depending once again on the various combinations of 'pair types' that are possible?

Research in this area is growing, and centres on formats that include the paired format, and the group format, where 3 test takers are asked to undertake a task. For this discussion we will not separate the paired and group formats. The same issues are at stake, and it is permissible to have three test takers in the UCLES tests.

Folland and Robertson (1976) were among the earliest writers to recommend the use of more than one test taker in speaking tests, primarily on the grounds that it would reduce test anxiety (Berkoff, 1985). There have been reports of the successful use of such tests not only from UCLES, but in the Israeli school context (Reves, 1980, 1991; Shohamy *et al.*, 1986), Zambia (Hilsdon, 1991), Italy (Lombardo, 1984), and Hong Kong (Morrison and Lee, 1985). However, most of these reports were experiential, rather than based on research.

Fulcher (1996a) looked at the group discussion, in which two or three test takers were asked to discuss a topic after a 10-minute preparation period. They also took a picture description task, and a traditional interview test. The 47 students involved completed a questionnaire on each of the task types, and a sample of students provided stimulated recall data on their experiences (see Chapter 8). Fulcher reported that students generally thought the group-discussion task generated the most natural discourse, that it created the least pre-test anxiety, and that over half the test takers preferred the discussion to other task types. While studies of learner perception are important, the Fulcher study did not manipulate key variables such as personality or proficiency level.

Berry (1995, 1997, 1998) has undertaken extensive research into the interaction of introvert and extrovert students, and found that discourse varies according to the pairing. She has found that both introverts and extroverts performed better when placed in homogeneous pairs, whereas in mixed pairs introverts did not perform as well as extroverts. Further, the performance of introverts is affected more depending upon the degree of extroversion of the partner. Nevertheless, both introverts and extroverts performed better in a paired test than they did in a one-to-one interview. Investigating the impact of ability level, Iwashita (1998) discovered that lower ability test takers talked more when paired with a higher ability test taker, but that amount of talk was not related to test score. O'Sullivan (2002) investigated the impact of degree of familiarity of the test takers in paired speaking tests, hypothesising that performance (particularly in terms of grammatical accuracy) will improve when speakers are paired with a test taker with whom they are familiar. He concluded that female Japanese test takers receive higher scores when paired with a friend than with a stranger (whether the stranger is male or female). However, he acknowledges that the significant differences between the scores amounted to a very small real difference on the score range. O'Sullivan relies entirely upon significance statistics to conclude that there is very real concern that pairing a test taker with a stranger could lower the score. A reanalysis of his raw data yields a Cohen's D of 0.5, and an effect size of 0.24 (Cohen, 1988, 1992). Effect sizes frequently show that we cannot rely purely on significance statistics (p values), but should go on to see the size of the significant effect on the test scores. In this case, the effect size is medium, indicating that the scores of approximately 24 per cent (just over 1 in 5) of test takers *may* be affected by a familiarity factor. However, O'Sullivan only used 32 Japanese test takers in his study. Both the sample size and the fact that familiarity is more likely to be an important variable in the Japanese population, do not justify the conclusion that using unfamiliar partners is likely to be a potentially serious problem more generally. Indeed, evidence from the second-language acquisition literature provides evidence to support the use of unfamiliar pairs because each partner 'assumes a greater burden for the smooth flow of the conversation than in those conversations in which partners know one another' (Plough and Gass, 1993: 46).

The negotiation of meaning that takes place in paired or group interactions is increasingly being researched. It is claimed that this negotiation fuels second language acquisition (Swain and Lapkin, 2001). It is not surprising that the format is recommended for speaking tests on the grounds that 'dialogues construct cognitive and strategic processes which in turn construct student performances, information which may be invaluable in validating inferences drawn from test scores' (Swain, 2001: 274). In other words, the pair or group format may generate language performances that allow us to test much more complex constructs than in a traditional OPI. The problem would lie in defining constructs that recognise the 'co-construction' of discourse and meaning, where the speech sample(s) to be assessed are essentially seen as produced through interaction, collaboration, and support (McNamara, 1997).

The paired format has attracted significant criticism, but it opens up the possibility of enriching our construct definition, and hence the meaning of test scores. The validity argument is plausible given our current state of knowledge. As further research is conducted it may get stronger, or weaker.

INDIRECT SPEAKING TESTS

As we noted at the beginning of this chapter, in what follows, 'indirect' is used to mean a test in which there is no face-to-face interaction with an interlocutor, and is equivalent to the use of 'semi-direct' in some of the literature. The use of the term 'direct' only means that there is face-to-face interaction with a human interlocutor. We have discussed the tendency to associate 'direct' with 'valid', but in this discussion no such association is intended. A 'simulated oral proficiency interview' (SOPI) is an indirect test that tries to simulate a direct OPI in its structure, through the phases of warm-up, prompts of increasing difficulty (level checks/probes), and wind down.

While many speaking tests require the test taker to speak to a rater/interlocutor or with another test taker, there are many speaking tests in which the test taker is asked to speak into a microphone after being given a prompt to speak. These tests may be computer- or tape-mediated. We have seen examples of these tests in Chapter 3, primarily the PhonePass test (Ordinate) and the Test of Spoken English (Educational Testing Service). Some language testers favour speaking tests where there is interaction, as we have seen above when discussing the paired format. Others are equally adamant that the indirect test is preferable. Sometimes the preference relates entirely to practical considerations: an indirect test is used because a direct test would be too expensive, or because there aren't enough speakers of the target language in the place where the test will take place. But sometimes the difference grows out of very real philosophical differences. As we have seen, McNamara (1997) would almost always prefer face-to-face interaction using simulations and role plays where possible because the co-construction of meaning in discourse is seen as essential to communication. Stansfield (1991) and Stansfield and Kenyon (1992a, 1992b, 1992c), on the other hand, argue that the simulated oral proficiency interview is preferable to face-to-face tests because the variability that we have seen to be present with a human interlocutor introduces a threat to reliability. While one side of the argument places the interaction between human speakers at the heart of the testing speaking enterprise, the other wishes to remove the human element as a source of potential error.

Research into the indirect testing of speaking has mainly been concerned with comparing indirect tests to a range of face-to-face tests, and much of this has been correlational. Clark (1975: 19) claimed in the 1970s that the research necessary to investigate the relationship between indirect and face-to-face tests was 'for the most part lacking'. However, there was one exception. Carroll (1967) compared the Modern Language Association (MLA) Proficiency Battery (1965) with FSI-type oral interviews in four languages, and reported correlation coefficients of between 0.66 and 0.82. A study by Clifford (1978) also compared an FSI-type oral interview with the MLA Co-operative Proficiency Test in German, producing a correlation coefficient of 0.83. This was the only additional study that Clark could quote in 1979 (Clark, 1979: 40). Clifford's study was repeated by Dugan (1988) using the MLA English test and an ACTFL OPI, in which moderate correlations in the region of 0.7 were reported.

Cartier (1980: 8) reported correlations of 0.74 and 0.72 between the Defense Language Institute's Taped Oral Proficiency Test of Spanish (TOPT) and FSI interviews, and Lowe and Clifford (1980: 37) reported a correlation of 0.90 (using 27 students) in a comparison of the Recorded Oral Proficiency Examination (ROPE) developed for TESOL, and the Central Intelligence Agency version of the FSI Oral Proficiency Interview.

The motivation for these early studies was one of practicality. The methodology was correlation because the researchers wanted to decide whether or not an indirect test could legitimately substitute for a longer and more costly test.

Clark (1979: 48) for instance, states that:

> Semi-direct tests may be proposed as second-order substitutes for direct techniques when general proficiency measurement is at issue but it is not operationally possible to administer a direct test. In these instances, it is considered highly important to determine – through appropriate experimental means – a high level of correlation between the two types of instruments when used with representative examinee groups.

The position that indirect tests are 'second-order substitutes' for interviews has been repeated since (Clark, 1988b: 197, Clark and Lett, 1988: 13), and considerable evidence has been collected to show that correlations above 0.8 can be achieved fairly systematically on well-designed indirect tests of second-language speaking.

For example, the final version of the Test of Spoken English (TSE) was validated against the FSI with correlations ranging from 0.73 to 0.77 (Clark and Swinton, 1980a). The two research reports of Clark and Swinton (1980a and 1980b) are still regularly quoted as evidence for the validity of the TSE. Clark and Lett (1988: 13) report on the development of tests of Chinese. Clark (1986b, 1998b) and Clark and Li (1986) correlated the Chinese test with AEI tests, reporting correlations of 0.89 to 0.96.

While the motivation was practical, we can see that the approach begs many questions. Firstly, it is assumed that the FSI Oral Proficiency Interview is valid because it is a 'direct measure' (see the preceding discussion in this chapter). It is treated as the 'gold standard' to which other tests can be compared. Secondly, high correlations between two tests do not necessarily mean that we can draw the same or similar inferences from the test scores. Correlational evidence only indicates association and not causality. As Burroughs (1971: 263) wrote: 'the correlation between spelling ability and height is very large, but this is only because each is correlated with age'. We are reminded of Kaulfers (1944) reference to the 'correlational fallacy' discussed in Chapter 1.

Significant work has been done on the development of simulated oral proficiency interviews (SOPIs) (Stansfield, 1989), the aim of which is to model face-to-face communication as closely as possible, pitched at the Intermediate, Advanced and Superior levels of the ACTFL Guidelines. Stansfield (1990a: 229) specifically refers to the work of Clark (1986b, 1998b) and Clark and Li (1986) as the beginning of the SOPI, and which inspired the development of the Portuguese Speaking Test (PST). Correlations between the PST and the OPI were found to be of the order of 0.93 (Stansfield, 1990b). This led to the development of further SOPIs in other languages including the Hebrew Speaking Test (HeST) (Shohamy *et al.*, 1989) which produced correlations of 0.90 (Israeli version) and 0.94 (US version) with the OPI (although Shohamy and Stansfield, 1990: 87 report these as 0.89 and 0.93 respectively, with a sample of only 20 students in each category, while Shohamy *et al.* (1991: 6) confirm the second set of correlations but claim the use of 40 students), and Indonesian and Hausa (Stansfield and Kenyon, 1989).

Stansfield (1990a: 232–3) argues that because the SOPI uses the format of an OPI, and similar tasks:

> it seems time to reconsider Clark's characterization of semi-direct tests as 'second-order substitutes' for the direct OPI. While this characterization may be applicable to semi-direct tests in general, it does not seem to apply to the SOPI.

Advantages of the SOPI over the OPI are stated to be increased reliability because of the removal of the interlocutor as a confounding factor, the standardisation of delivery and content, and the increased amount of language sampled (Stansfield, 1990a: 232; Shohamy and Stansfield, 1990: 81–2). However, Shohamy *et al.* (1991) report that despite the much longer time spent doing the SOPI there was no significant difference in the amount of language sampled when compared with an OPI.

Shohamy *et al.* (1991) were the first to go beyond correlational studies, and compared the SOPI and the OPI in terms of functions and topics, linguistic errors and discourse features in test-taker speech. They also examined it for 'features of orality'. In terms of functions, they found that high-level OPI students are asked to perform more functions than would be the case on a SOPI, but low and intermediate level students would perform more on the SOPI than the OPI. Trivial topics were reserved for weaker test takers on the OPI, while in the SOPI all students are exposed to the same topics. Shohamy *et al.* see this as an advantage of the OPI, which is 'adaptive' to the level of the test taker. No significant differences were discovered between the two tests in terms of the number of linguistic errors made although, when turning to discourse features, self correction and paraphrasing were reported to occur more often in the SOPI, while shift to L1 was more frequent in the OPI. The explanation given for this by Shohamy *et al.* is that test takers view

the SOPI as an elicitation procedure in which they are encouraged to concentrate on accurate production, while OPI test takers are involved in a
communication activity and must focus on the production and negotiation of
meaning.

With reference to recent debates regarding the cline between oracy and
literacy, and the features of each which are manifested in different contexts,
(Halliday, 1985), Shohamy *et al.* and Shohamy (1994) found that the SOPI
contains fewer oral features than the OPI, in that the latter contains a higher
ratio of grammatical (function) items to lexical items, it is more contextualised and there is more personal involvement on the part of the test taker,
including paralinguistic behaviour and the expression of personal views and
emotions.

This evidence suggests that even though the SOPI and the OPI correlate
highly, they measure different constructs. However, Shohamy *et al.* (1991)
found no significant differences in scores between the SOPI and OPI scores.
This is a common feature of research in the testing of speaking, as we have
seen in Chapter 4 when considering task difficulty. One reason is likely to be
that the speech samples from both the OPI and SOPI were rated on the same
scale – the ACTFL, by trained raters.

The work of Shohamy *et al.* (1991) and Shohamy (1994) show that it is
important to consider factors other than purely correlation. Luoma (1997)
looked at the direct and indirect versions of the Finnish National Certificate
in Language Proficiency, and found that, while they correlated highly, the
indirect test contains more situations and elicited more functions. However,
the direct test was found to be more interactive (unsurprisingly), and the
discourse produced by the two tests was also found to be different. O'Loughlin
(2001) uses a much wider range of methods than previous researchers to
investigate semi-direct tests in his study of the *access:* test designed to test
skilled migrant workers wishing to enter Australia. These methods included
an analysis of the test specifications for the direct and indirect forms, correlational analysis, multifaceted Rasch analysis, the discourse features of
test-taker speech across forms, lexical density of speech, and individual case
studies of test-taker processes in taking each form of the test. O'Loughlin
found that they were not equivalent, that discourse features varied across
forms, and different test-taking processes were involved. He concluded
that, despite the problem of interlocutor variability in the direct form of the
test, a face-to-face speaking test is to be preferred in most situations where
practical considerations allow one to be used, because the semi-direct test
taps monologic speech rather than the crucial component of co-constructed
interaction that 'is seen as integral to the construct of oral proficiency and
not simply an optional component' (O'Loughlin, 2001: 169).

Given our current state of knowledge, we can only conclude that, while
scores on an indirect test can be used to predict scores on a direct test, the
indirect test is testing something *different* from the direct test. Growing evidence has undermined the validity argument for indirect tests *as substitutes for
direct tests.* However, this does not mean that we should abandon indirect

testing. If the construct is different we need to revisit the construct definition of an indirect test to ensure that inferences drawn from scores on the test do not generalise beyond that construct definition. A new validity argument needs to be constructed around a non-interactive definition of the construct, in which the extent of intended score generalisability is explicitly stated, and for which new evidence can be gathered.

We can see in the case of indirect testing that all the research to which I have referred has contributed to our growing knowledge about the type of inferences we can make on the basis of test scores. The later research that questioned the earlier validity argument also shows us that a crucial part of the enterprise is to question the weakest parts of validity arguments in a process to expand our understanding. As Kane (1992: 530) puts it:

> Validity evidence is most effective when it addresses the weakest parts of the interpretive argument. Evidence that provides further support for a highly plausible assumption does not add much to the overall plausibility of the argument. The most questionable assumptions deserve the most attention. An assumption can be questioned because of existing evidence indicating that it may not be true, because of plausible alternative interpretations that deny the assumption, because of specific objections raised by critics, or simply because of a lack of supporting evidence.

A VALIDITY MODEL

The examples in this chapter have shown how some of the assumptions underlying validity arguments are made, and what types of evidence are collected to suggest that they are plausible. In this final short section we set out a model that may help us to consider what types of evidence we would need to collect to support a validity argument, and what types of evidence we might collect to challenge a validity argument. We have chosen to outline the model of Messick (1989, 1992, 1995, 1996), which remains one of the most influential. This model is not specific to testing second-language speaking, or indeed language testing. It is a generic model that can be applied to all educational testing and assessment (Miller and Linn, 2000).

In Chapter 5 we saw that Messick (1989: 13) defined construct validity as 'an integrated evaluative judgement of the degree to which empirical evidence and theoretical rationales support the adequacy and appropriateness of inferences and actions based on test scores or other modes of assessment'. Validity is a unified concept for Messick, and this has largely been incorporated into the Standards for Educational and Psychological Testing (1999: 9). However, no validity argument for a speaking test is supported by every type of evidence that could possibly be collected to support or question its assumptions. Decisions have to be made about what type of evidence should be collected to support the meaning of test scores in a specific context of test use. Messick outlines six aspects of validity, which are summarised and illustrated below. These aspects of validity provide a model that aids the researcher to select the kinds of evidence needed to support the validity argument for a particular test.

Substantive aspect

The Standards for Educational and Psychological Testing (1999: 12) define the substantive aspect of validity as the 'theoretical and empirical analyses of the response processes of test takers [which] can provide evidence concerning the fit between the construct and the detailed nature of performance or response actually engaged in by examinees'. This has been one of the most difficult aspects of validity to study. We have to ask the question: how do we know that the processes test takers use when responding to the tasks in the speaking test match the construct definition? O'Loughlin's (2001) observations of how test takers approached both direct and indirect tests is an example of an investigation into the substantive aspect of validity.

Structural aspect

The structural aspect of validity concerns the internal structure of the test, and is relevant to the scoring procedure and how scores are reported. For example, if a speaking test is constructed of multiple tasks, each of which is designed to elicit a different aspect of the construct, it should be possible (at least in principle) to show that the scores from the different parts of the test reflect the aspect of the construct it is designed to test. In our discussion of the paired speaking format, we saw that Saville and Hargreaves (1999) argue that the different parts of the FCE speaking component are designed to assess different construct features. The internal structure of the test is also directly related to the scoring system. If the construct is as broad as 'speaking', a holistic scale is most often used, and a single score reported to test takers and score users. If the construct is as complex as that claimed for the FCE it may be necessary to use multiple trait scales (one for each part of the test), and report a number of scores, as a test-taker 'profile'.

Content aspect

The content of the speaking test should have a strong relationship with test construct. If a speaking test is designed to measure achievement on a particular programme of study, we must ask to what extent the test content provides the opportunity for the test takers to demonstrate that their ability on the constructs of interest have improved. If the scores are going to be used to make a judgement about whether a test taker can successfully deal with general enquiries as a hotel concierge, test content should be representative of the domain to which the test scores are to be generalised. Content is normally investigated using expert judges, and the type of discourse generated by the task through discourse analysis, such as that reported in Taylor (2000), Shohamy *et al.* (1991) and Shohamy (1994).

Generalisability aspect

Generalisability is the extent to which we can say that scores are meaningful beyond the immediate context of a speaking test. As we have seen the score can be affected by the rater(s), the interlocutor, the specific task(s) used, and the interaction between the rater(s) and task(s). In many situations the test taker may also be a variable, particularly in the paired format. The number of variables that could affect the score is potentially very large, but we would only wish to investigate those that may be expected to have a significant affect in a particular context. Generalisability is investigated whenever it is necessary to claim that the score obtained in one testing context would mean the same in another testing context with a different rater and different tasks (written to the same specifications). This increases the plausibility of an assumption that the test score can be generalised to non-test contexts. Dandonoli and Henning (1990) and O'Loughlin (2001) used multifaceted Rasch to investigate the generalisabilty of scores across test facets, although we have seen that in the former of these two studies the facets of the test were not adequately specified.

External aspect

This concerns the relationship of the speaking test, or its parts, to other tests or variables outside the test. This typically employs correlation to investigate the strength of the association between tests that are said to assess the same construct. We have seen that this was the main source of evidence to support the validity argument for the indirect/semi-direct speaking test. A high correlation between direct and indirect tests was used to claim that they both tapped the same construct, and this is usually called 'convergent' evidence for validity. However, it is only part of the external aspect. While we would expect two tests based on the same construct to be highly associated, we would expect two tests based on different constructs to correlate less highly. This is 'divergent' evidence for validity (Campbell and Fiske, 1959). With a range of tests, some of which are based on the same construct but use different task types, some of which are based on different constructs but use the same task type, on the basis of the construct definitions it is possible to make a series of hypotheses about how they will correlate. Testing these hypotheses about high, medium and low correlations provides evidence for the external aspect of validity. Bachman and Palmer's (1981, 1983) investigation of the relationship between speaking and reading tests, using the FSI, translation and self-ratings is a classic example of a study into the external aspect of validity (see Chapter 8).

Consequential aspect

As we noted earlier in this chapter, the consequential aspect of validity is receiving increased attention in language testing (Alderson and Hamp-Lyons,

1996; Alderson and Wall, 1993; Bailey, 1996; Messick, 1996; Wall, 1997, 2000). The consequences of test use may be intended or unintended. An intended consequence of the use of a new speaking test may be to increase the attention paid to speaking in the language classroom, or to change the way in which speaking is currently taught to a more 'communicative' approach. Unintended consequences are more difficult to investigate, simply because they are unintended. Unintended consequences may be internal or external to the test. An example of an internal unintended consequence would be bias in some of the tasks that depressed (or inflated) the scores of some subgroup of the test-taking population for construct-irrelevant reasons. One task, for example, may be easier for males rather than females. If the test is used for university entrance more males would be accepted than females on the basis of unsupported inferences. This is a question of fairness. An external unintended consequence occurs when agencies decide to use a test for a purpose that was not originally intended by the test designers, and for which there is no validity argument. For example, a university wishes to restrict access to places on its medical programme for funding reasons. It decides to use the University English speaking placement test to exclude approximately 20 per cent of applicants with non-English L1s. This type of unintended consequence (gatekeeping) is usually outside the control of the test designer, but it can be guarded against by explicitly stating in a test manual what the test should not be used for. Shohamy (2001) discusses these aspects of consequential validity and fairness at length.

DIGEST

We began this chapter by arguing that to decide whether a test is useful for a particular purpose we must evaluate the plausibility of the validity argument, and the quality of the evidence presented to support its assumptions. We then looked at three illustrative examples of how validity arguments are made and questioned.

In the FSI tradition we saw that there is a heavy reliance on the argument of experience, which assumes that those who spend many years working with the test internalise standards and meanings, and apply them consistently. The rating system and descriptors are assumed to describe progress in learning any language. It is also assumed that the use of the Guidelines in curriculum planning will improve language teaching and learning. Evidence to support the position comes in the form of inter-rater correlations (reliability), group discrimination studies (weak consequential aspect), and multitrait-multimethod studies (external aspect). We have seen that the assumptions of the validity argument have been subjected to intense scrutiny, undermining the theoretical rationales, and calling the quality of much of the evidence into question.

The second example focused on the use of the paired format for the speaking tests in the University of Cambridge Local Examinations Syndicate suite of tests. The validity argument is that the format makes it possible to have a much more complex and richer construct definition. The assumptions are that the sample of language elicited from the test takers is larger and richer than other formats, the unequal power relationship which exists in the traditional interview no longer plays an important role in the co-construction of discourse, and that test takers' anxiety will be reduced. The evidence to support the assumptions (much unpublished) include studies of relative turn length across format types, amount of talking time for participants, and range of functions used (content aspect), test-taker preferences and anxiety across formats (consequential aspect). Evidence calling the argument into question relates to test-taker personality, and familiarity as sources of construct-irrelevant variance (generalisability). The published evidence questioning the validity argument is so far extremely limited.

The primary validity argument for the indirect test was that it could be used as a substitute for a direct speaking test. The main assumption was that the indirect test measures the same construct as the direct test. The evidence used to support the assumption was the high correlation between direct and indirect tests that was consistently discovered in a large number of studies (external aspect). The evidence presented to undermine the assumption consisted of discourse studies of the speech samples elicited by indirect and direct tests (content aspect), analysis of test specifications (substantive and content aspects), and test-taker processes (substantive aspect). We noted, however, that this does not 'invalidate' the use of indirect tests, merely shows that the construct definitions cannot be identical.

Finally, we outlined Messick's validity model as a useful framework for looking at the types of evidence that may be provided to support a validity argument. We have seen that any single validity argument does not address all aspects of validity, but those that are particularly relevant to the purpose of a particular test. When we evaluate the usefulness of the test for a particular purpose we need to consider the theoretical rationales and empirical evidence presented to support the validity argument, and make an informed judgement about its plausibility.

In the next chapter we turn our attention to the nature of evidence. The chapter considers a range of techniques that have been used to study the testing of second-language speaking.

Chapter 8

Researching second language speaking tests

In the last chapter we saw that evaluating the usefulness of a test can be a complex process, part of which is the evaluation of the evidence presented to support a validity argument. However, just the fact that we have placed so much emphasis on the quality of the evidence requires some comment. Language testing researchers are increasingly understanding that what they do and how they do it requires a philosophical basis, and this is not only within the growing field of ethics in language testing (see *Language Testing*, 14(3)). One of the most appealing epistemologies for modern language testing is Pragmatism (Davidson and Lynch, 2002: 121; Oller *et al.*, 2000a, 2000b, 2001). Peirce (1905: 264) wrote that

> if one can define accurately all the conceivable experimental phenomena that the affirmation or denial of a concept could imply, one will have therein a complete definition of the concept, and there is absolutely nothing more in it.

Peirce (1897) had argued that there were four ways of knowing. The first is the method of tenacity, in which individuals claim to know something because that is what they have always believed. The second is the method of authority, by which what we know is defined and taught by an authoritative institution as 'the truth'. The third is the *a priori*, or intuitive method. We accept as true what appears 'agreeable to reason' (Peirce, 1897: 131). The fourth is the scientific method, which requires the collection of evidence in support or denial of hypotheses by a community of researchers whose collective efforts will push forward our understanding of the object of enquiry. Peirce argues that it is necessary to accept that our beliefs will change in the light of the growing body of evidence. He avoided the two extremes of equating 'truth' with 'reality' on the one hand (a strong correspondence theory of truth), and that truth is dependent upon how we think, our cultural background, and myriad other variables on the other. Rather, 'truth' was the hypothetical result of an endless scientific investigation in which more evidence is collected, beliefs change and more evidence is again collected, in an endless process to improve our knowledge (Dancy and Sosa, 1993: 353). While a discussion of the mutability of truth is beyond the scope of this chapter, Peirce's epistemology is one that sits easily with our current understanding of validity.

So it is not at all surprising that language testers who write about the construction of validity arguments, testing its assumptions, refining arguments, testing again, or abandoning arguments and creating new ones, find in Pragmatism a philosophical home. As an entry for *Baldwin's Dictionary of Philosophy* published in 1902, Pierce defined Pragmatism as:

> The opinion that metaphysics is to be largely cleared up by the application of the following maxim for attaining clearness of apprehension: 'Consider what effects, that might conceivably have practical bearings, we conceive the object of our conception to have. Then our conception of these effects is the whole of our conception of the object.' (Pierce, 1902: 300)

In language testing it is difficult not to think in terms of the 'practical bearings' on the lives of test takers (and stakeholders) if things go wrong in high-stakes testing, which is why Messick (1989) put consequential validity into the unified conception of validity. The way in which testing is conducted, because of its potential consequences for test takers, is also being framed within an ethical framework to which practitioners in the International Language Testing Association assent (ILTA, 2000).

The evidence that we collect to support validity arguments is not of any *particular* type. All evidence is valuable, whether it comes from the application of quantitative and/or qualitative methods. The use of 'quantitative' and 'qualitative' is not meant to imply a strict dichotomy. It is merely a useful artifice for description and classification. In all quantitative methods qualitative judgements are made when selecting variables for investigation, and the interpretation of results. The point is that language testing as an enterprise is committed to collecting evidence in systematic, defensible ways. The value of a particular method is the utility of the tool to answer the questions we pose.

In what follows we will use the 'quantitative' and 'qualitative' artifice to describe a number of methods that have been successfully used to investigate the quality of validity arguments for speaking tests (see Bachman and Eignor, 1997 and Banerjee and Luoma, 1997 for overviews in language testing generally). For each heading we provide references for further reading, and use selected examples of studies that have employed a method. Many of the examples have already been encountered in other parts of this book. Statistical formulae and computations are avoided as much as possible when discussing quantitative methods. Nor do I include discussions of all the variations of the methods presented. Readers who wish to pursue this should consult the relevant books available in the language testing literature (Bachman, 2003). The focus in this chapter is the potential use of each method in researching speaking tests, and the aim is to provide understandable explanations of approaches and methods so that the reader will be able to evaluate other studies that they find in the literature.

We should also remember, as we have seen in Chapter 7, that the use of any single method of analysis may lead to conclusions that can easily be questioned later. This is particularly the case if a validity argument rests on evidence drawn from only one quantitative method. Davidson's (2000: 616) reminder is particularly appropriate in this context:

> The practice of language testing should be monitored and modified such that determining the world from statistical evidence is balanced by knowledge and perspectives from other worldviews. From time to time a new statistical procedure will emerge that passes the test of epistemological flexibility. Even still, at the end of the day, it is probably best never to rely on a single tool or even a single toolbox, alone.

The mix of evidence required to support or question a validity argument will vary from one context to another.

QUANTITATIVE METHODS

In this section we consider methods that are primarily quantitative. The methods have been selected because of the frequency with which they are used to research tests of speaking. We first consider correlation, which is the basis for factor analysis and multitrait-multimethod studies that follow. Next we outline Generalisability Theory, and conclude with multifaceted Rasch analysis.

Correlation

The correlation coefficient is one of the statistics that appears most frequently in the literature on testing second language speaking. In Chapter 7 we reviewed the large number of correlational studies that were conducted to show that the indirect speaking test could be used as a substitute for the direct speaking test, or OPI. Correlation is a measure of the association of variables, in this case of two tests. It has also been widely used in the testing of speaking to assess the extent to which raters agree on scores. Do sets of raters tend to 'covary', or vary together in how they score performances? The correlation coefficient is frequently reported as a measure of inter-rater reliability.

The correlation coefficient is presented as a number from +1 to −1. If a coefficient of +1 is reported this means that there is a direct linear relationship between the two variables: as one rater's scores increases, the second rater's scores increase in direct proportion. If a −1 were to be reported, the two raters would 'completely disagree': the best performance for rater 1 would be the worst for rater 2, and so on. If a coefficient of 0 is reported, there is no relationship at all between the scores awarded by the two raters.

Correlating variables is an important tool in any situation where we wish to know whether two variables are associated, and the degree or strength of their association. However, interpreting correlations is not as easy as this description suggests. In order to interpret a correlation coefficient we need more information than just the number from +1 to −1.

- A correlation coefficient takes no account of the mean or standard deviation of the scores. In the case of the two raters, the correlation coefficient would tell us the degree to which the two sets of scores were associated, but nothing about the differences in rater severity, as discussed in Chapter 6. All methods of calculating correlations rank persons according to scores, and compare the ranks. If correlational evidence is presented, we should also look for descriptive statistics, such as the mean score awarded by each rater, and the standard deviation of the scores. We could then see whether one rater is harsher or more lenient than another.

- Correlations are, however, extremely sensitive to the number of cases in the study, often referred to as the *n*-size. The smaller the number of cases, for example students in a study, the more likely we are to see high positive or negative correlations occur purely by chance. For this reason, we need to know if a correlation is statistically significant, and this is done by looking at a table of 'critical values' (see Brown, 1996: 164, 175). For example, if a correlation coefficient of 0.60 is reported, this would be significant if there were 10 test takers in the study, but not if there were 9.

- Correlations are also sensitive to restrictions in the range of scores, or truncated samples. If a study uses test takers who are fairly homogeneous, or at about the same level of language ability, low correlations will be reported just because there is no spread of scores.

- No test is completely reliable. There is always error, however much test designers try to reduce it. Correlations are also affected by error. In the case where the correlation is used to investigate the relationship between tests it is advisable to correct the correlations for attenuation (alter the correlations to take error into account). Henning (1987: 85–6) reports a hypothetical investigation into the relationship of a speaking test with a test of reading and a test of grammar. Each test has a different reliability. The correlation matrix shows that speaking is more highly correlated with reading than grammar, but once the correlations have been corrected for attenuation the speaking test correlates more highly with the test of grammar than with the test of reading.

- A correlation coefficient is not directly interpretable. However, the square root of the correlation coefficient can be interpreted directly as the proportion of shared variance between two variables. When Meredith (1990) reported a correlation of 0.57 between the variables of ACTFL ratings and length of study (see Chapter 7), we discover that the shared variance, or the degree to which these two variables 'overlap' is 0.32. We can say that length of study time and scores on the speaking test tend to vary together in about 32 per cent of cases. Even if a correlation of 0.57 is statistically significant this shows that it is not legitimate to make a strong claim about the relationship between study time and getting a better score on the test.

- Correlational studies cannot be used to support claims that one of the variables 'causes' the change in the second variable to which it is related. There is always the possibility that hidden variables or factors cause the association between the variables in a study. For example, in a concurrent validity study of the Australian Second Language Proficiency Rating system the ASLPR was correlated with the Comprehensive English Language Test (CELT) (Ingram, 1984, 1985b, 1990). The CELT is a three-part test consisting of listening, structure and vocabulary (Oxford, 1987). A correlation of 0.83 was reported between the CELT structure subtest and the ASLPR of 0.83 when using test takers following courses in Australia. When using a different population of students in China the correlations were generally much lower (Ingram, 1985b: 249–50). The findings were explained in terms of the difference in the syllabuses/course types being followed in the two countries. In Australia grammar and speaking were both taught, and learners tend to improve in both simultaneously. In China there was little emphasis on teaching speaking. This is a particularly clear example of how correlations can be affected by a third (hidden) variable. It is also acts as a very useful warning against interpreting relationships between variables as in some way reflecting psychological reality, unless we know a great deal about the nature of the sample in the study and the population from which it is drawn. The naive assumption that a high correlation between two tests indicates that the two are measuring the same thing was pointed out early in the history of testing speaking by Kaulfers (1944: 138):

> The tests must not be guilty of the 'correlation fallacy', the common delusion that a certain level of ability on a pencil-and-paper test of vocabulary, grammar, or reading comprehension can automatically be interpreted to mean a corresponding level of ability to understand the spoken language, or to speak the language fluently.

Correlation has been a useful tool in researching tests of speaking, and will remain so. But we have seen that interpreting correlations is not as easy as it appears at first sight. It is necessary to make careful judgements about whether reported correlations provide evidence of the quality required for the validity argument that is being constructed. Correlations are also the basis for more complex approaches to looking at data, such as Factor analysis and the multitrait-multimethod matrix, which we consider below. If the correlations that are used in these approaches are suspect, the outcomes of the studies are likely to be spurious.

Factor analysis

Factor analysis is a widely used approach to the analysis of test scores that uses the correlation matrix as a starting point for the analysis. Factor analysis is never done by hand because of the complexity of the process, but can be undertaken using standard statistical packages such as SPSS. Factor analysis is

> a data-reduction procedure that allows researchers to collapse large numbers of variables into smaller, more meaningful underlying constructs. The procedure provides a means for conceptually related variables to cluster so that the researcher can come to a better understanding of the relationship among those variables.   (Hinofotis, 1983)

The simplest way to understand factor analysis is through presenting an example and annotating it. For those who wish to read a detailed but clear exposition of the mathematics of factor analysis, see Child (1970).

The example I have chosen is from Hinofotis (1983) because of its clarity, and the completeness of the data that is presented. Hinofotis was investigating the communication problems of Teaching Assistants (TAs) at the University of California at Los Angeles. Videotaped role plays were made before and after a speaking course, and rated by six instructors before the speaking course and ten freshman native speakers after the speaking course. Ratings of the videotapes was done on a nine-point scale for the following constructs:

- Vocabulary (voc)
- Grammar (gra)
- Pronunciation (pro)
- Flow of speech (flo)
- Eye contact (eye)
- Nonverbal aspects (non)
- Confidence in manner (con)
- Presence (pre)
- Development of explanation (dev)
- Use of supporting evidence (evi)
- Clarity of expression (cla)
- Ability to relate to students (rel)

We are not concerned at the moment with the definition of the constructs in the Hinofotis study. Rather, we will look at the factor analysis of the test scores given by the instructors to the TAs on these constructs in order to explain the method, and then return to a discussion of what it all means. First, Hinofotis constructed a correlation matrix by calculating the correlation of every variable with every other variable. In the factor analysis the researcher tries to discover if there are a small number of 'factors' (constructs) that can account for the data in the correlation matrix. In Table 8.1 is a slightly adapted version of the factor matrix from Hinofotis (1983: 174).

Five factors have been extracted in this analysis. In the following annotation to Table 8.1 we will look at what the table means.

1. In the left-hand column we find the codes for the rating categories used in the speaking test, listed in the first 12 rows. These are essentially being treated as 12 separate tests. As there are 12 tests, the maximum variance is 12, with a figure of 1 for each test.
2. In the next five columns we have five factors, F1 to F5. In the cells we have figures that look like correlation coefficients and are called 'factor loadings'. Indeed, the factor loading can be understood as the correlation between the actual test and the factor. In the first row, which is Vocabulary, we see that it loads most heavily on factor 4 at 0.79 (shaded), or that it correlates more highly with factor 4 than any of the other factors. The maximum value that can occur in any cell is 1. If a 1 did occur, this factor would account for all the variance in the test scores.

Table 8.1 A factor matrix for ratings of TA performances

Variables	F1	F2	F3	F4	F5	h^2
voc	0.36	0.25	0.30	0.79	0.17	0.94
gra	0.37	0.18	0.18	0.61	0.44	0.77
pro	0.21	0.33	0.25	0.27	0.80	0.93
flo	0.31	0.67	0.24	0.35	0.36	0.86
eye	0.30	0.20	0.78	0.17	0.22	0.82
non	0.28	0.32	0.68	0.22	0.11	0.70
con	0.13	0.87	0.33	0.27	0.13	0.97
pre	0.46	0.72	0.17	0.00	0.23	0.81
dev	0.78	0.21	0.34	0.30	0.15	0.88
evi	0.83	0.27	0.23	0.30	0.15	0.93
cla	0.66	0.35	0.41	0.30	0.28	0.89
rel	0.62	0.28	0.53	0.22	0.23	0.86
Eigenvalues	2.94	2.73	2.08	1.66	1.30	10.36
% variance	28	23	20	16	13	

From *Issues in Language Testing Research, 1st Edition*, by Oller © 1983. Reprinted with permission of Heinle, a division of Thomson Learning: www.thomsonrights.com. Fax 800 730-2215.

3. In the final column h^2, we find what is called the 'communality'. The maximum value of any cell in this column is 1. In the case of Vocabulary the figure is 0.94, and this tells us how much of the score variance for vocabulary is accounted for by the five factors. If the value was 1, the five factors would account for all score variance, for each of the 'tests' = 1. The communality is calculated by squaring and adding the factor loadings in a row.

4. In row 13 we have eigenvalues. These are the contribution of each factor to explaining total score variance, and so the size of the eigenvalue indicates the importance of the factor. The eigenvalue for factor 1 is 2.94 (out of a possible value of 12), which means that it accounts for 28 per cent of the score variance across all tests. The eigenvalue is calculated by squaring and adding the factor loadings in a column. We should also note that no factor has an eigenvalue of less than 1. This is one of the most common principles used to decide how many factors should be used to 'explain' the correlation matrix that is used in a factor analysis: no factor should account for less variance than a single test. However, there are problems with this method of extracting factors of which readers who intend to use factor analysis should be aware (Kerlinger and Lee, 2000: 836).

5. At the intersection of the eigenvalue row and the h^2 column is the figure 10.36. This is the sum of the eigenvalues *and* the sum of the communalities. 10.36 is 86 per cent of 12, telling us that the five factors account for 86 per cent of the score variance in the 12 tests. We therefore know that 14 per cent of score variance in the tests is not accounted for by these factors, but by something else that will include error.

In the left-hand column we have real tests, in this case scores on rating scales for vocabulary, and so on. These have been correlated with factors, and we can see how much of score variance is accounted for by factors × individual tests, by factors × all tests, and by all factors × all tests.

This is as far as factor analysis takes us. In the introduction to this chapter we claimed that the distinction between quantitative and qualitative methods was a useful fiction, but only that. Perhaps factor analysis shows this better than any other quantitative method, for we are faced with the very real problem of what a factor is. McNemar (1951) argues that when interpreting factors researchers 'struggle and struggle and struggle' to try to interpret the factors in relation to their theories and hypotheses. In other words, interpreting the factors is a matter of judgement and argumentation.

Perhaps it is easiest to think of a factor as an 'ideal test' of a construct, and the factor loadings as the correlation between the actual test and the ideal test of the construct. In Table 8.1 I have added shading to the highest factor loadings in each column. This is the argument that Hinofitis puts forward.

Factor 1: The largest loadings are on development of explanation, use of supporting evidence, clarity of explanation and ability to relate to students. This factor is labelled 'Communication of Information'.

Factor 2: The largest loadings are on flow of speech, confidence in manner and presence. This factor is labelled 'Delivery'.

Factor 3: The largest loadings are on eye contact, non-verbal aspects and ability to relate to students. This factor is labelled 'Non-verbal aspects'.

Factor 4: The largest loadings are on vocabulary and grammar. This factor is labelled 'Language Proficiency'.

Factor 5: The largest loading is on pronunciation. This factor is labelled 'Pronunciation'.

In the factor matrix only the pronunciation test is unifactorial (loads on only one factor). One test, ability to relate to students, loads highly on factor 1 and factor 3, which 'suggests that the variable may share attributes with both factors' (Hinofotis, 1983: 174).

When evaluating a factor analysis the main question is whether the interpretation provided through the labelling of factors is plausible in the light of theory, other empirical findings, the hypotheses of the researchers, the quality of the tests and the data. Hinofotis had hypothesised that there would be three factors: Language Proficiency (vocabulary, grammar, pronunciation and flow of speech), Delivery (eye contact, non-verbal aspects, confidence in manner and presence), and Communication of Information (development of explanation, use of supporting evidence, clarity of expression and ability to relate to students). From the data it may be surmised that non-verbal aspects are not part of the construct of 'delivery', and that pronunciation is a construct in its own right rather than being part of the 'language proficiency'

construct. Other tests have shifted into different factors from those hypothesised. The task of the reader is to decide whether they find Hinofotis'
arguments plausible to support the validity argument that there are five
constructs that can account for the scores in the UCLA speaking test for TAs.
If the argument is plausible, Hinofotis has succeeded in presenting evidence
to support an inference from the score to its meaning.

Factor analysis is a useful tool for simplifying and explaining data, but the
results of factor analysis are always subject to replication. Kerlinger and Lee
(2000: 856) provide the following warning:

> In considering the scientific value of factor analysis, the reader must be cau-
> tioned against attributing 'reality' and uniqueness to factors. The danger of
> reification is great. It is easy to name a factor and then to believe there is reality
> behind the name. But giving a factor a name does not give it reality. Factor
> names are merely attempts to epitomize the essence of factors. They are always
> tentative, subject to later confirmation or disconfirmation.

Multitrait-multimethod studies

The multitrait-multimethod approach to investigating validity is another extension of correlation. Classically expounded by Campbell and Fiske (1959), the
method is specifically designed to provide both convergent and divergent evidence to support a validity argument. In correlational studies the researchers
are normally concerned to show a high correlation between two tests that
they hypothesise measure the same construct. Campbell and Fiske argued
that this 'convergent' evidence is not enough. It is also necessary to show
that a test of a particular construct has low correlations with tests of other
constructs, or that it 'diverges' from them. Next, they argued that each test
or task is a 'trait-method unit', a combination of the construct of interest,
and a method (task or item type) for collecting evidence from which we may
make inferences to the construct. In order to show both convergent and
divergent validity they say that it is necessary to use more than one trait or
construct, and more than one method. If two tests that use the same method
or task types correlate highly it could be because the methods are identical
or similar. This is a variant of the problem we discussed above: the high
correlation could be caused by test method rather than the construct of
interest.

> When a dimension of personality is hypothesized, when a construct is pro-
> posed, the proponent invariably has in mind distinctions between the new
> dimension and other constructs already in use. One cannot define without
> implying distinctions, and the verification of these distinctions is an important
> part of the validation process.   (Campbell and Fiske, 1959: 84)

The best way to understand the argument is to consider a real example
from Bachman and Palmer (1981, 1983), which has already been discussed
in Chapter 7. Bachman and Palmer wished to study the validity of the FSI
oral interview. In this study, to support the validity of the FSI speaking test

there should be convergent evidence (the FSI correlates more highly with other tests of speaking using different methods) and divergent evidence (the FSI has low correlations with tests of reading even when they share the same method). In the following discussion the terms 'trait' and 'construct' are used interchangeably, and no difference in meaning is intended. The use of one or the other term is merely dependent upon the terminology adopted by particular researchers. Campbell and Fiske, for example, always use the term 'trait', and this is preserved in this discussion.

Bachman and Palmer constructed a multitrait-multimethod matrix with two traits (constructs), speaking and reading, and three methods, the FSI interview, translation and self-rating. Both constructs were measured by each of the methods, giving six trait-method units. Each interview was rated by two raters, and each translation test was rated by two raters. Each of the trait-method units had high reliability and so it was not necessary to correct the correlations for attenuation. The correlation matrix is reproduced in Table 8.2.

Table 8.2　Multitrait-multimethod matrix

		Speaking (A)					Reading (B)				
		Int1 1	Int2 2	Tra1 3	Tra2 3	Self 5	Int1 1	Int2 2	Tra1 3	Tra2 4	Self 5
A	1	1	0.88	0.77	0.76	0.51	0.54	0.56	0.58	0.52	0.44
	2	0.88	1	0.72	0.72	0.56	0.45	0.46	0.61	0.55	0.45
	3	0.77	0.72	1	0.85	0.46	0.62	0.64	0.64	0.62	0.47
	4	0.76	0.72	0.85	1	0.53	0.65	0.67	0.68	0.69	0.51
	5	0.51	0.56	0.46	0.53	1	0.58	0.60	0.46	0.49	0.68
B	1	0.54	0.45	0.62	0.65	0.58	1	0.97	0.66	0.65	0.68
	2	0.56	0.46	0.64	0.67	0.60	0.97	1	0.65	0.65	0.68
	3	0.58	0.61	0.64	0.68	0.46	0.65	0.65	1	0.94	0.54
	4	0.52	0.55	0.62	0.69	0.49	0.65	0.65	0.94	1	0.54
	5	0.44	0.45	0.47	0.51	0.68	0.68	0.68	0.54	0.54	1

Before we can interpret this matrix it is necessary to introduce some terminology. This may look complex, but it is used in the language-testing literature that employs the multitrait-multimethod approach. Taking the time to understand the relationship between the terminology, the area of the correlation matrix to which it refers, and its meaning, is the only way to penetrate this literature and understand the types of validity claims that are being made.

Monotrait-heteromethod: The area of the matrix containing correlations between *the same construct measured by different methods*. These are the correlations within the triangles of Table 8.2.

Heterotrait-monomethod: The area of the matrix containing correlations between *different constructs measured by the same method*. These are the correlations between the two diagonal lines in the bottom left and top right of Table 8.2. These are the method diagonals.

Heterotrait-heteromethod: The area of the matrix containing correlations between *different constructs measured by different methods*. These are the correlations that are not enclosed in a triangle or between the diagonal lines.

In other words:

Monotrait   = same construct
Heterotrait   = different constructs
Monomethod   = same method
Heteromethod = different methods

Campbell and Fiske (1959) set out four criteria for making judgements about a multitrait-multimethod matrix. We will list these criteria, and gloss each one with reference to Table 8.2 and the claims made by Bachman and Palmer (1981, 1983).

1. The monotrait-heteromethod correlations should be significantly different from zero. This is evidence for convergent validity. As we explained above, this is the relationship between the same construct measured by different methods. If these correlations are high and significant, the two operationalisations of the same construct are not associated, and so cannot be measures of 'the same construct'.

   The lowest value in the 'validity triangles' is 0.46 and the highest 0.97. Bachman and Palmer therefore claim that there is evidence for convergent validity for both speaking and reading.

2. The monotrait-heteromethod correlations should be higher than correlations found in the heterotrait-heteromethod area of the matrix. If this were not the case a trait-method unit would be more highly associated with other trait-method units that share neither trait nor method in common. In other words, it would be impossible to interpret the correlation matrix in any meaningful way.

   To investigate this we look at a correlation in one of the triangles and compare it with correlations in its row and column in the heterotrait-heteromethod areas of the matrix. If we therefore compare the correlation A1 with A2 at 0.88 (first row second column) with its column A1 with

B2, etc. we see that 0.88 is higher than 0.56, 0.58, 0.52 and 0.44. Similarly with its row, 0.88 is higher than 0.45, 0.61, 0.55 and 0.45. Although there are some correlations that are very low (0.46 between A3 and A5) where this pattern is not sustained, Bachman and Palmer claim that the matrix provides this type of evidence for divergent validity.

3. The monotrait-heteromethod correlations should be higher than those in the heterotrait-monomethod area of the matrix, or more simply, independent attempts to measure the same construct should be more highly associated than measures of different constructs that happen to employ the same method. This is strong evidence for divergent validity.

When Bachman and Palmer compare the correlations in the triangles with the correlation in the method diagonals (both row and column), they claim that this criterion is met 13 of 20 times for speaking, and 12 of 20 times for reading. Using the 0.88 between A1 and A2 again, this is larger than both 0.54 and 0.46. Bachman and Palmer therefore claim to have presented strong evidence for divergent validity.

4. The heterotrait correlations should show the same patterns across monomethod and heteromethod areas of the matrix. If there are large differences between correlations this is evidence for a method effect impacting upon scores. That is, the method of measuring the trait affects the scores as much as, or more than, the construct that the method is supposed to measure. This is usually classified as construct irrelevant variance.

The patterns here are considerably different. Of particular concern are the higher correlations in the method diagonal for translation and self-assessment, showing a strong method effect. Bachman and Palmer conclude on the basis of the evidence from the method diagonal that the interview is the most appropriate method for testing speaking.

The multitrait-multimethod matrix is a powerful tool for the analysis of validity questions. In particular, it allows the researcher to see to what extent a task type (method) affects the scores. The use of this method assumes that we wish to classify method variance as error variance, which may not always be the case, as in tests of speaking for specific purposes. The results of an analysis are also dependent upon the correlation matrix and the sample of test takers from which they were generated. We have discussed the problems associated with interpreting a correlation, and those problems need to be dealt with before doing, or interpreting, a multitrait-multimethod matrix.

Generalisability studies

In Classical Test Theory (CTT) reliability is conceptualised as random error that makes it difficult to know what a test taker's true score is. Put another way, the observed score (the score the test taker actually gets) is made up of two components: the true score (true ability on the construct) and random error. The weakness of the CTT definition of reliability is that it leaves the error undifferentiated, and assumes that it is random. Generalisability Theory is an extension of CTT that asks to what extent a test score, given under a specific set of conditions, will generalise across those conditions. In other words, it takes into account that error may be random or systematic and provides a methodology for investigating the structure and strength of the error. As we have seen before, we may be interested in whether a score on a speaking test will generalise across raters and tasks. That is, how likely would it be that a test taker would get the same score if they took the test with a different rater/interlocutor, with another form of the test? In this simple two-facet model, we wish to ask how much each facet contributes to test score variance. Generalisability Theory also helps us to answer questions such as how many raters we would need to achieve the reliability we need, or how many tasks a speaking test should contain before we can say that a test score is meaningful across the range of possible task types that could be included in the test.

In Generalisability Theory the true score of CTT is replaced by the notion of the 'universe score'. The universe score would be the one obtained if a test taker could take an infinite number of tasks (generated by the test specifications) with an infinite number of potential raters/interlocutors. The infinite number of tasks and raters/interlocutors specified as facets in the design of the study is referred to as the 'universe of admissible observations' (Bachman, 1997).

A Generalisability Study starts with the specification of the facets over which the score should be generalisable. The score on the speaking test is treated as a dependent variable, and each of the facets as an independent variable, in an Analysis of Variance (ANOVA). ANOVA is explained in the standard textbooks for language testers and applied linguists. ANOVA is easily calculated using standard statistical packages (such as SPSS), and provides an estimate of how much score variance can be attributed to each of the facets in the design of the study. From these estimates of variance a generalisability coefficient can be easily calculated by hand, which informs the researcher of the extent to which scores on the test can be generalised to the universe of admissible observations. If the variance associated with raters is high, we would know that the rater makes a difference to test scores. If the variance associated with tasks is high, we would know that it makes a difference which task a test taker is given. Additionally, if there is an interaction effect between raters and tasks, we would know that some raters grade differently depending upon which task the test takers are attempting. With this information it is possible to conduct a Decision Study (D-Study) to discover how many raters, or how many tasks, are needed to reduce the variance components associated with these facets and increase the generalisability coefficient. In other words, it is another way of trying to reduce construct-irrelevant variance, as described in Chapter 2.

Bolus *et al.* (1981) worked on a speaking test for international TAs recruited to the University of California at Los Angeles. They were concerned about the generalisability of scores across raters, and the occasion on which the rating was given. Role-plays with potential TAs were recorded on video and all performances were rated by 6 judges on a nine-point scale on two separate occasions a month apart. The variance components in this design, along with the variance estimates, are presented in Table 8.3.

Table 8.3 Results of the Bolus *et al.* Generalisability Study

Source of variance	Variance component estimates
Person (construct-related variance)	1.99
Rater	0.05
Occasion	0.00
Person × rater	1.5
Person × occasion	0.06
Rater × occasion	0.05
Residual (random error)	0.64

The person estimate is acceptably high compared to other components, but the high interaction effect between person and rater indicates that raters are responding differentially to some of the test takers. Having identified this worrying source of score variance Bolus *et al.* calculated the generalisability coefficient and used it to estimate the number of raters that would be needed to reduce rater × person variance and increase the generalisability coefficient. Using a single rater the generalisability coefficient was found to be 0.48, which is very low. Using 3 raters this could be increased to 0.72, and with 5 raters would reach 0.8. This is a valuable insight for the test developer. With fewer raters the score is not generalisable, meaning that it would make a difference to a test taker which rater he had. The rating may change wildly with a different rater. It would be unwise to make decisions on the basis of these test scores. However, to improve the generalisability, many raters are needed. To reach a coefficient of 0.9 (highly reliable in CCT terminology) Bolus *et al.* calculated that they would need to have 10 raters observing each TA on two separate occasions. In Chapter 6 we have seen there is significant cost in developing a speaking test; although we did not proceed to prepare a budget for operational test delivery the cost of using this number of raters can be imagined. If 0.9 is required for a very high-stakes test, but the cost is potentially too much to achieve that, it may be back to the drawing board.

Generalisabilitiy Theory is a very powerful and flexible approach to the identification and analysis of facets of speaking tests. As a methodology it also shows that the traditional division between reliability and validity cannot often be maintained. While the generalisability coefficient is often seen as being equivalent to reliability in CTT it is much more than this. Far from being a measure of internal consistency, it represents the degree to which score meaning is dependent upon facets other than person variance on the construct the speaking test is designed to measure. These facets can be defined in terms of the test environment, but it is also possible to imagine studies that consider personality variables, environment variables, or level of inter-locutor support. Generalisability Theory also offers very practical information about the number of raters, observations (occasions) or tasks that are needed to reach acceptable levels of generalisability for the purpose of the test.

Multifaceted Rasch analysis

As in Generalisability Theory, multifaceted Rasch analysis lets the researcher look at a range of facets and how they contribute to score variance. However, multifaceted Rasch analysis is from a different family of statistical models (Pollitt, 1997), which is probabilistic. It is an extension of a rating-scale model (Linacre, 1989) that calculates the probability of a test taker achieving a certain score on a speaking test as a function of test-taker ability, task difficulty and rater severity. Additionally, each facet can be given a value on a common interval scale, and other facets can be added when needed. Un-like Generalisability Theory, multifaceted Rasch analysis can reveal which particular raters are harsher or more lenient than others, and show whether the harshness or leniency occurs at particular points on a rating scale. We have already encountered multifaceted Rasch analysis, and provided a brief description of it, when discussing the work of North in Chapter 4. This section will expand upon that section, but readers who wish to know more should consult the literature that deals specifically with the use of Rasch models in performance assessments (McNamara, 1996; McNamara and Adams, 1991).

Analyses are always conducted using specialist computer programs, particularly FACETS (Linacre, 1991). The results of a multifaceted Rasch analysis can

> allow inspection of the likelihood of a candidate of a particular ability achieving a particular score on an item of given difficulty, with a judge of given harshness.
> (McNamara and Adams, 1991: 3)

The example we will use to illustrate the type of information that is pro-duced by a multifaceted Rasch analysis is taken from McNamara (1996: 135). The study concerns the Australian *access:* test, which we have come across before in Chapter 7. Table 8.4 is a Facets map for the *access:* data. In the first column of the table we have the scale against which test takers, raters and tasks are measured, from −4 to +4. (This is just another kind of scale, but the metric is in logits. These units are the probabilities of getting a particular score expressed as natural logarithms. See Baker, 1997 for an introduction to understanding Rasch measurement.) In the second column we have the test takers, ranked against the scale according to ability. The higher up the scale, the more able the test taker, so test takers ID 24, 40 and 94 are the most able, while test taker ID 47 is the least able. The third column contains the four raters A, B, C and D. Rater B is the harshest, and rater C the most lenient. In the final column we find the prompts used in the speaking test, labelled as 'items'. Item 9 is the most difficult, and item 23 the easiest. One of the main

Table 8.4   A Facets map (McNamara, 1996: 135)

Measure (logits)	Test taker	Rater	Item
6			
	24 40 94		
	90		
5			
	28		
	37		
	77		
	1 53		
4	9		
	27 46		
	42 61 93		
	14		
	78 86		
3			
	20 62 7 73 82 89		
	23 68		
	31 65		
	17 32 4 56 6 83		
2	11		
	36 39 45		
	15 29 85		
	12 30	B	
	22 34 79 81		9
1	19 5 66 64 67 69		
	13 33 49 8		11
	44 63 75		19 14 5 6 17
	3 54 92	A	2 12
	66 80		22 3
0	2 21 52 72 84 87 91		8 20 15
	26 59		10
	10 41		21 7
			13 16
		D	1 4
–1	16	C	18
			23
	51		
	25		
–2			
	57		
	88		
–3			
	18		
–4	47		

advantages of this method is that test takers, items and raters, can all be measured on the same scale.

In probabilistic models we talk about the chances of doing well on a particular task, or with a particular rater. Using this table, we will first consider test taker ID 3, whose ability estimate is 0.43. If this test taker is given item 2 with a difficulty estimate of 0.46 and rated by rater A with a severity estimate of 0.41, there is roughly a 50/50 chance that test taker ID3 will get a particular score. As the estimated ability level of the test taker increases in logits, the chances increase that the score will rise, and as the ability level decreases so does the chance that the score will decrease. However, if test taker ID3 is matched with rater B and item 9, the chances of getting the same score seriously decreases. There is one problem, however, with interpreting Table 8.4. McNamara does not provide the raw scores (bands on the rating scale) that correspond to the logits. Any band would cover a 'range' of logits on the map. We cannot therefore see from the map at what point the probability of getting one particular score would be lower than getting the score immediately above it. When presenting the results of a Facets analysis, it is usually advisable to provide information on the relationship between raw scores and logits for clarity.

One of the most obvious uses of this method is in rater training. Wigglesworth (1993) reported giving feedback to raters following such an analysis, and found that it reduced the degree of bias in their rating. Lumley and McNamara (1995) used the technique to investigate the degree to which raters shifted in severity as a result of training, and reported that what little changes they observed were 'non-uniform'. However, if severity were found to remain relatively stable over a period it would be possible to use the severity statistics to alter scores for exceptionally severe or lenient raters. In other words, as long as intra-rater reliability is established, with the information provided by multifaceted Rasch analysis lack of inter-rater reliability (severity) can be corrected (see Chapter 6).

Summary of quantitative methods

We have considered a number of quantitative methods commonly used in the study of second language speaking tests. They have in common the assumption that the variance we observe in test scores is made up from variance that is attributable to the construct we wish to measure, and variance that is attributable to other factors which are not part of our construct definition (see Bachman and Eignor, 1987: 232). Quantitative techniques can be used primarily to investigate score variance, separating construct-relevant variance from construct-irrelevant variance. In this, all the quantitative methods provide evidence about the construct validity of a test. Those methods that allow us to measure the degree of variance attributable to construct-irrelevant factors, such as the rater, provide valuable information which can be used to reduce the variance caused by the source, thus increasing the construct validity.

QUALITATIVE METHODS

The use of qualitative methods in studying tests of second language speaking is a much more recent phenomenon, but one that has contributed a great deal of understanding to validity. When we discussed quantitative methods we saw that there is almost always a qualitative element present, especially when making judgements about the meaning of statistics. Similarly, data from qualitative studies is often (but not always) subjected to statistical analysis. In this section we will look at qualitative studies that are commonly used to study speaking tests: expert judgement, questionnaires and interviews, discourse analysis, and verbal protocol analysis.

Expert judgement

Although expert judgement is widely used in testing second language speaking it is uncommon to find descriptions of the processes used. Most of the intuitive methods for scale development described in Chapter 4 rely on expert judgement, for example, but precisely how individuals or committees come to agreement on the descriptors for rating scales is not reported.

> We have scoured the educational measurement and language testing literature and have found very little information and guidance on how people write tests in groups.   (Davidson and Lynch, 2002: 98)

The exceptions to this rule are cases where experts are specifically asked to make judgements about speech samples. Alderson (1991b: 81) reports asking ELTS raters to identify 'key sample scripts' for each band level on the developmental IELTS speaking and writing tests, and identifying features that were typical of samples. In the development of empirically derived, binary-choice, boundary-definition scales (Upshur and Turner, 1995), experts were asked to place speech samples into 'better' and 'poorer' piles, following the method of Thurstone (1928) as described in Chapter 4. North (1996/2000) also used experts during Phases A and B of the construction of the Common European Framework, also described in detail in Chapter 4. In Chapter 5 we saw that experts are used regularly in the design of test specifications and task types in an iterative process that involves piloting, review and revision. Although not in the context of testing speaking, Alderson (1990) reports on three studies where experts were asked to make judgements. In the first study, teachers familiar with language testing were asked to identify what items on a reading test were testing. In the second experts who were and were not familiar with a new test in Sri Lanka were asked to estimate the difficulty of the test items. And in the third study experienced test designers were asked to set grade boundaries for a national test. Alderson reports that in none of the studies could high levels of agreement be reached, and in the first two, agreement was low. Alderson (1990: 47) argues that:

so-called professional judgments are frequently flawed or in serious conflict with other professionals' judgments, and that language testers must be alert to the need to corroborate and validate the professional judgments we so frequently make.

Davidson and Lynch (2002) devote a whole chapter to how expert groups can be used in writing test specifications. They consider the literature on group dynamics, processes and synergies, and report on a study of how a group of specification writers operated as a group. This involved recording the process of test-specification writing, transcribing and coding data. Important variables were the size of the group and the relative expertise of the members, the roles played by individuals, and the impact on group cohesiveness and goal achievement. One critical observation is that it is necessary to record how an expert group arrives at decisions. The rationales for decision-making form part of the validity argument, and should be available for scrutiny.

Given the central role that decisions made by experts/expert judges has in the whole process of writing, piloting and studying speaking tests, it is surprising that more information is not available in the public domain. What published research and discussion is available suggests that expert judgement should be used with care and caution, that it should not be the only source of evidence for decision-making, and that the rationales for all decisions based on expert judgement should be carefully recorded as an important source of validity evidence.

Questionnaires and interviews

Collecting information through questionnaires and interviews is an important method in understanding test-taker preferences and opinions, or discovering how a variety of stakeholders react to new speaking tests. Where test takers are concerned, what has been termed 'response validity' is important (Henning, 1987: 96). This is defined as:

> the extent to which examinee responses to a test or questionnaire can be said to reflect the intended purpose in measurement. Lack of adequate instructions, incentives, task familiarity, or courtesy could invalidate responses.
>
> (Henning, 1987: 196)

In short, if test takers don't take the test seriously, if they don't understand what to do, if content is unfamiliar, or something about the test or testing context is offensive, it is unlikely that the test scores will reflect their ability on the construct of interest.

In Chapter 7 we discussed the growing use of the paired and group format to speaking tests. Fulcher (1996a) reported on a study that used both a questionnaire and an interview to investigate the reactions of test takers to three task types: a picture description, an interview and a group discussion. A total of 47 test takers attempted all three tasks, and were asked to complete a questionnaire after each task. A smaller number of test takers selected for their ability to verbalise their opinions were interviewed after completing all three tasks. The questionnaire used was adapted from Scott (1986), and is reproduced in Appendix 9. The questionnaire is an attempt to look at a range of test-taker-related facets across task types, including anxiety generated by task, testing occasion, the perception of whether the test would elicit a performance that could be scored in terms of time and quality, perception of whether the interlocutor/rater was an important variable, the difficulty of the task, the fairness of the topics chosen, and perceptions of relevance to what the test takers were studying in their language programme.

In this particular study task difficulty and test-taker ability was estimated using multifaceted Rasch analysis, so that perceptions of task difficulty could be compared with actual task difficulty. In addition, responses to the questionnaire were analysed using factor analysis in order to investigate whether groups of questions were related. The use of quantitative methods to aid the interpretation of qualitative data is commonplace in such studies. Fulcher reported that responses could be classified into three main categories:

Anxiety   Related to the interlocutor, the presence of recording equipment, the task and personal matters of self-confidence. The group discussion generated the least anxiety, and difficulty estimates for that task showed it to be the easiest of the three.

Validity   Perception of the validity of task 1 to generate a performance that could be fairly scored was found to be related to test-taker ability. Low-scoring test takers perceived the task as valid, but as ability increased the task was seen to be less valid. All test takers perceived task 2 as valid, but low-ability test takers reported that it was too difficult. Task 2 showed the highest difficulty estimates of the three tasks. All test takers considered task 3 valid.

Enjoyment   Task 3 was perceived as the most enjoyable task, and preferred by more than half of the test takers. Those who preferred task 1 were test takers with lower ability estimates who reported finding it easier than the other tasks.

Fulcher (1996a) did not publish transcripts of the interview with the test takers once they had completed all three tasks (in a different order), but summarised some of the main comments under each of the categories listed above. Fulcher showed selected test takers videotapes of their performances on the three tasks and then conducted a structured interview. Extracts from the interviews are provided below, which show how important this type of qualitative data can be to understanding perceptions and processes. Interviewer talk is recorded in [square brackets].

Extract 1. Student 2, Question 2

[If you could do the test again, with exactly the same material, would you do anything differently?]

Maybe. I don't think so. Well, now that I've looked at it again I know some words that I could use, better words. And if two people do an interview it's better I think because if you don't know what to say there comes a time when you don't speak and you don't know what to say, the other he speaks and fills the gap. [Did you like in the discussion task having the time to prepare?] Yeah, it was very useful. It was something to think of what we were going to say so we didn't have a gap. [When you were preparing for that, how did you go about preparing it?] We said that er one was going to er be on one side and the other going to be on the other side; to have a conversation we were going to be on the opposite er . . . side.

Extract 2. Student 3, Question 1

[What were you thinking about during the test?]

What a terrible experience (laughter) well er, I don't know, maybe I was trying to guess the next question to answer er while I was looking at the pictures. I was trying to think about the possible questions you know and think about the possible answers erm . . . I was thinking I think a bit more than er the usual one because I was trying to speak right and not make so many mistakes. And I think that's why I couldn't speak very much. [Do you find tasks where you are given planning time easier?] Yes. But it depends on the subject, like the pictures I don't think I need to prepare myself. I mean they were easy questions about my life so I didn't have to be prepared, but about the other subjects I think it was easier because it was about the university so I had to plan what I was going to say. To organise my ideas and . . .

Extract 3. Student 4, Question 2

[If you could do the test again, with exactly the same material, would you do anything differently?]

Yes, I want to do something different but I don't think I would do anything different. Maybe I would talk louder. I don't think I would do anything else. [Yes, you have got a very quite voice, and are you shy generally?] Yes. [Do you think that would influence an examiner?] Yes, definitely, because if I don't have fluency that means I won't get any marks. [So just for a test you think that you have to alter your character?] Yes. I try to but I don't think I can do anything different, because I don't feel it's natural. When I talk with others I feel it's more natural than in the interview. I just don't like it. [I hope you don't mind if I follow this one. When you're outside say just with friends, you don't have the same problems with talking and expressing yourself?] It depends with what friends because let's say er the friends here at the English Institute are not too close to me but the others at school are. I've known them for many years so it's different. But still I'm shy. In the interview because I'm shy I'm nervous because I think that I won't like it. That's why. I'm nervous and I don't talk. [Can you think of anything that the interviewer could look for when you go for an interview that would tell him or her that you were shy rather than unable to talk freely? Do you understand what I mean?] Yes. Well, it depends on the examiner. If he or she is just looking for er grammar or vocabulary erm they won't understand that I'm shy. But if he knows something about psychology they would understand.

Extract 4. Student 8, Question 3

[Are you nervous when doing speaking tests?]

Well, it could be an easy thing, but it usually I can't talk I can't pronounce words correctly because my tongue gets a bit . . . and er and also when you talk you have to think fast, you have to talk a lot, talk fast, and if it isn't your native language, your first language, er you have to think a bit more. It's difficult to do all these things at the same time and talk er good English. [So the anxiety you felt is something that no one can do anything about. It's there because you are learning a second language?] I think if the er the examiner is friendly and er an he doesn't keep marking you all the time you'll feel like you're talking to a friend of yours or someone and you won't be that nervous and you won't think about the marks. It's a conversation and not a marking session so I think you'll do much better. If a person is friendly I think it's okay. If he drinks tea all the time or talks with an Oxford accent then . . .

These extracts show that test takers can be sophisticated commentators on the test-taking experience. They provide valuable information on the time allowed for a task, why they prefer one task over another (e.g. 'filling the gaps'), the types of interlocutor/rater behaviour that may help reduce anxiety, and on how they think personality factors may affect test scores. Such studies should be conducted in the very early stages of test design, when learners are first asked to take prototype tasks. Findings from questionnaires and interviews can be used to improve tasks and the test-taking experience, improve response validity and increase the likelihood that the inferences we draw from scores are valid.

Discourse analysis

Throughout this book reference has been made to the place of discourse analysis in testing second language speaking. In Chapter 2 we considered discourse as part of the definition of the speaking construct, and the role discourse definition may play in testing speaking for specific purposes. In Chapter 3 we discussed the discourse likely to be generated by different task types, and the arguments that have been put forward for including multiple-task types in speaking tests to elicit a range of discourse styles irrespective of whether changes in discourse affect test score. Also in Chapter 3 we reviewed discourse studies that have shown the OPI to generate a 'test discourse'. The role of discourse analysis in the construction of rating scales was reviewed in Chapter 4, and its place in the design of test specifications and piloting prototype tasks was outlined in Chapter 5. In Chapter 6 we returned to a consideration of interview discourse with a review of studies in interlocutor support and accommodation. The type of discourse elicited by direct and indirect tests was reviewed in Chapter 7, as was the claim that the paired interview format produces co-constructed discourse which makes it possible to assess more complex constructs.

It would not be appropriate to go back over the chapters and provide another summary of a continuous theme. We will therefore take a single study that shows the ongoing importance of discourse analysis to our under-standing of testing speaking, in the important field of the co-construction of speaking.

Work by Brown (2003) was discussed in Chapter 6. She considers the variation in interlocutor discourse, how this affects test-taker discourse, and the extent to which such variation affects scores. The study analyses the discourse of two interviews with the same test taker, conducted by two interviewers who are significantly different in harshness (as established by a multifaceted Rasch analysis). Rater 1 had an estimated difficulty of −0.86, and rater 2 an estimated difficulty of 0.75, making rater 2 much harsher. The test taker, not surprisingly, received a higher score with rater 1 than rater 2.

Brown's focus is on the interaction between the test taker and the interlocutor, with a special concern for how the interlocutor is responsible for 'constructing' the perception of the test taker's proficiency in English. In the case of rater 1 Brown reports the following discourse features:

- Topicalisation of new information and elicitation of extended responses (topic priming)
- Extension of a response by asking for additional information
- Providing a summary of previous talk (formulation)
- Topic recycling
- Assessing content (e.g. 'that's great')
- Breaking down complex questions into short explicit open questions
- Clear markers of topic change
- Natural use of backchannelling (e.g. 'hmm', 'yeah')
- Natural use of newsmakers (e.g. 'really')

These features are considered to be very supportive, maintaining and enhancing the discourse that is co-constructed between the test taker and the interlocutor. The discourse features of rater 2 are noticeably different. These can be summarised as:

- Use of echo-tag questions after closed questions, which do not elicit an extended response but are seen as confirmation checks. Brown notes that this leads to minimal responses and long pauses
- Overuse of closed questions
- Use of statements as questions that are pragmatically misunderstood
- Use of unexplicit questions
- Sudden topic shifts with unclear markers
- Use of backchannelling and newsmarkers as indicators that an extended response is expected
- Failure to reformulate failed prompts

Brown characterises the style of rater 1 as 'teacherly' and supportive, and that of rater 2 as 'casual' and more typical of interaction between two first-language speakers of English. Whether this is an accurate characterisation is an empirical question, but there can be little doubt that in this important study of one test taker and two interlocutor/raters Brown has shown that in some cases discourse variation affects test score. This and other discourse studies provide support for the introduction of interlocutor frames by the University of Cambridge Local Examinations Syndicate, an example of which can be found in Chapter 3. More importantly, she provides data that explicitly challenges us to consider the extent to which variation that can be traced to the co-construction of discourse in a speaking test should be defined as construct-relevant, or controlled as construct-irrelevant (see the discussion in Chapter 2).

Finally, we should also note that the interpretation of this data is meaningful because Brown also had quantitative information about the ability estimate of the test taker and the relative harshness of the two raters. She also analysed verbal reports from the two raters to discover their perception of the test taker, thereby combining information from two qualitative and one quantitative analysis. Even with only one test taker, this approach has considerably strengthened the plausibility of the evidence presented, and shows the value of discourse-based evidence in studying speaking tests.

Verbal protocol analysis

Interview and verbal protocol analysis (VPA) are two separate approaches to collecting information. They differ in that:

> VPA distinguishes itself from other techniques that employ verbal data because, in the case of VPA, inferences are actually made about the cognitive processes that produced the verbalisation. In this way, it differs from techniques, such as discourse analysis or interviewing, which focus primarily on linguistic content and structure, and the formation of what is said.   (Green, 1998: 1)

Verbal reporting is therefore a type of introspection that assumes the test takers are capable of verbalising their cognitive processes, or at least providing information from which the researcher is able to uncover their cognitive processes. This has been controversial, not least because of problems associated with reliability (both the reliability of the individual who is introspecting and the researcher who is interpreting). Disquiet has also been voiced over the implicit assumption that verbalisation of cognitive processes can be 'direct' rather than mediated through the natural human tendency to 'make sense' of whatever it is we pay attention to. In other words, when the focus is specifically on cognitive processes, there is a question about whether verbal data can really count as 'direct evidence'. For an extensive discussion of these theoretical issues, as well as an excellent account of the methodology of VPA and stimulated recall in general, the reader should consult Gass and Mackey (2000).

Ericsson and Simon (1987) present the basic model for VPA, in which it is assumed that when undertaking a task the individual is constructing 'silent speech'. 'Talk aloud' is a method in which the researcher gets the individual to verbalise that silent speech. If the individual pays attention to anything other than the silent speech, the method is called 'Think aloud'. Green (1998: 8) notes that it is not always possible to separate Talk Aloud from Think Aloud, and in principle it seems unlikely that asked to verbalise thoughts anyone would not immediately begin to think about (and so interpret or explain) 'pure' silent speech. This is more likely to be the case when using VPA in testing second language speaking. Neither Talk Aloud nor Think

Aloud can be used concurrently, as the test taker is already speaking. VPA therefore has to be retrospective, taking place after the testing event. The lack of immediacy means that the test taker will already have begun to interpret and explain what happened in the test.

The research that is conducted in testing second language speaking is therefore always retrospective recall that is usually stimulated through the use of a structured interviews. The result of this is that cognitive processes are rarely, if ever, studied. The focus is always on *test-taking processes* (see O'Loughlin, 2001: 134–5) rather than *test takers' cognitive processes*, and the method really counts as an 'interview' rather than 'VPA'.

However, when looking at rater processing it is possible to use concurrent Think Aloud protocols, as we have seen in Chapter 6. This is the only area in the testing of second language speaking where VPA (strictly speaking) has made an impact.

Orr (2002) explicitly claims to use VPA to investigate how raters make decisions *while they are in the process of rating*. Orr played videotapes of two FCE-type paired performances and asked 32 experienced raters to award grades to the test takers. The raters were asked to verbalise the decision-making process, which was videotaped and transcribed for analysis. Orr discovered that the raters paid attention to many facets of the performances that are not present in the rating scale. These included test-taker 'presentation', defined as how much effort they were perceived as making, their body language, and eye contact. It also appears that some of the raters were comparing the performances of the two test takers in order to decide how to rank them, and even comparing the test takers with students that the raters had taught in the recent past. One of the raters also reported being 'sympathetic' to the more nervous and weaker test taker of a pair.

This type of qualitative data has serious implications for the degree to which we are able to make correct inferences from test scores. Firstly, the test score may not have been arrived at on the basis of the descriptors in the rating scale. If this is the case when it is reported that the test taker 'can do' something, it may be that they 'can do' something else, which may not be related to the reporting descriptors. Secondly, the same score may be awarded to different test takers by raters who have 'heeded' different aspects of the performance. The same score could mean different things for different test takers. Thirdly, the rater training process is called into question. It would appear, at least from Orr's sample, that rater training has not succeeded in socialising the raters into a common understanding of the descriptors in the rating scale.

Verbal protocol analysis has much to offer in testing second language speaking. Progress has been made in the investigation of how raters arrive at decisions, which will help improve rater training and possibly the design of rating scales. More research is required into how VPA can be used to investigate test-taker cognitive processes, rather than their perceptions of tests, tasks or the speaking test format.

Summary of qualitative methods

Qualitative approaches provide insights that cannot be gained from statistical analysis. The methods we have reviewed here provide insights into how experts make judgements (critical at all stages of test development), the perceptions of test takers, the quality of co-constructed performances and the nature of interlocutor support, the processes of test taking and the process of rating. These insights, carefully documented, provide additional evidence to support a validity argument. Qualitative methods also play a significant role in appreciating how score users (such as university admissions officers, or officials in Ministries of Education) understand and use scores (Shohamy, 1997, 2001). Therefore they also have a key role in understanding the consequential validity of test use.

DIGEST

At the end of Chapter 7 we outlined Messick's validity model for the evaluation of second language speaking tests. The type of validity evidence presented in any of these categories to support the assumptions of a validity argument is dependent upon the purpose of the test, the nature of the inferences that we wish to draw from scores, and the decisions that are going to be made on the basis of test scores. In this chapter we have presented some of the more common approaches to collecting evidence that may support validity arguments. However, there is no one-to-one mapping between the categories of the model in Chapter 7 and the methods presented in this chapter. In principle, any of the methods could be adapted to collect evidence to be entered under any of the aspects of validity.

For example, while it may seem obvious from our example (Bachman and Palmer, 1981, 1983) that the multitrait-multimethod matrix is suited to collecting evidence about the external aspect of validity, there is no reason in principle why this method could not be used for investigating the structural aspect of validity. The only changes from the example in this chapter would be the selection of the trait-method units. That is, instead of 'speaking' and 'reading' the traits could be 'fluency' and 'strategy use'. The onus lies upon the researcher to select a method that is most likely to generate data that will help to refine and extend a validity argument.

Decisions about the type of validity evidence that is required for a particular speaking test, and which methods to use, are a matter of judgement. Whether the methods are primarily quantitative or qualitative, human judgement is required. As Davidson and Lynch (2002: 609) wisely reminds us:

> There is a theme that runs through common everyday use of statistics by language testers: the problems encountered and the solutions rendered are far more of a human than a mathematical challenge. Human nature is the driving force, not the technical demands of calculation.

We began this chapter with a consideration of why evidence is so important. Language testing is a public activity, and test scores usually have serious consequences for the lives of individuals. The institutions that use test scores have a responsibility to understand the utility and the limitation of test-score meaning for decision-making. And the societies that utilise tests in the larger sociopolitical framework have a responsibility to avoid the misuse of tests to achieve political agendas (Hawthorne, 1997; Shohamy, 1997, 2001; Davidson and Lynch, 2002: 77–97). Standards documents, the ILTA Code of Ethics, and Codes of Practice, have come into being to direct the practice and use of language testing to protect individuals from the misuse of test scores. They do this by laying down guidelines for how test development, test practice and score use should be conducted *in principle*. A critical part of the framework is the provision of evidence to support score meaning and use. Together with rationales, evidence should be open to public and expert scrutiny. This is a requirement for a public activity where our beliefs about the meaning of test scores impact upon the lives of others. The provision of evidence is a requirement of social justice.

The 1958 FSI band descriptors

Level 1: Elementary Proficiency. Able to satisfy routine travel needs and minimum courtesy requirements.

Can ask and answer questions on topics very familiar to him; within the scope of his very limited language experience can understand simple questions and statements, allowing for slowed speech, repetition or paraphrase; speaking vocabulary inadequate to express anything but the most elementary needs; errors in pronunciation and grammar are frequent, but can be understood by a native speaker used to dealing with foreigners attempting to speak his language; while topics which are 'very familiar' and elementary needs vary considerably from individual to individual, any person at Level 1 should be able to order a simple meal, ask for shelter or lodging, ask and give simple directions, make purchases and tell time.

Level 2: Limited Working Proficiency. Able to satisfy routine social demands and limited work requirements.

Can handle with confidence but not with facility most social situations including introductions and casual conversations about current events, as well as work, family and autobiographical information; can handle limited work requirements, needing help in handling any complications or difficulties; can get the gist of most conversations on non-technical subjects (i.e. topics which require no specialized knowledge) and has a speaking vocabulary sufficient to express himself simply with some circumlocutions; accent, though often quite faulty, is intelligible; can usually handle elementary constructions quite accurately but does not have thorough or confident control of the grammar.

Level 3: Minimum Professional Proficiency. Able to speak the language with sufficient structural accuracy and vocabulary to participate effectively in most formal and informal conversations on practical, social and professional topics.

Can discuss particular interests and special fields of competence with reasonable ease; comprehension is quite complete for a normal rate of speech; vocabulary is broad enough that he rarely has to grope for a word; accent may be obviously foreign; control of grammar good; errors never interfere with understanding and rarely disturb the native speaker.

Level 4: Full Professional Proficiency. Able to use the language fluently and accurately on all levels normally pertinent to professional needs.

Can understand and participate in any conversation within the range of his experience with a high degree of fluency and precision of vocabulary; would rarely be taken for a native speaker, but can respond appropriately even in unfamiliar situations; errors of pronunciation and grammar quite rare; can handle informal interpreting from and into the language.

Level 5: Native or Bilingual Proficiency. Speaking proficiency equivalent to that of an educated native speaker.

Has complete fluency in the language such that his speech on all levels is fully accepted by educated native speakers in all its features, including breadth of vocabulary and idiom, colloquialisms and pertinent cultural references.

FSI component scales

Accent

1. Pronunciation frequently unintelligible.
2. Frequent gross errors and a very heavy accent make understanding difficult, requires frequent repetition.
3. 'Foreign accent' requires concentrated listening and mispronunciations lead to occasional misunderstanding and apparent errors in grammar or vocabulary.
4. Marked 'foreign accent' and occasional mispronunciations which do not interfere with understanding.
5. No conspicuous mispronunciations, but would not be taken for a native speaker.
6. Native pronunciation, with no trace of 'foreign accent'.

Grammar

1. Grammar almost entirely inaccurate except in stock phrases.
2. Constant errors showing control of very few major patterns and frequently preventing communication.
3. Frequent errors showing some major patterns uncontrolled and causing occasional irritation and misunderstanding.
4. Occasional errors showing imperfect control of some patterns but no weakness that causes misunderstanding.
5. Few errors, with no patterns of failure.
6. No more than two errors during the interview.

Vocabulary

1. Vocabulary inadequate for even the simplest conversation.
2. Vocabulary limited to basic personal and survival areas (time, food, transportation, family, etc.).
3. Choice of words sometimes inaccurate, limitations of vocabulary prevent discussion of some common professional and social topics.
4. Professional vocabulary adequate to discuss special interests; general vocabulary permits discussion of any non-technical subject with some circumlocutions.

5. Professional vocabulary broad and precise; general vocabulary adequate to cope with complex practical problems and varied social situations.
6. Vocabulary apparently as accurate and extensive as that of an educated native speaker.

Fluency
1. Speech is so halting and fragmentary that conversation is virtually impossible.
2. Speech is very slow and uneven except for short or routine sentences.
3. Speech is frequently hesitant and jerky; sentences may be left uncompleted.
4. Speech is occasionally hesitant, with some unevenness caused by rephrasing and groping for words.
5. Speech is effortless and smooth, but perceptibly non-native in speed and evenness.
6. Speech on all professional and general topics is as effortless and as smooth as a native speaker's.

Comprehension
1. Understands too little for the simplest type of conversation.
2. Understands only slow very simple speech on common social and touristic topics: requires constant repetition and rephrasing.
3. Understands careful, somewhat simplified speech directed to him, with considerable repetition and rephrasing.
4. Understands quite well normal educated speech directed to him, but requires occasional repetition and rephrasing.
5. Understands everything in normal educated conversation except for very colloquial or low-frequency items, or exceptionally rapid or slurred speech.
6. Understands everything in both formal and colloquial speech to be expected of an educated native speaker.

Appendix 3

The ACTFL Guidelines 1986

Novice: The Novice level is characterized by an ability to communicate minimally with learned material.

Novice Low: Oral production consists of isolated words and perhaps a few high-frequency phrases. Essentially no functional communicative ability.

Novice Mid: Oral production continues to consist of isolated words and learned phrases within very predictable areas of need, although quantity is increased. Vocabulary is sufficient only for handling simple, elementary needs and expressing basic courtesies. Utterances rarely consist of more than two or three words and show frequent long pauses and repetition of interlocutor's words. Speaker may have some difficulty producing even the simplest utterances. Some Novice Mid speakers will be understood only with great difficulty.

Novice High: Able to satisfy partially the requirements of basic communicative exchanges by relying heavily on learned utterances but occasionally expanding these through simple recombinations of their elements. Can ask questions or make statements involving learned material. Shows signs of spontaneity, although this falls short of real autonomy of expression. Speech continues to consist of learned utterances rather than of personalized, situationally adapted ones. Vocabulary centers on areas such as basic objects, places, and most common kinship terms. Pronunciation may still be strongly influenced by first language. Errors are frequent and, in spite of repetition, some Novice High speakers will have difficulty in being understood even by sympathetic interlocutors.

Intermediate: The intermediate level is characterized by an ability to
- create with the language by combining and recombining learned elements, though primarily in a reactive mode
- initiate, minimally sustain and close in a simple way basic communicative tasks, and
- ask and answer questions

Intermediate Low: Able to handle successfully a limited number of interactive, task-oriented social situations. Can ask and answer questions, initiate and respond to simple statements, and maintain face-to-face conversation, although in a highly restricted manner and with much linguistic inaccuracy. Within these limitations, can perform such tasks as introducing self, ordering a meal, asking directions and making purchases. Vocabulary is adequate to express only the most elementary needs. Strong interference from native language may occur. Misunderstandings frequently arise, but with repetition, the Intermediate Low speaker can generally be understood by sympathetic interlocutors.

Intermediate-Mid: Able to handle successfully a variety of uncomplicated, basic communicative tasks and social situations. Can talk simply about self and family members. Can ask and answer questions and participate in simple conversations on topics beyond the most immediate needs; e.g. personal history and leisure-time activities. Utterance length increases slightly, but speech may continue to be characterized by frequent long pauses, since the smooth incorporation of even basic conversational strategies is often hindered as the speaker struggles to create appropriate language forms. Pronunciation may continue to be strongly influenced by first language and fluency may still be strained. Although misunderstandings still arise, the Intermediate Mid speaker can generally be understood by sympathetic interlocutors.

Intermediate High: Able to handle successfully most uncomplicated communicative tasks and social situations. Can initiate, sustain, and close a general conversation with a number of strategies appropriate to a range of circumstances and topics, but errors are evident. Limited vocabulary still necessitates hesitation and may bring about slightly unexpected circumlocution. There is emerging evidence of connected discourse, particularly for simple narration and/or description. The Intermediate High speaker can generally be understood even by interlocutors not accustomed to dealing with speaking at this level, but repetition may still be required.

Advanced: The Advanced level is characterized by an ability to
* converse in a clearly participatory fashion
* initiate, sustain, and bring to closure a wide variety of communicative tasks, including those that require an increased ability to convey meaning with diverse language strategies due to a complication or an unforeseen turn of events
* satisfy the requirements of school and work situations, and
* narrate and describe with paragraph-length connected discourse

Advanced: Able to satisfy the requirements of everyday situations and routine school and work requirements. Can handle with confidence but not facility complicated tasks and social situations, such as elaborating, complaining and apologizing. Can narrate and describe with some details, linking sentences together smoothly. Can communicate facts and talk casually about topics of current public and personal interest, using general vocabulary. Shortcomings can often be smoothed over by communicative strategies, such as pause fillers, stalling devices and different rates of speech. Circumlocution which arises from vocabulary or syntactic limitations very often is quite successful, though some groping for words may still be evident. The Advanced level speaker can be understood without difficulty by native interlocutors.

Advanced Plus: Able to satisfy the requirements of a broad variety of everyday, school and work situations. Can discuss concrete topics relating to particular interests and special fields of competence. There is emerging evidence of ability to support opinions, explain in detail and hypothesize. The Advanced Plus speaker often shows a well-developed ability to compensate for an imperfect grasp of some forms with confident use of communicative strategies, such as paraphrasing and circumlocution. Differentiated vocabulary and intonation are effectively used to communicate fine shades of meaning. The Advanced Plus speaker often shows remarkable fluency and ease of speech, but under the demands of Superior Level, complex tasks, language may break down or prove inadequate.

Superior: The Superior level is characterized by an ability to
• participate effectively in most formal and informal conversations on practical, social, professional and abstract topics, and
• support opinions and hypothesize using native-like discourse strategies

Superior: Able to speak the language with sufficient accuracy to participate effectively in most formal and informal conversations on practical, social, professional and abstract topics. Can discuss special fields of competence and interest with ease. Can support opinions and hypothesize, but may not be able to tailor language to audience or discuss in depth highly abstract or unfamiliar topics. Usually the Superior level speaker is only partially familiar with regional or other dialectical variants. The Superior level speaker commands a wide variety of interactive strategies and shows good awareness of discourse strategies. The latter involves the ability to distinguish main ideas from supporting information through syntactic, lexical and suprasegmental features (pitch, stress, intonation). Sporadic errors may occur, particularly in low-frequency structures and some complex high-frequency structures more common to formal writing, but no patterns of error are evident. Errors do not disturb the native speaker or interfere with communication.

The Revised ACTFL Guidelines 1999

SUPERIOR

Speakers at the Superior level are able to communicate in the language with accuracy and fluency in order to participate fully and effectively in conversations on a variety of topics in formal and informal settings from both concrete and abstract perspectives. They discuss their interests and special fields of competence, explain complex matters in detail, and provide lengthy and coherent narrations, all with ease, fluency and accuracy. They explain their opinions on a number of topics of importance to them, such as social and political issues, and provide structured argument to support their opinions. They are able to construct and develop hypotheses to explore alternative possibilities. When appropriate, they use extended discourse without unnaturally lengthy hesitation to make their point, even when engaged in abstract elaborations. Such discourse, while coherent, may still be influenced by the Superior speakers' own language patterns, rather than those of the target language. Superior speakers command a variety of interactive and discourse strategies, such as turn-taking and separating main ideas from supporting information through the use of syntactic and lexical devices, as well as intonational features such as pitch, stress and tone. They demonstrate virtually no pattern of error in the use of basic structures. However, they may make sporadic errors, particularly in low-frequency structures and in some complex high-frequency structures more common to formal speech and writing. Such errors, if they do occur, do not distract the native interlocutor or interfere with communication.

ADVANCED HIGH

Speakers at the Advanced High level perform all Advanced-level tasks with linguistic ease, confidence and competence. They are able to consistently explain in detail and narrate fully and accurately in all time frames. In addition, Advanced High speakers handle the tasks pertaining to the Superior level but cannot sustain performance at that level across a variety of topics.

They can provide a structured argument to support their opinions, and they may construct hypotheses, but patterns of error appear. They can discuss some topics abstractly, especially those relating to their particular interests and special fields of expertise, but in general, they are more comfortable discussing a variety of topics concretely. Advanced High speakers may demonstrate a well-developed ability to compensate for an imperfect grasp of some forms or for limitations in, vocabulary by the confident use of communicative strategies, such as paraphrasing, circumlocution and illustration. They use precise vocabulary and intonation to express meaning and often show great fluency and ease of speech. However, when called on to perform the complex tasks associated with the Superior level over a variety of topics, their language will at times break down or prove inadequate, or they may avoid the task altogether, for example, by resorting to simplification through the use of description or narration in place of argument or hypothesis.

ADVANCED MID

Speakers at the Advanced Mid level are able to handle with ease and confidence a large number of communicative tasks. They participate actively in most informal and some formal exchanges on a variety of concrete topics relating to work, school, home and leisure activities, as well as to events of current, public and personal interest or individual relevance. Advanced Mid speakers demonstrate the ability to narrate and describe in all major time frames (past, present and future) by providing a full account, with good control of aspect, as they adapt flexibly to the demands of the conversation. Narration and description tend to be combined and interwoven to relate relevant and supporting facts in connected, paragraph-length discourse. Advanced Mid speakers can handle successfully and with relative ease the linguistic challenges presented by a complication or unexpected turn of events that occurs within the context of a routine situation or communicative task with which they are otherwise familiar. Communicative strategies such as circumlocution or rephrasing are often employed for this purpose. The speech of Advanced Mid speakers performing Advanced-level tasks is marked by substantial flow. Their vocabulary is fairly extensive although primarily generic in nature, except in the case of a particular area of specialization or interest. Dominant language discourse structures tend to recede, although discourse may still reflect the oral paragraph structure of their own language rather than that of the target language. Advanced Mid speakers contribute to conversations on a variety of familiar topics, dealt with concretely, with much accuracy, clarity and precision, and they convey their intended message without misrepresentation or confusion. They are readily understood by native speakers unaccustomed to dealing with non-natives. When called on to perform functions or handle topics associated with the Superior level, the quality and/or quantity of their speech will generally decline. Advanced Mid speakers are often able to state an opinion or cite conditions; however, they lack the ability to consistently provide a structured argument in extended discourse. Advanced Mid speakers may use a number of delaying strategies, resort to narration, description, explanation or anecdote, or simply attempt to avoid the linguistic demands of Superior-level tasks.

ADVANCED LOW

Speakers at the Advanced Low level are able to handle a variety of communicative tasks, although somewhat haltingly at times. They participate actively in most informal and a limited number of formal conversations on activities related to school, home and leisure activities and, to a lesser degree, those related to events of work, current, public and personal interest or individual relevance. Advanced Low speakers demonstrate the ability to narrate and describe in all major time frames (past, present and future) in paragraph-length discourse, but control of aspect may be lacking at times. They can handle appropriately the linguistic challenges presented by a complication or unexpected turn of events that occurs within the context of a routine situation or communicative task with which they are otherwise familiar, though at times their discourse may be minimal for the level and strained. Communicative strategies such as rephrasing and circumlocution may be employed in such instances. In their narrations and descriptions, they combine and link sentences into connected discourse of paragraph length. When pressed for a fuller account, they tend to grope and rely on minimal discourse. Their utterances are typically not longer than a single paragraph. Structure of the dominant language is still evident in the use of false cognates, literal translations or the oral paragraph structure of the speaker's own language rather than that of the target language. While the language of Advanced Low speakers may be marked by substantial, albeit irregular flow, it is typically somewhat strained and tentative, with noticeable self-correction and a certain 'grammatical roughness'. The vocabulary of Advanced Low speakers is primarily generic in nature. Advanced Low speakers contribute to the conversation with sufficient accuracy, clarity and precision to convey their intended message without misrepresentation or confusion, and it can be understood by native speakers unaccustomed to dealing with non-natives, even though this may be achieved through repetition and restatement. When attempting to perform functions or handle topics associated with the Superior level, the linguistic quality and quantity of their speech will deteriorate significantly.

INTERMEDIATE HIGH

Intermediate High speakers are able to converse with ease and confidence when dealing with most routine tasks and social situations of the Intermediate level. They are able to handle successfully many uncomplicated tasks and social situations requiring an exchange of basic information related to work, school, recreation, particular interests and areas of competence, though hesitation and errors may be evident. Intermediate High speakers handle the tasks pertaining to the Advanced level, but they are unable to sustain performance at that level over a variety of topics. With some consistency, speakers at the Intermediate High level narrate and describe in major time frames using connected discourse of paragraph length. However, their performance of these Advanced-level tasks will exhibit one or more features of breakdown, such as the failure to maintain the narration or description semantically or syntactically in the appropriate major time frame, the disintegration of connected discourse, the misuse of cohesive devices, a reduction in breadth and appropriateness of vocabulary, the failure to successfully circumlocute, or a significant amount of hesitation. Intermediate High speakers can generally be understood by native speakers unaccustomed to dealing with non-natives, although the dominant language is still evident (e.g. use of code-switching, false cognates, literal translations, etc.), and gaps in communication may occur.

INTERMEDIATE MID

Speakers at the Intermediate Mid level are able to handle successfully a variety of uncomplicated communicative tasks in straightforward social situations. Conversation is generally limited to those predictable and concrete exchanges necessary for survival in the target culture; these include personal information covering self, family, home, daily activities, interests and personal preferences, as well as physical and social needs, such as food, shopping, travel and lodging. Intermediate Mid speakers tend to function reactively, for example, by responding to direct questions or requests for information. However, they are capable of asking a variety of questions when necessary to obtain simple information to satisfy basic needs, such as directions, prices and services. When called on to perform functions or handle topics at the Advanced level, they provide some information but have difficulty linking ideas, manipulating time and aspect, and using communicative strategies, such as circumlocution. Intermediate Mid speakers are able to express personal meaning by creating with the language, in part by combining and recombining known elements and conversational input to make utterances of sentence length and some strings of sentences. Their speech may contain pauses, reformulations and self-corrections as they search for adequate vocabulary and appropriate language forms to express themselves. Because of inaccuracies in their vocabulary and/or pronunciation and/or grammar and/or syntax, misunderstandings can occur, but Intermediate Mid speakers are generally understood by sympathetic interlocutors accustomed to dealing with non-natives.

INTERMEDIATE LOW

Speakers at the Intermediate Low level are able to handle successfully a limited number of uncomplicated communicative tasks by creating with the language in straightforward social situations. Conversation is restricted to some of the concrete exchanges and predictable topics necessary for survival in the target language culture. These topics relate to basic personal information covering, for example, self and family, some daily activities and personal preferences, as well as to some immediate needs, such as ordering food and making simple purchases. At the Intermediate Low level, speakers are primarily reactive and struggle to answer direct questions or requests for information, but they are also able to ask a few appropriate questions. Intermediate Low speakers express personal meaning by combining and recombining into short statements what they know and what they hear from their interlocutors. Their utterances are often filled with hesitancy and inaccuracies as they search for appropriate linguistic forms and vocabulary while attempting to give form to the message. Their speech is characterized by frequent pauses, ineffective reformulations and self-corrections. Their pronunciation, vocabulary and syntax are strongly influenced by their first language but, in spite of frequent misunderstandings that require repetition or rephrasing, Intermediate Low speakers can generally be understood by sympathetic interlocutors, particularly by those accustomed to dealing with non-natives.

NOVICE HIGH

Speakers at the Novice High level are able to handle a variety of tasks pertaining to the Intermediate level, but are unable to sustain performance at that level. They are able to manage successfully a number of uncomplicated communicative tasks in straightforward social situations. Conversation is restricted to a few of the predictable topics necessary for survival in the target language culture, such as basic personal information, basic objects and a limited number of activities, preferences and immediate needs. Novice High speakers respond to simple, direct questions or requests for information; they are able to ask only a very few formulaic questions when asked to do so. Novice High speakers are able to express personal meaning by relying heavily on learned phrases or recombinations of these and what they hear from their interlocutor. Their utterances, which consist mostly of short and sometimes incomplete sentences in the present, may be hesitant or inaccurate. On the other hand, since these utterances are frequently only expansions of learned material and stock phrases, they may sometimes appear surprisingly fluent and accurate. These speakers' first language may strongly influence their pronunciation, as well as their vocabulary and syntax when they attempt to personalize their utterances. Frequent misunderstandings may arise but, with repetition or rephrasing, Novice High speakers can generally be understood by sympathetic interlocutors used to non-natives. When called on to handle simply a variety of topics and perform functions pertaining to the Intermediate level, a Novice High speaker can sometimes respond in intelligible sentences, but will not be able to sustain sentence-level discourse.

NOVICE MID

Speakers at the Novice Mid level communicate minimally and with difficulty by using a number of isolated words and memorized phrases limited by the particular context in which the language has been learned. When responding to direct questions, they may utter only two or three words at a time or an occasional stock answer. They pause frequently as they search for simple vocabulary or attempt to recycle their own and their interlocutor's words. Because of hesitations, lack of vocabulary, inaccuracy or failure to respond appropriately, Novice Mid speakers may be understood with great difficulty even by sympathetic interlocutors accustomed to dealing with non-natives. When called on to handle topics by performing functions associated with the Intermediate level, they frequently resort to repetition, words from their native language or silence.

NOVICE LOW

Speakers at the Novice Low level have no real functional ability and, because of their pronunciation, they may be unintelligible. Given adequate time and familiar cues, they may be able to exchange greetings, give their identity and name a number of familiar objects from their immediate environment. They are unable to perform functions or handle topics pertaining to the Intermediate level, and cannot therefore participate in a true conversational exchange.

Appendix 5

Sample rating scales

THE BACHMAN AND PALMER SCALE (1982)*

Sociolinguistic competence

Main trait rating	Distinction of formulaic	Register substantive	Nativeness	Cultural references
4	Control of both formal and informal registers	Control of both formal and informal registers	No non-native but grammatical structures	Full control
3		Evidence of two registers, and control of formal or informal	Rare non-native but grammatical structures	Some control
2	Evidence of two registers, and control of formal or informal	Evidence of two registers	Frequent non-native but grammatical structures	
1	Evidence of two registers	Evidence of only one register	or impossible to judge because of interference from other factors	No control
	Evidence of only one register			
0				

Grammatical competence

Main trait rating	Range	Accuracy
6	Complete range of morphologic and syntactic structures	No errors not expectable of a native speaker.
5		Control of most structures used with few error types.
4	Large, but not complete, range of both morphologic and syntactic structures.	
3		Control of some structures used, but with many error types.
2	Limited range of both morphologic and syntactic structures, but with some systematic evidence.	
1	No systematic evidence of morphologic and syntactic structures.	Control of few or no structures. Errors of all or most possible types frequent.
0		

Pragmatic competence

Main trait rating	Vocabulary	Cohesion	Organization
4	Extensive vocabulary	Excellent cohesion using a variety of appropriate devices	Excellent ability to organize consciously
3	Large vocabulary	Good cohesion, including subordination.	Moderate ability to organize consciously
2	Vocabulary of moderate size	Moderate cohesion, including coordination.	
1	Small vocabulary	Very little cohesion; relationships between structures not adequately marked.	Natural organization only (i.e. not consciously imposed) or
0	Limited vocabulary (A few words and formulate phrases)	Language completely disjointed	Poor ability to organize consciously

ILR SCALE, 1991

---

5   **Functional Native Proficiency**. Speaking proficiency is functionally equivalent to that of a highly articulate, well-educated native speaker and reflects the cultural standards of the country where the language is natively spoken. The individual uses the language with complete flexibility and intuition, so that speech on all levels is fully accepted by well-educated native speakers in all of its features, including breadth of vocabulary and idiom, colloquialisms and pertinent cultural references. Pronunciation is typically consistent with that of well-educated native speakers of a non-stigmatised dialect.

4+   **Advanced Professional Proficiency, Plus**. Speaking proficiency is regularly superior in all respects usually equivalent to that of a well-educated, highly articulate native speaker. Language ability does not impede the performance of any language-use task. However, the individual would not necessarily be perceived as culturally native.

Examples: The individual organises discourse well, employing functional rhetorical speech devices, native cultural references and understanding. Effectively applies a native speaker's social and circumstantial knowledge. However, cannot sustain that performance under all circumstances. While the individual has a wide range and control of structure, an occasional non-native slip may occur. The individual has a sophisticated control of vocabulary and phrasing that is rarely imprecise, yet there are occasional weakness in idioms, colloquialisms, pronunciation and cultural reference, or there may be occasional failure to interact in a totally native manner.

---

4   **Advanced Professional Proficiency**: Able to use the language fluently and accurately on all levels normally pertinent to professional needs. The individual's language usage and ability to function are fully successful. Organises discourse well, using appropriate speech devices, native cultural references and understanding. Language ability only rarely hinders him/her in performing any task requiring language, yet the individual would seldom be perceived as a native. Speaks effortlessly and smoothly and is able to use the language with a high degree of effectiveness, reliability and precision for all representational purposes within the range of personal and professional experience and scope of responsibilities. Can serve as an informal interpreter in a range of unpredictable circumstances. Can perform extensive, sophisticated language tasks, encompassing most matters of interest to well-educated native speakers, including tasks which do not bear directly on a professional speciality.

Examples: Can discuss in detail concepts which are fundamentally different from those of the target culture and make those concepts clear and accessible to the native speaker. Similarly, the individual can understand the details and ramifications of concepts that are culturally or conceptually different from his/her own. Can set the tone of interpersonal official, semi-official and non-professional verbal exchanges with a representative range of native speakers (in a range of varied audiences, purposes, tasks and settings). Can play an effective role among native speakers in such contexts as conferences, lectures and debates on matters of disagreement. Can advocate a position at length, both formally and in chance encounters, using sophisticated verbal strategies. Can understand and reliably produce shifts of both subject matter and tone. Can understand native speakers of the standard and other major dialects in essentially any face-to-face interaction.

3+ **General Professional Proficiency, Plus**: Is often able to use the language to satisfy professional needs in a wide range of sophisticated and demanding tasks.

Examples: Despite obvious strengths, may exhibit some hesitancy, uncertainty, effort or errors which limit the range of language-use tasks that can be reliably performed. Typically, there is particular strength in fluency and one or more, but not all, of the following: breadth of lexicon, including items of low and medium frequencies, especially sociolinguistic/cultural references and nuances of close synonyms; structural precision, with sophisticated features that are readily, accurately and appropriately controlled (such as complex modifications and embedding in Indo-European languages); discourse competence in a wide range of contexts and tasks, often matching a native speaker's strategic and organisational abilities and expectations. Occasional patterned errors occur in low-frequency and highly complex structures.

3   **General Professional Proficiency**: Able to speak the language with sufficient structural accuracy and vocabulary to participate effectively in most formal and informal conversations on practical, social and professional topics. Nevertheless, the individual's limitations generally restrict the professional contexts of language use to matters of shared knowledge and/or international convention. Discourse is cohesive. The individual uses the language acceptably, but with some noticeable imperfections; yet, errors virtually never interfere with understanding and rarely disturb the native speaker. The individual can effectively combine structure and vocabulary to convey his/her meaning accurately. The individual speaks readily and fills pauses suitably. In face-to-face conversations with natives speaking the standard dialect at a normal rate of speech, comprehension is quite complete. Although cultural references, proverbs and the implications of nuances and idioms may not be fully understood, the individual can easily repair the conversation. Pronunciation may be obviously foreign. Individual sounds are accurate; but stress, intonation and pitch control may be faulty.

Examples: Can typically discuss particular interests and special fields of competence with reasonable ease. Can use the language as part of normal professional duties such as clarifying points, answering objections, justifying decisions, understanding the essence of challenges, stating and defending policy, conducting meetings, delivering briefings, or other extended and elaborate informative monologues. Can reliably elicit information and opinion from native speakers. Structural inaccuracy is rarely the major cause of misunderstanding. Use of structural devices is flexible and elaborate. Without searching for words or phrases, the individual uses the language clearly and relatively naturally to elaborate concepts freely and make ideas easily understandable to native speakers. Errors occur in low-frequency and highly complex structures.

2+ **Limited Working Proficiency, Plus**: Able to satisfy most work requirements with language usage that is often, but not always, acceptable and effective. The individual shows considerable ability to communicate effectively on topics relating to particular interests and special fields of competencies. Often shows a high degree of fluency and ease of speech, yet when under tension or pressure, the ability to use the language effectively may deteriorate. Comprehension of normal native speech is typically nearly complete. The individual may miss cultural and local references and may require a native speaker to adjust to his/her limitations in some ways. Native speakers often perceive the individual's speech to contain awkward or inaccurate phrasing of ideas, mistaken time, space and person references, or to be inappropriate in some way, if not strictly incorrect.

Examples: Typically, the individual can participate in most social, formal and information interactions; but limitations either in range of contexts, types of tasks or level of accuracy hinder effectiveness. The individual may be ill at ease with the use of the language either in social interaction or in speaking at length in professional contexts. He/she is generally strong in either structural precision or vocabulary, but not in both. Weakness or unevenness in one of the foregoing, or in pronunciation, occasionally results in miscommunication. Normally controls, but cannot always easily produce, general vocabulary. Discourse is often incohesive.

2 **Limited Working Proficiency**: Able to satisfy routine social demands and limited work requirements. Can handle routine work-related interactions that are limited in scope. In more complex and sophisticated work-related tasks, language usage generally disturbs the native speaker. Can handle with confidence, but not facility, most normal high-frequency social conversational situations, including extensive but casual conversations about current events, as well as work, family and autobiographical information. The individual can get the gist of most everyday conversations but has some difficulty understanding native speakers in situations that require specialised or sophisticated knowledge. The individual's utterances are minimally cohesive. Linguistic structure is usually not very elaborate and not thoroughly controlled; errors are frequent, vocabulary use is appropriate for high-frequency utterances, but unusual or imprecise elsewhere.

Examples: While these interactions will vary widely from individual to individual, the individual can typically ask and answer predicable questions in the workplace and give straightforward instructions to subordinates. Additionally, the individual can participate in personal and accommodation-type interactions with elaboration and facility; that is, can give and understand complicated, detailed and extensive directions and make non-routine changes in travel and accommodation arrangements. Simple structures and basic grammatical relations are typically controlled. However, there are areas of weakness. For example, in the commonly taught languages, these may be simple markings such as plurals, articles, linking words and negatives or more complex structures such as tense/aspect usage, case morphology, passive constructions, word order and embedding.

1+   **Elementary Proficiency, Plus**: Can initiate and maintain predictable face-to-face conversations and satisfy limited social demands. He/she may, however, have little understanding of the social conventions of conversation. The interlocutor is generally required to strain and employ real-world knowledge to understand even some simple speech. The speaker at this level may hesitate and may have to change subjects due to lack of language resources. Range and control of the language are limited. Speech largely consists of a series of short, discrete utterances.

Examples: The individual is able to satisfy most travel and accommodation needs and a limited range of social demands beyond exchange of skeletal biographic information. Speaking ability may extend beyond immediate survival needs. Accuracy in basic grammatical relations is evident, although not consistent. May exhibit the more common forms of verb tenses, for example, but may make frequent errors in formation and selection. While some structures are established, errors occur in more complex patterns. The individual typically cannot sustain coherent structures in longer utterances or unfamiliar situations. Ability to describe and give precise information is limited. Person, space and time references are often used incorrectly. Pronunciation is understandable to natives used to dealing with foreigners. Can combine most significant sounds with reasonable comprehensibility but has difficulty in producing certain sounds in certain positions or in certain combinations. Speech will usually be laboured. Frequently has to repeat utterances to be understood by the general public.

1   **Elementary Proficiency**: Able to satisfy minimum courtesy requirements and maintain very simple face-to-face conversations on familiar topics. A native speaker must often use slowed speech, repetition, paraphrase or a combination of these to be understood by this individual. Similarly, the native speaker must strain and employ real-world knowledge to understand even simple statements/questions from this individual. The speaker has a functional, but limited proficiency. Misunderstandings are frequent, but the individual is able to ask for help and to verify comprehension of native speech in face-to-face interaction. The individual is unable to produce continuous discourse except with rehearsed material.

Examples: Structural accuracy is likely to be random or severely limited. Time concepts are vague. Vocabulary is inaccurate, and its range is very narrow. The individual often speaks with great difficulty. By repeating, such speakers can make themselves understood to native speakers who are in regular contact with foreigners, but there is little precision in the information conveyed. Needs, experience or training may vary greatly from individual to individual; for example, speakers at this level may have encountered quite different vocabulary areas. However, the individual can typically satisfy predictable, simple, personal and accommodation needs; can generally meet courtesy, introduction and identification requirements; exchange greetings and elicit and provide, for example, predictable and skeletal biographical information. He/she might give information about business hours, explain routine procedures in a limited way and state in a simple manner what actions will be taken. He/she is able to formulate some questions even in languages with complicated question constructions. Almost every utterance may be characterised by structural errors and errors in basic grammatical relations. Vocabulary is extremely limited and characteristically does not include modifiers. Pronunciation, stress and intonation are generally poor, often heavily influenced by another language. Use of structure and vocabulary is highly imprecise.

0+ **Memorised Proficiency**: Able to satisfy immediate needs using rehearsed utterances. Shows little real autonomy of expression, flexibility or spontaneity. Can ask questions or make statements with reasonable accuracy only with memorised utterances or formulas. Attempts at creating speech are unsuccessful.

Examples: The individual's vocabulary is usually limited to areas of immediate survival needs. Most utterances are telegraphic: that is, functors (linking words, markers and the like) are omitted, confused or distorted. An individual can usually differentiate most significant sounds when produced in isolation, but, when combined in words or groups of words, errors may be frequent. Even with repetition, communication is severely limited even with persons used to dealing with foreigners. Stress, intonation, tone, etc., are usually quite faulty.

0 **No Proficiency**: Unable to function in the spoken language. Oral production is limited to occasional isolated words. Has essentially no communicative ability.

Appendix 6

International second language proficiency ratings

0	ZERO PROFICIENCY	Unable to communicate in the language.
0+	FORMULAIC PROFICIENCY	Able to perform in a very limited capacity within the most immediate, predictable areas of need, using essentially formulaic language.
1–	MINIMUM 'CREATIVE' PROFICIENCY	Able to satisfy immediate, predictable needs, using predominantly formulaic language.
1	BASIC TRANSACTIONAL PROFICIENCY	Able to satisfy basic everyday transactional needs.
1+	TRANSACTIONAL PROFICIENCY	Able to satisfy everyday transactional needs and limited social needs.
2	BASIC SOCIAL PROFICIENCY	Able to satisfy basic social needs, and routine needs pertinent to everyday commerce and to linguistically undemanding 'vocational' fields.
2+	SOCIAL PROFICIENCY	
3	BASIC 'VOCATIONAL' PROFICIENCY	Able to perform effectively in most informal and formal situations pertinent to social and community life and everyday commerce and recreation, and in situations which are not linguistically demanding in own 'vocational' fields.
3+	BASIC 'VOCATIONAL' PROFICIENCY PLUS	
4	'VOCATIONAL' PROFICIENCY	Able to perform very effectively in almost all situations pertinent to social and community life and everyday commerce and recreation, and generally in almost all situations pertinent to own 'vocational' fields.
4+	ADVANCED 'VOCATIONAL' PROFICIENCY	
5	NATIVE-LIKE PROFICIENCY	Proficiency equivalent to that of a native speaker of the same sociocultural variety.

Appendix 7

A sample transcript

A> Hello:: I'm (NAME) B> I'm (NAME) not (NAME) A> (NAME) [yes B> yeah] A> that's what that's what I've got that's [what B> ah] A> that's what I said [the B> but] they called me (NAME) A> ah yeah they it was the the person who I asked him to call you but er never mind: anyway I understand you're a pharmacist B> yeah A> is that right tell me something about your work B> ah: erm /2/ I work at I don't know if you know Cyprus at all A> yes I do B> I work at (NAME) hospital A> hm m B> and I work as a pharmacist as a hospital pharmacist we are three pharmacists there we actually erm /2/ dispense medicines and er: /4/ of course we have other things like preparing: some kinds of medicines the (inaudible) A> yeah B> sceptic solution: A> hm: so it's generally dealing with drugs in the hospital that B> yeah and of course we supply the medicines to most other wards and casualty and we're actually responsible: A> yeah so you have to check to make sure that none of them go missing B> yeah but their expiry dates erm: /4/ if they're kept well if they're kept properly A> yeah it sounds very interesting is (NAME) a big hospital B> no actually it it's a small one A> hm: right but you you live out there in (NAME) B> I have to (laughter) A> yeah B> because I am er: I am /2/ on call every other day A> yeah B> er but I I /4/ come from Nicosia A> hm so you would you like to transfer to Nicosia General if [you B> yeah] were given half [the chance B> for sure] A> or Makarios probably even nicer B> yes [(laughter)] A> yeah because Makarios is a modern hospital whereas Nicosia is beginning to fall to bits B> yes A> a little isn't it B> one of the most er: /3/ it's the most A> yeah okay B> but I'm interesting in drug quality control A> hm: okay well I'll ask you about that in a in a few minutes B> ah A> but you you chose to do the medicine the medical version this morning B> (laughter) yes A> so I'm going to ask you to have another look at this could you turn to page one it's the very first page in there B> first page yeah A> yeah you remember reading this this morning very [quickly B> yes] A> I guess B> very very quickly [(laughter)] A> yeah B> that was the trick A> okay well this was about plutonium in the body: and I'm going to have to ask you about this diagram here er again: in the bottom left hand side left hand corner down here there's a box with an X in it: my first question is can you identify what X [is B> bones] A> the bones B> yeah A> okay can you tell me how the bones how how it how it's related to the rest of the diagram I mean what happens to plutonium and how it gets into the bones and so on B> ah: er /2/ plutonium enters the body through inhalation: okay A> hm hm B> I start from the beginning [(laughter A> okay] B> erm /2/ then it goes to the digestive system A> hm hm B> and to the (inaudible) lungs some in the lungs:: /2/ from the lungs it goes er /2/ through the reticuloendothelial system A> hm which is: [what B> erm] /2/ A> does that what does it mean that word B> well ah it's a system that er /2/ has to do with erm: /5/ fibrocytosis: A> no you're going to have to explain for me B> erm: consisted for from er: /2/ cells A> hm hm B> that actually are responsible for er: /6/ to take: er foreign material A> hm hm B> out of the body erm /4/ and this is done: er /2/ when they put into the circulation A> okay right B> (laughter) A> I think I've got that B> yeah: and er /2/ from that system goes to the blood A> hm hm B> and from the circulation: er /2/ to bones kidneys and the liver A> yes okay how's erm: you you said that that plutonium was taken into the body through inhalation B> yeah A> yeah: does that mean to say that plutonium is in the air:: [I mean we breathe it in B> there is some] there: yes plutonium exists there in very small quantities very small quantities A> but not enough to damage us: B> oh no I don't think so A> hm B> except if you live near or next to nuclear reactors where plutonium [(laughter)] A> yes but we don#t have any nuclear reactors in Cyprus B> no A> so this is not a problem that would come up in: would you you we would find in Cyprus at all B> no no A> if erm let's imagine that you did come across a case like this B> yes A> what kind of drug would you treat it with would you treat it with drugs at all: B> drugs A> yes B> I mean do you mean plutonium poisoning A> yeah:: B> the symptoms yes: A> hm B> but not actually not the er: /4/ the real disease A> hm what what would the symptoms be B> oh: it might be symptoms of er: radiation exposure like diarrhoea vomiting A> hm B> headaches and er: /4/ ataxia erm:: /4/ convulsions sweating A> it sounds pretty horrible B> yeah it is [(laughter)] A> okay well I'll leave that now I I won't I won't press you any farther on plutonium poisoning the course you're going to going to you want to take in England I I presume B> yeah A> yeah what what is it B> it's a course on I'm not sure because er /7/ it says United Kingdom or or Denmark Denmark /7/ I think A> sorry I I didn't B> er it was for United Kingdom or Denmark A> or Denmark B> yeah A> so you don't know which one you're going to B> no A> do you speak Danish B> no (laughter) A> probably the United Kingdom well unless of course they [teach B> many] teach A> yeah [they might B> (inaudible)] A> teach [it B> yeah] A> in En in En in English in Denmark but but you don't know where you're going to do it B> no not [yet A> no] hm how about the the course itself quality control: drugs B> yeah A> well what does it involve B> erm: ah /2/ first we've to control drugs A> hm B> ah you want me to say what we mean by quality control [something A> yeah] B> like that A> please B> we mean ah: we mean /2/ (inaudible) and testers tests which are used to to determine the density purity potency quantity and of course quality of pharmaceutical preparations A> okay I I thought that most pharmaceutical preparations they

were produced by companies B> yeah A> and then they were sold I mean
does this mean to say that: say you were going to buy a drug from an English
company or a company from the States: but when it came to Cyprus you you
would have to check it first: before you actually used it in Cyprus [or are B>
or yeah] A> you checking the quality of [drugs produced B> the first time]
A> in Cyprus B> yes A> [I mean erm: B> (inaudible)] A> quality of what I
mean [to say (inaudible) B> I mean all] pharmaceutical companies have
their own: er /2/ quality control departments A> yeah B> they check their
products for their quality but er all products registered and sold in the
Cyprus market: /2/ they are first checked from their quality and then registered here A> right B> I mean: for the first time A> that sounds sensible B>
yeah A> hm B> and of course: /4/ I mean the government (inaudible): er er
/2/ has two pharma two: erm /5/ labs two laboratories the pharmaceutical
laboratories and the chemical state laboratory A> hm B> in the pharmaceutical laboratory are checked are checked er /6/ products for (inaudible) A>
hm B> you see and: erm also on erm: /4/ medicines bought by the government for the use of to be used in /6/ the hospitals A> hm it sounds like very
interesting work B> it is A> quite [fascinating B> yeah] A> erm B> has to do
with chemical reactions A> yeah hm: yes it it's fascinating I think it's much
more it's much more interesting than being involved in this side of hospital
work than perhaps er you know the medical practitioners going around and
seeing patients and things I mean I would find this more [fascinating B> yes
it's] more fascinating A> yeah: but are yeah it's B> fascinating with chemical
reactions er: /1/ A> yeah B> erm: /4/ has to do with photometric methods
[and A> hm:] B> (inaudible) A> yeah: okay well I don't think I need to ask
you anything else B> yeah A> unless you have anything to ask me B> (laughter) no A> (laughter) [okay B> do you] live in Cyprus A> yes I do B> really
A> yes B> oh I thought you were coming from England A> well yes I I am I
am English because all all examiners for this have to be English but I've lived
in Cyprus for: almost nine years now B> you like it A> of course I'm more
Cypriot than English now (laughter) [I'm B> you] don't speak Greek do you
A> yes I do B really A> yes my wife er is a Cypriot B> oh A> as well and [er
B> because it's a very very difficult language A> not particularly no it's very
rule governed: erm so once you get the hang of the rules you're okay B>
(laughter) A> but er: er no I've never I've [never B> (inaudible)] A> yeah I
mean it's very it's a nice language but er no I've never worked in England
and I feel er I I all my working life has been in Cyprus B> oh A> I I know
Cyprus better than I know England [(laughter)] anyway er B> did I pass the
exams A> can't tell you that [(laughter) B> yeah] A> because of course I
don't know erm B> well I mean your part A> oh: (laughter) you're you're a
good speaker: I I mean I shouldn't worry too much: but for the rest of it I
don't know B> yeah A> I don't mark the rest of it B> thank you very much
A> okay bye B> bye

Category	1	2	3	4	5	6	7	8
Tally	0	18	1	10	2	3	2	0

Appendix 8

The fluency rating scale

Band 0

Candidates in band 0 do not reach the required standard to be placed in band 1.

Band 1

The candidate frequently pauses in speech before completing the propositional intention of the utterance, causing the interviewer to ask additional questions and/or make comments in order to continue the conversation [categories 1 and 8]. (Utterances tend to be short), and there is little evidence of candidates taking time to plan the content of the utterance in advance of speaking [category 2]. However, hesitation is frequently evident when the candidate has to plan the utterance grammatically [category 3]. This often involves the repetition of items, long pauses and the reformulation of sentences.

Misunderstanding of the interviewer's questions or comments is fairly frequent, and the candidate sometimes cannot respond at all, or dries up part way through the answer [categories 1 and 8]. (Single-word responses followed by pauses are common), forcing the interviewer to encourage further contribution. It is rare for a band 1 candidate to be able to give examples, counter examples or reasons, to support a view expressed [category 4].

Pausing for grammatical and lexical repair is evident, i.e. selection of a new word or structure when it is realised that an utterance is not accurate or cannot be completed accurately [category 6].

Candidates at band 1 may pause because of difficulty in retrieving a word, but when this happens will usually abandon the message rather than attempt to circumlocute. It is rare for a band 1 candidate to express uncertainty regarding choice of lexis or the propositional content of the message [category 5]. (The message itself is often simple.)

Band 2

A band 2 candidate will almost always be able to complete the propositional intention of an utterance once started, causing no strain on the interviewer by expecting him/her to maintain the interaction [category 8]. However, just like a band 1 candidate, a band 2 candidate will frequently misunderstand the interviewer's question or be completely unable to respond to the interviewer's question, requiring the interviewer to repeat the question or clarify what he/she wishes the candidate to do [category 8]. Similarly (single-word responses are common), forcing the interviewer to encourage further contribution.

Although the candidate will spend less time pausing to plan the grammar of an utterance, it will be observed that there are many occasions on which the candidate will reformulate an utterance having begun using one grammatical pattern and conclude with a different form [categories 3 and 6]. Similarly, with lexis, there will be evidence that the candidate pauses to search for an appropriate lexical item and, if it is not available, will make some attempt to circumlocute even if this is not very successful [categories 5 and 6]. From time to time a band 2 candidate may pause to consider giving an example, counter example or reason for a point of view. However, this will be infrequent and when it does occur the example or reason may be expressed in very simplistic terms and may lack relevance to the topic [category 4].

Band 3

A candidate in band 3 will hardly ever misunderstand a question or be unable to respond to a question from the interviewer. On the odd occasion when it does happen a band 3 candidate will almost always ask for clarification from the interviewer [category 8].

Most pauses in the speech of a band 3 candidate will occur when they require 'thinking time' in order to provide a propositionally appropriate utterance [category 2]. Time is sometimes needed to plan a sentence grammatically in advance, especially after making an error which the candidate then rephrases [category 3].

A band 3 candidate is very conscious of his/her use of lexis, and often pauses to think about the word which has been used, or to select another which they consider to be better in the context. The candidate may even question the interviewer overtly regarding the appropriacy of the word which has been chosen [category 5].

Often candidates in this band will give examples, counter examples or reasons to support their point of view [category 4].

(At band 3 and above there is an increasing tendency for candidates to use 'backchannelling' – the use of 'hm' or 'yeah' – when the interviewer is talking, giving the interview a greater sense of normal conversation, although many better candidates still do not use this device.)

Band 4

A band 4 candidate will only very rarely misunderstand a question of the interviewer, fail to respond or dry up in the middle of an utterance [categories 1 and 8].

A candidate in this band will exhibit a much greater tendency than candidates in any other band to express doubt about what they are saying. They will often use words such as 'maybe' and 'perhaps' when presenting their own point of view or opinion [category 7]. More often than not, they will back up their opinion with examples or provide reasons for holding a certain belief [category 4]. They will pause frequently to consider exactly how to express the content of what they wish to say and how they will present their views [category 2]. (They will only rarely respond with a single word unless asked a polar question by the interviewer.)

There will be far fewer pauses to consider the grammatical structure of an utterance [category 3] and pausing to consider the appropriacy of a lexical item chosen is rare [category 5]. A candidate in this band will reformulate a sentence from time to time if it is considered to be inaccurate or the grammar does not allow the candidate to complete the proposition which he/she wishes to express [category 6].

Band 5

A candidate at band 5 almost never misunderstands the interviewer, fails to respond or dries up when speaking [categories 1 and 8]. The majority of pauses or hesitations which occur will be when the candidate is considering how to express a point of view or opinion [category 2], or how to support a point of view or opinion by providing appropriate examples or reasons [category 4]. However, a candidate at band 5 will not express uncertainty regarding these views or opinions as frequently as a candidate at band 4, and so there are fewer hesitations when introducing new propositions [category 7].

Very rarely does a band 5 candidate have to pause to consider the grammatical structure of an utterance [category 3] and almost never hesitates regarding choice of lexis [category 5]. Band 5 candidates demonstrate a confidence in their ability to get things right the first time. While they do sometimes pause to reformulate sentences this is always because they cannot put across the propositional content of their utterance without changing grammatical form [category 6].

It may be noticed by the interviewer that the candidate responds to questions and prompts so quickly and efficiently that the next question or prompt has not been prepared, resulting in a pause in the interview while the interviewer plans his/her next utterance [category 1].

Band 6

Candidates in band 6 reach a standard higher than that described in band 5.

Appendix 9

Questionnaire

Questions 1–15 were asked for each task taken by the students. Questions 16–19 were separate questions added to the end of the three other questionnaires. This example is from task 1.

Please complete these details

Name:
Age:
Class at School:

Please complete the following by placing a circle around the most appropriate answer

For example:

Question: It is useful to study the day before an oral test

| Strongly Agree | Agree | No Opinion | Disagree | Strongly Disagree |

1. I believe that the picture task would provide an examiner with an accurate idea of my ability to speak English.

| Strongly Agree | Agree | No Opinion | Disagree | Strongly Disagree |

2. I felt nervous before the picture task.

| Strongly Agree | Agree | No Opinion | Disagree | Strongly Disagree |

3. I felt nervous while I was doing the picture task.

| Strongly Agree | Agree | No Opinion | Disagree | Strongly Disagree |

4. I believe I did well on the picture task.

| Strongly Agree | Agree | No Opinion | Disagree | Strongly Disagree |

5. If I had done the picture task on another day, I would have done better.

| Strongly Agree | Agree | No Opinion | Disagree | Strongly Disagree |

6. I believe that the picture task provided me with an adequate opportunity to demonstrate my ability to speak English.

| Strongly Agree | Agree | No Opinion | Disagree | Strongly Disagree |

Please explain why:

7. The time allowed for the picture task was too short.

| Strongly Agree | Agree | No Opinion | Disagree | Strongly Disagree |

8. I liked doing the picture task.

| Strongly Agree | Agree | No Opinion | Disagree | Strongly Disagree |

Please explain why:

9. I understood what I was supposed to do in the picture task.

| Strongly Agree | Agree | No Opinion | Disagree | Strongly Disagree |

10. I thought that the picture task was related to what I learn in class.

| Strongly Agree | Agree | No Opinion | Disagree | Strongly Disagree |

11. If a different teacher had conducted the picture task, I would have done better.

| Strongly Agree | Agree | No Opinion | Disagree | Strongly Disagree |

12. I thought that the picture task was too difficult.

| Strongly Agree | Agree | No Opinion | Disagree | Strongly Disagree |

Please explain why:

13. I thought that the picture task was interesting.

| Strongly Agree | Agree | No Opinion | Disagree | Strongly Disagree |

14. I thought that doing the picture task was an unpleasant experience.

| Strongly Agree | Agree | No Opinion | Disagree | Strongly Disagree |

15. Did you think that the subject chosen for the picture task was particularly fair or unfair? Please give your reasons.

| Very fair | Fair | No opinion | Unfair | Very unfair |

Reasons:

16. If you were going to take an oral test in an examination, which of the three tasks would you prefer to do? Put a '1' next to the task you would prefer most, a '2' next to your second choice, and a '3' next to the task you would least like to do.

Task 1: Picture task

Task 2: Discussion of passage

Task 3: Group discussion

17. If you felt nervous during any of the tasks, what would have made you feel less nervous?

18. How would you rate your own proficiency in spoken English?

Generally:	Very good	Good	Average	Poor	Very poor
Accuracy:	Very good	Good	Average	Poor	Very poor
Fluency:	Very good	Good	Average	Poor	Very poor

19. For how many years have you been studying English?

References

ACTFL Provisional Guidelines 1984 In Higgs, T. V. (ed.) 1984 *Teaching for Proficiency, the Organizing Principle*. Lincolnwood, IL: National Textbook Company, 219–226.

ACTFL 1986 ACTFL Proficiency Guidelines. Hastings-on-Hudson, NY: American Council on the Teaching of Foreign Languages.

ACTFL 1999 Revised ACTFL Proficiency Guidelines – Speaking. Yonkers, NY: American Council on the Teaching of Foreign Languages.

Adams, M. L. (1978) Measuring foreign language speaking proficiency: a study of agreement among raters. In Clark, J. L. D. (ed.) *Direct testing of speaking proficiency: theory and application*. Princeton, NJ: Educational Testing Service, 129–49.

Adams, M. L. (1980) Five cooccurring factors in speaking proficiency. In Frith, J. R. (ed.) *Measuring Spoken Language Proficiency*. Washington DC: Georgetown University Press, 1–6.

Adams, M. L. and Frith, J. R. (1979) *Testing Kit: French and Spanish*. Washington DC: Department of State and the Foreign Services Institute.

Adams, R. J., Griffin, P. E. and Martin, L. (1987) A latent trait method for measuring a dimension in second language proficiency. *Language Testing*, 4(1): 9–27.

AERA, APA and NCME (1985) *Standards for Educational and Psychological Testing*. 5th edn. Washington DC: American Educational Research Association.

AERA, APA and NCME (1999) *Standards for Educational and Psychological Testing*. 6th edn. Washington DC: American Educational Research Association.

Agard, F. and Dunkel, H. (1948) *An investigation of second language teaching*. Chicago, IL: Ginn.

Alderson, J. C. (1981) Report of the discussion on general language proficiency. In Alderson, J. C. and Hughes, A. (eds) *Issues in Language Testing*. London: The British Council, 187–94.

Alderson, J. C. (1983) Who needs jam? In Hughes, A. and Porter, D. (eds) *Current Developments in Language Testing*. London: Academic Press, 87–92.

Alderson, J. C. (1990) Judgments in language testing. In Douglas, D. and Chapelle, C. (eds) *A New Decade of Language Testing Research*. Washington DC: TESOL, 46–57.

Alderson, J. C. (1991a) Language testing in the 1990s: How far have we come? How much further have we to go? In Anivan, S. (ed.) *Current Developments in Language Testing*. Singapore: Seameo Regional Language Centre.

Alderson, J. C. (1991b) Bands and scores. In Alderson, J. C. and North, B. (eds) *Language Testing in the 1990s*. London: Modern English Publications and the British Council, 71–86.

Alderson, J. C. (1991c) Dis-sporting life. Response to Alastair Pollitt's paper: Giving students a sporting chance: Assessment by counting and by judging. In Alderson, J. C. and North, B. (eds) *Language Testing in the 1990s*. London: Modern English Publications and the British Council, 60–70.

Alderson, J. C., Clapham, C. and Wall, D. (1995) *Language Test Construction and Evaluation*. Cambridge: Cambridge University Press.

Alderson, J. C. and Hamp-Lyons, L. (1996) TOEFL preparation courses: a study of washback. *Language Testing*, 13(3): 280–97.

Alderson, J. C. and Wall, D. (1993) Does washback exist? *Applied Linguistics*, 14(2): 115–29.

American Council on the Teaching of Foreign Languages, New York (1999) *ACTFL Proficiency Guidelines: Speaking*.

Anderson, A. and Lynch, T. (1988) *Listening*. Oxford: Oxford University Press.

Angiolillo, P. (1947) *Armed Forces Foreign Language Teaching*. New York: Vanni.

Austin, J. L. (1962) *How to do things with words*. Oxford: Oxford University Press.

Bachman, L. F. (1981) An experiment in a picture-stimuli procedure for testing oral communication. In Palmer, A. S., Groot, P. J. J. and Trosper, G. A. (eds) *The Construct Validation of Tests of Communicative Competence*. Washington DC: TESOL, 140–8.

Bachman, L. F. (1988) Problems in examining the validity of the ACTFL Oral Proficiency Interview. *Studies in Second Language Acquisition*, 10(2): 149–64.

Bachman, L. F. (1990) *Fundamental Considerations in Language Testing*. Oxford: Oxford University Press.

Bachman, L. F. (1997) Generalizability theory. In Clapham, C. and Corson, D. (eds) *Encyclopedia of Language and Education*, Vol. 7: *Language Testing and Assessment*. Amsterdam: Kluwer Academic Publishers, 255–62.

Bachman, L. F. (2002) Some reflections on task-based language performance assessment. *Language Testing*, 19(4): 453–76.

Bachman, L. F. (2003) *Statistical analyses for language assessment*. Cambridge: Cambridge University Press.

Bachman, L. F., Davidson, F., Ryan, K. and Choi, I-C. (1995) *An investigation into the comparability of two tests of English as a foreign language*. The Cambridge-TOEFL comparability study. Cambridge: Cambridge University Press.

Bachman, L. F. and Eignor, D. (1997) Recent advances in quantitative test analysis. In Clapham, C. and Corson, D. (eds) *Encyclopedia of Language and Education*, Vol. 7: *Language Testing and Assessment*. Amsterdam: Kluwer Academic Publishers, 227–42.

Bachman, L. F., Kunan, A., Vanniarajan, S. and Lynch, B. (1988) Task and ability analysis as a basis for examining content and construct comparability in two EFL proficiency test batteries. *Language Testing*, 5(2): 160–86.

Bachman, L. F., Lynch, B. and Mason, M. (1995) Investigating variability in tasks and rater judgements in a performance test of foreign language speaking. *Language Testing*, 12(2): 238–57.

Bachman, L. F. and Palmer, A. S. (1981) The construct validity of the FSI oral interview. *Language Learning*, 31(1): 67–86.

Bachman, L. F. and Palmer, A. S. (1982) The construct validation of some components of communicative proficiency. *TESOL Quarterly*, 16(4): 409–65.

Bachman, L. F. and Palmer, A. S. (1983) The construct validity of the FSI oral interview. In J. Oller (ed.) *Issues in Language Testing Research*. Rowley, MA: Newbury House Publishers, 154–69.

258 References

Bachman, L. F. and Palmer, A. S. (1996) *Language Testing in Practice.* Oxford: Oxford University Press.

Bachman, L. F. and Savignon, S. J. (1986) The evaluation of communicative language proficiency: a critique of the ACTFL Oral Interview. *Modern Language Journal,* 70: 380–90.

Bailey, K. M. (1996) Working for washback: A review of the washback concept in language testing. *Language Testing,* 13(3): 257–79.

Baker, R. (1997) *Classical Test Theory and Item Response Theory in Test Analysis.* Lancaster University, Language Testing Update, Special Report No. 2.

Banerjee, J. and Luoma, S. (1987) Qualitative approaches to test validation. In Clapham, C. and Corson, D. (eds) *Encyclopedia of Language and Education,* Vol. 7: *Language Testing and Assessment.* Amsterdam: Kluwer Academic Publishers, 275–87.

Barnwell, D. (1986) Who is to judge how well others speak? An experiment with the ACTFL/ETS Oral Proficiency Scale. Paper presented at the Eastern States Conference on Linguistics, Pittsburgh, PA.

Barnwell, D. (1987) Oral proficiency testing in the United States. *British Journal of Language Teaching,* 25(1): 35–42.

Barnwell, D. (1989) Naive native speakers and judgements of oral proficiency in Spanish. *Language Testing,* 6(2); 152–63.

Barnwell, D. (1996) *A History of Foreign Language Testing in the United States.* Tempe, AZ: Bilingual Press.

Bartz, W. M. (1979) Testing oral communication in the foreign language classroom. *Language in Education: Theory and Practice 17.* Arlington, VA: ERIC Clearinghouse on Languages and Linguistics.

Bejar, I. I. (1985) *A Preliminary Study of Raters for the Test of Spoken English.* Princeton, NJ: Educational Testing Service.

Berkoff, N. A. (1985) Testing oral proficiency: A new approach. In Lee, Y. P. (ed.) *New Directions in Language Testing.* Oxford: Pergamon Institute of English, 93–100.

Berry, V. (1995) A qualitative analysis of factors affecting learner performances in group oral tests. Paper presented at the 17th Language Testing Research Colloquium, Long Beach, CA.

Berry, V. (1997) Ethical considerations when assessing oral proficiency in pairs. In Huhta, A., Kohonen, V., Kurki-Suonio, L. and Luoma, S. (eds) *Current Developments in Language Testing.* Jyväskylä: Jyväskylä University Press, 107–23.

Berry, V. (1998) Personality and oral test score variability. Paper presented at TESOL '98 Conference, Seattle, WA.

Berwick, R. and Ross, S. (1996) Cross-cultural pragmatics in oral proficiency interview strategies. In Milanovic, M. and Saville, N. (eds) *Performance Testing, Cognition and Assessment.* Selected papers from the 15th Language Testing Research Colloquium. Cambridge: Cambridge University Press, 34–54.

Biber, D. (1988) *Variation across speech and writing.* Cambridge: Cambridge University Press.

Bolus, R. E., Hinofotis, F. and Bailey, K. M. (1981) An introduction to generalizability theory in second language research. *Language Learning,* 32(1): 245–58.

Brazil, D. A. (1985) *The Communicative Value of Intonation in English.* University of Birmingham, English Language Research. Discourse Analysis Monograph 8.

Brazil, D. A. (1995) *A Grammar of Speech.* Oxford: Oxford University Press.

Brennan, R. L. (1996) Generalizability of performance assessments. In Phillips, G. W. (ed.) *Technical issues in large-scale performance assessment.* Washington DC: National Center for Education Statistics (NCES 96-802), 19–58.

Brereton, J. L. (1944) *The Case for Examinations*: An acccount of their place in education with some proposals for their reform. Cambridge: Cambridge University Press.

Brigham, C. C. (1923) *A Study of American Intelligence*. Princeton, NJ: Princeton University Press.

British Council (1983) *VOTE: Oral Testing*. London: British Council English Languages Services Department and the Design, Production and Publishing Department.

Brod, R. (1982) Building a language profession. *ADFL Bulletin*, 14(1): 10–13.

Brown, A. (2000) An investigation of rater's orientation in awarding scores in the IELTS interview. In Tulloch, R. (ed.) *IELTS Research Reports*, Vol. 3. Canberra: IELTS Australia Pty, 30–49.

Brown, A. (2003) Interviewer variation and the co-construction of speaking proficiency. *Language Testing*, 20(1): 1–25.

Brown, A. and Hill, K. (1998) Interviewer style and candidate performance in the IELTS oral interview. In Woods, S. (ed.) *IELTS Research Reports*, Vol. 1. Sydney: ELICOS, 173–91.

Brown, A. and Lumley, T. (1997) Interviewer variability in specific-purpose language performance tests. In Kohonen, V., Huhta, A., Kurki-Suonio, L. and Luoma, S. (eds) *Current Developments and Alternatives in Language Assessment*. Jyväskylä: University of Jyväskylä Press, 137–50.

Brown, A., McNamara, T., Iwashita, N. and O'Hagan, S. (2001) Investigating raters' orientations in specific-purpose task-based oral assessment. *Final report to TOEFL 2000 RDOC*. Princeton, NJ: Educational Testing Service.

Brown, G. and Yule, G. (1983) *Teaching the Spoken Language*: An approached based on the analysis of conversational English. Cambridge: Cambridge University Press.

Brown, J. D. (1996) *Testing in Language Programs*. Upper Saddle River, NJ: Prentice Hall Regents.

Brown, J. D., Hudson, T. and Norris, J. (1999) Validation of test-dependent and task-independent ratings of performance assessment. Paper presented at the 21st Language Testing Research Colloquium, Tsukuba, Japan.

Brown, J. W. (1985) RSVP: Classroom oral interview procedure. *Foreign Language Annals*, 18(6): 481–6.

Brumfit, C. (1984) *Communicative Methodology in Language Teaching*: The roles of fluency and accuracy. Cambridge: Cambridge University Press.

Buck, G. (2001) *Assessing Listening*. Cambridge: Cambridge University Press.

Burroughs, G. E. R. (1971) *Design and Analysis in Educational Research*. Educational Monograph 8. Birmingham: University of Birmingham Press.

Butler, F., Eignor, D., Jones, S., McNamara, T. and Suomi, B. K. (2000) *TOEFL 2000 Speaking Framework: A Working Paper*. Princeton, NJ: Educational Testing Service. TOEFL Monograph Series Ms. 20. Available online at ftp://ftp.ets.org/pub/toefl/253716.pdf.

Bygate, M. (1987) *Speaking*. Oxford: Oxford University Press.

Byrnes, H. (1987) Second language acquisition: Insights from a proficiency orientation. In Byrnes, H. and Canale, M. (eds) *Defining and Developing Proficiency: Guidelines, Implementations and Concepts*. Lincolnwood, IL: National Textbook Company, 107–31.

Campbell, D. T. and Fiske, D. W. (1959) Convergent and discriminant validation by the multitrait–multimethod matrix. *Psychological Bulletin*, 56(2): 81–105.

Canale, M. and Swain, M. (1980) Theoretical bases of communicative approaches to second language teaching and testing. *Applied Linguistics*, 1: 1–47.

Candlin, C. N. (1987) Towards task-based language learning. In Candlin, C. N. and Murphy, D. F. (eds) *Language Learning Tasks.* Lancaster Practical Paper in English Language Education, Vol. 7. Englewood Cliffs, NJ: Prentice Hall International, 5–22.

Carroll, B. J. (1980) *Testing Communicative Performance.* An Interim Study. Oxford: Pergamon Press.

Carroll, B. J. (1981) Specifications for an English language testing service. In Alderson, J. C. and Hughes, A. (eds) *Issues in Language Testing.* London: The British Council, 66–110.

Carroll, B. J. and Hall, P. J. (1985) *Make Your Own Language Tests.* A practical guide to writing language performance tests. Oxford: Pergamon Press.

Carroll, J. B. (1967) The foreign language attainments of language majors in the senior year: A survey conducted in US colleges and universities. *Foreign Language Annals,* 1(2): 131–51.

Carroll, J. B. (1968) The psychology of language testing. In Davies, A. (ed.) *Language Testing Symposium.* Oxford: Oxford University Press, 46–69.

Cartier, F. A. (1980) Alternative methods of oral proficiency assessment. In Frith, J. R. (ed.) *Measuring Spoken Language Proficiency.* Washington DC: Georgetown University Press, 7–14.

Chalhoub-Deville, M. (1995a) Deriving oral assessment scales across different tests and rater groups. *Language Testing,* 12(1): 16–33.

Chalhoub-Deville, M. (1995b) A contextualized approach to describing oral language proficiency. *Language Learning,* 45(2): 251–81.

Chapelle, C. (1998) Construct definition and validity inquiry in SLA research. In Bachman, L. F. and Cohen, A. D. (eds) *Interfaces Between Second Language Acquisition and Language Testing Research.* Cambridge: Cambridge University Press, 32–70.

Chapelle, C. (1999a) From reading theory to testing practice. In Chalhoub-Deville, M. (ed.) *Issues in computer-adaptive testing of reading.* Cambridge: Cambridge University Press, 150–66.

Chapelle, C. (1999b) Validity in language assessment. *Annual Review of Applied Linguistics,* 19: 254–72.

Chastain, K. (1980) Native speaker reaction to instructor-identified student second language errors. *Modern Language Journal,* 64(2): 210–15.

Child, D. (1970) *The Essentials of Factor Analysis.* London and New York: Holt, Rinehart & Winston.

Clahsen, H. (1985) Profiling second language development: a procedure for assessing L2 proficiency. In Hyltenstam, K. and Pienemann, M. (eds) *Modelling and assessing second language acquisition.* San Diego, CA: College Hill Press.

Clapham, C. (1981) Reaction to the Carroll Paper I. In Alderson, J. C. and Hughes, A. (eds) *Issues in Language Testing.* London: The British Council, 111–16.

Clapham, C. (2000) Assessment for academic purposes: Where next? *System,* 28(4): 511–21.

Clark, J. L. D. (1975) Theoretical and technical considerations in oral proficiency testing. In Jones, R. L. and Spolsky, B. (eds) *Testing Language Proficiency.* Arlington, VA: Center for Applied Linguistics, 10–28.

Clark, J. L. D. (1979) Direct versus semi-direct tests of speaking ability. In Biere, E. J. and Hinofotis, F. B. (eds) *New Concepts in Language Testing: Some Recent Studies.* Washington DC: TESOL, 35–49.

Clark, J. L. D. (1980) "Toward a common measure of speaking proficiency." In Frith, J. R. (ed.) *Measuring Spoken Language Proficiency.* Georgetown: Georgetown University Press, 15–26.

Clark, J. L. D. (1986a) *Handbook for the Development of Tape-Mediated, ACTFL/ILR Scale-Based Tests of Speaking Proficiency in the Less Commonly Taught Languages.* Washington DC: Center for Applied Linguistics.

Clark, J. L. D. (1986b) Development of a tape-mediated, ACTFL/ILR scale-based test of Chinese speaking proficiency. In Stansfield, C. W. (ed.) *Technology in Language Testing.* Washington DC: TESOL.

Clark, J. L. D. (1988a) *The Proficiency-Oriented Testing Movement in the United States and its Implications for Instructional Program Design and Evaluation.* Mimeo: Defense Language Institute, Monterey, CA.

Clark, J. L. D. (1988b) Validation of a test of Chinese speaking proficiency. *Language Testing*, 5(2): 187–205.

Clark, J. L. D. and Lett, J. A. (1988) *Research Issues in Second Language Proficiency Testing.* Mimeo: Defense Language Institute, Monterey, CA.

Clark, J. L. D. and Li, Y. C. (1986) *Development, validation and dissemination of a proficiency-based test of speaking ability in Chinese and an associated assessment model for other less commonly taught languages.* Washington DC: Center for Applied Linguistics.

Clark, J. L. D. and Swinton, S. S. (1980a) *An Exploration of Speaking Proficiency Measures in the TOEFL Context.* TOEFL Research Report 4, Princeton, NJ: Educational Testing Service.

Clark, J. L. D. and Swinton, S. S. (1980b) *The Test of Spoken English as a Measure of Communicative Ability in English-Medium Instructional Settings.* TOEFL Research Report 7, Princeton, NJ: Educational Testing Service.

Clifford, R. T. (1978) Reliability and validity aspects contributing to oral proficiency of prospective teachers of German. In Clark, J. L. D. (ed.) *Direct testing of speaking proficiency: theory and application.* Princeton, NJ: Educational Testing Service, 191–209.

Cohen, J. (1988) *Statistical Power Analysis for the Behavioural Sciences.* Hillsdale, NJ: Erlbaum.

Cohen, J. (1992) A power primer. *Psychological Bulletin*, 112(1): 155–9.

College Entrance Examination Board (1939) *Thirty Ninth Annual Report of the Secretary.* New York: College Entrance Examination Board.

Committee on Resolutions and Investigations (1917) Report of committee on resolutions and investigations appointed by the Association of Modern Language Teachers of the Middle States and Maryland. *Modern Language Journal* 1, 250–61.

Coolidge, C. (1923) Annual Message. Available online: http://www.theamerican-presidency.net/1923.htm

Cooper, C. R. (1977) Holistic evaluation of writing. In Cooper, C. R. and Odell, L. (eds) *Evaluating Writing: Describing, measuring, judging.* Urbana, IL: NCTE, 3–22.

Council of Europe (1996) *A Common European Framework for Language Learning and Teaching.* Draft 1 of a Framework Proposal. Strasbourg: Council of Europe.

Council of Europe (2001) *Common European Framework of Reference for Languages: Learning, teaching, assessment.* Cambridge: Cambridge University Press.

Cumming, A., Kantor, R. and Powers, D. (2001) *Scoring TOEFL Essays and TOEFL 2000 Prototype Writing Tasks:* An Investigation into Raters' Decision Making and Development of a Preliminary Analytical Framework. Princeton, NJ: Educational Testing Service. TOEFL Monograph Series Ms. 22. Available online at ftp://ftp.ets.org/pub/toefl/990630.pdf.

Dancy, J. and Sosa, E. (1993) *A Companion to Epistemology.* Oxford: Blackwell.

Dandonoli, P. and Henning, G. (1990) An investigation of the construct validity of the ACTFL Proficiency Guidelines and Oral Interview Procedure. *Foreign Language Annals*, 23(1): 11–22.

Davidson, F. [online] *The Virtual Specbank.* http://ux6.cso.uiuc.edu/~fgd/ltvshome.htm.

Davidson, F. (2000) The language tester's statistical toolbox. *System,* 28(4): 605–17.

Davidson, F. and Bachman, L. F. (1990) The Cambridge-TOEFL Comparability Study: An example of the cross-national comparison of language tests. In de Jong, J. H. A. L. (ed.) *Standardization in Language Testing. AILA Review.* Amsterdam: Free University Press, 24–45.

Davidson, F. and Lynch, B. K. (2002) *Testcraft. A Teacher's Guide to Writing and Using Language Test Specifications.* New Haven, CT and London: Yale University Press.

Davies, A. (1990) *Principles of Language Testing.* Oxford: Basil Blackwell.

Davies, A. (1991) *The native speaker in applied linguistics.* Edinburgh: Edinburgh University Press.

Davies, A., Brown, A., Elder, C., Hill, K., Lumley, T. and McNamara, T. (1999) *Dictionary of Language Testing.* Cambridge: Cambridge University Press.

de Charruf, L. F. (1984) Oral testing. *MEXTESOL Journal,* 8(2): 63–79.

Douglas, D. (1997) *Testing Speaking Ability in Academic Contexts: Theoretical Considerations.* Princeton, NJ: Educational Testing Service. TOEFL Monograph Series Ms. 8. Available online at ftp.ets.org/pub/toefl/Toefl-MS-8.pdf.

Douglas, D. (1998) Language for specific purposes. In Clapham, C. and Corson, D. (eds) *Language Testing and Assessment,* Vol. 7 of the *Encyclopedia of Language and Education.* Dordrecht: Kluwer Academic Publishers, 111–19.

Douglas, D. (2000) *Assessing Languages for Specific Purposes.* Cambridge: Cambridge University Press.

Douglas, D. and Selinker, L. (1992) Analyzing Oral Proficiency Test performance in general and specific purpose contexts. *System,* 20(3): 317–28.

Douglas, D. and Smith, J. (1997) *Theoretical Underpinnings of the Test of Spoken English Revision Project.* TOEFL Monograph Series 9. Princeton, NJ: Educational Testing Service.

Dugan, J. S. (1988) Standardized tests as an alternative to the oral interview. *Proceedings of the 7th Annual Eastern Michigan University Conference on Languages for Business and the Professions,* Ypsilanti, MI.

Elder, C., Iwashita, N. and McNamara, T. (2002) Estimating the difficulty of oral proficiency tasks: what does the test-taker have to offer? *Language Testing,* 19(4): 347–68.

Ellis, R. (1985) A variable competence model of second language acquisition. *IRAL,* 23: 47–59.

Ericsson, K. and Simon, J. (1987) Verbal reports on thinking. In Færch, C. and Kasper, G. (eds) *Introspection in second language research.* Clevedon: Multilingual Matters, 24–53.

Ervin-Tripp, S. M. (1968) Sociolinguistics. In Berkowitz L. (ed.) *Advances in experimental social psychology,* Vol. 4. New York: Academic Press, 91–165.

ETS (1999a) *Policy Statement for Documentation of a Learning Disability in Adolescents and Adults.* Office of Disability Policy, Princeton, NJ: Educational Testing Service.

ETS (1999b) Policy Statement for Documentation of Attention-Deficit/Hyperactivity Disorder in Adolescents and Adults. Office of Disability Policy, Princeton, NJ: Educational Testing Service.

ETS (2000a) *Test of Spoken English Sample Paper.* Princeton, NJ: Educational Testing Service.

ETS (2000b) *ETS Standards for Quality and Fairness.* Princeton, NJ: Educational Testing Service.

ETS, (2001) *Guidelines for Documentation of Psychiatric Disabilities in Adolescents and Adults.* Office of Disability Policy, Princeton, NJ: Educational Testing Service.

Færch, C. and Kasper, G. (1983) *Strategies in Interlanguage Communication.* London: Longman.

Folland, D. and Robertson, D. (1976) Towards objectivity in group oral testing. *English Language Teaching Journal,* 30(2): 156–67.

Foot, M. C. (1999a) Relaxing in pairs. *ELT Journal,* 53(1): 36–41.

Foot, M. C. (1999b) Reply to Saville and Hargreaves. *ELT Journal,* 53(1): 52–3.

Foster, P. and Skehan, P. (1996) The influence of planning on performance in task-based learning. *Studies in Second Language Acquisition,* 18: 299–324.

Fulcher, G. (1987) Tests of oral performance: the need for data-based criteria. *English Language Teaching Journal,* 41(4): 287–91.

Fulcher, G. (1989) *Lexis and Reality in Oral Testing.* Washington DC: ERIC Clearing-house for Languages and Linguistics, ERIC_NO: ED298759.

Fulcher, G. (1993) The construction and validation of rating scales for oral tests in English as a foreign language. University of Lancaster, UK: unpublished PhD thesis.

Fulcher, G. (1995) Variable competence in second language acquisition: A problem for research methodology? *System,* 23(1): 25–33.

Fulcher, G. (1996a) Testing tasks: issues in task design and the group oral. *Language Testing,* 13(1): 23–51.

Fulcher, G. (1996b) Does thick description lead to smart tests? A data-based approach to rating scale construction. *Language Testing,* 13(2): 208–38.

Fulcher, G. (1996c) Invalidating validity claims for the ACTFL Oral Rating Scale. *System,* 24(2): 163–72.

Fulcher, G. (1997) The testing of speaking in a second language. In Clapham, C. and Corson, D. (eds) *Encyclopedia of Language and Education,* Vol. 7: *Language Testing and Assessment.* Amsterdam: Kluwer Academic Publishers, 75–85.

Fulcher, G. (1998) Widdowson's model of communicative competence and the testing of reading: an exploratory study. *System,* 26: 281–302.

Fulcher, G. (1999) Assessment in English for academic purposes: Putting content validity in its place. *Applied Linguistics,* 20(2): 221–36.

Fulcher, G. (2000) The communicative legacy in language testing. *System,* 28(4): 479–82.

Fulcher, G. (2002) Managers face the tests. *EL Gazette, EL Teaching Matters Supplement,* 3 (April).

Fulcher, G. (2003) Interface design in computer based language testing. *Language Testing,* 20, 4.

Fulcher, G. and Bamford, R. (1996) I didn't get the grade I need. Where's my solicitor? *System,* 24(4): 437–48.

Fulcher, G. and Márquez Reiter, R. (2003) Task difficulty in speaking tests. *Language Testing,* 20, 3.

Gass, S. M. and Mackey, A. (2000) *Simulated Recall Methodology in Second Language Research.* Mahwah, NJ: Lawrence Erlbaum Publishers.

Geddes, M. and Sturtridge, G. (1979) *Listening Links.* London: Heineman.

Gitomer, D. H. and Bennett, R. E. (2001) *Unmasking constructs through new technology, measurement theory, and cognitive science.* Princeton, NJ: Research Memorandum RM-02-01.

Goddard, H. H. (1919) *Psychology of the Normal and the Subnormal* (reprinted, 1999). London: Routledge & Kegan Paul.

Goffman, E. (1976) Replies and responses. *Language in Society*, 5: 257–313.

Gould, S. J. (1981) *The Mismeasure of Man.* London: Penguin Books.

Green, A. (1998) *Verbal protocol analysis in language testing research.* Cambridge: Cambridge University Press.

Grice, H. P. (1975) Logic and conversation. In Cole, P. and Morgan, J. L. (eds) *Syntax and Semantics*, Vol. 3: *Speech Acts.* New York: Academic Press, 41–58.

Griffin, P. E., Adams, R. J., Martin, L. and Tomlinson, B. (1988) An algorithmic approach to prescriptive assessment in English as a Second Language. *Language Testing*, 5(1): 1–18.

Hall, J. K. (1995) (Re)creating our worlds with words: A sociocultural perspective of face-to-face interaction. *Applied Linguistics*, 16: 206–32.

Halliday, M. A. K. (1985) *Spoken and written language.* Melbourne, Victoria: Deakin University Press.

Hamp-Lyons, L. (1987) Cambridge First Certificate in English. In Alderson, J. C., Krahnke, K. J. and Stansfield, C. W. (eds) *Reviews of English Language Proficiency Tests.* Washington DC: TESOL Publications, 18–19.

Hamp-Lyons, L. (1991) Scoring procedures for ESL contexts. In Hamp-Lyons, L. (ed.) *Assessing Second Language Writing in Academic Contexts.* Norwood, NJ: Ablex, 241–76

Harrison, A. (1982) The assessment of communicative exchanges. *Language Testing Newsletter*, 3: 2–5.

Hatch, E. (1974) Second language universals. *Working Papers on Bilingualism*, 3: 1–17.

Hawthorne, L. (1997) The political dimension of English language testing in Australia. *Language Testing*, 14(3): 248–60.

He, A. W. (1998) Answering questions in LPIs: A case study. In Young, R. and He, A. W. (eds) *Talking and Testing. Discourse Approaches to the Assessment of Oral Proficiency.* Amsterdam: John Benjamins, 101–16.

He, A. W. and Young, R. (1998) Language proficiency interviews: A discourse approach. In Young, R. and He, A. W. (eds) *Talking and Testing. Discourse Approches to the Assessment of Oral Proficiency.* Amsterdam: John Benjamins.

Hendricks, D., Scholz, G., Spurling, R., Johnson, M. and Vandenburg, L. (1980) Oral proficiency testing in an intensive English Language Program. In Oller, J. and Perkins, K. (eds) *Research in Language Testing.* Rowley, MA: Newbury House Publishers, 77–90.

Henning, G. (1987) *A Guide to Language Testing: Development, evaluation, research.* Rowley, MA: Newbury House.

Henning, G. (1988) The influence of test and sample dimensionality on latent trait person ability and item difficulty calibrations. *Language Testing*, 5(2): 83–99.

Henning, G. (1989) Meanings and implications of the principle of local independence. *Language Testing*, 6(1): 95–108.

Henning, G. (1992a) Dimensionality and construct validity of language tests. *Language Testing*, 9(1): 1–11.

Henning, G. (1992b) The ACTFL oral proficiency interview: validity evidence. *System*, 20(3): 365–72.

Heyden, P. M. (1920) Experience with oral examiners in modern languages. *Modern Language Journal*, 5: 87–92.

Hieke, A. E. (1985) A componential approach to oral fluency evaluation. *Modern Language Journal*, 69(2): 135–42.

Hilsdon, J. (1991) The group oral exam: Advantages and limitations. In Alderson, J. C. and North, B. (eds) *Language Testing in the 1990s.* London: Modern English Publications and the British Council, 189–97.

Hinofotis, F. B. (1983) The structure of oral communication in an educational environment: a comparison of factor-analytic rotational procedures. In Oller, J. W. (ed.) *Issues in Language Testing Research.* Rowley, MA: Newbury House, 170–87.

Hudson, R. A. (1980) *Sociolinguistics.* Cambridge: Cambridge University Press.

Hughes, A. (1989) *Testing for Language Teachers.* Cambridge: Cambridge University Press.

Hymes, D. (1971) On communicative competence. Philadelphia, PA: University of Philadelphia Press. Reprinted extracts in Brumfit, C. J. and Johnson, K. (eds) *The Communicative Approach to Language Teaching.* Oxford: Oxford University Press.

ILTA (2000) *Code of Ethics.* International Language Testing Association.

Ingram, D. (1982) *Introduction to the ASLPR.* Mimeo: Department of Immigration and Ethnic Affairs, Canberra: Australian Government Publishing.

Ingram, D. (1984) *Report on the formal trialling of the Australian second language proficiency ratings (ASLPR).* Studies in adult migrant education, Department of Immigration and Ethnic Affairs, Canberra: Australian Government Publishing Service.

Ingram, D. (1985a) Assessment and the ASLPR. Paper to the conference of the Curriculum Area Committee Languages, Senior Secondary Assessment Board of South Australia, Adelaide.

Ingram, D. (1985b) Assessing proficiency: an overview on some aspects of testing. In Hyltenstam, K. and Pienemann, M. (eds) *Modelling and assessing second language acquisition.* San Diego, CA: College Hill Press, 215–76.

Ingram, D. (1990) The Australian Second Language Proficiency Ratings. In de Jong, J. H. A. L. (ed.) *Standardization in Language Testing. AILA Review.* Amsterdam: Free University Press, 46–61.

Iwashita, N. (1998) The validity of the paired interview in oral performance assessment. *Melbourne Papers in Language Testing,* 5(2): 51–65.

Iwashita, N., McNamara, T. and Elder, C. (2001) Can we predict task difficulty in an oral proficiency test? Exploring the potential of an information processing approach to task design. *Language Learning,* 51(3): 401–36.

Jacoby, S. and McNamara, T. (1999) Locating competence. *English for Specific Purposes,* 18(3): 213–41.

Jacoby, S. and Ochs, E. (1995) Co-construction: An introduction. *Research on Language and Social Interaction,* 28(3): 171–83.

Jafarpur, A. (1988) Non-native raters determining the oral proficiency of EFL learners. *System,* 16(1): 61–8.

James, C. (1998) *Errors in Language Learning and Use: Exploring Error Analysis.* New York: Addison Wesley.

Jarvis, G. A. (1986) Proficiency testing: A matter of false hopes? *ADFL Bulletin,* 18(1): 20–1.

Jefferson, G. (1993) Caveat speaker: Preliminary notes on recipient topic-shift implicature. *Research on Language and Social Interaction,* 26: 1–30.

Johnson, M. (2001) *The Art of Non-conversation.* New Haven, CT: Yale University Press.

Jones, K. (1982) *Simulations in Language Teaching.* Cambridge: Cambridge University Press.

Jones, R. L. (1975) Testing language proficiency in the United States Government. In Jones, R. L. and Spolsky, B. (eds) *Testing Language Proficiency.* Arlington VA: Center for Applied Linguistics, 1–9.

Jones, R. L. (1981) Scoring procedures in oral language proficiency tests. In Read, J. A. S. (ed.) *Directions in Language Testing* (Anthology Series 9) RELC: Singapore University Press, 100–7.

Joreskog, K. G. (1969) A general approach to confirmatory maximum likelihood factor analysis. *Psychometrika*, 34(2): 183–202.

Kachru, B. B. (1992) World Englishes: approaches, issues and resources. *Language Teaching*, 25: 1–14.

Kane, M. T. (1992) An argument-based approach to validity. *Psychological Bulletin*, 122(3): 527–35.

Kasper, G. and Kellerman, E. (1997a) *Communication Strategies: Psycholinguistic and Sociological Perspectives*. London, Longman.

Kasper, G. and Kellerman, E. (1997b) Introduction: approaches to communication strategies. In Kasper, G. and Kellerman, E. (eds) *Communication Strategies: Psycholinguistic and Sociological Perspectives*. London, Longman, 1–13.

Katz, I., Xi, X., Hyun-Joo, K. and Cheng, P. (in press) *Elicited Speech from Graph Items on the Test of Spoken English*. Princeton, NJ: Educational Testing Service.

Kaulfers, W. V. (1944) War-time developments in modern language achievement tests. *Modern Language Journal*, 70(4): 366–72.

Kelly, G. A. (1955) *The psychology of personal constructs*, Vols I and II. New York: Norton.

Kenyon, D. (1992) Introductory remarks at symposium on development and use of rating scales in language testing. Paper delivered at the 14th Language Testing Research Colloquium, Vancouver, 27 February–1 March.

Kerlinger, F. N. and Lee, H. B. (2000) *Foundations of Behavioral Research. Fourth Edition*. Orlando, FL: Harcourt Brace.

Kirk, R. E. (1996) Practical significance: a concept whose time has come. *Educational and Psychological Measurement*, 56(5): 746–59.

Kirsch, I. (2001) *The international adult literacy survey (IALS): understanding what was measured*. Princeton, NJ: ETS Research Report RR-01-25.

Kramsch, C. J. (1986a) Proficiency versus achievement: Reflections on the proficiency movement. *ADFL Bulletin*, 18(1): 22–4.

Kramsch, C. J. (1986b) From language proficiency to interactional competence. *Modern Language Journal*, 70(4): 366–72.

Kramsch, C. J. (1993) *Context and culture in language teaching*. Oxford: Oxford University Press.

Labov, W. and Fanshel, D. (1977) *Therapeutic Discourse*. New York: Academic Press.

Lado, R. (1957) *Linguistics across Cultures*. Ann Arbor, MI: University of Michigan Press.

Lado, R. (1961) *Language Testing*. London: Longman.

Lambert, R. D., Elinor, G., Barber, E. J., Merrill, M. B. and Twarog, L. I. (1984) *Beyond Growth: The Next Stage in Language and Area Studies*. Washington DC: Association of American Universities.

Lantolf, J. P. and Frawley, W. (1985) Oral proficiency testing: A critical analysis. *Modern Language Journal*, 69(4): 337–45.

Lantolf, J. P. and Frawley, W. (1988) Proficiency: understanding the construct. *Studies in Second Language Acquisition*, 10(2): 181–95.

Lazaraton, A. (1992) The structural organization of a language interview: A conversation analytic perspective. *System*, 20(3): 373–86.

Lazaraton, A. (1996a) Interlocutor support in oral proficiency interviews. The case of CASE. *Language Testing*, 13(2): 151–72.

Lazaraton, A. (1996b) A qualitative approach to monitoring examiner conduct in the Cambridge assessment of spoken English (CASE). In Milanovic, M. and Saville, N. (eds) *Performance Testing, Cognition and Assessment: Selected papers from the 15th Language Testing Research Colloquium*. Cambridge: Cambridge University Press, 18–33.

Lee, T., Wylie, E. and Ingram, D. (1998) Mapping rates of progress in proficiency. Paper to the 20th Annual Language Testing Research Colloquium. Monterey, CA, 9–12 March.

Leech, G. N. (1983) *Principles of Pragmatics*. London: Longman.

Levinson, S. (1983) *Pragmatics*. Cambridge: Cambridge University Press.

Lewkowicz, J. A. (1997) Authenticy for whom? Does authenticity really matter? In Huhta, A., Kohnen, V., Lurki-Suonio, L. and Luoma, S. (eds) *Current developments and alternatives in language assessment*. Jyväskylä: Jyväskylä University Press, 165–84.

Lewkowicz, J. A. (2000) Authenticity in language testing: some outstanding questions. *Language Testing*, 17(1): 43–64.

Lightbrown, P. (1985) Great expectations: Second language acquisition research and classroom teaching. *Applied Linguistics*, 6: 171–89.

Linacre, J. M. (1989) *Multi-faceted measurement*. Chicago, IL: MESA Press.

Linacre, J. M. (1991) *FACETS computer program for many-faceted Rasch measurement*. Chicago, IL: Mesa Press.

Linacre, J. M. and Wright, B. D. (1990) *Facets: Many-Faceted Rasch Analysis*. Chicago, IL: Mesa Press.

Liskin-Gasparro, J. E. (1984a) The ACTFL proficiency guidelines: Gateway to testing and curriculum. *Foreign Language Annals*, 17(5): 475–89.

Liskin-Gasparro, J. E. (1984b) The ACTFL proficiency guidelines: A historical perspective. In Higgs, T. V. (ed.) *Teaching for Proficiency, the Organizing Principle*. Lincolnwood, IL: National Textbook Company, 11–42.

Lombardo, L. (1984) Oral testing: getting a sample of the real language. *English Teaching Forum*, 22(1): 2–6.

London Chamber for Commerce and Industry (1999) *English Language Skills Assessment, Information for Candidates*. London: LCCI.

Long, M. (1983) Inside the 'Black Box': Methodological issues in classroom research on language learning. In Seliger, H. W. and Long, M. (eds) *Classroom Oriented Research in Second Language Acquisition*. Rowley, MA: Newbury House Publishers, 3–36.

Lowe, P. (1983) The ILR oral interview: origins, applications, pitfalls, and implications. *Die Unterrichtspraxis*, 16: 230–44.

Lowe, P. (1985a) The ILR proficiency scale as a synthesizing research principle: The view from the mountain. In James, C. J. (ed.) *Foreign Language Proficiency in the Classroom and Beyond*. Lincolnwood, IL: National Textbook Company, 9–53.

Lowe, P. (1985b) *ILR Handbook on Oral Interview Testing* (final version). Washington DC: DLI/LS Oral Interview Project.

Lowe, P. (1986) Proficiency: panacea, framework, process? A reply to Kramsch, Schulz, and particularly Bachman and Savignon. *Modern Language Journal*, 70(4): 391–7.

Lowe, P. (1987) Interagency Language Roundtable Proficiency Interview. In Alderson, J. C., Krahnke, K. J. and Stansfield, C. W. (eds) *Reviews of English Language Proficiency Tests*. TESOL, 43–7.

Lowe, P. and Clifford, R. T. (1980) Developing an indirect measure of overall oral proficiency. In Frith, J. R. (ed.) *Measuring Spoken Language Proficiency*. Washington DC: Georgetown University Press, 31–9.

Lowe, P. and Liskin-Gasparro, J. (1986) *Testing Speaking Proficiency: The oral interview*. Washington DC: ERIC Digest.

Lumley, T. and McNamara, T. F. (1995) Rater characteristics and rater bias: implications for training. *Language Testing*, 12(1): 54–71.

Luoma, S. (1997) Comparability of a tape-mediated and face-to-face test of speaking: A triangulation study. Unpublished licentiate thesis. Jyväskylä: Jyväskylä University Centre for Applied Language Studies.

McCarthy, M. (1991) *Discourse Analysis for Language Teachers.* Cambridge: Cambridge University Press.

McCarthy, M. (1998) *Spoken Language and Applied Linguistics.* Cambridge: Cambridge University Press.

McNamara, T. (1995) Modelling performance: Opening Pandora's box. *Applied Linguistics,* 16(2): 159–79.

McNamara, T. F. (1996) *Measuring Second Language Performance.* London: Longman.

McNamara, T. F. (1997) 'Interaction' in second language performance assessment: Whose performance? *Applied Linguistics,* 18(4): 446–65.

McNamara, T. F. and Adams, M. J. (1991) Exploring rater behaviour with Rasch techniques. Paper presented at the 13th Language Testing Research Colloquium, Educational Testing Service, Princeton, NJ, 21–23 March.

McNamara, T. F. and Lumley, T. (1997) The effect of interlocutor and assessment mode variables in overseas assessments of speaking skills in occupational settings. *Language Testing,* 14: 140–56.

McNemar, Q. (1951) The factors in factoring behavior. *Psychometrika,* 16: 353–9.

MacPhail, J. (1985) Oral assessment interviews: Suggestions for participants. Unpublished MA dissertation, University of Lancaster: Department of Linguistics and Modern English Language.

Madsen, H. S. (1983) *Techniques in Testing.* Oxford: Oxford University Press.

Magnan, S. S. (1986a) Assessing speaking proficiency in the undergraduate curriculum: Data from French. *Foreign Language Annals,* 19(5): 429–38.

Magnan, S. S. (1986b) From achievement to proficiency through multi-sequence evaluation. In James, C. J. (ed.) *Foreign Language Proficiency in the Classroom and Beyond.* Lincolnwood, IL: National Textbook Company, 117–45.

Mandinach, E. B., Cahalan, C. and Camera, W. J. (2002) *The Impact of Flagging on the Admission Process: Policies, Practices, and Implications.* College Board Research Report No. 2002-2, ETS RR-02-03. New York: College Entrance Examination Board.

Markee, N. (2000) *Conversation Analysis.* Mahwah, NJ: Lawrence Erlbaum Associates.

Matthews, M. (1990) The measurement of productive skills: doubts concerning the assessment criteria of certain public examinations. *English Language Teaching Journal,* 44(2): 117–21.

Meredith, R. A. (1978) Improved oral test scores through delayed response. *Modern Language Journal,* 62(7): 321–7.

Meredith, R. A. (1990) The Oral Proficiency Interview in real life: Sharpening the scale. *Modern Language Journal,* 74(3): 288–96.

Messick, S. (1989) Validity. In Linn, R. L. *Educational Measurement.* New York: Macmillan/American Council on Education, 13–103.

Messick, S. (1992) The interplay of evidence and consequences in the validation of performance assessments. *Educational Researcher,* 23(2): 13–23.

Messick, S. (1995) Validity of psychological assessment: Validation of inferences from persons' responses and performances as scientific inquiry into score meaning. *American Psychologist,* 50, 741–9.

Messick, S. (1996) Validity and washback in language testing. *Language Testing,* 13(3): 241–56.

Milanovic, M. and Saville, N. (1994) An investigation of marketing strategies using verbal protocols. Paper presented at the 1994 Language Testing Research Colloquium, Washington DC, March.

Milanovic, M., Saville, N., Pollitt, A. and Cook, A. (1992) Developing rating scales for CASE: theoretical concerns and analyses. Paper presented at the 14th Language Testing Research Colloquium, Vancouver, 27 February–1 March.

Miller, M. D. and Linn, R. L. (2000) Validation of performance-based assessments. *Applied Psychological Measurement*, 24(4): 367–78.

Mislevy, R. J., Steinberg, L. S. and Almond, R. G. (1999a) Design and analysis in task-based language assessment. *Language Testing*, 19(4): 477–96.

Mislevy, R. J., Steinberg, L. S., and Almond, R. G. (1999b) *On the Roles of Task Model Variables in Assessment Design*. Los Angeles, CA: National Center for Research on Evaluation, Standards and Student Testing, CSE Technical Report 500.

Mislevy, R. J., Steinberg, L. S., Breyer, F. J., Almond, R. G. and Johnson, L. (1998) *A Cognitive Task Analysis, with Implications for Designing a Simulation-Based Performance Assessment*. Los Angeles, CA: National Center for Research on Evaluation, Standards and Student Testing, CSE Technical Report 487.

Morrison, D. M. and Lee, N. (1985) Simulating an academic tutorial: A test validation study. In Lee, Y. P. (ed.) *New Directions in Language Testing*. Oxford: Pergamon Institute of English, 85–92.

Morrow, K. (1979) Communicative language testing: Revolution or evolution? In Brumfit, C. K. and Johnson, K. (eds) *The Communicative Approach to Language Teaching*. Oxford: Oxford University Press, 143–59.

Morrow, K. (1982) Testing spoken language. In Heaton, J. B. (ed.) *Language Testing*. London: Modern English Publications, 56–8.

Moss, P. (1992) Shifting conceptions of validity in educational measurement: Implications for performance assessment. *Review of Educational Research*, 62(3): 229–58.

Moss, P. (1994) Can there be validity without reliability? *Educational Researchers*, 23(2): 5–12.

Mullen, K. A. (1978a) Determining the effect of uncontrolled sources of error in a direct test of oral proficiency and the capability of the procedure to detect improvement following classroom instruction. In Clark, J. L. D. (ed.) *Direct testing of speaking proficiency: theory and application*. Princeton, NJ: Educational Testing Service, 171–89.

Mullen, K. A. (1978b) Direct evaluation of second language proficiency: The effect of rater and scale in oral interviews. *Language Learning*, 28(2): 301–8.

Mullen, K. A. (1980) Rater reliability and oral proficiency examinations. In Oller, J. and Perkins, K. (eds) *Research in Language Testing*. Rowley, MA: Newbury House Publishers, 91–101.

Munby, J. (1978) *Communicative syllabus design*. Cambridge: Cambridge University Press.

North, B. (1993) *Scales of language proficiency: A survey of some existing systems*. Strasbourg: Council of Europe, Council for Cultural Cooperation, CC-LANG (94) 24.

North, B. (1995) The development of a common framework scale of descriptors of language proficiency based on a theory of measurement. *System*, 23(4): 445–65.

North, B. (1996) The development of a common framework scale of descriptors of language proficiency based on a theory of measurement. In Huhta, A. Kohonen, V., Kurki-Suonio, L. and Luoma, S. (eds) *Current Developments and Alternatives in Language Assessment*. Jyväskylä: University of Jyväskylä, 423–7.

North, B. (1996/2000) *The development of a common framework scale of descriptors of language proficiency based on a theory of measurement.* PhD thesis, Thames Valley University/New York: Peter Lang.

North, B. and Schneider, G. (1998) Scaling descriptors for language proficiency scales. *Language Testing*, 15(2): 217–63.

Nunan, D. (1989) *Designing Tasks for the Communicative Classroom.* Cambridge: Cambridge University Press.

Oller, J. W., Kim, K. and Choe, Y. (2000a) Testing verbal (language) and non-verbal abilities in language minorities: a socio-educational problem in historical perspective. *Language Testing*, 17(3): 341–60.

Oller, J. W., Kim, K. and Choe, Y. (2000b) Applying general sign theory to testing language (verbal) and nonverbal behaviours. *Language Testing*, 17(4): 377–96.

Oller, J. W., Kim, K., Choe, Y. and Jarvis, L. H. (2001) Testing relations between language (verbal) and nonverbal abilities in children and adults acquiring a non-primary language. *Language Testing*, 18(1): 33–54.

O'Loughlin, K. (2001) *The equivalence or direct and semi-direct speaking tests.* Studies in Language Testing 13. Cambridge: Cambridge University Press.

Ordinate (no date) *PhonePass: Test of Spoken English Skills by Telephone.* Menlo Park, CA.

Orr, M. (2002) The FCE speaking test: using rater reports to help interpret test scores. *System*, 30: 143–54.

O'Sullivan, B. (2002) Learner acquaintanceship and oral proficiency test pair-task performance. *Language Testing*, 19(3): 277–95.

Oxford, R. (1987) Comprehensive English Language Test. In Alderson, J. C., Krahnke, K. J. and Stansfield, C. W. (eds) *Reviews of English Language Proficiency Tests.* TESOL, 22–4.

Peirce, C. S. (1897) The fixation of belief. In Moore, C. E. (ed.) (1998) *The Essential Writings: Charles S. Peirce.* New York: Prometheus Books, 120–37.

Peirce, C. S. (1902) Pragmaticism. In Moore, C. E. (ed.) (1998) *The Essential Writings: Charles S. Peirce.* New York: Prometheus Books, 300–2.

Peirce, C. S. (1905) What Pragmaticism is. In Moore, C. E. (ed.) (1998) *The Essential Writings: Charles S. Peirce.* New York: Prometheus Books, 262–81.

Pendergast, T. M. (1985) OLAF N.73: A computerized oral language analyser and feedback system. In Lee, Y. P. (ed.) *New Directions in Language Testing.* Oxford: Pergamon Institute of English, 101–7.

Perren, G. E. (1968) Testing spoken language: Some unresolved problems. In Davies, A. (ed.) *Language Testing Symposium.* Oxford: Oxford University Press, 107–16.

Perrett, G. (1990) The language testing interview: A reappraisal. In de Jong, J. H. A. L. and Stevenson, D. K. (eds) *Individualizing the Assessment of Language Abilities.* Philadelphia, PA: Multilingual Matters, 225–38.

Phillips, S. E. (1994) High-stakes testing accommodations: Validity versus disabled rights. *Applied Measurement in Education*, 7(2): 93–120.

Pica, T., Kanagy, R. and Falodun, J. (1993) Choosing and using communication tasks for second language instruction and research. In Crookes, G. and Gass, S. M. (eds) *Tasks and Language Learning: Integrating Theory and Practice.* Cleveland, OH: Multilingual Matters, 9–34.

Pienemann, M., Johnston, M. and Brindley, G. (1988) Constructing an acquisition-based procedure for second language assessment. *Studies in Second Language Acquisition*, 10: 217–34.

Plough, I. and Gass, S. M. (1993) Interlocutor and task familiarity: Effects on interactional structure. In Crookes, G. and Gass, S. M. (eds) *Tasks and Language*

Learning. Integrating Theory and Practice. Cleveland, OH: Multilingual Matters, 35–56.

Pollitt, A. (1991a) Giving students a sporting chance: Assessment by counting and judging. In Alderson, J. C. and North, B. (eds) *Language Testing in the 1990s.* London: Modern English Publications in Association with the British Council, 46–59.

Pollitt, A. (1991b) Response to Charles Alderson's paper: Bands and scores. In Alderson, J. C. and North, B. (eds) *Language Testing in the 1990s.* London: Modern English Publications and the British Council, 87–94.

Pollitt, A. (1997) Rasch measurement in latent trait model. In Clapham, C. and Corson, D. (eds) *Encyclopedia of Language and Education,* Vol. 7: *Language Testing and Assessment.* Amsterdam: Kluwer Academic Publishers, 243–53.

Pollitt, A. and Murray, N. L. (1993) What raters really pay attention to. Paper presented at the Language Testing Research Colloquium, Cambridge, August.

Popham, W. J. (1978) *Criterion Referenced Measurement.* Englewood Cliffs, NJ: Prentice Hall.

Powers, D. E., Albertson, W., Florek, T., Johnson, K., Malak, J., Nemceff, B., Porzuc, M., Silvester, D., Wang, M., Weston, R., Winner, E. and Zelazny, A. (2002) *Influence of Irrelevant Speech on Standardized Test Performance.* TOEFL Research Report 68. Princeton, NJ: Educational Testing Service.

Quinones, J. (no date) Independent rating in oral proficiency interviews. Washington DC: Central Intelligence Agency.

Reed, D. J. and Halleck, G. B. (1997) Probing above the ceiling in oral interviews: What's up there? In Kohonen, V., Huhta, A., Kurki-Suonio, L. and Luoma, S. (eds) *Current Developments and Alternatives in Language Assessment.* Jyväskylä: University of Jyväskylä Press, 225–38.

Reves, T. (1980) The group-oral test: an experiment. *English Teachers' Journal,* 24: 19–21.

Reves, T. (1991) From testing research to educational policy: A comprehensive test of oral proficiency. In Alderson, J. C. and North, B. (eds) *Language Testing in the 1990s.* London: Modern English Publications and the British Council, 178–88.

Roach, J. O. (1945) *Some problems of oral examinations in modern languages. An experimental approach based on the Cambridge examinations in English for Foreign Students.* University of Cambridge Examinations Syndicate: Internal report circulated to oral examiners and local representatives for these examinations.

Rorty, R. (1999) *Philosophy and Social Hope.* London: Penguin.

Rosenfeld, M., Leung, S. and Oltman, P. K. (2001) *The Reading, Writing, Speaking and Listening Tasks Important for Academic Success at the Undergraduate and Graduate Levels.* Princeton, NJ: Educational Testing Service. TOEFL Monograph Series Ms. 21. Available online at ftp://ftp.ets.org/pub/toefl/990629.pdf.

Ross, S. (1992) The discourse of accommodation in oral proficiency interviews. *Studies in Second Language Acquisition,* 14: 159–76.

Ross, S. (1998) Divergent frame interpretations in language proficiency interview interaction. In Young, R. and He, A. W. (eds) *Talking and Testing: Discourse approaches to the assessment of oral proficiency.* Amsterdam: John Benjamins, 333–53.

Ross, S. and Berwick, R. (1992) The discourse of accommodation in oral proficiency interviews. *Studies in Second Language Acquisition,* 14(2): 159–76.

Rubin, D. L. and Schramm, G. (1997) The testing of L1 speaking. In Clapham, C. and Corson, D. (eds) *Encyclopedia of Language and Education,* Vol. 7: *Language Testing and Assessment.* Amsterdam: Kluwer Academic Publishers, 29–37.

Sacks, H., Schegloff, E. and Jefferson, G. (1974) A simplest systematics for the organization of turn-taking for conversation. *Language*, 50(4): 696–735.

Saville, N. and Hargreaves, P. (1999) Assessing speaking in the revised FCE. *ELT Journal*, 53(1): 42–51.

Schärer, R. (1996) A European language portfolio. In Huhta, A. Kohonen, V., Kurki-Suonio, I. and Luoma, S. (eds) *Current Developments and Alternatives in Language Assessment*. Jyväskylä: University of Jyväskylä, 449–64.

Schärer, R. and North, B. (1992) *Towards a Common European Framework for Reporting Language Competency*. Washington DC: National Foreign Language Center, occasional papers.

Schegloff, E. and Sacks, H. (1973) Opening up closings. *Semiotica*, 7(4): 289–327.

Schulz, R. A. (1986) From achievement through proficiency through classroom instruction: some caveats. *Modern Language Journal*, 70(4): 373–79.

Scott, M. L. (1986) Student affective reactions to oral language tests. *Language Testing*, 3: 99–118.

Searle, J. (1969) *Speech Acts: An Essay in the Philosophy of Language*. Cambridge: Cambridge University Press.

Seliger, H. W. (1980) Utterance planning and correction behaviour: its function in the grammar construction process for second language learners. In Dechert, H. and Raupach, M. (eds) *Towards a Cross-Linguistic Assessment of Speech Production*. Frankfurt: Peter Lang.

Sheorey, R. (1986) Error perceptions of native-speaking and non-native speaking teachers of ESL. *English Language Teaching Journal*, 40(4): 306–12.

Shohamy, E. (1983a) Interrater and intrarater reliability of the oral interview and concurrent validity with cloze procedure in Hebrew. In Oller, J. W. (ed.) *Issues in Language Testing Research*. Rowley, MA: Newbury House, 229–36.

Shohamy, E. (1983b) The stability of oral proficiency assessment in the oral interview procedure. *Language Learning*, 33(4): 527–40.

Shohamy, E. (1988) A proposed framework for testing the oral language of second/foreign language learners. *Studies in Second Language Acquisition*, 10: 165–79.

Shohamy, E. (1990) Language testing priorities: a different perspective. *Foreign Language Annals*, 23(5): 365–94.

Shohamy, E. (1994) The validity of direct versus semi-direct oral tests. *Language Testing*, 11(2): 99–123.

Shohamy, E. (1997) Testing methods, testing consequences: are they ethical? Are they fair? *Language Testing*, 14(3): 340–9.

Shohamy, E. (2001) *The Power of Tests: A critical perspective on the uses of language tests*. London: Longman.

Shohamy, E., Gordon, C., Kenyon, D. and Stansfield, C. (1989) The development and validation of a semi-direct test for assessing oral proficiency in Hebrew. *Bulletin of Hebrew Higher Education*, 4(1): 4–9.

Shohamy, E., Reves, T. and Bejerano, Y. (1986) Introducing a new comprehensive test of oral proficiency. *English Language Teaching Journal*, 40: 212–20.

Shohamy, E., Shmueli, D. and Gordon, C. (1991) The validity of concurrent validity of a direct vs. semi-direct test of oral proficiency. Paper presented at the 13th Language Testing Research Colloquium, Educational Testing Service, Princeton, NJ.

Shohamy, E. and Stansfield, C. W. (1990) The Hebrew speaking test: An example of international cooperation in test development and validation. In de Jong, J. H. A. L. (ed.) *Standardization in Language Testing: AILA Review*. Amsterdam: Free University Press, 79–90.

Silverman, D. (1976) Interview talk: bringing off a research instrument. In Silverman, D. and Jones, J. (eds) *Organizational Work: the language of grading, the grading of language*. London: Collier Macmillan, 133–50.

Skehan, P. (1998a) *A Cognitive Approach to Language Learning*. Oxford: Oxford University Press.

Skehan, P. (1998b) Processing perspectives to second language development, instruction, performance and assessment. London: Thames Valley Working papers in Applied Linguistics, 4: 70–88.

Skehan, P. (2001) Tasks and language performance assessment. In Bygate, M., Skehan, P. and Swain, M. (eds) *Researching Pedagogic Tasks. Second Language Learning, Teaching and Testing*. London: Longman, 167–85.

Skehan, P. and Foster, P. (1997) The influence of planning and post-task activities on accuracy and complexity in task-based learning. *Language Teaching Research*, 1: 185–211.

Sollenberger, H. E. (1978) Development and current use of the FSI oral interview test. In Clark, J. L. D. (ed.) *Direct Testing of Speaking Proficiency: Theory and Application*. Princeton, NJ: Educational Testing Service, 1–12.

Spolsky, B. (1985) The limits of authenticity in language testing. *Language Testing*, 2(1): 31–40.

Spolsky, B. (1995) *Measured Words*. Oxford: Oxford University Press.

Spolsky, B. (2001) Tests of the speaking construct: an historical perspective. Paper delivered at the LTRC-AAAL Symposium on the Speaking Construct, St Louis, MO, February.

Stansfield, C. W. (1989) Simulated Oral Proficiency Interviews. *ERIC Digest*. Washington DC: ERIC Clearinghouse for Languages and Linguistics and the Center for Applied Linguistics.

Stansfield, C. W. (1990a) An evaluation of simulated oral proficiency interviews as measures of spoken language proficiency. In Alatis, J. E. (ed.) *Linguistics, language teaching and language acquisition: The interdependence of theory, practice and research*. Georgetown University Round Table on Languages and Linguistics. Washington DC: Georgetown University Press, 228–34.

Stansfield, C. W. (1990b) The development and validation of the Portuguese Speaking Test. *Hispania*, 73(3): 641–51.

Stansfield, C. W. (1991) A comparative analysis of simulated and direct proficiency interviews. In Anvian, S. (ed.) *Current Developments in Language Testing*. Singapore: SEAMEO Regional Language Centre, Anthology Series, 25: 199–209.

Stansfield, C. W. and Kenyon, D. M. (1989) *Development of the Hausa, Hebrew and Indonesian speaking tests*. Washington DC: Center for Applied Linguistics.

Stansfield, C. W. and Kenyon, D. (1992a) Comparing scales of speaking tasks by language teachers and by the ACTFL guidelines. Paper presented at the 14th Language Testing Research Colloquium, Vancouver, 27 February–1 March.

Stansfield, C. W. and Kenyon, D. M. (1992b) The development and validation of a simulated oral proficiency interview. *The Modern Language Journal*, 72(2): 129–41.

Stansfield, C. W. and Kenyon, D. M. (1992c) Research on the comparability of the oral proficiency interview and the simulated oral proficiency interview. *System*, 20(3): 347–64.

Stansfield, C. W. and Rivera, C. (2001) *Test Accommodations for LEP Students. ERIC Digest*, ED458280. College Park, MD: ERIC Clearinghouse on Assessment and Evaluation.

Stevenson, D. K. (1981) Beyond faith and face validity: the multitrait–multimethod matrix and the convergent and discriminant validity of oral proficiency tests. In Palmer, A. S., Groot, P. M. J. and Trosper, G. (eds) *The Construct Validation of Tests of Communicative Competence.* Washington DC: TESOL, 37–61.

Stevenson, D. K. (1985a) Authenticity, validity and a tea party. *Language Testing,* 2(1): 41–7.

Stevenson, D. K. (1985b) Pop validity and performance testing. In Lee, Y. P. (ed.) *New Directions in Language Testing.* Oxford: Pergamon Institute of English, 111–18.

Swain, M. (2001) Examining dialogue: another approach to content specification and to validating inferences drawn from test scores. *Language Testing,* 18(3): 275–302.

Swain, M. and Lapkin, S. (2001) Focus on form through collaborative dialogue: Exploring task effects. In Bygate, M., Skehan, P. and Swain, M. (eds) *Researching Pedagogic Tasks: Second language learning, teaching and testing.* London: Longman, 99–118.

Tarone, E. (1983) On the variability of interlanguage systems. *Applied Linguistics,* 4: 142–63.

Tarone, E. (1985) Variability in interlanguage use: a study of style-shifting in morphology and syntax. *Language Learning,* 35: 373–403.

Tarone, E. (1987) Methodologies for studying variability in second language acquisition. In Ellis, R. (ed.) *Second Language Acquisition in Context.* Hemel Hempstead: Prentice Hall International, 35–40.

Tarone, E. (1988) *Variation in Interlanguage.* London: Edward Arnold.

Tarone, E. (1998) Research on interlanguage variation: Implications for language testing. In Bachman, L. F. and Cohen, A. D. (eds) *Interfaces between Second Language Acquisition and Language Testing Research.* Cambridge: Cambridge University Press, 71–89.

Taylor, L. (2000) Investigating the paired speaking test format. University of Cambridge Local Examinations Syndicate Research Notes 2, 14–15. Available online at: http://www.cambridge-efl.org/rs_notes/0002/rn2.pdf

Thomas, J. (2003) *Applied Cross-cultural Pragmatics Studies in Spoken, Situated Interaction.* London: Longman.

Thurstone, L. L. (1928) Attitudes can be measured. *American Journal of Sociology,* 33: 529–54.

Thurstone, L. L. (1959) *The Measurement of Values.* Chicago, IL: Chicago University Press.

Trim, J. L. M. (1997) The proposed Common European Framework for the description of language learning, teaching and assessment. In Huhta, A. Kohonen, V., Kurki-Suonio, L. and Luoma, S. (eds) *Current Developments and Alternatives in Language Assessment.* Jyväskylä: University of Jyväskylä, 415–22.

Tsui, A. B. M. (1994) *English Conversation.* Oxford: Oxford University Press.

Turner, C. and Upshur, J. (1996) Scale development factors as factors of test method. Paper given at the 18th Language Testing Research Colloquium, Tampere, Finland, August 1996.

Underhill, N. (1982) The great reliability validity trade-off: Problems in assessing the productive skills. In Heaton, B. (ed.) *Language Testing.* London: Modern English Publications, 17–23.

Underhill, N. (1987) *Testing Spoken Language: A handbook of oral testing techniques.* Cambridge: Cambridge University Press.

University of Cambridge Local Examinations Syndicate (1988) *Communicative Use of English as a Foreign Language, Test of Oral Interaction Basic Level 0203/1.* Cambridge: UCLES.

University of Cambridge Local Examinations Syndicate (1997) *Business English Certificate I*, Handbook and Sample Papers. Cambridge: UCLES.

University of Cambridge Local Examinations Syndicate (2001) *Preliminary English Test Handbook*, Sample Materials. Cambridge: UCLES.

University of Cambridge Local Examinations Syndicate (2002a) *Certificate of Proficiency in English Test*, Handbook and Sample Materials. Cambridge: UCLES.

University of Cambridge Local Examinations Syndicate (2002b) *Certificate of English Language Skills Test*, Handbook and Sample Materials. Cambridge: UCLES.

Upshur, J. (1971) Productive communication testing: Progress report. In Perren, G. E. and Trim, J. L. *Applications of Linguistics*. Cambridge: Cambridge University Press, 345–441.

Upshur, J. and Turner, C. (1995) Constructing rating scales for second language tests. *English Language Teaching Journal*, 49(1): 3–12.

Upshur, J. A. and Turner, C. E. (1999) Systematic effects in the rating of second-language speaking ability: test method and learner discourse. *Language Testing*, 16(1): 82–111.

Valdman, A. (1988) The assessment of foreign language oral proficiency: introduction. *Studies in Second Language Acquisition*, 10(2): 221–8.

Valette, R. M. (1997) *Modern Language Testing*. San Diego, CA: Harcourt Brace Jovanovich.

van Lier, L. (1989) Reeling, writhing, drawling, stretching, and fainting in coils: Oral Proficiency Interviews as conversation. *TESOL Quarterly*, 23(3): 489–508.

van Patten, B. (1986) The ACTFL proficiency guidelines: Implications for grammatical accuracy in the classroom? *Studies in Second Language Acquisition*, 8: 56–7.

Váradi, T. (1983) Strategies of target language learner communication: Message adjustment. In Færch, C. and Kasper, G. (eds) *Introspection in second language research*. Clevedon: Multilingual Matters, 79–99.

Varonis, E. M. and Gass, S. (1985) Non-native/Non-native conversations: A model for negotiation of meaning. *Applied Linguistics*, 6(1): 71–90.

Vollmer, H. J. (1983) The structure of foreign language competence. In Hughes, A. and Porter, D. (eds) *Current Developments in Language Testing*. London: Academic Press, 3–30.

Wall, D. (1997) Impact and washback in language testing. In Clapham, C. M. and Corson, D. (eds) *Language Testing and Assessment, Encyclopedia of Language and Education*, Vol. 7. Dordrecht: Kluwer, 291–302.

Wall, D. (2000) The impact of high-stakes testing on teaching and learning: can this be predicted or controlled? *System*, 28(4): 499–510.

Waters, A. (1996) *A Review of Research into Needs in English for Academic Purposes of Relevance to the North American Higher Education Context*. Princeton, NJ: Educational Testing Service. TOEFL Monograph Series Ms. 6. Available online at ftp:// ftp.ets.org/pub/toefl/Toefl-MS-6.pdf.

Weigle, S. C. (1994) Using FACETS to model rater training effects. Paper presented at the 16th Annual Language Testing Research Colloquium, Washington DC, March.

Weinstein, A. I. (1979) Steps in a speaking test. In Frith, J. R. (ed.) *Testing Kit: French and Spanish*. Washington DC: Department of State, 106–10.

Weir, C. (1988) *Communicative Language Testing*. Exeter: Exeter University Press.

Weir, C. (1993) *Understanding and Developing Language Tests*. New York and London: Prentice Hall International.

Widdowson, H. G. (1983) *Learning Purpose and Language Use*. Oxford: Oxford University Press.

Wigglesworth, G. (1993) Exploring bias analysis as a tool for improving rater consistency in assessing oral interaction. *Language Testing*, 10: 305–35.

Wigglesworth, G. (2001) Influences on performance in task-based oral assessments. In Bygate, M., Skehan, P. and Swain, M. (eds) *Researching Pedagogic Tasks. Second Language Learning, Teaching and Testing.* London: Longman, 186–209.

Wilds, C. (1975) The oral interview test. In Jones, R. L. and Spolsky, B. (eds) *Testing Language Proficiency.* Arlington, VA: Center for Applied Linguistics, 29–44.

Wilds, C. (1979) The measurement of speaking and reading proficiency in a foreign language. In Adams, M. L. and Frith, J. R. (eds) *Testing Kit: French and Spanish.* Department of State: Foreign Services Institute, 1–12.

Wilkinson, A. (1968) The testing of oracy. In Davies, A. (ed.) *Language Testing Symposium.* Oxford: Oxford University Press, 117–32.

Winter, E. O. (1978) A look at the role of certain words in information structure. In Jones, K. P. and Horsnell, V. (eds) *Informatics*, 3. London: ASLIB, 86–97.

Wolfson, N. (1983) Rules of speaking. In Richards, J. C. and Schmidt, R. W. (eds) *Language and Communication.* London: Longman.

Wood, B. D. (1927) *New York Experiments with New-Type Modern Language Tests.* New York: Macmillan.

Wright, B. D. and Masters, G. N. (1982) *Rating Scale Analysis.* Chicago, IL: MESA Press.

Wright, T. (1987) Instructional task and discoursal outcome in the L2 classroom. In Candlin, C. N. and Murphy, D. F. (eds) *Language Learning Tasks.* Lancaster Practical Paper in English Language Education, Vol. 7. Englewood Cliffs, NJ: Prentice Hall International, 47–68.

Yerkes, R. M. (ed.) (1921) Psychological examining in the United States Army. *Memoirs of the National Academy of Sciences*, Vol. 15.

Yoshida-Morise, Y. (1998) The use of communication strategies in language proficiency interviews. In Young, R. and He, A. W. (eds) *Talking and Testing. Discourse Approaches to the Assessment of Oral Proficiency.* Amsterdam: John Benjamins, 205–38.

Young, R. (1995) Conversational styles in language proficiency interviews. *Language Learning*, 45(1): 3–42.

Young, R. (2002) Discourse approaches to oral language assessment. *Annual Review of Applied Linguistics*, 22: 243–62.

Young, R. and Halleck, G. B. (1998) 'Let them eat cake!' or how to avoid losing your head in cross-cultural conversations. In Young, R. and He, A. W. (eds) *Talking and Testing. Discourse Approaches to the Assessment of Oral Proficiency.* Amsterdam: John Benjamins, 355–82.

Young, R. and He, A. W. (1998) *Talking and Testing. Discourse Approaches to the Assessment of Oral Proficiency.* Amsterdam: John Benjamins.

Young, S. and Milanovic, M. (1992) Discourse variation in oral proficiency interviews. *Studies in Second Language Acquisition*, 14(4): 403–24.

Yule, G. and Tarone, E. (1997) Investigating communication strategies in L2 reference: pros and cons. In Kasper, G. and Kellerman, E. (eds) *Communication Strategies: Psycholinguistic and Sociological Perspectives.* London, Longman, 17–30.

Zappala, S. P. J. (1979) Interpreter situations. In Adams, M. L. and Frith, J. R. (eds) *Testing Kit: French and Spanish.* Department of State: Foreign Services Institute, 111–17.

Index

'ability/interaction' approach, 90–1
ability level, 189
abstract level, 14
accent, 12, 228
accommodations, test, xv
  interlocutor and, 147–8, 149
  test takers with disabilities, 155–6
    flagging, 156–9
accuracy, 26–30, 48
  Functional Trisection, 175–6
achievement strategies, 31–2, 48
activity costs, 161–9
Adams, M. J., 142, 213
Adams, M. L., 9, 10, 13, 93, 140, 182, 183
Adams, R. J., 175
addition of examples, 101–2, 103–4
address terms, 39
adequacy, 64
adjacency pairs, 34, 36–7
adjuncts, 27
administration, 152–3
  documents, 166
Adult Immigrants on a Conversation Course Exit Test, 123–6
advanced level, 175, 231–2, 233–5
advanced professional proficiency, 241
AEI approach (ACTFL/ETS/IRL), 94–5
  evaluation of AEI tradition, xv, 146, 171, 173–86
  see also American Council on the Teaching of Foreign Languages; Educational Testing Service; Inter-agency Language Roundtable
Agard, F., 7

Alderson, J. C., 1, 89, 90, 95, 97, 120, 144, 145, 153, 156, 216–17
American Council of Learned Societies, 9
American Council on the Teaching of Foreign Languages (ACTFL), 11, 12, 93, 140, 143, 171
  rating scale, 15–16, 230–8
    Guidelines 1986, 11, 16, 230–2
    Revised Guidelines 1999, 11, 16, 233–8
  validity study, xv, 146, 171, 173–86
American with Disabilities Act, 156, 158
analysis of variance (ANOVA), 211
analytic rating scales, 89–91
Anderson, A., 34
Angiolillo, P., 6
anxiety, 218
appropriacy, 39–42
approximation, 32
Army Alpha and Beta tests, 3
Army Education Corps, 8
Army Specialized Training Program (ASTP), 6–8
assessor-oriented scales, 89
Association of College Registrars, 2, 5
Association of Modern Language Teachers, 2
aural tests, 2
Austin, J. L., 42
Australian *access:* test, 193, 213–15
Australian Second Language Proficiency Ratings (ASLPR), 93–4, 141, 203
authenticity, 54–5, 61
authority, 199
  pragmatic appropriacy, 41–2

automaticity, 24, 30
avoidance strategies, 32–4, 48

Bachman, L. F., 19, 31, 44, 45, 49, 51,
    53–6, 60, 63, 65, 66, 67, 90, 91,
    94, 120, 123–6, 128, 131, 145,
    152, 154, 160, 180, 181, 182–4,
    185, 186, 196, 200, 207–10, 211,
    215, 224, 239–40
Bailey, K. M., 211–12
Bamford, R., 169
band descriptors
    ACTFL, 15–16, 230–8
    categories and, 103–4
    costs of designing, 165
    FSI, 13–14, 95, 226–7
    ILR, 14–15, 241–5
    link with language elicited by tasks,
        174–5
    scaling descriptors method, 92, 107–13
    terminology, 96–7
Barnwell, D., 7–8, 10, 94, 96, 140, 143,
    178, 179, 186
Bartz, W. M., 185
basic user, 112
being, expressing, 43–4
Bejar, I. I., 142
Bejarano, Y., 131, 141
Berkoff, N. A., 188
Berry, V., 188–9
Berwick, R., 147, 148
bias, test, 9
Bolus, R. E., 211–12
Brazil, D. A., 26, 27, 28, 34
Breimhorst v. ETS, 158
Brennan, R. L., 145
Brigham, C. C., 4–5
British Council Oral Testing video,
    150–1, 153–4
Brod, R., 178
Brown, A., 144, 149, 220–2
Brown, G., 60–1
Brown, J. D., 202
Brown, J. W., 177
Buck, G., 35
budgeting for test design, xv, 159–69
Burroughs, G. E. R., 191
Butler, F., 20–1
Bygate, M., 24, 47
Byrnes, H., 143

Campbell, D. T., 183, 196, 207, 208,
    209–10
Canale, M., 31, 44
Candlin, C. N., 51, 61
Carroll, B. J., 119, 121–3
Carroll, J. B., 11, 190–1
Cartier, F. A., 191
categories, explanatory, 99–102, 103–4
Central Intelligence Agency (CIA), 10
Certificate of Proficiency in English
    (CPE), 5–6, 8, 76–8
certification, 145
Chalhoub-Deville, M., 65, 146
Chapelle, C., 19, 62, 65, 66, 117, 181
Chastain, K., 179
Child, D., 204
choices, 24–5
Civil Service Commission, 9
Clahsen, H., 26
Clapham, C., 64, 120, 123, 145
Clark, J. L. D., 13, 140, 178, 190, 191,
    192
Clifford, R. T., 191
closed tasks, 52
closings, 38
co-construction, 45–6, 57, 189
code complexity, 61
code switching, 32
codes of practice, 225
coding speech data, 98–102
    quality control, 102–3
cognitive load, 61
Cohen, J., 189
Cold War, 9–10
college admissions, 157, 158
College Entrance Examination
    Board English Competence
    Examination, 2–3, 5
committee rating scale design, 92
Common European Framework, 111–13,
    146, 216
common reference levels, 111–13
communality, 205
communication goal, 52–3
    see also goal orientation
communication of information, 205,
    206
communication strategies (CS), 20,
    31–4, 48
communicative competence, 7–8, 9, 51

communicative effectiveness, 105, 106
communicative language ability models, 45
communicative potential, 52
communicative stress, 60
Communicative Use of English as a Foreign Language (CUEFL) test, 59–60
competence
  communicative, 7–8, 9, 51
  interactional, 34, 44–6, 49
  language competence, 9, 25–31, 48
  and performance, 20
'competent' individuals, 6
complex and numerous operations, 63
component scales of FSI, 12–14, 228–9
comprehension, 12, 229
Comprehensive English Language Test (CELT), 203
concrete level, 14
consciousness-raising, 23
consequential validity, 196–7
constatives, 42
construct definition, xiv, 3, 18–49, 62
  accuracy and fluency, 26–31, 48
  costs, 163–4
  defining speaking, 23–5
  framework for, 48, 49
  interactional competence, 34, 44–6, 49
  learning to speak, 21–3
  pronunciation and intonation, 25–6
  speaking in context, 39–44
  strategies for speaking, 31–4, 48
  structuring speech, 34–8, 48
construct-equivalent validity, 172
construct-irrelevant variance, 3, 47–9, 138, 210
construct underrepresentation, 47
constructor-oriented scales, 89
content-oriented tasks, 52
content-planning hesitation, 30–1, 100–1, 103–4
content validity, 195
context
  construct definition and contextual factors, 19
  educational contexts, 10–11
  Functional Trisection, 175–6
  of speaking, 39–44

contextualised judgements, 143
contrast, 26
control, 135–7
convergent validity, 196, 207, 209
conversation, 2, 3
  directed conversation, 8
co-occurring features, 106
Coolidge, C., 4
Cooper, C. R., 89
cooperative strategies, 32
correlation, 190–2, 201–3
correlation fallacy, 7, 203
cost-benefit scale, 40–1
costs, xv, 159–69
court cases, 157, 158, 169
criterion-reductive tests, 179–80
critical values table, 202
cross-contamination, 90
curriculum, 176–8

Dancy, J., 199
Dandonoli, P., 146, 181–2, 196
data-based scale development, 92, 97–104
Davidson, F., xiii, xv, 121, 127–9, 130, 131, 134, 135, 201, 216, 217, 224
Davies, A., 88–9, 94
de Charruf, L. F., 141
decision study (D-Study), 211
declarative sentences, 42
Defense Language Institute (DLI), 10, 191
descriptions, 60–1
descriptors *see* band descriptors
delivery, 205, 206
design team, 117
  costs, 161–2
dialect, 21
dictation, 2, 3
differentiated outcomes, 63
difficult requests, role-playing, 127–9
diplomatic personnel, 9, 84
directed conversation, 8
directness
  face validity and direct tests, 181, 185
  input-response relationship, 56
  see also indirect speech acts; indirect speaking tests; indirectness scale
disabilities, test takers with, 155–9

discourse
  changes in and changes in task,
    64–5
  features and indirect speaking tests,
    192–3
discourse analysis, 220–2
discriminant analysis, 102–3, 182,
    183
discussion, 85–6, 188
divergent validity, 196, 207, 210
documentation
  cost of writing administration
    documents, 166
  preparation of test specifications,
    117–20
double blind coding, 102–3
Douglas, D., 19, 64, 66
Dugan, J. S., 191
Dunkel, H., 7

educated native level, 15, 93–5
educational contexts, 10–11
Educational Testing Service (ETS), 11,
    120, 190
  Breimhorst case, 158
  Maps and Graphs, 70–3
  Standards for Quality and Fairness,
    119–20, 157
eigenvalues, 205
Eignor, D., 215
Elder, C., 63–4
elementary proficiency, 226, 244
eliciting of speech, 50–1
Ellis, R., 61
embedded adjacency pairs, 37
empirical rating scale design, 91–2,
    97–113
empirically derived, binary-choice,
    boundary definition scales
    (EBBs), 92, 104–7
end-of-turn pauses, 100, 103–4
English for Academic Purposes (EAP)
    tests, 64
English Language Testing Service
    (ELTS), 98
  specifications, 121–3
enjoyment, 218
environment, 138–9, 153–5
Ericsson, K., 222
error gravity, 27–8

errors, 179, 192
  accuracy, 26–30
  rules of speaking, 39–40
Ervin-Tripp, S. M., 39
European Framework, 111–13, 146, 216
evaluation, xv, 171–98
  FSI tradition, xv, 146, 171, 173–86
  indirect speaking tests, xv, 172, 190–4
  testing in pairs, xv, 172, 186–90
  validity model, 194–7
evidence *see* research
evidence-centred design, 119, 129
expected response, characteristics of, 55
experience, 185, 186
experiential rating scale design, 92,
    92–7
expert judgement, 92, 216–17
'experts', 6
explanatory categories, 99–102, 103–4
expressing being, 43–4
extended discourse tasks, 61
external aspect of validity, 196
external/internal distinction, 20
extroverts, 188–9

face validity, 10, 181, 185–6
factor analysis, 203–7
factor loadings, 204, 205
fairness, 197
familiar information, 63
familiarity, 57
  interlocutor status and, 57, 58, 60,
    68–86 *passim*
  pairing, 189
Fanshel, D., 43
First Certificate in English (FCE), 6,
    187
Fiske, D. W., 183, 196, 207, 208, 209–10
flagging, 156–9
fluency
  Common European Framework
    fluency scale, 112
  construct definition, 26–7, 30–1, 48
  FSI rating scale, 12, 14, 229
  rating scale, 250–2
    development, 97, 98, 98–102,
      103–4
focus of rating scales, 90–1
Folland, D., 188
Foot, M. C., 172, 187–8

Foreign Service Institute (FSI), 9–10,
  10–11, 186
  evaluation of FSI tradition, xv, 146,
    171, 173–86
    curriculum, 176–8
    face validity, 185–6
    Functional Trisection, 175–6, 177
    language acquisition, 179–80
    link between descriptors and
      language elicited, 174–5
    validity concerns, 181–4
  Oral Proficiency Interview *see* Oral
    Proficiency Interview (OPI)
  rating scale, 11–14
    band descriptors, 13–14, 95,
      226–7
    component scales, 12–14, 228–9
    development, 92–7
formal avoidance, 33
Foster, P., 27, 63
Frawley, W., 94, 178–9, 179–80
freedom, 135–7
Frith, J. R., 10, 93
Fulcher, G., 1, 11, 14, 28, 30, 41, 53, 61,
    64, 65, 66, 66–7, 86, 89, 96–7, 98,
    99, 103, 104, 107, 113, 117, 142,
    146, 160, 169, 178, 180, 182, 185,
    188, 217–20
full professional proficiency, 227
functional avoidance, 33
functional native proficiency, 241
Functional Trisection, 175–6, 177
functions, 192

Gass, S., 67, 147, 189, 222
gatekeeping, 197
Geddes, M., 53
general description (GD), 130
general professional proficiency, 242
generalisability, 61–2, 65–6, 196
generalisability studies, 210–13
goal orientation, 52–3, 57, 58, 60
  task types 68–86 *passim*
Goddard, H. H., 4
grammar, 12, 13–14, 205, 206, 228
grammatical accuracy, 105, 106
grammatical competence, 240
grammatical-planning hesitation, 101,
  103–4
Green, A., 118, 222

Goffman, E., 36–7
Gordon, C., 172, 192–3
Grice, H. P., 39, 40
Griffin, P. E., 175
group discussion, 188

Hall, J. K., 22
Hall, P. J., 119
Halleck, G. B., 36, 43
Halliday, M. A. K., 193
halo effect, 90
Hamp-Lyons, L., 89–90, 187
Hargreaves, P., 36, 78, 187, 195
Harrison, A., 140
Hatch, E., 26
He, A. W., 37, 45–6
Hendricks, D., 140–1
Henning, G., 108, 146, 181–2, 196, 202,
  217
hesitation, 30–1, 98, 99–102, 103–4
heterotrait-heteromethod, 209
heterotrait-monomethod, 209
Heyden, P. M., 2
hidden variables, 202–3
Hieke, A. E., 97
Hill, K., 149
history of testing, xiv, 1–17
  before 1939, 1–6
  Cold War, 9–10
  educational contexts, 10–11
  focus on rating scales, 11–16
  war years, 6–8
Hinofotis, F. B., 203, 204–7, 211–12
holistic rating scales, 9, 89–91
holistic scoring, 90
Hudson, R. A., 35
Hughes, A., 117
human judgement, 224
Hymes, D. 39

idiolect, 21
immediacy, 64
Immigration Act 1924 (US), xiv, 4–5
immigration policy, 2–5
implicature, 40
imposition, 66–7
independent user, 112
indirect speaking tests, xv, 172, 190–4
indirect speech acts, 42–3
indirectness scale, 40–1

information
  communication of, 205, 206
  familiar, 63
Information Gap task, 80–2
Ingram, D., 93–4, 95–6, 141, 203
input, characteristics of, 54
input-response relationship, 55–6
instructions, 60–1
instrumental motivation, 22–3
integrative motivation, 22–3
integrative speaking tests, 84
intelligence testing, 3–4
intended consequences, 197
interactional activity, 52–3, 57–8
interactional competence, 34, 44–6, 49
interactional competence theory (ICT),
    45–6
interactional relationship 57, 58, 59
  task types 68–86 *passim*
interactionism, 62, 66
Interagency Language Roundtable
    (ILR), 10, 11, 93
  rating scale, 14–15, 15, 90–1, 241–5
interlocutor frames, 74, 147, 151, 221
interlocutors, xv, 138
  status and familiarity, 57, 58, 60
    task types 68–86 *passim*
  testing in pairs, 187–8
  training, 147–52, 167–8
  variation and discourse analysis,
    220–2
intermediate level, 174, 175, 230–1,
    235–7
internal/external distinction, 20
International English Language Testing
    System (IELTS), 64
International Language Testing
    Association (ILTA), 200, 225
International Second Language
    Proficiency Ratings (ISLPR), 94,
    246
interpretative density, 61
interpreting/translating tasks, 83–4
interpretive argument, 171
inter-rater reliability, 8, 10, 140–2,
    143–4, 215
interview talk, 185
interviews, 217–20
  see also Oral Proficiency Interview
    (OPI)

intonation, 25–6, 34
introverts, 188–9
intuitive analysis, 108–9
intuitive method, 199
intuitive rating scale design, 91–2, 92–7
item response theory (IRT), 108
Iwashita, N., 63–4, 189

Jacoby, S., 45, 46
Jafarpur, A., 142
James, C., 27
Jarvis, G. A., 94, 174
Jefferson, G., 34, 100, 149
jigsaw task, 53
Johnson, M., xiii, 45
Jones, K., 83
Jones, R. L., 95
Joreskog, K. G., 183
judgements
  contextualised, 143
  expert, 92, 216–17
  human, 224

Kachru, B. B., 94
Kane, M. T., 117, 171, 194
Kasper, G., 20, 31
Katz, I., 119
Kaulfers, W. V., 6–7, 149–50, 192, 203
Kellerman, E., 20, 31
Kelly, G. A., 144
Kenyon, D., 107, 113, 149, 190, 192
Kerlinger, F. N., 18, 205, 207
knowledge base, complexity of, 63
Kramsch, C. J., 9, 45, 66, 186

Labov, W., 43
Lado, R., 18–19, 46
Lambert, R. D., 178
language acquisition
  AEL rating scales and, 179–80
  primary, 21–2
  second *see* second language
    acquisition
language awareness approaches, 23
language competence, 9, 25–31, 48
language for specific purposes (LSP),
    testing, 64, 178
Lantolf, J. P., 94, 178–9, 179–80
Lapkin, S., 189
Lazaraton, A., 148, 151, 152

Lee, H. B., 18, 205, 207
Lee, N., 141–2
Leech, G. N., 40–1
Lett, J. A., 191
Levinson, S., 37, 38
Lewkowicz, J. A., 54
Li, Y. C., 191, 192
limited working proficiency, 226, 243
Linacre, J. M., 108, 213
Linn, R. L., 194
Liskin-Gasparro, J. E., 9, 10, 11, 93, 140, 141, 174, 175, 177, 179
literal utterances, 43
local performance conditions, xv, 138–9, 152–5
London Chamber of Commerce and Industry (LCCI), 69–70
Long, M., 99–100
Lowe, P., 10, 14–15, 15, 16, 93, 94–5, 96, 139, 141, 144, 173, 176, 176–7, 179, 184, 186
Lower Certificate in English (LCE), 6
Lumley, T., 215
Luoma, S., 193
Lynch, B., 65
Lynch, B. K., xv, 121, 130, 131, 134, 135, 216, 217
Lynch, T., 34

Mackey, A., 222
Magnan, S. S., 178, 182, 184
Mandinach, E. B., 157
Maps and Graphics test, 70–3
Markee, N., 34, 44
Márquez Reiter, R., 41, 65, 66–7, 89
Mason, M., 65
Masters, G. N., 105
Matthews, M., 13, 96
McNamara, T., 44, 45, 46, 58, 63–4, 82–3, 107, 113, 142, 142–3, 144, 145, 189, 190, 213–15
McNemar, Q., 206
meaning, negotiation of, 189
memorised proficiency, 14, 245
Meredith, R. A., 99, 182, 184, 202
Messick, S., 47, 116–17, 129, 138, 173, 194–7, 200
Milanovic, M., 107, 146, 149
military personnel, 6–8, 9, 84
Miller, M. D., 194

minimum professional proficiency, 226–7
miscommunication, 25–6
Mislevy, R. J., 118, 129, 134
model of speaking test performance, 113–15
Modern Language Association (MLA), 190–1
monotrait-heteromethod, 209–10
morphological creativity, 32
Morrison, D. M., 141–2
Morrow, K., 54, 185
Moss, P., 143, 144
motivation, 22–3
Mullen, K. A., 97, 140, 141
multifaceted Rasch analysis, 107–8, 110, 142, 213–15
multiple-trait scoring, 90
multitrait-multimethod (MTMM) studies, 181–2, 182–4, 207–10, 224
Munby, J., 121
Murray, N. L., 144

n-size, 202
narrative tasks, 60, 69–70
native speaker level, 15, 93–5, 227, 241
native speakers: reactions to errors, 179
negative politeness, 40
negotiation of meaning, 189
'new behaviourism', 62, 65
no proficiency, 14, 245
noise, 154
non-linguistic strategies, 32
non-verbal aspects, 205, 206
North, B., 107, 108–11, 112–13, 146, 180, 216
notional/functional approach, 10
novice level, 174, 175, 230, 237–8
Nunan, D., 51–2

Occupational English Tests (OETs), 44, 82–3
Ochs, E., 45
O'Loughlin, K., 118, 149, 193, 195, 196, 223
omission, 28
open tasks, 52
openings, 38
optionality scale, 40–1

oracy, 192–3
Oral Proficiency Interview (OPI), xiii, 8,
    78–9
  comparison with indirect tests, 190–1,
    192–3
  evaluation, 171, 173–86
  MTMM study, 207–10
  rater reliability, 139–41
oral tests, 2, 5
Ordinate, 58–9, 68, 190
orientation of rating scales, 89–90, 91
Orr, M., 144, 223
O'Sullivan, B., 189
overgeneralisation, 32
Oxford, R., 203

pairs, xv, 78, 172, 186–90
Palmer, A. S., 19, 31, 49, 51, 53–6, 90,
    120, 123–6, 128, 131, 152, 154,
    160, 182–4, 196, 207–10, 224,
    239–40
paraphrase, 32
particularity, 61
pauses, 99–102, 103–4
Peace Corps, 10
pedagogy
  task difficulty, 60–2
  tasks, 50–3
Peirce, C. S., 199–200
perceptions, rater, 144
performance
  and competence, 20
  model of speaking test performance,
    113–15
performance conditions, 56–7, 63–4
performance testing, 6–7, 62–3
performatives, 42–3
Perren, G. E., 93
perspective, 64
Phillips, S. E., 159
PhonePass test, 58–9, 68, 190
phonology, 25–6, 48
Pica, T., 52–3, 81
picture description tasks, 7, 131–3, 135
Picture Prompts, 73–6
Pienemann, M., 96, 97–8, 173, 180
piloting prototype tasks, 118
  costs of, 164–5
planning time, 64
Plough, I., 189

politeness principle, 40–1
Pollitt, A., 62–3, 144, 180, 213
Popham, W. J., 121, 128, 130
Portuguese Speaking Test (PST), 192
Powers, D. E., 154
pragmatic competence, 240
pragmatic knowledge, 39–44, 48
Pragmatism, 199–200
pre-activity costs, 161
pre-closings, 38
prepositions, 29–30
presentation tasks, 76–8
President's Commission on Foreign
    Language and International
    Studies, 11
primary language learning, 21–2
primary-trait scoring, 9, 90
'procedure' specification, 131
Proficiency Movement, 11, 176–9
proficiency scales *see* rating scales
proficient user, 112
progression, 95–6
prompt attributes (PA), 130
pronouns, 28–9
pronunciation, 2, 25–6, 205, 206
prototype tasks, 118
  costs of designing, 164
  piloting, 118, 164–5
psycholinguistic categories, 63
purpose of testing, 47
  defining, 162–3

qualitative analysis, 109
qualitative research methods, xv–xvi,
    216–24
  discourse analysis, 220–2
  expert judgement, 216–17
  questionnaires and interviews, 217–20
  verbal protocol analysis, 222–3
quality control, 102–3
quantitative analysis, 109–11
quantitative research methods, xv–xvi,
    201–15
  correlation, 190–2, 201–3
  factor analysis, 203–7
  generalisability studies, 210–13
  multifaceted Rasch analysis, 107–8,
    110, 142, 213–15
  multitrait-multimethod studies, 181–2,
    182–4, 207–10, 224

questionnaires, 109–11, 217–20, 253–5
Quinones, J., 10

race, 3–4
Rasch model *see* multifaceted Rasch
    analysis
raters, xv, 113, 114, 115, 139–47
    costs of training, 167–8
    decision making, 223
    perceptions, 144
    reliability, 139–42
    severity, 142, 215
    training, 142–7, 215
rating scales, xiv, 9, 11–16, 65–6,
    88–115, 144, 173, 239–45
    ACTFL, 11, 15–16, 230–8
    approaches to design, 91–113
        data-based scale development, 92,
        97–104
        EBBs, 92, 104–7
        intuitive and experiential, 92,
        92–7
        scaling descriptors, 92, 107–13
    Bachman and Palmer, 90–1,
        239–40
    costs of designing, 165
    defining, 88–9
    evaluation, 173–86
    FSI, 11–14, 92–7, 226–9
    ILR, 14–15, 15, 90–1, 241–5
    ISPLR, 94, 246
    types of, 89–91
reactivity, 55–6, 57–8
reading aloud, 8
reading tasks, 2–3
'real-world' approach, 90–1
Recorded Oral Proficiency Exam
    (ROPE), 191
reduction strategies, 32–4, 48
relative clauses, 28–9
reliability, 1–2, 10, 202
    generalisability studies, 210–13
    inter-rater reliability, 8, 10, 140–2,
        143–4, 215
    rater, 139–42
    task difficulty and, 61–2
repeat the sentence tasks, 68
replication, 111
reporting scores, 156–9
representation level, 14

research, xv–xvi, 199–225
    costs of basic research, 168
    and designing test specifications,
        118–19
    qualitative methods, xv–xvi, 216–24
        discourse analysis, 220–2
        expert judgement, 216–17
        questionnaires and interviews,
        217–20
        verbal protocol analysis, 222–3
    quantitative methods, xv–xvi, 201–15
        correlation, 190–2, 201–3
        factor analysis, 203–7
        generalisability studies, 210–13
        multifaceted Rasch analysis, 107–8,
        110, 142, 213–15
        multitrait-multimethod studies,
        181–2, 182–4, 207–10, 224
resources, costs of, 162
response, expected, 55
response attributes (RA), 130–1, 134
    sample transcript, 134, 247–9
response-input relationship, 55–6
response validity, 217
restructuring, 32
Reves, T., 131, 141
Rivera, C., 155
Roach, J. O., 5, 8
Robertson, D., 188
role, 43–4
role play, 44, 82–3
    difficult requests, 127–9
Rorty, R., 19
Ross, S., 147, 148
Rubin, D. L., 22
rubrics, characteristics of, 53–4
rules of speaking, 39–42

Sacks, H., 34, 35, 100
sample item (SI), 130, 131
samples, speech *see* speech samples
Savignon, S. J., 66, 94, 180, 181, 185,
    186
Saville, N., 36, 78, 146, 187, 195
scaling descriptors, 92, 107–13
Schegloff, E., 34, 100
Schneider, G., 109–10, 112–13
Schramm, G., 22
Schulz, R. A., 96
scientific method, 199

scope, 56
scoring, 89–90, 91
scoring rubrics *see* rating scales
Scott, M. L., 218
Searle, J., 43
second language acquisition, 22–3
    task difficulty, 60–2
    tasks, 50–3
Second World War, 6–8
Seliger, H. W., 26
Selinker, L., 66
setting, characteristics of, 53
severity, rater, 142, 215
Shmueli, D., 172, 192–3
Shohamy, E., xiv, 64, 131, 141, 159, 172,
    192–3, 195, 197, 224
Simon, J., 222
simulated oral proficiency interviews
    (SOPIs), 190, 192–3
simulations, 44, 83
situations, 57, 58
    task types, 68–86 *passim*
Skehan, P., 27, 63, 65, 113–14
skills-oriented tasks, 52
social distance/status, 35–6, 41–2, 43–4,
    66–7
socialisation, 143–4, 145
sociolinguistic competence, 239
sociolinguistic knowledge, 48
Sollenberger, H. E., 9, 13
Sosa, E., 199
speaking construct *see* construct
    definition
specification supplement (SS), 130, 131
specificity, 64, 66, 134
speech
    nature of, 23–5
    rules of, 39–42
    strategies for, 31–4, 48
    structure of, 34–8, 48
    variability in, 21–2
speech act theory, 42–3
speech acts, assessment of, 127–9
speech samples
    coding, 98–102
    test specifications, 134
    transcript, 134, 247–9
Spolsky, B., 2, 5, 55
standards, 8
    documents, 225

Standards for Educational and
    Psychological Testing, 117, 155,
    156–7, 194, 195
Stansfield, C. W., 107, 149, 155, 172,
    190, 192
status, 57
    interlocutor status and familiarity, 57,
        58, 60, 68–86 *passim*
    social, 35–6, 41–2, 43–4, 66–7
Stevenson, D. K., 186
strategic competence, 31
strategies for speaking, 31–4, 48
stress, 25–6
structural validity, 195
structure of speech, 34–8, 48
structured tasks, 63
student visas, 5
study, years of, 184
Sturtridge, G., 53
substantive validity, 195
superior level, 175–6, 232, 233
support, interlocutor, 148
survival level, 14
sustained speech, 7–8
Swain, M., 31, 44, 62, 189
Swinton, S. S., 13, 140, 191
syllabuses, 120
syntax, 34

'talk aloud' method, 222–3
Taped Oral Proficiency Test of Spanish
    (TOPT), 191
target language use (TLU) checklists,
    53–6
Tarone, E., 61
task banks, 135, 136
task orientation, 57, 58, 59
    task types, 68–86 *passim*
task performance conditions, 56–7,
    63–4
task-specific variance, 66
tasks, xiv, 50–87
    in second language acquisition and
        pedagogy, 50–3
    specifications at the level of task,
        131–4
    task difficulty, 60–7
        in language testing, 62–7
        in pedagogy and second language
            acquisition, 60–2

tasks (*continued*)
task types in speaking tests, 67–86
test task characteristics, 53–60
Taylor, L., 186–7, 195
teaching
and level of specificity, 134
Proficiency Movement, 11, 176–8
teaching assistants (TAs), 204–7, 211–12
tenacity, 199
tense, 29
terminology, 96–7
test accommodations *see*
accommodations, test
test bias, 9
Test of English for Educational
Purposes, 78
test genre, 43
test rubrics, characteristics of, 53–4
test specifications, xiv–xv, 116–37
control and freedom, 135–7
costs of writing, 166–7
defining, 120–9
at the level of test and/or task, 131–4
response attributes and speech
samples, 134
teaching and the level of specificity,
134
and testing environment, 154
validity argument, 116–20
writing, 129–34
Test of Spoken English (TSE), 191
Testing Kit Workshops, 10
'think aloud' method, 222–3
Thomas, J., 39
Thurstone, L. L., 105, 144, 216
topics, 57, 58, 60, 192
task types, 68–86 *passim*
training
costs, 167–8
interlocutors, 147–52, 167–8
raters, 142–7, 215
training materials, 145, 150–1, 153–4
costs of designing, 167
trait theory, 18–19, 62
transcript, 134, 247–9
transition relevance places (TRPs),
34–6, 37
translating/interpreting tasks, 83–4
true score, 210–11
Tsui, A. B. M., 36

turn taking, 34–6
Turner, C., 65, 104, 105–6, 144, 216

Underhill, N., xiii, 23, 85, 138, 186
unintended consequences, 197
United Kingdom (UK), 5–6, 8
United States (USA), xiv, 155, 156, 158
development of testing second
language speaking, xii, 1–5, 6–8,
9–11
universe of admissible observations, 211
universe score, 211
University of Cambridge Business
English Certificate, 80–2
University of Cambridge Certificate in
English Language Skills, 85–6
University of Cambridge Local
Examinations Syndicate
(UCLES), 86, 120, 147, 151, 221
CPE, 5–6, 8, 76–8
CUEFL, 59–60
pairs, 78, 172, 186–7
Picture Prompts, 73–6
Preliminary English Test, 73–6
presentations, 76–8
unpredictability, 34
Upshur, J., 65, 104, 105–6, 144, 216
user-oriented scales, 89
usher, 153

Valdman, A., 174
Valette, R. M., 50–1
validity, 136, 171, 218
argument, xiii, 116–20
rater training and, 145–7
concerns and FSI approach, 181–4
construct-equivalent, 172
convergent, 196, 207, 209
divergent, 196, 207, 210
face validity, 10, 181, 185–6
response validity, 217
see also evaluation; research
validity model, xv, 194–7
van Lier, L., 79
Van Patten, B., 12, 179
variability
interlocutors and, 220–2
in speech, 21–2
in test performance by task
characteristics/conditions, 61–2

variationism, 61, 62
Varonis, E. M., 67, 147
verbal protocol analysis (VPA), 222–3
verbal reporting techniques, 147, 222–3
Vietnam War, 10
vocabulary, 12, 205, 206, 228 9
Vollmer, H. J., 180
Vygotsky, L. S., 45

Wall, D., 120, 145
weakness (in rating scales), 173
weighting table, 12
Weigle, S. C., 142
Weinstein, A. I., 78–9
Weir, C., 56–7, 78
Wigglesworth, G., 65, 215
Wilds, C., 11, 12, 92–3, 93, 95, 96, 139,
     185
Wilkinson, A., 113, 142, 144
Winter, E. O., 102

Wolfson, N., 39
Wood, B. D., 2
words
   expressing being, 43–4
   order, 27, 28
   speech act theory, 42–3
   word coinage, 32
Wright, B. D., 105
Wright, T., 52
written language, 23–4
written tests, 3, 5

years of study, 184
Yerkes, R. M., 3–4
Yoshida-Morise, Y., 33
Young, R., 36, 43, 45–6, 149
Young, S., 149
Yule, G., 60–1

Zappala, S., 83